The Power and the Money

By the Same Author

Win At Any Cost: The Sellout of College Athletes

The Power and the Money

Inside the *Wall Street Journal*

Francis X. Dealy, Jr.

A Birch Lane Press Book
Published by Carol Publishing Group

A Birch Lane Press Book
Published by Carol Publishing Group
Birch Lane Press is a registered trademark of Carol Communications, Inc.
Editorial Offices: 600 Madison Avenue, New York, N.Y. 10022
Sales and Distribution Offices: 120 Enterprise Avenue, Secaucus, N.J. 07094
In Canada: Canadian Manda Group, P.O. Box 920, Station U, Toronto, Ontario M8Z 5P9
Queries regarding rights and permissions should be addressed to Carol Publishing
Group, 600 Madison Avenue, New York, N.Y. 10022

Carol Publishing Group books are available at special discounts for bulk purchases, for
sales promotion, fund-raising, or educational purposes. Special editions can be created
to specifications. For details, contact: Special Sales Department, Carol Publishing
Group, 120 Enterprise Avenue, Secaucus, N.J. 07094

Manufactured in the United States of America
10 9 8 7 6 5 4 3 2 1

Library of Congress Cataloging-in-Publication Data

Dealy, Francis X.
        The power and the money : inside the Wall Street Journal / by
    Francis X. Dealy.
            p.   cm.
"A Birch Lane Press bo k."
ISBN 1-55972-118-9
1. Wall Street Journal. I. Title.
PN4899.N42W25   1993
071'.3.--dc20   92-35893
                                                          CIP

To ELLEN, again

Contents

1. Mr. Dow Meets Mr. Jones: Then and Now   1
2. The Potentate: Clarence Barron, Publisher (1912–28)   16
3. The Debacle   32
4. The Resurrection and Barney Kilgore, President (1941–65)   44
5. Grasp for Power   54
6. The First Huckster   61
7. The Formidable Vermont Connecticut Royster   70
8. Barney Falters   78
9. The Ultimate Follower: Warren Phillips, Publisher (1975–91)   91
10. The Second Huckster   110
11. The First Dauphin   127
12. The Second Dauphin   143
13. *Book Digest*: Compounding Disaster   163
14. High Tech and a Rodeo for Suits   180
15. Ascent of the First Dauphin: Peter Kann, Publisher (1991–Present)   189
16. Mr. Peepers, the Zany Editorialist   206
17. The Column Heard Round the World   218

18. Taken for a Ride in the Trump Helicopter   236
19. Black Monday   253
20. Nepotism: Peter Kann and Karen Elliott House   265
21. Wooing the Wrong Foreign Relations   279
22. Why the *Journal* Missed the Savings and Loan
    Scandal   292
23. Michael Milken: The Exposé That Never
    Happened   304
24. A Pulitzer Prize: Just One More Time   314
25. Telerate and FNN: Too Little and Too Late   325
26. The *Wall Street Journal*: Today and Tomorrow   344
    A Note on the Research   350
    Notes   352
    Bibliography   366
    Index   368

Acknowledgments

———

I wish to thank the many people at Dow Jones & Company, Inc., and the *Wall Street Journal* who granted me virtually unlimited access.

I also wish to thank Michael Sheraton and Daniel F. Fairbanks, Sc.D., who are unusually competent researchers.

And, finally, I wish to thank Jack Scharf and Sarah Auchincloss for their belief in me and this project.

The Power and the Money

1

Mr. Dow Meets Mr. Jones:
Then and Now

Five million of the richest, most influential people in America begin their day reading the *Wall Street Journal*.

Journal subscriber surveys say that virtually all the leaders of Wall Street and corporate America, plus a surprising number of important people from law, politics, education, and medicine, spend at least forty-five minutes each weekday morning perusing the *Wall Street Journal*.

And apparently it's time well spent.

The average *Journal* subscriber possesses net assets worth $1.2 million, owns a principal residence and a summer home, together worth $925,000, and drives a $43,000 car, according to these same surveys.

No wonder the advertising industry, whenever it wants to convey worldly achievement, uses the *Wall Street Journal* as a prop. Aided by this image, which is further reinforced by the *Journal's* front page, with its robber baron logo and its six photographless columns of solid type, the *Wall Street Journal* represents the best virtues of capitalism. It is an institution that deserves U. S. historical landmark status.

Besides being the country's newspaper of record for business and finance, the *Wall Street Journal* is an excellent general newspaper as well.

In fact, the paper's nonbusiness news stories, profiles, whimsical features, controversial editorials, columns, and cultural reviews are why media polls consistently name the *Wall Street Journal* one of the country's top three general newspapers. In the news capital of the world, Washington, the *Journal's* bureau ranks second to none. The *Journal's* bureau chief, Al Hunt, has entertained President and Mrs. Bush in his home. On the international front, the *Journal's* eighty-seven-person foreign correspondents corps, residing in seventy-three countries, is as competent and as extensive as any television network's. For example, London bureau's Tony Horowitz and Geraldine Brooks, a husband-and-wife team, rivaled CNN in their coverage of the Gulf War.

Today's typical *Journal* reader—a white forty-four-year-old male MBA from Wharton who works for General Electric in strategic planning and lives in Fairfield County, Connecticut—relates to the *Wall Street Journal* the same way he relates to his company: General Electric's policies are law; the *Journal's* stories are gospel.

It's the *Journal's* front page in particular which engenders his devotion. It may look like a newspaper, but it reads like a magazine.

By design, on any given day, four of the *Journal's* six front-page columns are devoted to articles which have nothing to do with either business or the immediate news of the day. These essays, routinely requiring months to prepare, revisit a news event a week to a year after the fact, explaining its underlying influences which the daily press often fail to report. While the front page of the *New York Times* might be filled with stories concerning Bosnia, Somalia, President-elect Clinton's latest appointment, Yeltsin, Israel and the Palestinians, the *Wall Street Journal's* front page will be devoted to such diverse stories as how McDonald's and Burger King's fat-laden hamburgers contribute to the strife of inner cities; how President-elect Clinton spent his Christmas holidays; how Linda Gosden Robinson, a public relations padrona, trades off her husband's reputation to gain clients; and how Jordan's King Hussein endures frustrations from enemy and ally alike to bring peace to the Middle East. And always, to add levity to this otherwise serious fare, the front page's column four is devoted to a subject that is either amusing, quirky, or both.

All *Journal* articles exhibit a common thread—brilliant writing. That's why, in the early seventies, high school teachers of creative writing would bring the *Wall Street Journal*, not the *New Yorker*, to class. In fact, during the *Journal's* golden age of writing, roughly from the mid-sixties to the mid-seventies, when people still read newspapers, such *Journal* reporters, correspondents, and columnists as Vermont Royster, Peter Kann, Lindley Clark, Steve Lovelady, Bill Blundell, and Jim Perry routinely "outtyped" David Halberstam, Peter Arnett, Norman Mailer, Truman Capote, and others.

The *Journal's* obsession with its writing began after Pearl Harbor, when, in its own fight for survival, a young editor conceded that the *Journal* was a "second newspaper," read only after the major daily had been consulted. By acknowledging this seemingly inferior role, the *Journal* was then free to stake out an entirely new territory for a national daily publication—reporting the underlying causes and effects of events—leaving the reporting of the often boring who-what-why-and-hows to the dailies. The key to this daring decision, of course, was to write about causes and effects so brilliantly that the reader relished the chance to revisit an event with which his daily newspaper had already acquainted him.

In the early 1940s, the *Journal* had maybe three people on staff capable of brilliant writing. They were assigned to the copy desk and virtually rewrote every reporter's draft from that day forward. Since then, the *Journal* has been an editor's, not a bureau chief's or a reporter's, newspaper.

More often than any reader might suspect, copy that a reporter submits to an editor, which an editor then submits to a reader, is transformed beyond recognition, save for the subject and certain quotes. This explains why, today, nearly two hundred of the news department's six-hundred-person staff do nothing but refine or rewrite reporters' drafts. It also explains why a page-one story, like a salmon fighting upstream, pushes through five layers of editors before the associate managing editor finally approves it for publication.

Though the editor's mark on a piece is often transforming, it is always anonymous. When Karen Elliott House won a Pulitzer Prize for the *Journal* in 1984 for her series on Jordan's King Hussein, copy editor Dan Kelly stayed up all night rewriting House's submission, condensing it from three to two articles, before page-one editor Glynn Mapes would publish them. Yet Kelly never received a mention in Karen Elliott House's effusive Pulitzer heraldry.

Until recently, the *Journal's* brilliant writing and ambitious reporting made it preeminent. It beat the *New York Times* or the *Los Angeles Times* mercilessly in business and finance coverage, while matching them in national and international coverage.

Uniqueness and technology also contributed to the *Journal's* supremacy. Until 1982, the *Wall Street Journal* was the country's only national daily newspaper, a superlative made possible by a leased satellite floating 25,000 miles above the earth. The satellite faxes, page by page, an issue of the *Journal* to a network of printing plants strategically placed throughout the country. In turn, each plant prints and distributes its regional share of the *Journal's* total daily circulation, which back then was 2.1 million copies. (Today it's 1.8 million; 1.59 million subscribers and 230,000 newsstand purchasers.) Thus, *Journal* buyers in Portland, Oregon, read the same newspaper that their Portland, Maine, counterparts receive.

In many areas, the local postal service was too slow, so the *Journal* created its own door-to-door delivery service. Today 900,000 *Journal* copies bypass the post office daily.

But beginning in the early eighties, when Wall Street and corporate America became front-page news for everyone, the *Journal* allowed several publications to make incursions into its once exclusive province. What began as curiosities, sources of wary amusement for the *Journal's* management, turned into full-scale competition.

First, *USA Today* came on the scene. Considered "too down scale" by the *Journal* to be a competitor for readers, *USA Today* became a competitor for advertisers soon enough. Ironically, Al Neuharth, *USA Today's* founder, credits the *Journal* with a portion of his newspaper's early success. "The *Journal* showed us how to use satellite technology so we, too, could print and distribute nationally,"[1] Neuharth said, smiling.

Another national business newspaper, *Investor's Daily*, launched in the early eighties, made inroads as well because of its superior stock tables and other statistics.

Two other newspapers discovered that expanded business coverage meant expanded circulation. In 1976, the *Los Angeles Times* had twelve business reporters and editors; by 1983, it had sixty-nine. The *New York Times* averted its near demise in the late seventies after it introduced its separate business section, "Business Day." Other newspapers soon followed suit, and, together, the major dailies began to cut into the *Journal's* readership.

About this time, the CRT, the cathode ray tube, and more important, the information it conveyed, replaced the printed word. The CRT allowed a large segment of Wall Street professionals to turn to a small green desk-top screen that transmits the purest form of information—statistics—as quickly as it becomes available. *On-line* and *real time*, computerese for *instantaneous*, came into the business vernacular. As the CRT replaced the *Journal's* statistics pages, Wall Street's bond with its favorite newspaper changed from utter dependence to nonchalant affection.

These competitive incursions, and their weakening effects on the *Journal*, resulted from a smugness and a lack of judgment that began to infect the Dow Jones senior management ranks in the mid-sixties.

These attitudes became more manifest in 1976, the year Dow Jones left the Over-the-Counter Market for the New York Stock Exchange, a move which symbolized the beginning of Dow Jones's transformation from an entrepreneurial, one-product company, the *Wall Street Journal*, to a full-fledged member of bureaucratic corporate America.

In that same year, 1976, Warren Phillips began his reign as Dow Jones's chief executive officer. A former *Journal* managing editor, Phillips had risen to power on the coattails of William Kerby, also a former *Journal* managing editor, who had risen to power on the coattails of Barney Kilgore, one of two *Journal* saviors who rescued the newspaper from certain death. The other savior, Clarence Barron, had done the same thing in 1912.

Phillips ran Dow Jones for the next fifteen years, during which period both Dow Jones and the *Wall Street Journal* experienced much of what Wall Street and the rest of corporate America experienced: great triumphs and even greater humiliations.

But unlike Wall Street and corporate America, few people knew about Dow Jones's failures, because the *Wall Street Journal* rarely reported them. And when it did, the spin control was shameless. When a *Journal* reporter confessed to participating in an insider-trading scandal in 1983, the *Journal* conducted its own front-page investigation, arraignment, indictment, prosecution, and sentencing with such thunderous indignation that most people were distracted from asking what, if any, responsibility the *Journal's* management had had in the affair.

And when the *Journal* failed to monitor and report the excesses of the eighties, for example, the Milken and the savings-and-loan scandals, the paper resorted to the same deluge of after-the-fact but Pulitzer Prize–winning coverage. A distracted nation forgot to ask: Why didn't America's newspaper of record for business and finance reveal these stories sooner, when real trouble could have been avoided?

In addition to these reversals, from 1976 to today Dow Jones has certainly grown bigger, but not smarter or better. In 1976, Dow Jones earnings-per-share were $1.91. In 1991, they had dropped to $.71 per share, a forty-five-year low. During this same period, the company's revenues increased sixfold, from $270 million to $1.7 billion. In 1976, Dow Jones employed 4,096 people. Today, 9,500 people work in one of three Dow Jones operating or product groups: Business Publications; Community Newspapers; and Information Services.

Dow Jones's Business Publications Group consists, first and foremost, of the *Wall Street Journal*, still the country's largest daily newspaper despite a 14.3 percent circulation decline in the last ten years. The *Journal* offers four regional editions that are printed at eighteen printing plants throughout the country. The *Journal* offers advertisers the flexibility of choosing one or all of sixteen localized editions for their advertisements to run in. In addition to its domestic edition, the *Journal* also publishes a European and an Asian edition, which, according to Phillips, makes the *Journal* "a global newspaper."

In addition to the global *Journal*, Dow Jones publishes *Barron's National Business and Financial Weekly*, with a circulation of 237,700. The newsweekly for Wall Street professionals, *Barron's* has had the same loyal following for sixty-five years, mesmerized no doubt by its irreverent editor, Alan Abelson, and before him, the equally controversial Robert Bleiberg. But as much influence as *Barron's* wields on Wall Street, it is neglected inside Dow Jones. Since its founding in 1889, Dow Jones's senior management has always focused on the *Journal*.

The next Dow Jones operating group, Community Newspapers, is a management consulting firm's euphemism for the Ottaway Community Newspapers, a chain of twenty-three small-town papers whose median circulation is 22,000.

Acquired during a golf game by Dow Jones chairman Bill Kerby, Ottaway Newspapers has always been too small to affect Dow Jones one way or another. But the Ottaway family has done well by Dow Jones. Today the Ottaways own 5.1 million shares of Dow Jones stock worth $150 million, which, next to Clarence Barron's descendants, makes them the second-largest Dow Jones shareholder. Kerby bought Ottaway Newspapers in 1970 for $36 million worth of Dow Jones stock, a price equivalent to twenty-four times Ottaway's earnings. At the time, the average deal's multiple was twelve times earnings.

The third Dow Jones operating group, Information Services, deals with anything that distributes information electronically.

Since its inception in 1974, like *Barron's*, ISG has always felt like a second-class citizen, jealous of Dow Jones's adoration of the *Wall Street Journal*. Until 1990, ISG had been, for the most part, a collection of promises, space-age projects whose profits were always going to be materialize tomorrow while their expenses were always realized today.

One notable exception was the Dow Jones News Service, the "ticker," which was established in 1897 by Charles Dow, Edward Jones, and the unacclaimed Charles Bergstresser, the same three men who founded the *Wall Street Journal* eight years before. Today the ticker distributes business and financial news stories to 131,000 teleprinters and video displays worldwide. It's an invaluable news and information service to the professional financier, and its profits, though small, have been steady for nearly a century. The ticker has a number of product extensions, including the Professional Investor wire, the AP–Dow Jones ticker, which serves much of Europe and Asia, DowVision, which communicates with desktop computers, and DowPhone, a subscription-based telephone service.

Another product of the Information Services Group is the Dow Jones News Retrieval Service, a distributor of data bases to corporations. Initiated in 1978, the Retrieval Service has never fulfilled its potential because of a lack of marketing common sense. The service keeps adding data bases to its inventory and increasing its rates to pay for them. Right now, the Retrieval Service charges $600 per hour, a rate so expensive that only the biggest or most imprudent corporations can afford it.

The newest, biggest, and most problematic service to be added to the Dow Jones Information Services Group is Telerate, which Dow Jones acquired, piecemeal, over four years for $1.6 billion. Telerate is an electronic or real-time distributor of various financial market statistics, including the prices of U.S. government securities, foreign exchange, international government bonds, global equities, energy, mortgage-backed securities and a variety of money-market instruments. Telerate also provides an "analytic service," whereby its customers can use special Telerate–provided software to analyze its data further.

Since completing the acquisition in 1990, Dow Jones has replaced three Telerate executives: its founder and chairman, Neil Hirsch; its president, Joe Terranova; and its executive vice president, John

Jessop. All three men left Dow Jones unhappy with being forced to do business "the Dow Jones way." Dow Jones was unhappy because many unexpected reversals surfaced, they claim, only after the final acquisition installment sum was paid.

In addition to its structure and breadth, Dow Jones has changed in other ways, too.

For years, Dow Jones was headquartered above a five-and-ten on a Wall Street side street. In 1984, Dow Jones moved into its own building, a marble octagon resembling an Italian cathedral located in the new and fashionable Wall Street neighborhood.

In 1976, Dow Jones had 15.9 million shares outstanding, of which the descendants of Clarence Barron, mostly the Cox and the Bancroft families, held 9.5 million shares, or 60 percent of the company. By 1991, Dow Jones had two types of stock, common and Class B common, to foil the efforts of hostile takeover artists. The Class B common had ten votes per share, while the common carried only one vote per share. After splitting two-for-one in 1983 and again in 1984, Dow Jones had 78.6 million shares of common stock outstanding and 22.6 million shares of Class B common stock outstanding. The Cox and Bancroft families owned 40 percent of the common stock, 77.1 percent of the Class B common stock, and 67 percent of all the shareholder votes. The descendants of Clarence Barron still owned the company, one of the few companies listed on the NYSE so dominated.

But unlike other newspaper families, the Barron descendants are not active in Dow Jones's day-to-day operations. They are happy to remain dormant, living off their nearly $50-million annual dividend income from Dow Jones stock alone, which explains why no one complained when in 1991 Dow Jones paid 76¢ per share in dividends when it earned only 71¢ per share.

Dow Jones's financial decline, which began in 1984, has not been obvious because the company has sold off assets each year to keep earnings artificially high. But finally, in 1991, Dow Jones ran out of salable assets or furniture to sell, revealing the company's operating truth—plummeting profits.

The recession has also helped hide Dow Jones's problems. It provided the perfect excuse as Dow Jones quarterly and annual reports cited "the worldwide advertising recessions" to explain its reversals. But Dow Jones's advertising reversals began in 1984, at the height of Wall Street's prosperity. And there has been no mention to date that despite 1991 and 1992 being banner years for Wall Street, Dow Jones and the *Journal* are still stuck in the doldrums.

Besides lack of judgment, Dow Jones's management is plagued by the same villains that attack the rest of corporate America—the Wall Street establishment. Phillips, and now Peter Kann, Dow Jones's new CEO, spend all their time making presentations to analysts. They have no time to manage the business.

When Barney Kilgore, the *Journal's* great architect, ran Dow Jones, he and a handful of key associates pored over that day's *Journal* every morning, second-guessing the managing editor. Often Kilgore would stroll down two floors to the newsroom and deliver praise or censure to the appropriate person, face-to-face. Back then, quarterly earnings were rarely discussed. These men were journalists who dedicated their lives to making the *Journal* one of the best-written, most accurate, informative, and entertaining newspapers in the world.

Today, like much of corporate America, layer upon layer of reporters, bureau chiefs, subeditors, department editors, senior editors, associate managing editors, deputy managing editors, associate vice presidents, divisional vice presidents, divisional presidents, corporate vice presidents, and, finally, corporate presidents separate Peter Kann, a former Pulitzer Prize–winning correspondent, from the *Journal's* newsroom or the daily management of Telerate.

But Dow Jones's problems today far exceed the trials and tribulations that spring from becoming a fat, smug bureaucracy.

Like IBM, General Motors, and American Express, Dow Jones has been victimized by a singular management ineptness resulting from choosing the wrong man to lead the company. Barney Kilgore was a legitimate hero who single-handedly saved the *Journal* in the early forties. But Kilgore made one mistake, choosing William Kerby as his successor. As the father's sins are visited on the son, Kerby repeated the same mistake by choosing Warren Phillips to succeed him in 1976, as did Phillips in choosing his heir, Peter Kann, in 1989.

Peter Kann lacks the rudiments of business sense and, worst of all, the humility and the tolerance to learn. Kann has surrounded himself with weak men whose only aim is to maintain their untroubled relation with the boss. Also, in what is the most conspicuous and destructive case of nepotism in corporate America today, Kann permits his wife, Karen Elliott House, to terrorize the *Journal*.[2]

In a short span of twenty-four years, the lack of judgment of Kerby,

Phillips, and Kann, individually and collectively, has violated the ethical legacies of Kilgore and set Dow Jones adrift. Also, in selecting the wrong managing editor for the eighties, Phillips and Kann are responsible for compromising the *Journal's* integrity and putting its once eminent journalism in question.

With its more recent, permissive, go-go journalism, the *Journal* has been too busy pandering to hostile-takeover artists to reveal the excesses of the last decade. Most sinful of all, the Milken and savings-and-loan scandals occurred right under the *Journal's* nose without so much as a mention.[3] The slowest news medium of all, the book, was the first to tell the story of Michael Milken and the $500 billion savings-and-loan collapse.

Also, when it came to the business of managing Dow Jones or deciding what acquisitions to make, at what price, and how to integrate them, Phillips and then Kann have made the wrong decision every time.

But unlike IBM, General Motors, and American Express, whose mistakes have been well chronicled, Dow Jones's deficiencies have remained largely unreported.[4] Most press accounts of the company are either fawning or timid. Because the *Journal* is always a potential employer or reviewer of books, everyone treads lightly. The *Journal*, together with Dow Jones, is just too powerful. If the press in general is the fourth estate, the *Wall Street Journal* is the fifth estate.

American financial journalism started in May 1789, shortly after traders began selling stocks and bonds under sycamore trees at the corner of Broad and Wall streets.

In the fall of that same year, the traders shifted their operations indoors to several different locations, creating an information gap. At first, traders dispatched clerks to other offices to exchange notes that chronicled the latest trading information. By 1827, Wall Street had grown so much that the streets of lower Manhattan were clogged with clerks-turned-publishers delivering up to ten handwritten bulletins each day to their subscribers.

In 1872, Thomas Alva Edison invented a system whereby the latest stock prices could be sent to subscribers via electrical impuses. Each subscriber was equipped with a paper-tape printing machine that converted the impulses into text. As the tape emerged from the press, it made a ticking sound that gave the machine its name. Because the data conveyed by ticker were limited to symbols and digits, the service augmented, rather than replaced, the bulletins.

In November 1882, Charles Dow, Edward Jones, and Charles Bergstresser defected from the leading financial publisher of the day, Kiernan News Agency, to form Dow Jones & Company, Inc.

While at Kiernan, Charles Bergstresser developed a stylus that could record the news onto thirty-five sheets or bulletins simultaneously, a technique that quadrupled productivity. When Kiernan refused Bergstresser's proposal for equity partnership in exchange for his time-saving invention, Bergstresser persuaded Dow and Jones, two Kiernan reporters, to help him form a new venture.

The increased delivery speed owed to Bergstresser's pen made Dow Jones & Company an immediate success, although its bulletins were hardly editorial masterpieces.

Bulletin Dow Jones & Company, Inc. September 5, 1883.
 12.05 P.M. "Hatch & Foote have announced their suspension."
 12.35 P.M. "The rumor that Peters, Wetmore & Schenck were in any trouble are [sic] absolutely false."
 1:05 P.M. "The House of Cook endangered by Northern Pacific."
 2:05 P.M. "Hatch & Foote have announced their reinstatement."

A year after Dow Jones was founded, Bergstresser convinced his partners to become the first Wall Street news service to acquire a printing press, an investment that doubled the firm's publishing productivity. The typeset word, compared to the hand written, improved the bulletin as well.

Dow Jones exploited the telegraph to become the first American financial publisher to cover London. Edward Jones struck an arrangement with an employee of the *Times* of London to telegraph the market summaries every day after the newspaper was distributed. Five hours ahead of New York, once the *Times*'s market-page information became part of the public domain, Jones felt free to use it.

The telegraph also enabled Dow Jones to be the first New York financial publisher to cover Boston, an important banking and manufacturing center. In 1897, for ten cents a word, Clarence Barron, proprietor of the Boston News Service, began wiring news items to New York for Dow Jones's Afternoon News Letter. "*Barron's* fees," claimed Dow, the partner in charge of news, "were more than paid for through increased circulation tariffs."[5]

In the spring of 1889, Bergstresser identified a gap in the financial news market. The one-page bulletins conveyed news as it happened; ticker services offered even terser and faster news summaries; but no medium reported the events of an entire day. Thus, Bergstresser again convinced Charles Dow and Edward Jones to invest in additional printing presses, to start Wall Street's first afternoon newspaper.

The first issue of the *Wall Street Journal* appeared on July 8, 1889. The new printing press, fast and powerful, enabled the *Journal* to be distributed by 3:15 P.M., fifteen minutes after the New York Stock Exchange closed and an hour before the *New York Sun*, the *New York Commercial Bulletin*, and the *Daily Financial News World* appeared. This earlier delivery time also allowed the *Journal* to travel to neighboring cities, such as Philadelphia and Syracuse.

The *Journal*'s early issues were little more than duplications of the Dow Jones bulletins, with sentences so laconic they sometimes obfuscated their meaning. Whatever circulation gains the *Journal* achieved, then, were due more to its printing press than its printed word.

Coinciding with the founding of the *Wall Street Journal*, the company introduced the Dow Jones averages, a measurement of how twelve stocks listed on the New York Stock Exchange fared on any given day.

Dow Jones also continued to publish its bulletins throughout the day, thanks to its new printing press, with quadrupled frequency. Every fifteen minutes, a bulletin was printed and distributed.

And through its use of the telegraph, the *Journal* had expanded its corps of correspondents to include employees in most major cities in the United States and Europe by 1890.

In 1897, Bergstresser introduced the broad-tape ticker, an improvement over existing ticker services because it could accommodate text as well as symbols and digits. Dow Jones advertised its new service with the slogan, News Carried by Electricity, Printed by Electricity. With Bergstresser's latest innovation, Dow Jones became a three-product company: bulletins, ticker, and the *Wall Street Journal*.

A year later, the *Wall Street Journal* introduced a morning edition, again because a newly acquired printing press provided additional production capacity. By 1899, between the morning and afternoon editions the *Journal*'s circulation had climbed to 11,000, and the paper was thriving. Demand to advertise in the *Journal*, for example, became so great that Edward Jones, the partner who headed advertising, usurped six of the front page's seven columns to accommodate ads.

But this success spawned enmity. Jones's incursions in the front page deeply offended Charles Dow, head of news. "He [Jones] just wanted the short-term gains from advertisers and to hell with the reader,"[6] Dow confided to Thomas F. Woodlock, a *Journal* editor.

In February 1899, there was an explosion. It was the same old fight: Jones's disregard for Dow's editorial wishes versus Bergstresser's desire to acquire equipment. "Jones, who was volatile to begin with, became irrational when Bergstresser suggested we buy another printing press," Dow told Woodlock. "And when I suggested that we should stop coddling advertisers, Jones stormed out of the office."[7]

By June, Edward Jones had sold his interest in the company. Bergstresser moved to Paris to become an absentee owner, leaving Charles Dow in New York to manage Dow Jones and the *Wall Street Journal*.

Thus, despite twenty years of success, the struggle between editorial demands and technology seriously weakened the basic Dow Jones structure. It also started a tradition still existent today: Editorial, above all else, is the most essential *Journal* discipline.

2

The Potentate: Clarence Barron, Publisher (1912–28)

The walruslike tycoon often appeared to be in a quandary, plagued by the choices success had come to offer him. He hated to interrupt his work routine, for example, to pursue other obsessions, such as swimming, eating, travel, or devotion to his two stepdaughters.

That's why Clarence Barron, chairman of the Boston News Bureau, astonished beachgoers whenever he went swimming. Clad in a black one-piece bathing unit that barely contained his five-foot five-inch, 350-pound girth, Barron would dictate to two male secretaries perched on a nearby raft while he floated in the surf. Regardless of where he went, Barron always had a coterie of male secretaries in tow, taking down his unending stream of ideas and commentaries. That's how Barron could send upwards of a hundred memos to his editors each day and still write several news stories and editorials himself.

One of the first financial journalists in America, the Boston-based Barron rose to prominence as he reported and explained the industrial revolution, much of which occurred in New England.

Though he comported himself like a potentate, Clarence Walker Barron was born into an itinerant Irish family on July 2, 1855 in Boston's North End, not far from Faneuil Hall and the wharves. His parents, Henry and Elana Barron, had recently come to Boston in search of work. But so had thousands of other unskilled Irish workers who, fleeing the Great Irish Potato Famines of 1847, glutted New England's already underutilized labor pool. Boston's employers, largely white Anglo-Saxons, expressed their resentments by displaying attitudes and signs that said: "Irish need not apply."

As a consequence, Henry Barron was forced to be a dockworker, an unsteady, low-paying position that jeopardized his ability to provide for a family. In fact, when Clarence was born, the Barrons asked friends, the Clarence Walkers, to raise their son, a wrenching hardship that explains, among several things, how Barron got his name.

Eventually, Henry Barron's fortunes changed, and he was able to reclaim his son, who, through the encouragement of his second foster family, had become an inveterate reader. When he reached twelve, after impressing a teacher with his familiarity with the novels of Charles Dickens, young Barron was invited to attend Boston's English High School, a school for gifted students.

While at English, Barron demonstrated both his writing skills and his cunning by winning an essay competition. Later explaining to a friend how he won, Barron said: "I knew Mr. Lambeth, the most influential judge, taught mythology and that he had very little interest in my passion, railroads. So I contrived a metaphor he could relate to."[1] Barron's essay compared the economic effect of the railroad to Prometheus's gift of fire.

In addition to Latin, Greek, English composition, and mathematics, Barron took shorthand, the only boy to do so. Impervious to the usual jeers, Barron pursued stenography so diligently that by the time he graduated from English in 1873, he could transcribe most conversations verbatim.

Barron would practice his stenography by recording the proceedings of the Middlesex Courthouse. Once, the court stenographer unexpectedly fell ill, and the judge asked Barron to replace the stricken man.

In June 1870, thanks to his note-taking skills and aggressiveness, Barron landed a reporter's position with the *Boston Daily News*.

Two months into the job, Barron came across a debate on the industrial revolution between the abolitionist William Lloyd Garrison and Wendell Phillips, a leading orator of the day.[2] Believing there was little reader interest in the topic, most other Boston papers failed to cover it. But Barron reported on the debate, relating how this seemingly arcane subject affected daily life. To the surprise of everyone, the issue sold out.

Noting this and other indications of reader demand for more business news, the *Boston Transcript* established a separate business section and hired Barron, then twenty-one, to be its editor. Within months, the *Transcript's* circulation, already at the respectable level of 56,700, increased 15 percent, due to the newspaper's expanded coverage.

Barron's fearlessness made him an outstanding journalist. As if divinely inspired, he believed it was his mission to interview heads of states and corporations. And once in the presence of interviewees— the more important or famous the better—Barron treated them like lodge brothers.

His close relationship with Alexander Graham Bell, a professor of speech and vocal physiology at Boston University, enabled him to be the first to report Bell's inaugural telephone conversation: "Mr. Watson, come here. I want you."[3]

Touched by Barron's interest in his work, Professor Bell continued to reward Barron with exclusive interviews throughout much of his career. Besides writing a series that predicted the future economic effects of the telephone, Barron also detailed for *Transcript* readers how Bell went from rags to riches after the Bell Telephone Company was founded. Another notable *Transcript* scoop occurred when Thomas Alva Edison leaked to Barron that J. P. Morgan would finance the founding of the Edison Illuminating Company.

Despite his alliances with many powerful business leaders, Barron remained objective. He never protected a friend, a virtue that tested the resolve of the *Transcript's* owners. Cornelius Vanderbilt, the nation's railroad czar, was a case in point.

Prompted by the Panic of 1873, Vanderbilt had engaged in a stock-watering scheme to refinance the debt incurred several years before to acquire the New York Central Railroad. Clarence Barron caught wind of the scam and exposed his erstwhile friend in the *Boston Transcript*. In return, Vanderbilt tried to get Barron fired by reminding the owners, a Vanderbilt-controlled bank was the newspaper's sole source of financing. Though shaken, the owners decided to stand by their reporter.

The panics of the mid 1870s, the first sobering episodes in the industrial revolution, were set off by Jay Cooke, a nineteenth-century Rockefeller who also was fond of Barron. Cooke had established the Northern Pacific Railroad Company right after the Civil War. But a decade later the railroad foundered, and not even Cooke's immense wealth could quell Wall Street's hysteria.

Under banner headlines, Barron wrote:

Today, the failed ambitions of Jay Cooke struck again. Swamped
by panic and disillusionment, the New York stock exchange shut
down, temporarily. In the last two weeks alone, Mr. Cooke's
failure to pay his debts has caused 5,000 commercial firms and
fifty-seven Stock Exchange firms to die violent deaths. In the
same period, European investors, long the source of much
needed capital, lost $600 million in United States railroad
stocks.[4]

Though enthralled by free enterprise, Barron never became a
cheerleader for business, no small accomplishment for a financial
journalist. By resisting this urge, Barron's reporting made a difference. The creation of the Interstate Commerce Commission, for
example, came about in part because of Barron's coverage of the
railroad industry.

In June 1887, after eleven years as the *Transcript's* financial editor,
Barron founded his own company, the Boston News Bureau, a service
that disseminated news of the Boston and New York stock exchanges
via a daily newspaper and messengered bulletins as needed. After six
months, Barron had 125 subscribers.

Throughout most of his life, Clarence Barron was fascinated by J. P.
Morgan, who had also attended Boston's English High School.
Barron relished covering J. P. Morgan, especially when he could also
add a gentle prod. "The market's symbol of optimism, the bull, was
adopted to represent J. P. Morgan, whose body, voice, and temperament are very bull-like indeed,"[5] Barron once wrote.

But Barron admired Morgan greatly. In reporting the economic
panics of the early 1890s, caused by railroad overexpansion, Barron
reworked his earlier metaphor by heralding Morgan as "the nation's
Prometheus. By taking control of, or 'organizing,' bankrupt railroads
through voting trusts, J. P. Morgan has saved the country
singlehandedly."[6]

The American economy soared in the latter part of the nineteenth
century. In 1867 the United States produced 22,000 tons of steel; by
1900, steel production had risen to 11 million tons, a sum equal to the
combined output of England, France, and Germany.

Because the economy became an increasingly interesting news
story, Barron's news-service subscribers had increased to 5,123 by
1896.[7] The ticker had long ago replaced the hand-delivered bulletins,

a technological innovation which made for better informed subscribers and more profits for Barron. Not content to sit still, Barron
founded a similar financial news service in Philadelphia in 1896.

Throughout his business life, Barron exhibited impatience and
unreasonableness, common traits for entrepreneurs. Barron expected
his employees to share his ambition for making the Boston News
Bureau a success. But he was unwilling to share the Bureau's profits.

Only Barron had a clear vision of what the business should be, but
he lacked the temperament to pass this thinking on to his staff. Thus,
Barron's employees were always on tenterhooks, not knowing what he
expected of them. "Though business is booming, Mr. Barron is never
satisfied. And thus, neither is anyone else,"[8] wrote Edward Stein, a
secretary.

As Barron's prosperity grew, so did his waistline. By the late 1890s,
Barron had assumed the physiognomy of his idol, J. P. Morgan. He
stood five feet, five inches tall and weighed 300 pounds, a weight he
jokingly referred to as "my leanest." He kept six different wardrobes,
each successively bigger. When Barron could only fit into the biggest
set of clothes, he knew he weighed 350 pounds and that it was time to
diet. "His love of food was only matched by his devotion to my
grandmother and mother,"[9] said William Cox, step-great-grandson of
C. W. Barron.

Despite his newfound wealth, Barron continued to live in Mrs.
Jessie Waldron's boardinghouse as he had for the previous twelve
years. After her socially prominent but financially inept husband died
unexpectedly, Mrs. Waldron took in boarders in her stately Marlboro
Street town house, not far from the Boston Commons.

At first, Barron shared the Waldrons' hospitality with three other
men. But soon, Jessie Waldron, together with her two daughters, so
enthralled Barron that he plotted to drive his rivals away. Knowing
Jessie Waldron needed the income from four boarders to feel secure,
Barron suggested that if he were her only guest, he would gladly pay a
sum equal to five.

With each passing year as the star boarder, Barron became more
dependent on Jessie Waldron. "This woman has a surprising ability to
suggest just the right action," Barron once said. "We sit well into the
night, talking about my business problems. After hours of listening,
Jessie quietly says, 'Well, Clarence, it seems to me you should do
this. . . .' "[10]

Finally, in 1900, after living together platonically for fourteen years, Barron married Jessie Waldron and legally adopted her two daughters. To celebrate their new family status and to demonstrate his business success, the Barrons purchased a mansion in Boston's exclusive Back Bay section. "It's a fitting tribute to American free enterprise that I, a virtual waif thirty years ago, can now mingle with the Cabots and the Lowells,"[11] Barron wrote a friend. The Barron mansion was so large it required an elevator. It also boasted twenty-six rooms, eighteen telephones, a library, and a staff of twelve servants.

When Barron married, he was forty-five and wealthy, even by Boston's Back Bay standards. Middle age and success caused him to realize there was more to life than just business. Too fat and sedentary to engage in rigorous physical activity, Barron turned to the sea. He purchased the ninety-seven-foot yacht the *Hourless* and sailed it throughout the Northeast, in vain pursuit of Morgan's *Corsair*.

True to his nature, Barron became obsessed with sailing. Dressed in a commodore's uniform of gold-braided blue blazer, white trousers, and captain's hat, he would stand on the bridge and exhort his crew of eighteen to ever more exacting service. "Whenever C.W. was aboard the *Hourless*, his quest for domination became overwhelming,"[12] said Hugh Bancroft, Barron's unfavored son-in-law.

A gifted bridge player, Barron would remain aboard the *Hourless* for months at a time, sailing between Boston and New York, accumulating master bridge points with friends and business acquaintances. Occasionally, his two step-daughters and their beaus would accompany him, but his wife stayed at home.

In 1900, about the time Barron discovered sailing, his New York correspondent firm, Dow Jones & Company, Inc., was experiencing internal difficulty. The founding partners were still feuding. Several years before, Edward Jones had been forced to leave the firm because Charles Dow believed the ethics of their newspaper, the *Wall Street Journal*, were being compromised by Jones's advertising sales efforts. And now Dow, head of the newspaper's editorial department, and Bergstresser, head of production, were fighting over the same issue.

In ill health and fed up with the wrangling, Charles Dow traveled to Boston to ascertain if Barron would be interested in acquiring Dow Jones, a successful business news operation in New York. Feeling guilty because he was away from Jessie much of the time, Barron decided to buy the *Journal* and give it to her as a gift. He believed that since his wife was so valuable in building his business, she would do even better running her own.

By reacting to Charles Dow's overture with a polite lack of interest, Barron proved to be the shrewder negotiator. When Dow was just about to retract his invitation, Barron agreed to buy the *Wall Street Journal* and the Dow Jones Ticker Service for $156,000, with virtually no cash down and a series of personal IOUs pegged to the *Journal*'s future profits. Once the deal was concluded, Barron turned Dow Jones & Company, Inc. over to his wife, who, together with her future son-in-law, Hugh Bancroft, moved to New York to manage the company.

The term *profit* had a peculiar meaning to Clarence Barron. When calculating the *Journal*'s profits for his payments to Dow, Barron included any number of extraordinary expenses, including his wife's three-bedroom suite at the Waldorf-Astoria.

Irrespective of Mrs. Barron's long-distance commute and Clarence Barron's preoccupation with sailing, the couple still continued to cultivate their Boston social alliances, ties that eventually improved the family's blood lines greatly. In 1902, Jessie Waldron Barron's oldest daughter, Martha, married Horace W. Endicott, scion to the Endicott shoe fortune. Several years later, Jane married Hugh Bancroft, whose family went back to the first Pilgrims. Both weddings took place at the Barrons's summer estate in Cohassett overlooking the Atlantic, under huge pink-and-white-striped tents overflowing with food, flowers, and music.

But it was the guests who transformed these weddings into extraordinary affairs. First, there were the financial celebrities, tycoons from State Street, Wall Street, London, Paris, and Zurich. Then there were the Boston Brahmins, genteel descendants of Harvard Yard, Trinity Church, and Brattle Street. And then, most notably, there were the Irish from Boston's waterfront, Barron's relatives, unfettered by the whiskey and dance.

As warm and generous as Jessie Barron was in her private life, she was pragmatic, if not conniving, in business. Realizing the notion of a woman in business at the turn of the century was virtually unacceptable, Jessie Barron constructed an elaborate ruse involving her unsuspecting son-in-law Hugh Bancroft to circumvent this prejudice. She invited Bancroft to join the Dow Jones board of directors and help her manage the company. Tall, athletic, Harvard-educated, and a lawyer, Hugh Bancroft seemed to the outside world like the perfect leader. But Mrs. Barron knew that her son-in-law, like his father and grandfather before him, was the perfect follower.

Arriving on a ship that landed ten miles north of Boston in 1632, the Bancrofts were mainstays in the Pilgrim migration that imbued New England with much of its flinty morality and self-reliance. For the next fifty years, the family was the Massachusetts Bay Colony's sole exporter of sugar and tobacco, a trade that made them immensely wealthy. From then on, with money problems forever solved, the ensuing Bancrofts gravitated toward prestigious but largely ceremonial careers whose lack of challenge dulled their competitive edge. Hugh Bancroft's father, for example, served on the Board of Overseers of Harvard University.

Between Mrs. Barron's directives and Hugh Bancroft's compliant nature, Dow Jones and the *Wall Street Journal* experienced surprisingly good results for the first half-dozen years of their stewardship. So much so that, despite the terms militating against an early payment, Barron retired his IOUs far ahead of schedule.

Unfortunately, success lulled Mrs. Barron and Bancroft into a false state of confidence. They believed Dow Jones would prevail no matter what, a belief that caused them to relax unduly. An unexpected economic downturn, the Panic of 1907, proved them wrong and as quickly and as easily as success came, failure did, too. By 1912, virtually all Dow Jones profits had vanished, the *Journal's* circulation had slipped from a high of 11,000 to 7,500, and Dow Jones personnel had grown lazy and arrogant.

In the spring of that year, after lingering in the Boston background for years, Barron burst on the scene, intent on reviving Dow Jones and the *Journal.* A week later, Bancroft returned to Boston to head the city's transit authority.

Semiretirement did nothing for Barron's serenity. Enraged by the *Journal's* downward slide, Barron's first visit to the newsroom demonstrated his tyrannical lack of restraint. Words, spittle, and furniture flew as the 322-pound publisher stormed the aisles, at once chiding and exhorting all those who came into sight.

William Hamilton, the *Journal's* editor then, wrote: "C. W. Barron turned many reporters to petrified wood. With equal ferocity, he would persecute you one moment, praise you the next. Not many could adapt to his ups and downs. But those who did became better journalists."[13]

At the time, the *Wall Street Journal* was staffed by timid teenagers with little to no prior experience. These tyros did an adequate job of reporting market statistics, but lacked the analytic and writing skills to report cogently about business and finance, which was a particular strength of the *Journal of Commerce*, a feared competitor.

But those journalists who followed Barron's ubiquitous "Seven Points to Better Reporting and Writing" did eventually improve:

1. Be intrepid. You represent the *Wall Street Journal*, the premier financial publication of the day. Unlike a general assignment reporter, readers make financial decisions based on your efforts. Therefore, you have a responsibility to interview anyone and everyone.

2. No ego. Do not compete with Henry James or Ford Madox Ford when you take pen in hand.

3. Keep it simple. No adverbs, no adjectives, just simple declarative sentences in the active voice. There are exceptions, of course, but they are for the *New York Herald*.

4. Be lucid. Is what you've written what you want to say? Throw the baby out with the bathwater if it means sacrificing a brilliant metaphor for clarity.

5. Get it right. Editors can rewrite but only you can collect all the facts accurately. And they should be included in the first three paragraphs.

6. Tell a story. Quotes from identified sources are the most powerful narrative tool. And, of course, get them up high.

7. The lead is everything. Rework it thirty times. And invariably, on the thirty-first try, a perfect paragraph flows from somewhere.

Besides being the fattest publisher on Wall Street, Barron was also the most peripatetic. He never spent time sitting at his desk, preferring instead to roam about, questioning anyone who crossed his path. Since Barron's own job had ranged from copy boy to advertising salesman to editorial writer, he could tell instantly from the answers people gave him who was good and who was not.

Though Barron intimidated most of his employees, the outside world regarded him highly. Men like Theodore Roosevelt, William Howard Taft, and Woodrow Wilson counted Barron among trusted advisers, a status which carried mixed blessings. While it greatly enhanced Barron's celebrity, his penchant for cultivating affiliations with newsmakers gave detractors something to carp about.

James Gordon Bennett, Jr., publisher of the *New York Herald*, wrote in a dispatch from Paris:

While at the Ritz the other day, I could not help but note the frenzied arrival of America's foremost financial journalist, Clarence W. Barron, and his retinue. Curious, I asked, "Why are you here?" Barron replied, "So I might better inform my readers what to expect from Europe in the next ten years."

Mr. Barron then shared his itinerary, which included interviews with George V, Kaiser Wilhelm II, and several other reigning monarchs. While these names rolled off his enthusiastic and forceful tongue, I could not help but wonder if Mr. Barron would use his writing skills to manipulate royalty as he does in America with the likes of J. P. Morgan, Roosevelt, Taft, and other aspiring notables. The more powerful the subject, I'm told by my New York editors, the more flattering Mr. Barron's prose can be. And with heads of state, I imagine his prose will fairly soar. It's called "personal journalism"—a newspaper czar using his newspapers to beguile the mighty.

Regardless of Bennett's acid commentary, Barron did inform his readers that war on the Continent was imminent and it would begin by Germany invading Belgium.

During this European trip, Barron did not limit his observations to world politics. He occasionally wrote letters about what he liked and disliked in the arts. One cultural commentary marked the unveiling of a controversial painting:

For ten years now, ever since these chaps Braque and Picasso began foisting their distorted images on to the public as art— "Cubism" is what they call it—I have been content to remain privately amused at the boundless gullibility of those innocents in search of culture.

But today, having witnessed the unveiling of what was advertised as a seminal work of art—"Nude Descending a Staircase" by Marcel DuChamp—I have forsaken my vow of silence to warn the unsuspecting reader that these so-called Cubists are nothing but a band of out-of-work scoundrels skilled in promotion and deception.

The basis for my objection to Monsieur DuChamp's picture is entirely unrelated to probity. The title is highly misleading.

There is no nudity to be seen, no matter how hard, or at what angle, one stares at this tawdry canvas. The image, if one can call it that, is a series of rectangular lines which appear to trace, like a moving picture would, the continuous exposure of a figure without clothing sliding down a staircase. Any talentless fool can do this.

And I as much as said so to the perpetrator, Monsieur DuChamp, a wan, stringy-haired fellow. Lacking the courtesy to look me in the eye, this fellow fondled his pipe while he said, "Sir, I am an artist. That means whatever I do is a work of art. If I choose to hang a broom from the ceiling or display an ice-filled urinal, then by definition, both these items become objet d'arts."

Dazed, I stumbled into the adjoining gallery without further word. There, on the ceiling and on the floor, were a broom and a urinal.

Barron spent the better part of the next two years in Europe, reporting on the war. He returned to New York in early 1917, weeks before President Woodrow Wilson convinced Congress to authorize America's entry into World War I.

During this period, United States business flourished, manufacturing weapons and other war matériel for England and France. Dow Jones also experienced an upsurge in profits, marking the beginning of the correlation between the health of the nation's economy and the health of Dow Jones's profits. In 1917, the *Journal*'s circulation had climbed to 20,000, and Barron was earning in salary and dividends over $100,000 annually.

A year later, his beloved wife, Jessie, died of emphysema. Barron worshiped his wife to the end. In a letter to one of his stepdaughters, Barron wrote: "... your mother was greater than the Suffragettes. She single-handedly broke down Wall Street's all but impenetrable barriers against women."

Barron considered a good wife the secret to a good life. Often, before hiring a key executive, he would evaluate the man's wife as well.

By 1921, Barron took to defending Wall Street against regulation. In a *Journal* editorial, he wrote:

Capitalism—the sacred notion of free men and free markets— has enabled our economy to ascend from the third circle of Hell to Halcyon prosperity in fifty short years. But rather than continue the system exactly as is, there are those who would have the government intervene and control Wall Street, as if it were more illegal gamble than legitimate risk.... Like Moscow's new leaders, these people don't understand the cornerstones of free enterprise, supply and demand.

To the underutilized officials pursuing the regulation of our financial markets, we say, seek some other cause to get re-elected or promoted. Wall Street, because it is so free, provides all the information needed by any investor to prosper.

Later that same year, Dow Jones introduced a new publication, *Barron's*, a weekly magazine which offered tips to a throng of first-time investors anxious to take advantage of the Roaring Twenties prosperity. Also that same year, reflecting continuing record profits, the *Wall Street Journal* opened bureaus in Washington, D.C., Detroit, and Chicago.

By this time in his life, with Jessie no longer there to restrain him, Barron indulged his obsessions for food, work, and Germany's post-war problems with the fervor that plagues some geniuses. If judged by today's world, a therapist might diagnose him as a manic depressive because of his emotional highs and lows.

Barron manifested his depressive moods through an eating disorder. The fatter Clarence Barron became, the more melancholy he felt. Finally, after months of overeating and despondency, Barron discovered Dr. John H. Kellogg, a Battle Creek, Michigan, physician who specialized in treating obesity. The Pritikin of his day, Kellogg advocated grain as the mainstay of a healthy diet, a prescription which eventually led to corn flakes and the dry cereal industry.

Barron would visit Battle Creek twice a year, enduring Kellogg's diet and exercise regime for six weeks. Invariably, Barron would lose fifty to sixty pounds. But rather than carry Kellogg's program into his daily life, Barron would revert to ravenous eating as soon as he boarded his special train back to New York. Curiously, for a person who exhibited so much discipline in work, Clarence Barron could not or would not do the same for his personal life.

The Roaring Twenties, when America's middle class acquired comfort, if not affluence, was acknowledged by Barron in his many *Journal* articles extolling the recreational and investment opportunities of Florida. Lloyd Wendt, in his book *The Wall Street Journal*, quotes Barron as having said: "There are three great reasons for believing in Florida: January, February, and March."

Barron regarded Florida as a winter Wall Street where the fruits of capitalism enhanced the quality of daily life. He once told his step-granddaughter Jessie Cox, "The reason I worked so hard is so I can come to Palm Beach and enjoy the beauty, smell, and warmth of the place. And the middle class can do the same thing now."[14]

In 1921, Barron unexpectedly invited Hugh Bancroft back to Dow Jones. Though he still disliked Bancroft intensely, Barron preferred his son-in-law in New York so he could be closer to his grandchildren. In a moment of ebullience, Barron appointed Bancroft supervisor of the *Journal's* advertising and production functions. Later, Barron regretted this move: "Bancroft is not competent. Thank God I didn't make him editor."[15]

By relegating Bancroft to the *Journal's* business department, Barron demonstrated a prejudice that still pervades Dow Jones today: Compared to editorial people, business people are second-class citizens.

In 1923, Barron, then sixty-eight, realized he needed a successor. Convinced that Bancroft would never be that person, Barron went outside the company to look for an heir. Someone recommended Kenneth Craven Hogate, twenty-four, then a reporter on the *Detroit News* who enjoyed regular access to Henry Ford, someone Barron had never been able to interview.

After meeting Casey Hogate, Barron was ecstatic: "I could not have fathered a better son. He's bright and he even looks like me. And he's been a newspaper man all his life,"[16] Barron told Jane Bancroft.

A Phi Beta Kappa graduate of DePauw University, Casey Hogate was the quintessential midwesterner: competent, soft-spoken, and selfless. Hogate, also grossly overweight, was the heir to a newspaper family that had published a weekly, the *Republican*, in Danville, Indiana, for four generations. By age fourteen, Hogate knew how to set type, sell classifieds, and cover the Hendricks County courthouse beat.

In October 1923, Barron hired Hogate to be the *Journal's* Detroit reporter. Within his first month, Hogate persuaded Henry Ford to submit to an interview by Clarence Barron, the result of which was an editorial that praised Ford lavishly.

Shortly after the Ford interview, Barron appointed Casey Hogate managing editor of the *Wall Street Journal*. The first time Barron returned to Europe, Hogate used his absence to introduce many improvements in the *Journal*, including cartoons, stock-market quotations, and various columns, two of which still exist today: "Heard on the Street" and "Abreast of the Market." Hogate also predicted that someday Dow Jones would expand to include Boston, New York, and Philadelphia editions, making the *Journal* the nation's first national newspaper.

Stimulated by Hogate's innovations, the *Journal*'s circulation exceeded 24,000 by February 1926, double what it had been ten years before. That same year the paper charged $18 for a yearly subscription and 7¢ per copy on the newsstand.

Dow Jones's other news service, the ticker, was also doing well. Founded in 1897, the Dow Jones ticker had always been the quickest means to keep subscribers informed, a necessity for professional financiers who could not wait for the next day's *Journal* for information. Most brokerage houses and banks had at least one bell-shaped glass jar spewing forth ticker tape containing the latest financial news. Operating on long-distance telephone lines, the ticker news was provided by *Journal* reporters who, whenever they ran across a story, first had to phone the wire before writing it up for the *Journal*. Most reporters hated their ticker responsibility. It represented one more delay before they could see their byline in print; feeding the ticker required no creativity and offered even less glory.

The ticker prospered from the mid-twenties onward because of Joseph Ackell, Dow Jones's resident inventor. In early 1926, Ackell invented a ticker capable of receiving sixty words per minute, twice as fast as the nearest competitor's. As a consequence, ticker subscriptions swelled to 9,000, up 23 percent from the previous year. On the strength of this invention, Ackell was appointed head of the Dow Jones ticker service. By 1929, Ackell had linked ninety-three North American cities to the New York ticker newsroom via telegraph, creating the most comprehensive ticker bureau system in the country.

A Brooklyn native, Joseph J. Ackell joined Dow Jones as a stenographer in June 1923, fresh out of high school. His job was to type up story drafts and submit them to the copy desk for editing. By July, it was clear Ackell couldn't spell. "And since our reporters couldn't spell either, Ackell was a problem," William Hamilton, the *Journal*'s managing editor, once told a colleague.

One day an Ackell-transcribed article riddled with misspellings appeared on page one. The blunder infuriated Hamilton, who, perhaps unfairly, set out to fire Ackell.

But Ackell was not at his desk. Neither was anyone else visible. Finally, after touring the newsroom, Hamilton discovered the entire New York staff hovered around Dow Jones's central ticker, perplexed. As Hamilton poked his way through the circle, he learned the machine had just broken down, ten minutes before the noontime news was to go out. When Hamilton arrived in front of the ticker, he found Joe Ackell lying under it, covered in ink, grinning.

Everyone, including Hamilton, waited anxiously as Ackell tinkered away, oblivious to his short-lived career. After a few more minutes of tension, the ticker began to clack again. As Ackell stood up to cheers, Hamilton leaned forward and said, "You've found your calling, son."

From that day forward, Ackell maintained the newsroom's machinery. Soon he was devising machinery that could save time and labor as well.

Shortly thereafter, Ackell convinced the family to fund an unusual research project. He believed he could invent a system that would make the *Journal* a national newspaper. What was needed, he told the Bancrofts, was a means to send a "master copy" of a *Journal* issue from New York, where it was made up, to several plants strategically located throughout the country, which in turn would print and distribute that day's *Journal* in their regions.

While managing the Dow Jones ticker service by day, Ackell pursued his national newspaper project by night. Along the way he also invented automated mailing equipment and a calculator that posted Dow Jones's accounting ledgers and determined the Dow Jones averages automatically.

Despite the *Journal*'s and the ticker's strong performances, Barron's relationship with Bancroft remained problematic. Barron still exhibited an enmity towards Bancroft, as if his son-in-law were responsible for the Brahmin scourges of the Irish fifty years before. Barron's descendant, William Cox, recalled: "C.W. never got over the fact that my grandfather and my grand uncle [H. Wendell Endicott], for that matter, were to the manor born."[17]

As Barron aged, his intolerance for Bancroft increased. Finally, in 1926, Bancroft's name was removed from the newspaper's masthead, a significant demotion, and Hogate was elevated to a post that made him second only to Barron. With Bancroft banished and Hogate running the *Journal*, Barron spent the next several years in relative tranquillity, supporting capitalism, the Republican party, and Herbert Hoover's candidacy and indulging his passion for food.

On October 2, 1928, Barron, seventy-three, died in his sleep at Kellogg's sanitarium. A page-one obituary in the *New York Times* observed: "To a large extent he initiated the system of financial journalism in vogue today."

The *New York Post* was even more lavish in its praise: "Clarence W. Barron did for financial journalism what James Gordon Bennett did for general news.... Barron was one of the most picturesque figures that the starry skies of Wall Street ever produced."

America's economic power, as symbolized by Wall Street, had grown apace and thrived steadily until 1928. Few men understood and chronicled this miracle better than Clarence Barron.

A week after Barron's death, Hugh Bancroft's name reappeared on the *Wall Street Journal's* masthead. Bancroft was resurrected yet again to protect his wife, Jane's, stock holdings, which in 1928 generated more than $350,000 a year in dividends. Five years later, in the fall of 1933, with the *Journal* and the country floundering in the Great Depression, Hugh Bancroft died a suspected suicide. He was only fifty-three.

Two months later, another young man from the Midwest, Bernard Kilgore, joined Dow Jones. Eventually, Kilgore would eclipse even Barron in importance to the *Journal*.

3

The Debacle

In June 1935, on a summer day when Washington's humidity glistened on the Rose Room's walls, the President could barely conceal his exasperation as an aide wheeled him past the White House press corps. Late entrances into any room, especially when he was perspiring heavily, always set Roosevelt on edge. He much preferred to be standing coolly at the podium, wheelchair hidden, greeting the newsmen as they filed in. But this morning, at the briefing preceding the press conference, Secretary of the Treasury Henry Morgenthau taxed Roosevelt's patience and schedule by droning on about the Depression's latest crisis.

After struggling to the microphones, the President read a statement that promoted the latest triumph of the WPA, one of the more successful New Deal programs. The inexperienced members of the audience wrote down every word; the veteran reporters sat on their hands, skeptically waiting.

Referring to Roosevelt's attempt to garner positive headlines, Arthur Krock of the *New York Times* leaned over to Joseph Alsop and whispered, "Small price to pay. Remember, Hoover never even let us in here."

The moment the President concluded his statement, Walter Lippmann leapt to his feet and, ignoring the good news about the WPA, asked, "Mr. President, why are interest rates so high? Shouldn't they be lower to stimulate economic recovery?"

Tightening his grip on the podium, Roosevelt stared at Lippmann for a moment, registering his displeasure with the question and the manner with which it was asked. Then, smiling affectedly, the President replied: "I'm pleased my opening statement made such an impression on you, Mr. Lippmann." Roosevelt went on to chide Lippmann for his recent front-page story which misstated the administration's position on interest rates. As the President articulated the *Herald's* "egregious errors," Lippmann's face grew more contorted.

Lippmann finally interrupted. "Did anyone get the story right, sir?"

With a flourish, Roosevelt pointed to a young man sitting off by himself. "There... Kilgore... of the *Wall Street Journal*....He got it right," the president said. All eyes turned to examine Bernard Kilgore, twenty-six, newly appointed Washington bureau chief of the *Wall Street Journal*. What Krock, Lippmann, Alsop, and others saw that day was a man whose baleful eyes, nervous tick, and receding hairline made him look like a government clerk, not some journalist capable of earning a presidential compliment.

A man blessed with brightness, industry, and the rarest humility, Barney Kilgore affected his mentor, Casey Hogate, Dow Jones's president, the same way Hogate had affected Barron: He could do no wrong. And actually, Kilgore rarely did.

In September 1929, three months after graduating from DePauw University Phi Beta Kappa, Kilgore was recruited by Casey Hogate as a reporter trainee for the *Wall Street Journal*.

After six years of increasingly noteworthy service, first in San Francisco, where he initiated a column entitled "Dear George" that explained complicated financial issues in plain and understandable terms, and then in New York as an editor/columnist, Kilgore was transferred to Washington to head the *Journal's* talent-filled news bureau. Three members of the Washington staff, Vermont Connecticut Royster, William Henry Grimes, and Bill Kerby, would later become editor, managing editor, and chief executive officer of the *Journal* and Dow Jones, respectively.

By the mid-thirties, because of the Depression, Roosevelt, and the Securities & Exchange Commission, Washington, D.C., had become an important news center for every major daily, especially for the *Wall Street Journal*. The public's once great enthusiasm for the *Journal's* primary beat, news of the New York–based securities markets, had turned to apathy; the newspaper was suffering from the nation's backlash against anything that smacked of Wall Street. Consequently, the more the *Journal* could expand its coverage of Washington, reasoned Casey Hogate, the more chance it had for survival.

But contrary to its newfound significance, the Washington bureau still consisted of three drab rooms in the National Press Building, inadequate space for a staff of thirteen people. The biggest room was the wire room, where copy was edited and then transmitted to editors or the ticker in New York. The second room was for the staff; it had four used typewriters. The third room was a glass-enclosed cubicle that served as Kilgore's office. The lack of splendor did not bother Kilgore, the quintessential midwesterner, in the least. Like the rest of Dow Jones and *Journal* employees at the time, Kilgore never thought about his own symbols of power.

Leslie Bernard Kilgore grew up in South Bend, Indiana, the only son of Tecumseh and Lavina Kilgore. Even in his youth, Barney Kilgore's unassuming demeanor camouflaged a prodigious mind and a fun-loving spirit. In school, beginning with the first grade, Kilgore demonstrated he was a remarkable student, always at the head of his class and always exempt from examinations. While others studied for finals, Kilgore invented mechanical contraptions.

Every June, for instance, he built a railroad out of wagons and a gasoline engine powerful enough to transport adults. Wearing a floppy denim cap and a red handkerchief around his neck, Kilgore gave the whole neighborhood rides. With each passing year, the train got bigger and faster. In June 1920, Kilgore outdid himself. Tecumseh Kilgore once related to the *South Bend News*, "I finally had to put a stop to Barney's train the day he rounded a curve so fast that his mother landed in the rose bushes."[1]

In the fall, his father added, Kilgore would rig a bedsheet to his red wooden wagon and "sail over every square inch of South Bend's paved surfaces, scaring any number of dogs and garden club ladies along the way."

Largely self-educated, Tecumseh Kilgore did many things by day, from selling insurance to serving as a school superintendent. By night, he was an ambitious reader of the classics, relishing everything from Homer to Tolstoy.

"My father was extremely erudite," Kilgore told a friend once. "Even in the most casual conversations, he would reveal something new, something I didn't know. Once, when I was a teenager, a dinner guest asked him if he knew anything about Budapest. Dad talked about the city for over an hour. Even told us how the Danube River affected its development."[2]

His mother, Lavina Bodenhorn Kilgore, a pianist of considerable talent, attended New York's Julliard School of Music on a scholarship. Instead of pursuing a career, she returned to Indiana and Tecumseh Kilgore. However, Lavina did not neglect her talent. "My mother played the piano like most people talk," Kilgore was fond of saying. "I could tell her mood by what she was playing. Debussey meant things were fine. But Beethoven meant trouble."[3]

Taught by his mother, Kilgore became a skilled classical pianist, too. But when Kilgore went away to college, he switched to jazz. "My parents were disappointed, but jazz allowed me access to people," Kilgore remembered.

Later, when he became president of Dow Jones and wanted to know what his frontline reporters were thinking, Kilgore would travel to *Journal* outposts. "Barney would amble into the bureau, unannounced, and invite everyone out to dinner. We'd all drink too much and end up standing around a piano, listening to him. God, he could play! Then we'd spill our guts," said Fred Taylor, former *Journal* managing editor, recollecting Kilgore's visits to San Francisco.[4]

When Kilgore was fourteen, he contracted a mysterious, poliolike disorder which restricted his activities for the better part of a year. Though the disease left him as abruptly as it came, an involuntary tic remained.

The tic embarrassed Kilgore until his father told him how a Greek orator surmounted his handicap. "After Dad told me Demosthenes learned to speak clearly by putting pebbles in his mouth, I decided to learn how to overcome the shame rather than shrink from others," Kilgore remembered. He became a debater and in three years of high school debating competition, Kilgore never lost a contest.

Of his many influences, Tecumseh Kilgore's love of books had the most effect on young Kilgore. Anxious for his son to be a good writer, the elder Kilgore constantly recommended the style of his favorite author. "Whenever I had something to write for school, Dad would say: 'Remember Mark Twain. He loved verbs and simple declarative sentences. Hated adverbs. Most important, Twain could end a story when it was finished.'"[5]

After graduating from South Bend Central High School in 1925 with honors and an impressive record of extracurricular activities, Kilgore entered DePauw University, a distinguished liberal arts college in Greencastle, Indiana. There he served on the school newspaper, the *DePauw*, for four years, as reporter, sports editor, and in his senior year, editor in chief. The *Mirage*, the college yearbook, described him as "right out of 'Front Page,' with the brim to his fedora pushed back, his sleeves rolled up and coffee stains on his one, always loosened tie."

In his junior year, Kilgore served as editor of the yearbook, which he redesigned and copyrighted. When he graduated, Kilgore sold the rights of his design to the next class for $1,500.

Kilgore used his dual editorships to convince school officials he needed a car on campus. It was a rare exception which Kilgore used to his best advantage. One winter evening in 1928, Kilgore attached a sled to his Model T, "Pandora," and took three sorority sisters for a moonlit sleigh ride. At dawn, all four staggered back to campus, grinning. Pandora had run aground in a snowbank miles outside of Greencastle.

In Kilgore's senior year, DePauw hosted a series of lectures by distinguished alumni. Casey Hogate, class of 1918, then vice president and general manager of the *Wall Street Journal*, returned to Greencastle to speak about the freedoms and responsibilities of the press in America.

At the conclusion of his remarks, Hogate called for questions. One hand shot up.

"Mr. Hogate," Kilgore asked, "you didn't mention this, but does the *Wall Street Journal* have any special responsibilities to its readers, considering it's a financial newspaper?"

Acknowledging he had neglected an important point, Hogate went on to say the *Journal* maintained very strict standards for accuracy and impartiality, stricter even than the *New York Times*, because "unlike a general newspaper, many people make financial decisions based on what appears in each issue of the *Journal*."

The next day, after reading Kilgore's account of his speech, Hogate sought Kilgore out and complimented him on the piece. Three months later, the twenty-one-year-old Kilgore joined the *Journal* at Hogate's behest, one month before the Crash.

As a holdover from the Clarence Barron days, the *Journal* was still in the habit of hiring high school graduates proficient in stenography for $10 per week. Though Kilgore was several cuts above the normal recruit, he blended in nicely with his peers. No one suspected, for instance, that he was earning $40 per week or that he had earned a Phi Beta Kappa key. But Kilgore was not spared the hazing ritual of every new *Journal* hiree. His first two weeks on the job were spent in a windowless basement room noting the differences between Dow

Jones ticker and *Journal* stories. Kilgore was then shifted to the copy desk to learn the *Journal's* writing style.

The twenties became a particularly exciting time for Wall Street, especially when Barron was alive, always injecting color or controversy into the *Journal*. But Barron's successor, Casey Hogate, was overwhelmed by the Depression and was forced to delegate the day-to-day operation of the *Journal* news department to Cyril E. Kissane, a prosaic managing editor. As a partial consequence of Kissane's dullness, the *Journal's* news coverage throughout the early thirties consisted mostly of dry, statistics-laden accounts of which stocks were best and why. Also, the *Journal's* arid articles could be blamed on the quality of its staff. Former stenographers were adept at collecting facts and figures but lacked the creativity to write engagingly. Emulating what other newspapers did to solve this problem, the *Journal* editors created a style manual which insured uniformly grammatical, if not lyrical, prose. The *Journal's* copy desk implemented the rules of the style manual quite rigidly.

These rules required that the pertinent facts of a story be crammed into the first or second paragraph. The balance of the story elaborated on these facts. Talented writers were not persuaded by the editors' argument that this style, called the inverted pyramid, enabled readers to get the gist of an article in a glance. Reporters who could write creatively much preferred to tease a reader by starting off with an anecdote and then telling the story in a linear fashion, saving the denouement for the last paragraph.

Kilgore later admitted, "Mark Twain would not have written for the *Journal* then. And he certainly would not have read it."

After spending three months on the New York copy desk, Kilgore was shifted to the San Francisco bureau. The twenty-one-year-old cub reporter was relegated to reporting the quarterly earnings of the second- and third-tier banks, a dismal responsibility throughout the Depression. But within months, Kilgore developed a reputation for being an accurate and thorough fact gatherer. It was Kilgore, for instance, who began the *Journal* tradition of double-checking a company's released earnings against those contained in the company's audited statement. He discovered the Bank of America had been inflating its earnings in press releases for years.

But Kilgore's writing abilities languished. There was little opportunity to chronicle the human toll of the Crash. Aware he was still too inexperienced to be heard, Kilgore kept his frustration to himself.

But after fifteen months of compliance, he came upon a news story which he believed, if written in a certain way, would be an interesting page-one feature. At the time, there were no page-one features, interesting or otherwise; nothing but factual accounts of the markets, laced with prices and data, the type only professional financiers read.

When Kilgore handed in the unorthodox piece, Deac Hendee, Kilgore's immediate boss, rejected it out of hand. Undeterred, Kilgore quietly gave the article to Carl Miller, Hendee's boss. Miller read it through, wordlessly. When he finished, Miller took off his glasses and gently asked Kilgore to return to his desk. Two days later, this story appeared on the edition's front page, untouched. The story began:

> Five years ago, Oliver Twining rarely was early for work. As the chairman of Pacific Bank & Trust Company, Mr. Twining regularly strolled into his office twenty minutes late. "Rank has its privileges," he would explain.
>
> Today, however, Oliver Twining is rarely late for work.
>
> Now self-employed, he operates 14 hours per day on the corner of Church and California Streets, shouting "Apples for sale!"
>
> Oliver Twining is just one of many former bankers trying to piece their lives back together in the wake of 9,000 bank failures in the last three years.

Kilgore's feature continued to cite a half-dozen anecdotes which poignantly demonstrated the human cost of the Depression. Shortly thereafter, Kilgore returned to New York as special assistant to Casey Hogate. He was not in New York six weeks when Hogate asked Kilgore to accompany him to a meeting which the newly elected mayor of New York City, Fiorello La Guardia, had requested.

Hogate expected the occasion to be a routine, off-the-record visit where the *Journal* and the new mayor would get to know one another better. But when the three men met, Hogate and Kilgore were stunned by La Guardia's reception. Later, Kilgore wrote, "As we made our entrance, the mayor bounced from behind Teddy Roosevelt's enormous desk and, ignoring Casey's outstretched hand, accused him of harboring a criminal."

La Guardia, who had just exploited the anti–Wall Street sentiment to get elected, charged that *Journal* reporter Richard Edmonson, who wrote the weekly investor feature "Abreast of the Market" had regularly received bribes to tout certain stocks. Horrified, Hogate assigned the story to Kilgore, with instructions to report what he uncovered as if Edmonson worked for a rival newspaper. No fact was to be omitted, no favoritism shown.

Thirty-seven hours later, Kilgore's piece revealed the validity of La Guardia's allegations, resulting in Edmonson's subsequent termination from the *Journal*. The article also told of Dow Jones's newly created ethical guidelines, conflict-of-interest policies to which all employees would henceforth be bound. First among them were severe restrictions on the buying and selling of securities. Though the *Journal* reported the scandal candidly, the country was not mollified. People blamed the Depression on Wall Street, and now the *Wall Street Journal*, seemingly so incorruptible, had proved them right.

Kilgore remained in New York for the next two years, writing, editing, and authoring an economics column. Then, in January 1935, Hogate sent his protégé to Washington to relieve William Grimes, who was going to replace Cy Kissane as the *Journal*'s managing editor.

In competing with the likes of Arthur Krock of the *New York Times* and Walter Lippmann of the *New York Herald Tribune*, Kilgore and his bureau chronicled the New Deal with surprising fairness, particularly for a newspaper known to be rabidly Republican. "We did nothing but follow Hogate's rules of journalism," Kilgore later said. "The public confuses a reporter with an editorial writer. At the *Journal*, no two jobs could be more dissimilar. The Washington bureau neither agreed or disagreed with Roosevelt's programs. We merely reported them. By the same token, we were never swayed by a *Journal* editorial either."[6]

During his first eight years with the *Journal*, Barney Kilgore led two lives. By day, he was an industrious reporter with a penchant for well-written features. In the evening, he performed at various jazz clubs in San Francisco, Washington, and New York. If writing transported Barney Kilgore during the day, jazz allowed him to soar at night. He would play for hours, cigarette dangling from his mouth, his nervous tic barely visible, oblivious to everything except his music.

According to family legend, only one person, Mary Louise Throop, ever caused Barney Kilgore to look up from the keyboard. In December 1936, Kilgore and some friends were having a party in a private rail car they had rented to attend a reunion at DePauw of their fraternity, Sigma Delta Chi. Mary Throop and her sorority sisters were among the guests. As usual, Kilgore began playing the piano when the reflections of Mary's sequined black velvet dress caught his eye. Kilgore later told his son, James, "I looked up to see where those distracting flashes were coming from, and there was your mother, the prettiest, smartest-looking woman I had ever seen."

Besides being attractive, Mary Throop had a mind of her own. Unlike the typical DePauw coed at the time, she was not the least bit subservient, an attitude Kilgore enjoyed immensely. "Barney loved anyone who challenged him, and Mary did it better than most,"[7] said Eleanor Cammack, a DePauw classmate of Kilgore's.

Another observer of the thirties, Kit Melick, a *Journal* editorial assistant, agreed with Cammack. "I thought Barney was a nice man, but a little plain and simple. You know, like Hoosiers usually are. But when I met his Mary I was stunned. She was so beautiful, so sophisticated."[8]

L. Bernard Kilgore and Mary Louise Throop were married on October 1, 1938, in Greencastle, Indiana, home of DePauw University and the Throop family. Eventually, they had three children: Kathryn, James Bernard, and John Harvey.

As the Depression continued, so, too, did the decline of the *Journal*'s financial situation. The paper's circulation, which had reached a high in 1929 of 56,750, had fallen to 12,000 by 1936. And the *Journal*'s advertising pages and profits declined commensurately.

Remembering when their father, Hugh Bancroft, stepped in and botched the *Journal*, Jessie Cox and Jane Cook, granddaughters of Clarence Barron, remained on the sidelines, offering Hogate and his associates enthusiastic but noninterfering support. Bill Cox said recently, "Either courage or vanity caused my mother [Jessie Cox] and aunt [Jane Cook] to keep the *Journal* alive. In today's world, the *Journal* never would have survived."[9]

From 1936 to 1939, the *Journal* losses exceeded $5 million per year. The *Wall Street Journal*'s subscriber ranks now consisted solely of professional financiers. The Depression had killed off the bulk of the *Journal*'s former circulation, the small investor who played the market for his own benefit.

As the Depression began to take its toll on the *Journal*, the ticker began to gain favor within Dow Jones. Because of its speed in conveying information, subscribers considered the ticker more essential than the *Journal.* And when, as a result of their own Depression-wrought reversals, subscribers wanted to reduce expenses, they discontinued the *Journal,* not the Dow Jones ticker.

Once the ticker became Dow Jones's only source of profits, Jessie Cox and Jane Bancroft began to regard Ackell with new respect, a change that affected Ackell's ego. William Grimes, the *Journal's* managing editor, confided: "When the ladies started to pay attention to Joe, he became insufferable. He even took to telling reporters how to improve their wire coverage."[10]

Even Barney Kilgore, by now a respected Washington journalist, did not escape Ackell's scrutiny.

At about five o'clock on September 3, 1937, Roosevelt announced a new commissioner of the Tennessee Valley Authority, an important New Deal program. Kilgore reported the appointment to the Dow Jones ticker immediately before returning to his office three blocks away to write a more elaborate account of the event for the next day's *Journal.* In the ten minutes it took Kilgore to walk the distance, a press aide announced another, far less important TVA appointment. When Kilgore reached his office and learned of the second appointment, he did not bother to call the ticker again. However, he did include it in his story for the *Journal.*

About midmorning the next day, Kilgore received a telephone call from Ackell. The conversation began amiably enough, according to C. A. Mahoney, a reporter who happened to be sitting nearby. But then Kilgore's tic became increasingly evident as the young bureau chief attempted to explain, courteously at first, why the *Journal,* but not the ticker, had carried the second appointment.

Finally, Mahoney remembered, "Kilgore banged down the phone, but not before saying, 'I'm sorry, Mr. Ackell, but that's a journalistic decision beyond your depth.'"[11] Mahoney and several other reporters stood and cheered.

The next day, Kilgore received a call from Grimes, the managing editor. Grimes related how Ackell had complained to Hogate that "Kilgore became vicious when I merely offered a few words of encouragement and advice." Grimes added that Hogate wanted Kilgore to apologize that morning to preclude Ackell taking his grievance to the Bancrofts, the relatives of Clarence Barron who still owned Dow Jones.

Kilgore refused.

"Barney would not budge, not even for Hogate," Mahoney said.

"Another day passed, and then we heard Barney on the phone quietly saying, 'Yes, Mrs. Bancroft, I did say that. I meant no disrespect. But because the ticker is making money, that doesn't change the fact Mr. Ackell is an engineer, not a journalist. I would not tell him how to operate a piece of machinery. He should extend me the same courtesy.'"

Shortly thereafter, the ticker created its own staff of reporters.

As his reputation as a journalist grew, Kilgore began to voice his belief that the *Journal* needed to become more mainstream. Kilgore would say, "The *Journal's* audience is too small and rarefied. It's edited for bankers, not their depositors; for brokers, not their stockholders; for financiers, not middle class workers. And it's deadly dry sometimes. People, even business people, love to read stories. That's why Ovid, Homer, and Twain endure. They used simple, interesting tales to convey complicated abstractions. And what could be more complicated, more abstract than business and finance?"

Specifically, Kilgore wanted to make the *Journal's* front page, which he considered funereal at times, more accessible. Kilgore explained, "It is, at once, our greatest strength and greatest liability. It impresses people, they remember it. But I'm not sure they want to read it all the time."

To this end, Kilgore suggested putting the column "Washington Wire," a weekly summary of activities in Congress, the White House, and other pertinent government branches, on the front page. Besides acknowledging business people's interest in Washington, Kilgore suspected that the smartly written column would draw more readers into the page.

William Grimes, the managing editor and future Pulitzer Prizewinner, was aghast. He saw no reason to change. Grimes said, "What was good enough for Clarence Barron should be good enough for Barney Kilgore. It should stay put on the editorial page where it's been for the last six years."

Again, Kilgore disagreed with a managing editor and sought the opinion of a higher court. This time it was Hogate, Dow Jones's president, who saw the wisdom in Kilgore's reasoning. Several months after the "Washington Wire" column started to appear on the front page every Tuesday, letters to the editors indicated the change was a success. But Grimes did not take defeat graciously. He retaliated by reducing the Washington bureau's news space in the *Journal*.

By the late thirties, even the ticker fell into the red, and Hogate's health began to suffer from ten years of battling the effects of the Depression. Jessie Cox and Jane Bancroft Cook kept wrestling with the question: With an ailing publisher and an even more ailing readership, why keep the *Journal* open?

Unlike his mentor, Clarence Barron, Casey Hogate failed to select and groom a successor. Hogate had little time for any consideration other than the daily struggle of keeping Dow Jones alive. In September 1941, Cox and Cook decided to postpone closing the *Journal* for a few more months to see if the war in Europe would stimulate the economy and the *Journal's* prospects. In the interim, the two ladies wanted to install Joe Ackell as a replacement for Hogate, who by now was seriously incapacitated. When they confided their intentions to Hogate, he said little. He did not want to disparage Ackell's appointment for fear the ladies would immediately shut down the newspaper for lack of a viable alternative.

Torn between his loyalty to the Barron family and his belief Ackell would be a disaster, Hogate hatched a counterattack which, he hoped, could never be traced back to him. Within minutes of learning who his successor would be, Hogate invited Kilgore, who had just come to New York as the *Journal's* managing editor, to dinner at the Plaza Hotel in New York. When Kilgore walked into the Oak Room, he was mildly surprised to see his erstwhile detractor, William Grimes, flanking Hogate at a corner table.

During the course of the dinner, Hogate revealed his plan, which consisted of his calling Jessie Cox, the more malleable of the two sisters, and saying that Grimes had come forth when he heard the rumor that Ackell was about to succeed Hogate. According to Grimes, who had already consulted key news staffers, if Ackell became the boss, half the news department would resign.

While Hogate laid out his plan, Kilgore kept nodding his head. Everything Hogate said, including the threat of quitting, Kilgore agreed with unreservedly. Grimes, however, remained inscrutable.

Then Kilgore asked Hogate, "Of course, the sixty-four dollar question is, who's going to replace you?"

Kilgore strained to hear Hogate's reply.

Peremptorily, Grimes, Kilgore's old nemesis, leaned forward and said: "You are, Barney."

4

The Resurrection and Barney Kilgore, President (1941–65)

A month after Kilgore's dinner with Hogate at the Plaza, an official press release announced that Bernard Kilgore was appointed vice president and general manager of Dow Jones & Company, Inc., reporting to Kenneth C. Hogate, the company's president, whose illness confined him to home. Though Barron's descendants had authorized Kilgore to run Dow Jones as he saw fit, they were reluctant to give the thirty-two-year-old journalist complete authority. The family wanted the option of being able to call on Joe Ackell if Kilgore did not work out.

But this ambiguity was the least of Kilgore's concerns as he quietly took over Hogate's penthouse office on the eighth floor of the Dow Jones Building at 44 Broad Street, in the shadow of the New York Stock Exchange.

The nation's dread, which for so long had been focused on the Depression, switched to the war. For the past twelve years, the country had been intrigued by Roosevelt and how his government regulation and intervention were or were not solving the poverty and turmoil of the Depression. Now people were frightened by Hitler, the Rising Sun, and the possibility of their fathers, husbands, brothers, and friends being killed on some Pacific atoll or Sicilian battlefield.

It took time for people to realize that the war, though despicable, did revitalize the economy. As the United States began to emerge victorious, people wanted to know more about the wartime role of commerce. Consequently, the nation's apathy toward Wall Street in the thirties turned to curiosity about business in the forties. Satisfying this need, the *Journal*'s circulation had risen several thousand copies, to 35,000, by February 1943, a far cry from the 56,000 the *Journal* had attained in 1930, but a positive trend nonetheless.

But Kilgore knew this trend was temporary and that to increase circulation permanently the *Journal* would have to change from a financial trade publication to a general newspaper specializing in business and financial news.

On January 12, 1943, Kilgore spent his first hour as Dow Jones's new vice president and general manager lost in his favorite passion—shadow editing an issue of the *Wall Street Journal*. Oblivious to his new office, Kilgore sat hunched over the paper, his right knee pumping furiously, scrawling on the margin of every page.

At about 9:45 A.M., William Kerby, twenty-seven, a short man with a notably florid complexion, appeared in Kilgore's doorway. After Kilgore's promotion, Kerby had succeeded him as the *Journal*'s managing editor. Behind Kerby stood William "Henry" Grimes, fifty-one, now head of the editorial page. Grimes looked perturbed.

"Always the editor," Kerby said softly to Kilgore.

Kilgore suddenly looked up, smiled, and beckoned to the silver coffee service on the Chippendale sideboard. "Welcome to our first kaffeeklatsch," he said.

After helping themselves to coffee, the two visitors took seats at the table according to their enthusiasm for the meeting. Grimes sat down at the other end, by himself. Kerby went right to Kilgore's side.

As the men settled down, Kilgore asked offhandedly, "What did you think of today's issue?"

Kerby diplomatically waited for Grimes to respond. When he didn't, the younger man, eager to please, said, "I thought it was stronger than usual."

"Why?" Kilgore asked.

"Well, the column-six leader was an excellent analysis."

"What's going on here, Barney?" interrupted Grimes. "Casey [Hogate] never interfered. He ran the business and we ran the paper."

Smiling, Kilgore said to his one time boss, "And to think I worried you'd stop speaking up, Henry."

Eased by Kilgore's affability, Grimes replied, "I know you, Barney. You're always changing things. I'm worried you're going to change us right out of business."

"I'm worried about that, too," Kilgore replied. "But we're in such bad shape now, we've nothing to lose."

It was the start of a Dow Jones institution whereby every morning for the next forty-five years, editors-turned-executives would gather over coffee at Clarence Barron's enormous mahogany table to dissect that day's *Journal*. But this morning, Kilgore had an even more important agenda in mind. He was going to spell out his plan to save the *Journal*.

Kilgore began by trying to convince Grimes, a respected but truculent editor, the *Journal* was in trouble. In the past, when asked to explain the *Journal's* flagging performance, Grimes would shrug and cite the Depression. But that morning, Kilgore preempted Grimes by saying: "Blaming the Depression for our present state will only hasten our demise." Grimes became rigid, but Kerby nodded his agreement.

"It's true," Kerby said. "The Depression hurt us initially. But we kept running away from it long after we had to. Today, we're a jargon-laden trade sheet serving only Wall Street." Kerby tried to soften his words with a smile.

Grimes fairly shouted, "Thank God for Wall Street. It's part of our name, and it kept us going for the last ten years."

Kilgore replied gently, "We're not going to abandon our friends, Henry."

Kilgore then introduced his plan, which by any standard was breathtaking in sweep and risk. Its cornerstone called for the *Wall Street Journal* to become America's first national daily newspaper.

"Thanks to Joe Ackell," Kilgore said," in a few years we'll be able to print the *Journal* in Boston, Philadelphia, Los Angeles, and San Francisco for distribution in those and neighboring cities on the same day. Our circulation could leap to a hundred thousand in five years."

By modifying a principle of telegraphy, Kilgore's erstwhile rival, Joe Ackell, was close to inventing a technology which could convert an entire eighteen-page *Journal* issue into electrical impulses that would be transmitted via telegraph wires to various yet-to-be-built plants throughout the country. When received, the impulses would be converted into punched holes in paper tape, which would then be played through a typesetting machine the same way a paper roll operates a player piano.

"This is crazy, Barney. Crazy!" Grimes shouted, a gray forelock falling into his eyes, he was trembling so much. "One moment you're telling us we're about to go out of business because we talked only to Wall Street for the past ten years. And then the next moment you're telling us we're now going to expand throughout the country, the first newspaper ever to do so, carrying a logo that reminds everyone what caused the Depression."

"I agree, Henry. It is crazy," Kilgore said evenly. "I admitted that to the Bancrofts when I asked them to finance the plan. I said, 'It's either crazy or it's our only hope. We'll know one way or another in fifteen months.'"

But becoming a national newspaper would not, by itself, save the *Journal*, Kilgore added. Through a series of editorial changes, Kilgore hoped also to attract new readers "from commerce, government, law, education, and politics. People who are managers, owners of small businesses, middle class people who want to get ahead."

Kilgore's editorial changes focused on the *Journal's* front page. He told the two men, "Since most people read their hometown newspaper first, by the time they get to us they're in a different frame of mind. If something on our front page doesn't jump out at them, they're only too happy to be on their way."

Kilgore believed the front page had to persuade the reader to take an additional twenty to thirty minutes from his busy day to savor the *Journal*. To accomplish this, the *Journal* had to compete with the front pages of the dailies in at least one strategic area. Kilgore went on, "In the rush to meet their deadlines, dailies have all they can do to gather the bare-bone facts—the who-what-when-and-how—of a breaking story. They don't have time to explain why an event occurred, which is what people really want. In New York City alone, there are twelve papers telling people the facts. But none tell them why."

Kilgore then announced that the two outside columns of the *Journal's* front page, columns one and six would be dedicated to features which explained the "whys" behind selected news events and, more important, how they affected business. Heretofore, these columns had been used for breaking business news stories. Dubbed leaders, these column-one and -six pieces were to be longer than usual and contain two additional elements, a flashline and a nutgraf. The flashline, designed to catch the scanner's eye, consisted of two to three words below the headline that summed up the story. The nutgraf was a paragraph that told the reader why the story was important.

Again Grimes interrupted. "If we're going to run nothing but leaders on the front page, we might as well change our name to *Time* [magazine]!" he said.

Ignoring the sarcasm, Kilgore answered, "That's exactly right, Henry. We want the *Journal's* front page to look like a newspaper's and read like a magazine's."

By committing as much as 67 percent of the front page to leaders, stories that, unlike breaking news, need not be told immediately, the *Journal's* front page no longer would be ruled by the tyranny of deadlines. This gave *Journal* reporters enough time—a day, a week, a month, several months—to do a story properly. And since these stories could be stockpiled and published at will, the *Journal's* front page could be planned in advance. Both these time benefits would enhance the *Journal's* editorial content, which eventually would lead to increased readership.

But Kilgore went further. He insisted the *Journal's* front page amuse as well. "We need a little whimsy to leaven these serious why or situation features." Column four was slotted for lighthearted essays, called A-heds after the type of headline used to herald them. He then offered the following story, written by Bill Kerby, as an example of a *Journal* A-hed. The story began: "Donovan Saul shuffles down the road, his eyes glued to the ground. Suddenly, he jackknifes and scoops up from the roadside what appears to be a gobbet of Silly Putty." The subsequent paragraphs explained that Mr. Saul made his living catching and selling slugs to scientists, who used them for research.

"There's only one problem, Barney," Grimes said. "Who's going to write stories like that? We don't have the talent!"

Conceding that the new format was beyond the *Journal's* current capability in writing, Kilgore announced the establishment of a copy desk which would be manned by writers hired from other publications. "And some of these new copy desk people will be women. At least until the men return from war. Besides, some gals make terrific writers," said Kilgore.

The copy desk's job was to transform the reporters' rough drafts into lyrical prose. "The reporter will still have his byline on the story," Kilgore said, "but it will be written by the copy desk."

Kilgore did not alter the rest of the *Journal's* front page. As usual, columns two and three contained hard-news summaries, one to two sentences in length, which either referred the reader to full-length stories inside the paper or conveyed the gist of an event. Weekly columns, such as "Washington Wire" and "Taxes," appeared every day on a rotating basis in column five. Breaking business or "spot" news was relegated to the *Journal's* interior pages beginning with page three, which became the equivalent of other newspapers' front page.

As a result of these editorial changes, Kilgore said, the *Journal* should develop a reputation as "a newspaper brimming with integrity, accuracy, fearlessness, insight, comedy, and contradictions. That's why our editorials, for example, should continue to champion free markets and free men, even to the point of outrage." Grimes almost smiled.

But the *Journal* itself, not the staff, should have the personality, Kilgore quickly added. "In the best traditions of the Midwest, the *Journal* will be a company of competent but self-effacing newsmen who chronicle the news impartially. No stars, and certainly no radio appearances!"

Three years later, February 1945, the *Journal's* circulation had increased to 55,000 copies. Forty years later, February 1982, the *Journal's* circulation had increased to 2,010,000 copies, the largest newspaper in America. Both benchmarks were achieved by following Kilgore's formula.

Because Kilgore had transformed the *Journal* into a general newspaper, it became eligible for journalism's highest award. In 1947, William Henry Grimes won the *Journal's* first Pulitzer for his editorials espousing free men and free markets.

Considering the number of arguments he lost, and the people he lost them to, Grimes enjoyed a rare success throughout his thirty-five years with the *Wall Street Journal.* His sour and combative nature notwithstanding, Grimes progressed from reporter to Washington bureau chief to managing editor to editor because he was a man of conviction. Casey Hogate once said of Grimes, "Whether you like what he says or not, Henry is a good leavening influence around here. He speaks his mind."

Though loved by Hogate, Grimes was hated by Clarence Barron. "It was Henry's outspokenness. It rivaled Mr. Barron's,"[1] Hogate explained once. Others suspected Barron resented Grimes for his salary, which was ten times higher than the norm.

In 1923, during his first six months at the *Journal* as a reporter, whenever his byline appeared, Grimes would receive as many as ten memos from Barron, each successively sardonic, criticizing him for real or imagined mistakes. To heighten their demoralizing effect, the memos were always hand-delivered by one of Barron's secretaries.

Instead of being cowed, Grimes would read each memo in front of the secretary and then, with mock deliberation, tear it into shreds.

Incredulous that any employee could be so impudent, Barron, on his way out to the New York Yacht Club for luncheon one day, decided to deliver one of his notes himself.

Barron entered the newsroom and waddled down an aisle of disbelieving reporters to Grimes's desk, where he handed Grimes a memo. Grimes took the note nonchalantly, read it, shook his head in disagreement, and tore it up while eyeing Barron.

Like an enraged bull, Barron charged Grimes.

But before Barron could utter a word, Grimes stood up, snatched Barron's yachting cap off his head, threw it to the floor and repeatedly jumped up and down on it.

The room fell quiet, waiting for Barron's explosion.

Instead, the publisher turned and lumbered back down the aisle, saying to no one in particular, "The boy has spirit."

A graduate of Case Western Reserve University, Grimes worked for the United Press International for ten years before joining the *Journal* in 1923. Older and more experienced than the typical *Journal* recruit, Grimes, thirty-one, was hired by Casey Hogate as part of his effort to upgrade the newsroom, which was filled with teenage stenographers at the time. Irrespective of Barron's sentiments, Grimes immediately established himself as a star reporter.

Three years later, Hogate sent Grimes to Washington to replace the bureau chief, John Boyle, a beloved employee but hopeless alcoholic. Like every other journalist covering Washington during the thirties, Grimes's job was made easy by the President's love of the limelight. From 1932 onwards, most of the country's headlines chronicled how Roosevelt was coping with either the Depression or the threat of war.

By 1935, Grimes had built a staff of thirteen reporters. But Grimes was not an easy boss. Though reporters of average abilities liked the way he protected them from New York, people with talent, people who did not need protection from zealous copy editors, were sometimes alienated by Grimes's arbitrariness. Kilgore, for instance, almost quit several times because Grimes insisted on burying Kilgore's column, "Washington Wire," deep inside the paper. And Bill Kerby did in fact quit for a year because Grimes constantly disparaged Kerby's soft-news features. "We're a business newspaper, not some goddamned woman's magazine," Grimes would scream.

In September 1935, still blinded by affection for his protégé, Hogate promoted Grimes to managing editor in New York and sent Kilgore to Washington to replace Grimes as bureau chief. Much more in the spotlight then, Grimes's shortcomings still remained muted or hidden because the man he replaced, Cy Kissane, was notoriously second-rate.

From 1936 to 1941, Grimes and Kilgore clashed daily. It was a miracle neither man quit.

On his second day as managing editor, Grimes wrested power from the field by instituting a procedure whereby all bureau stories would be copyedited and fact-checked by a New York editor, activities which heretofore had been allocated to bureau chiefs. Most chiefs acted like barons and regarded their editing duties as inviolable, a task that demonstrated their authority and ensured their participation in the news.

In one fell swoop, Grimes stripped the barons of their glory, leaving blurred lines of authority and, some argued, weak news stories. "How can a New York copy editor know more about a news story than I? How can he decide what points to emphasize, what additional quotes to seek?" the bureau chiefs would ask.

Because Washington filed the largest news volume, no bureau chief was more vexed by Grimes than Barney Kilgore. Their conflict came to a head in 1937 when a Washington bureau member filed a feature on why Roosevelt sought to expand the Supreme Court.

After editing it himself, Kilgore filed the piece at 5:30 P.M., beating the first edition's lockup by forty-five minutes. A satisfied Kilgore was about to go home when the teletype machine clanked out a message from Grimes in New York. "Your piece rejected. Too frothy."

Kilgore leapt for the phone and placed a call to Grimes, who refused to take it. Kilgore then asked Grimes's secretary to switch him to Hogate, whereupon he said: "Casey, it's Barney. I'm sorry, I don't have time to explain, but unless our leader makes column six tomorrow, beginning next week, you can reach me at the *Times*."[2] The piece appeared the next day after Hogate persuaded both men to accept a compromise. From now on, the Washington bureau would have its own New York copy editor, Bill Kerby.

By 1941, realizing that Grimes was more trouble than he was worth, Hogate replaced Grimes with Kilgore as the *Journal*'s managing editor. To save face, he appointed Grimes Dow Jones executive editor, an imposing title that carried no responsibilities. Thereafter, this solution became a much-used way of dealing with a *Journal* executive who had failed. Rather than terminate him, the *Journal* would promote the miscreant to a position with a lofty title and nothing to do. The outside world, most Dow Jones staffers, and sometimes the person himself never suspected he had been exiled.

But within months of assuming his new post, Grimes realized it was a sinecure. Rather than sit back and do nothing, he persuaded Hogate to name him head of editorials, a new position for the *Journal*.

Before that time, the *Journal* had published many brilliant editorials, written by Clarence Barron, William Hamilton, Thomas Woodlock, and even Charles Dow. But these men also oversaw the entire newspaper and wrote editorials only when their moods and schedules allowed. With him as the *Journal*'s first full-time editorial-page editor, Grimes told Hogate, the consistency of the *Journal*'s commentary would improve markedly. Moreover, Grimes continued, the *Journal* needed a wall between news and editorial just as it had between advertising and editorial.

From 1941 to 1946, with Kilgore and Kerby preoccupied with the *Journal*'s front page, Grimes did what he pleased with the editorial page, which was well received. For the most part, *Journal* readers back then yearned for the days when taxation, government regulation, and liberals in power had been nonexistent, and these were Grimes's favorite themes.

Grimes was not known for his verbosity.

In September 1946, for example, Truman fired the liberal Henry Wallace from his administration. When Wallace joined the *New Republic* as editor, Grimes wrote: "Henry Wallace has become editor of the *New Republic*. We suggest that it serves both right."

The following year, 1947, Grimes won the *Journal*'s first Pulitzer

Prize. Some critics suggest the prize acknowledged the *Journal's* rebirth, not Grimes's talent. "Either Kilgore or Kerby deserved it more. But they were ineligible because they were management. So they searched the ranks and came up with Grimes," Buren McCormack, a *Journal* editor, said.

5

Grasp for Power

After World War II, the *Journal* made a remarkable recovery. While the front pages of other dailies were filled with the breaking and often tragic news of the day, the *Journal's* front pages were filled with more welcome news, long features which explained the astonishing progress of the U.S. economy.

As a result of arming the Allied forces, America's manufacturers now knew how to organize, how to automate. This technology spawned a new civilian battalion, corporate middle management, which absorbed millions of returning veterans. Many of these new corporate managers, anxious to get ahead, began reading the *Wall Street Journal.*

By the beginning of 1947, the *Journal's* circulation had rocketed to 72,000, more than double what it was when Kilgore took over five years before. Even the *Journal's* Pacific Coast edition, a separate entity founded before the Depression, was beginning to show signs of life as its circulation climbed above 10,000 for the first time.

Though Joseph Ackell, Dow Jones's inventor, was a few years away from perfecting his "national newspaper" technology, the *Journal's* recovery made it possible to start two new editions, Boston and Dallas, in the spring of 1947. The *Journal* also opened bureaus in St. Louis, Pittsburgh, Minneapolis, and Phoenix, bringing its worldwide total to twenty-three.

But, sadly, in the midst of all this felicity, Casey Hogate died in April 1947 at the age of fifty-one. Though he had not been seen for four years, Hogate was mourned by many staffers, Barney Kilgore most of all. A midwestern gentleman, quiet and unassuming almost to a fault, Hogate had been worn down by the stress of trying to hold Dow Jones together throughout the Depression. The first of Dow Jones's editors-turned-executives, Hogate was best remembered for contending with Clarence Barron and inventing the "What's News" summaries on page one.

Hogate's death, of course, meant that Barney Kilgore, then thirty-nine, would be named president of Dow Jones, though he had been functioning as such for years. Kilgore was now free, so he thought, to run the company as he saw fit, including picking his second-in-command.

That's why Kilgore was unprepared when Laurence M. Lombard, the Bancrofts' newest attorney, summoned him to Boston in April 1947.

Seated in the anteroom of Hemenway & Barnes, Lombard's law firm, Kilgore waited anxiously. Six months before, when it had finally become apparent that Casey Hogate was too ill to return to Dow Jones, Jessie Cox and Jane Bancroft retained Lombard to determine how the company should function after Hogate. Kilgore was stung that the owners had not consulted him.

Just then a slight, bearded man, a shorter version of George Bernard Shaw, entered the anteroom.

"Mr. Kilgore?" the man asked brightly.

"Mr. Lombard," Kilgore answered.

They shook hands, and Kilgore followed Lombard down a long corridor. As they walked, the two men used small talk to gain some measure of one another.

Soon they arrived at Lombard's corner office, filled with the memorabilia of a patrician: diplomas from Groton, Harvard College, and Harvard Law School and photographs of Lombard in earlier days skiing Tuckerman's Ravine.

As both men sat down, Lombard complimented Kilgore on the progress the *Journal* had made in the last five years.

Deftly, Lombard translated his compliment into hard numbers: "Your changes, of course, have resulted in an 83-percent increase in circulation revenues and a 62-percent increase in advertising revenues since 1941, and a dividend of $2.63, the first in twenty-three years."

Kilgore fended off Lombard's flattery with a modest nod, but he was impressed with the attorney's command of the facts.

Lombard proceeded to explain that he had recommended to the Bancrofts the need to appoint a second-in-command. "Therefore, when you become Dow Jones's chief executive officer next week, I'm going to recommend that Joe Ackell be made president."

An uncomfortable silence fell upon the room.

"Well, Mr. Kilgore?" Lombard finally asked.

Kilgore brushed his chin absentmindedly, preoccupied over how best to respond.

"Please, call me Barney," he said. Kilgore again paused before saying, "I'm reminded of a story my father used to tell me when I was growing up in Indiana. It's about Oliver Cromwell and the time he abandoned ship in a storm off the coast of Ireland. Cromwell almost drowned several times as he swam the half mile to shore. Finally, after the Lord Protector fought his way to safety, two able-bodied fishermen who had witnessed the entire incident rushed up to help him. But Cromwell waved them off, saying, 'Tis easy to rescue a drowning man when he's standing in the surf.'"

"What prompted that?" Lombard asked, nonplussed.

"It should be obvious," Kilgore answered.

"Not to me."

"Five years ago, when the *Journal* was about to sink, the Bancrofts approved and financed a radical plan to save it," Kilgore said. "Against all odds, the plan worked. Based on that success, one would expect we earned the ladies' confidence. Instead, now that we're standing safely in the surf, they hire you to rush in to rescue us."

The full force of Kilgore's resentment stunned Lombard.

"It all boils down to this, Mr. Lombard," Kilgore continued. "Who's running the *Journal*, you or me?"

"That's ridiculous!"

"Is it?"

"Yes, it is...ridiculous."

"Well, if it's so ridiculous, then why didn't the ladies ask me who my second-in-command should be?" Kilgore said, his voice trembling with anger.

"The ladies didn't approach you because they barely know you."

Kilgore's face was now iced fury.

"But quite apart from that," Lombard continued, "Mr. Ackell would make a superb president and, frankly, I'm astonished you don't agree."

"I know much better than you Joe Ackell's contributions," Kilgore said. "But that doesn't mean he should be president," Kilgore continued. "Dow Jones is a news organization and Joe's not a newsman. To name him president would be like naming me the senior partner of this law firm."

Lombard shook his head. "You're the journalist, Barney. Mr. Ackell balances your gaps."

"What does that mean?" Kilgore asked.

"What good is your editorial if people don't get it every day on time? What Ackell accomplishes is too important to ignore."

"I'm not proposing we ignore him. I'm just saying he shouldn't be president."

"Well, who should be, then?" Lombard asked defiantly.

"Bill Kerby."

Dismay swept over Lombard.

"Many people, myself included, think Kerby's a follower, not a leader," Lombard said.

"Who's the boss, you or me?" Kilgore said.

"You are, Barney. You are. But you're wrong on one count. Technology and Joseph Ackell are every bit as important as editorial and Bill Kerby."

Two weeks later, a news item buried inside the *Journal* disclosed that Kilgore, as planned, had replaced Hogate as Dow Jones chief executive officer and Kerby, not Ackell, had been named president, as Kilgore had wished.

By selecting the twenty-nine-year-old Kerby as president, Kilgore made several important statements.

Though mild-mannered and genial, Kilgore declared that he, not the Bancrofts, and certainly not Lombard, would run Dow Jones.

Kilgore also revealed a weakness that many chief executive officers share. Rather than have the best possible people as their immediate subordinates, some top executives choose lieutenants who make them comfortable, people who are soothers, not leaders. In this instance, Kilgore preferred Kerby—a talented feature writer and an accommodating friend, but a follower—over Ackell, who had managed a business, the ticker, successfully. Selecting key executives on the basis of friendship, not competence, would continue at Dow Jones for the next fifty years. As Kilgore did when defending his choice of Bill Kerby to Lombard, each succeeding Dow Jones management justified its executive selections in the belief that because the *Journal* is the heart and soul of Dow Jones, the company needs a journalist at the helm.

Throughout their long and close relationship, which began in the mid-thirties when both men worked in the *Journal's* Washington bureau, Kilgore harbored doubts about Kerby's abilities only once.

When Kilgore vacated his position as Washington bureau chief to take over the *Journal* in 1941, rather than appoint Kerby to succeed him, Kilgore recruited Gene Duffield, a talented journalist from the *Chicago Tribune* instead. "I'm not sure Bill can handle those prima donnas," Kilgore explained to Bill McSherry, his confidant at the time. "Besides, I think Gene Duffield can be my successor."

Kilgore's plans for a successor changed shortly after the war began when Duffield left the *Journal* for high-level government service, never to return. With Duffield gone and with the pressures of resurrecting the *Journal* mounting, Kilgore came to appreciate Kerby again, especially for his feature-writing ability. In early December 1941, Kilgore asked Kerby to take over the front page and make it more optimistic.

A week later, on Sunday, December 7, 1941, at 3:00 P.M., Kilgore and Kerby were both in the office when the ticker's bell clanged, signaling this headline on the broadtape: "Japan Attacks Pearl Harbor." In the next two hours, Kilgore and Kerby responded magnificently. They assigned and edited four front-page stories dealing with various aspects of the attack. But at 5:00 P.M., thirty minutes before the deadline, when it became apparent to Kilgore and Kerby that the front page needed a lead story summarizing how the war would affect business in the United States, Kilgore turned to Kerby and said, "Write it." With Kilgore copyediting the paragraphs as Kerby completed them, Kerby, then thirty-three, wrote a brilliant, Churchill-like story under the three-column headline "War With Japan Means Industrial Revolution in the United States."

> The American productive machine will be reshaped with but one purpose—to produce the maximum of things needed to defeat the enemy.
> It will be a brutal process.
> It implies intense, almost fantastic stimulation for some industries; strict rationing for others; inevitable, complete liquidation for a few.
> War with Japan will be a war of great distances.
> Thus, certainly in its preliminary stages and probably for the duration, it will be a war of the sea and the air.
> This means unlimited quantities of ships and shells, bombers and bombs, oil gasoline. Eventually, it will mean an army

dwarfing the present military establishment—5 million, 8 million. It's a guess. But that will come later."

All his life, Bill Kerby tried desperately not to follow two men, his father, Frederick M. Kerby, and Barney Kilgore. Judging from his constant search for recognition, Kerby never succeeded.

Bill Kerby was born in the summer of 1908 in Washington, D.C. Both his father and his mother, Helen Hunter Kerby, came from seventeenth-century Colonial families who retained their breeding, if not their money, down through the years. A man of varied interests, Frederick Kerby was the Washington manager for the Scripps-Howard News by day and an intellectual cheerleader by night. The Kerbys' apartment became Washington's answer to Gertrude Stein's Paris salon. Carl Sandburg, to name but one literary figure, was a frequent guest. The senior Kerby also venerated Eugene Debs, pacifism, and labor unions.

Like Kilgore's father, Frederick Kerby, who was self-educated and erudite, played an enormous role in his son's life.

By the time he was sixteen, Bill Kerby, at his father's urging, had read *Das Kapital*, Boccaccio, George Bernard Shaw, Arthur Conan Doyle, and Richard Harding Davis, a famous turn-of-the-century journalist, playwright, and novelist. When it came time for college, the senior Kerby persuaded his son to forsake the University of Virginia in favor of the University of Michigan.

Frederick Kerby also pulled strings and arranged for Bill Kerby's first job as a cub reporter for the *Washington Daily News* during his first summer in college. The next year, 1928, the senior Kerby asked his good friend, William Henry Grimes, to hire his son Bill as a summer intern for the Washington bureau of the *Wall Street Journal*.

At Michigan, Kerby worked on the student newspaper, the *Michigan Daily*, all four years and graduated Phi Beta Kappa with a degree in literature. One professor of rhetoric told Kerby, "You are a facile writer with no depth, no conviction."[1] Rather than be dismayed, Kerby took the appraisal as a compliment.

Kerby's first permanent employer after Michigan was his father, who, under an elaborate ruse, paid his son's salary as a reporter for the Federated Press News Service Agency. It seems the manager of the agency was yet another friend of Frederick Kerby's. Within months, the young Kerby went to the United Press, again through his father's intercession, where he became a credible reporter covering the House of Representatives during the Hoover and Roosevelt administrations. In the spring of 1933, his father convinced Henry Grimes to hire his son permanently.

Charles Sterner, a *Journal* deskman in the Washington bureau at the time, described young Kerby on his first day at work. "At first, I thought Bill Kerby looked like a salamander,"[2] Sterner later said, "with those bulging eyes, and those damn garish suspenders which elongated him, made him seem taller than his five-foot-five."

Kerby became a favorite of Henry Grimes's. Grimes helped the young Michigan graduate surpass his father as a journalist. With Grimes's encouragement, Kerby developed into a solid reporter, known especially for his graceful writing, a rare skill at the *Journal* back then. It was not uncommon for reporters to retype and publish under their name press releases that had been written by public relations flacks.

In contrast to this practice, Kerby regularly researched, reported, and wrote features that comprehensively explained many pertinent issues of the day. And then Grimes and Kerby, together, would scheme how to get these pieces approved by the *Journal*'s recalcitrant managing editor, Cy Kissane, whose nickname was "Stupid." One story that earned Kissane this nickname was Kerby's scoop on Roosevelt's undisclosed intent to devalue the dollar by manipulating the gold standard. A week after Kissane refused to publish it because it was too technical, the *New York Times* ran a similar story on its front page.

When Grimes replaced Kissane as managing editor in 1935, Grimes drafted Kerby, then twenty-seven, to be his assistant. Unfortunately, the promotion went to Kerby's head. "Bill Kerby became a dreadful egoist,"[3] recalled Kit Melick, a newsroom editorial assistant. Soon after arriving in New York, for example, Kerby clashed repeatedly with the *Journal*'s advertising director, Robert Feemster, over Feemster's perceived lack of respect for his new position. Thereafter, Kerby referred to Feemster derisively as "that huckster." The Kerby-Feemster feud marked the beginning of their antagonism, which to this day the *Journal*'s editorial and advertising departments still feel toward each other.

6

The First Huckster

Immediately following World War II, the *Journal*'s advertising sales department came into its own within Dow Jones. The advertising sales department would never usurp the supremacy of the news department, of course, but even rank-and-file reporters noted the impressive new stream of ads.

Barney Kilgore appreciated the *Journal*'s advertising sales department better than most because he saw how improved selling efforts had greatly increased advertising revenues and profits. By the end of 1947, for example, the *Journal*'s advertising revenues had risen to $2.4 million, a 600 percent increase from 1937, when the *Journal*'s sparse advertising consisted mostly of retail stockbrokers trying to trade their ad dollars for favorable press coverage.

After Kilgore determined the *Journal* would be a national newspaper, the ad sales department started to pursue a different type of advertiser, companies like General Motors and American Tobacco, which advertised in magazines, a medium with large national audiences. And since the *Journal* looked like a newspaper, a medium with small, localized audiences, it was not easy to convince the ad agencies for Chevrolet or Lucky Strikes that the *Journal* was, from an advertising point of view, like *Time* and not like the *New York Times*.

A good ad salesperson, Kilgore realized, needed intelligence to articulate the *Journal*'s uniqueness, a personality which was both likable and convincing, and a maturity to endure occasional humiliation. Kilgore also knew this rare combination of traits was often accompanied by other, less appealing characteristics.

But many *Journal* news people had less understanding, and therefore less tolerance, for their advertising sales counterparts. At best, they viewed advertising salespeople with ambivalence. While they recognized and admired the industry needed to bring in all the *Journal*'s advertisers, the typical news editor still didn't trust the process; it was more a question of seduction than honest persuasion. Somehow, the editor thought, the ad salesperson compromised the *Journal*'s editorial ethics.

These various attitudes and prejudices were displayed in a meeting held in the Dow Jones executive conference room on January 12, 1948. A five-foot five-inch, three-hundred-pound man wearing a cowboy hat named Robert Feemster, age thirty-eight, paced the floor, occasionally turning to yell and point his finger at Barney Kilgore, forty, and Bill Kerby, thirty-seven, who sat impassively by. Judging from his size and fury, one would think Feemster was Clarence Barron's grandson vilifying two subordinates. "You've no idea how hard it was to sell this ad. And now you're not going to back me up?" Feemster screamed, striding back and forth.

Kilgore appeared tranquil. Kerby, on the other hand, stared at a spot on the wall as if it could help him throttle Feemster.

"Let me explain this again," Feemster said in a slow, sarcastic tone. "Ford wants this ad to run on the back page. They know it's ordinarily a news page, but they want an exception just this once."

Kilgore remained still.

"If it were Dominick & Dominick or Merrill Lynch I wouldn't mind so much. But Ford represents a whole new category," Feemster said.

Then Kilgore interrupted gently, "Robert... Robert, please."

"I mean it, Barney," Feemster went on. "This job is tough enough without you turning down my ads."

Feemster fell into the chair next to Kilgore and removed his gray ten-gallon hat. With a red handkerchief the size of a small tablecloth, he mopped his forehead and the hat's interior sweatband. Then, with the insouciance of an archduke, Feemster put the hat back on.

"For an instant I thought you might be taking it off, it being indoors and all," Kerby interjected.

Kilgore grinned. Then he said, "I'm sorry, Robert. We can't make an exception for Ford."

"Well, Ford usually gets what it wants. That's why *Time* magazine, to name but one, goes out of its way for them. When Henry likes you, you get a ton of advertising, a ton," Feemster said. "And because

we're new to Ford we have to 'outcooperate' the competition,"
Feemster added, making the quote sign in the air.

"Somehow," Kilgore replied, "I can't see Henry Luce giving an
advertiser *Time*'s principle edit page, Robert. But no matter, we're
not going to do it. If we lose the business, then we lose the business."

Feemster's face turned red. "Christ! I bust my ass selling these
people and then my own people sabotage me."

"Don't make promises you can't keep," Kerby said, his eyes
flashing.

"Listen, Kerby, my ads are paying your salary, so I'd shut up if I
were you," Feemster cried.

"Reporters pay my salary, and yours, too," Kerby snapped back.

"That's enough...that's enough, goddammit," Kilgore yelled.

There was a pause. And then Feemster, looking chagrined,
struggled to his feet, removed his hat and said, "You're the boss,
Barney. I'll do whatever you want."

Then, like a dirigible, Feemster drifted out of the room.

Both Kilgore and Kerby remained seated, staring at the tops of
their hands.

"Why do you let him do that?" Kerby finally asked.

"I can't sell ads," Kilgore said, smiling.

"But he acts like Napoleon. And he treats you like a subordinate!"

Kilgore chuckled. "That reminds me. Last month, on the train
home one evening, this guy comes up and says, 'I met your boss, Bob
Feemster, today,'" Kilgore said.

"What did you say?" Kerby asked.

"I told the guy what a great boss he was," Kilgore replied, laughing
loudly.

Kerby shook his head disapprovingly.

"Perhaps," said Kilgore, "I should rein him in a bit. But you don't
see him the way I do."

"I didn't go to DePauw," Kerby said.

"Yeah, I suppose that's part of it."

"Old school ties aside, do you know he's having an affair with his
secretary?" Kerby asked.

"Yeah, I know," Kilgore said wearily.

"Well? Aren't you going to do anything?" Kerby persisted.

"It's none of my business, however it may upset me," Kilgore said
sadly. "I run a newspaper, not a domestic tribunal. Besides, his good
points outweigh the bad."

"Really?" Kerby said, raising his eyebrows.

"Whatever makes him wear cowboy hats and have affairs also makes him a brilliant salesman," Kilgore said.

"So, he's a good salesman!"

Shaking his head thoughtfully, Kilgore said, "I probably wouldn't let Feemster act the way he does if he were an editor or an accountant. But I can't sell ads. Neither can you. And since ad revenue is our economic lifeblood, we have to tolerate him."

"But surely others can sell advertising just as well."

"Maybe. But they could also be a whole lot more unmanageable."

"You're joking!" Kerby said.

"Think about it," Kilgore said as he stood to leave the room. "To sell advertising for the *Journal* requires a big ego, the type that often also wants to run the whole operation. We need someone who's got the ego, but who'll also comply. That's Feemster. Tolerating his foolishness is a small price to pay."

Throughout much of the early history of the financial press, territorial struggles such as this between editorial and advertising did not exist, simply because neither discipline had evolved to where its principles could be compromised.

Financial advertising in the United States began in 1827 when three firms—Spencer Trask & Co, Charles M. Whitney & Co., and Purnell & Hagaman—decided to join forces and publish one bulletin which conveyed the hourly stock prices. All three firms ran their letterheads on the bulletin's front page, creating the first ad.

By 1860, independent publishers had taken over most hand-delivered bulletins. But trading firms continued to run their letterheads, now for a fee, to remind themselves and competitors they were still part of the Wall Street community.

In 1889, when the *Wall Street Journal* was founded, reporters solicited both news and ads from firms. Again, the *Journal's* coverage of business had not reached a point where these dual responsibilities raised conflicts of interest.

During the *Journal's* first five years, subscription revenue remained the newspaper's main revenue source. As the *Journal* grew, Edward Jones came to realize that advertising could contribute substantially to the paper's profits. The hyperactive Jones pursued advertising at every turn, transforming the *Journal's* front page into a Wall Street bulletin board. By 1898, the *Journal* was grossing $175,000 per year, $95,000 of which came from advertising. But some critics suspected Jones may have been too aggressive. They claimed the *Journal's* editorial page treated a famous tycoon at the time,

James Keane, too kindly in exchange for advertising from companies he controlled.

In 1902, when Mrs. Barron took control of Dow Jones, her son-in-law, Hugh Bancroft, troubled by the *Journal's* pandering to advertisers, pared the front page down to one column of ads.

Then, in 1912, when Clarence Barron ousted Bancroft, the *Journal's* views toward advertising became more relaxed again. A notorious low payer, Barron encouraged reporters to augment their meager salaries with commissions earned from selling advertising. Sometimes this practice led to more serious abuse.

Besides being the *Journal's* most accomplished reporter and essayist, Barron also was the paper's most effective salesman. In one of the more revealing manifestations of the era's permissiveness, no one blanched when Clarence Barron would ask a company president to buy an ad at the conclusion of a news interview. The Ford Motor Company, for example, placed its first ad in the *Journal* shortly after Barron's laudatory profile of Henry Ford appeared in March 1923.

During Barron's reign, a *Journal* reporter, William Gomber, was cited by a special U.S. Senate committee investigating fraud on Wall Street. It alleged that from 1923 to 1927, Gomber wrote favorable articles about companies which placed their *Journal* ads through him. Invariably, Gomber's stories drove the companies' stock price up, though their performances did not merit these increases.

In 1928, when Hugh Bancroft returned to Dow Jones after Clarence Barron died, the *Journal* erected a wall between editorial and advertising, segregating news gathering from advertising solicitation. A reporter and ad salesman, for example, could be fired immediately if seen together. Bancroft also introduced rigid standards for advertising. He even went so far as to outlaw the advertising of "body contact" products such as unguents and deodorants, a rule the *Journal* still adheres to today.

After his initial reformation, Bancroft delegated advertising's day-to-day operations to Casey Hogate, then Dow Jones's general manager. In 1930, one of the first ad people Hogate hired was Robert McCleary Feemster, DePauw, '30.

"The other salesmen hated me because I was Hogate's recruit," Feemster later told a colleague. "And I hated them because I wanted to be a reporter. I felt selling was beneath me."

As the *Journal's* ad statistics showed, the last thing a firm wanted to do during the Depression was to spend money on advertising.

Feemster became a masterful salesman almost immediately, but not, as some suspected, because of his egomania. Rather than dominate a prospect on a sales call, Feemster would approach him humbly, ask a few questions, and then listen attentively. Later, at the appropriate time, he would tailor his sales recommendations to fulfill the needs the prospect had revealed, often obtaining the order, always creating a favorable impression.

In search of new advertisers, Feemster emigrated from Wall Street to Madison Avenue, where national advertisers and their advertising agencies resided. Madison Avenue represented uncharted waters for Feemster and the *Journal* in 1936. Up to that point, Feemster and the rest of the *Journal* salespeople had only solicited financial companies, which explains why the *Journal*'s advertising had dropped to a low of $325,000 in 1935, down from $1.9 million in 1928.

Feemster was the first to sell an important national advertiser, the American Tobacco Company, makers of Lucky Strike cigarettes, and the process revealed the depth of his determination.

Later, Feemster reminisced, "I staked out the offices of American Tobacco, knowing I would never get to see the chairman, George Washington Hill, in his office. One evening, as Mr. Hill came out of his building, I rushed up and introduced myself, gave him a copy of the *Journal* and asked him if he might like a ride uptown. (I had hired a big, black, shiny Packard.) Hill was so startled, he got in. He then asked, 'How can the *Wall Street Journal* afford this car?' I said, 'They don't know about it yet. But it's the only way I could get you alone for twenty minutes.' Mr. Hill cracked up. He couldn't get over my ballsyness. And, of course, by the time we get to Grand Central, we're great friends and he's bought an ad."

Besides Feemster's sales abilities, the *Journal* benefited from an unexpected source, the Securities Act of 1933, which requires full disclosure of planned or just-completed financial transactions. To guarantee compliance, Wall Street firms began buying advertising space to disclose their deals. The ads were dubbed tombstones, and they soon became the *Journal*'s biggest source of advertising revenue.

Later, in 1943, Feemster also devised a means to overcome the principal reason why companies with restricted trading areas would not advertise in the *Journal*. Since the newspaper's advertising rates, like those of all media, were pegged to the size of its circulation, a San Francisco retailer, for example, did not want to pay for New York City distribution. Feemster invented a scheme by which an advertiser could buy all or a portion of the *Journal*'s circulation. Gump's of San

Francisco, for example, could purchase the *Journal*'s northern California circulation, whereas American Tobacco (Lucky Strikes) could buy the national edition.

Based on these triumphs, Feemster leapfrogged three more senior men to become the *Journal*'s advertising manager in September 1936. Casey Hogate later told a colleague, "Feemster was delirious because he was now making more money than his arch-rival, Barney Kilgore, a fact he made known to everyone."

One of Feemster's first managerial acts caused an uproar throughout Dow Jones. Without consulting anyone, Feemster hired Batten, Barton, Durstine & Osborne, a Madison Avenue advertising agency, to promote the *Journal* to advertisers and ad agencies. The first time BBDO presented its advertising recommendations to Feemster, the agency nearly resigned the account. Under the direction of John Caples, an unassuming but talented writer, a team of BBDO writers and art directors had been working day and night for several weeks, creating a campaign that would impress Feemster, whose reputation had motivated them to even greater efforts.

The presentation took place at BBDO. At the appointed hour, the BBDO contingent filed into its vast, sumptuous presentation room and sat down, taking up one whole side of the table. For the next half hour, they waited anxiously for the client. Finally, the three-hundred-pound Feemster entered the room like a parade blimp. Without looking right or left, he glided to the head of the table and said, "Well?"

Caples greeted Feemster courteously and began to present what he and his colleagues regarded as an inspired advertising campaign.

Two minutes later, having only heard Caples's preliminary remarks, Feemster stood up and removed his suit jacket.

Three more minutes passed as Caples, always methodical, continued to explain the agency's reasoning behind the yet-unseen campaign. But by this time, the hyperactive Feemster had listened too long. It was now time for action, movement, objects to react to.

Feemster sprang to his feet and shrieked, "Where are the ads, goddammit? I'm here for the ads, not a lot of who-struck-John!"

Shaken, Caples quickly wheeled an easel holding a dozen prospective ads stacked one on top of the other to where Feemster sat. Assuming a machine gun–like delivery, Caples started to read the first ad's headline. But before he could utter the third word, "next" rang through the air—which is how Feemster responded to the other ads Caples presented.

As Caples placed the last board on the table, Feemster, scowling, said, "I hate 'em...all of 'em."

Unperturbed, Caples paused to settle the room and then asked, "Perhaps you have an idea or two, Mr. Feemster?"

Feemster called for some Scotch tape. He then took a crumpled copy of the *Journal* from his suit jacket, tore the front page off, and taped the page to the easel. Turning to the group, Feemster said, "This, gentlemen, is the *Journal's* first ad! It will run in the *New York Times.*"

The room fell silent.

"But that's the *Journal's* front page!" a disembodied voice exclaimed.

"Exactly," answered Feemster.

"And you want to run it with the *New York Times?*"

"Exactly."

"Without any explanations, any headlines. Nothing?" another puzzled voice asked.

"Exactly."

"Brilliant!" said John Caples.

Within hours of the ad's appearance, Madison Avenue was abuzz about the printer's error which placed the *Journal's* front page on the back page of the *New York Times.*

Jessie Cox, however, had a different reaction. When Mrs. Cox learned the ad was Feemster's idea, she instructed Kilgore to fire him. Kilgore refused. Instead, in 1942, Kilgore named Feemster Dow Jones's assistant general manager in charge of sales, a new position that made Feemster responsible for both advertising and circulation.

Feemster brought to the moribund world of circulation the same brash ingenuity he displayed in advertising. He commissioned John Caples to create a direct-mail campaign to lure new readers to the *Journal.* Appealing to a basic and powerful instinct, Caples created the milestone headline: "The Men Who Get Ahead in Business Read the *Wall Street Journal.*"

Spurred by these ads, a helpful economy, and Kilgore's formula, the *Journal's* circulation increased from a low of 28,000 in 1938 to 131,000 in 1948. In 1949, Kilgore named Feemster chairman of Dow Jones's executive committee to acknowledge that the *Journal's* advertising linage had surpassed $4 million.

Throughout the thirties and forties, Feemster dominated the *Journal* so much that people were always surprised to learn that others sold advertising for the *Journal* as well. Actually, Feemster was ably assisted by DePauw classmate Ted Callis and twenty-three salesmen who were content to remain in Feemster's shadow. However, one salesman in the Boston office, a World War ll veteran who spoke in Brooklynese streams of consciousness, Donald A. Macdonald, would eventually rival Feemster in flamboyance and ambition, but not in competence.

But as designing as both sales executives could be, Feemster and Macdonald always respected the *Journal* division that separates advertising from news, part of the checks and balances Kilgore created to restore the *Journal's* advertising sales ethics which the Gomber incident had tarnished in the thirties. Kilgore also erected another wall that separated the *Journal's* editorial page from the influence of the news department.

The Formidable Vermont Connecticut Royster

Like a submarine returning to port, the midnight-blue limousine, New York State license plate WSJ-1, glided through the Holland Tunnel traffic, wending its way northeastward to 44 Broad Street. It was the first week of June 1954.

Barney Kilgore, Dow Jones CEO, and Bill Kerby, president, sat in the back, each with a reading lamp aimed over his shoulder, absorbed in that day's *Journal*. As Kilgore came to the end of a story, he asked offhandedly: "What's this about General Motors canceling $250,000 worth of their ads?"

"Remember the piece we ran on them last week?" Kerby replied. "They didn't like us printing pictures of the new '55 models before the official announcement date."

"You'd think they would," Kilgore said, returning to his paper.

More silence passed. Then Kilgore, finishing another page, said, "Henry [Grimes, editorial-page editor] called last night upset. Apparently Roy wants to endorse integration by coming out in favor of *Brown v. Board of Education.*" Kilgore was referring to Vermont Connecticut "Roy" Royster, former Washington reporter and now an assistant editorial-page editor who had some revolutionary ideas for the *Journal* from time to time.

"Hmm..." Kerby murmured.

"Yeah, it surprised me, too."

"Could be a problem," Kerby said, putting his paper down.

Kilgore went back to reading the *Journal*. But he did say distractedly, "Well, I asked both of them up for coffee this morning."

When Kilgore and Kerby entered the penthouse, Grimes, fifty-three, and Royster, forty-one, were waiting. As always, Grimes looked gray and agitated, while Royster seemed detached.

"Is this worse than the Truman-MacArthur fight?" Kilgore asked, grinning. "We get upset when our only two Pulitzers are quarreling." Royster had won a Pulitzer the year before for general excellence in editorials. It was the *Journal*'s second Pulitzer Prize, the first going to Grimes in 1947, also for editorials.

"Roy's got this wild-ass idea to endorse the desegregation decision," Grimes hollered.

"Is that right, Roy?" Kilgore asked mildly.

Wordlessly, Royster began to distribute carbon copies of the editorial.

But Kilgore held his hand up, saying, "I don't want to read it now. Whatever we decide, I'll read about it tomorrow along with everyone else." Kilgore was referring to his policy of never approving an editorial beforehand.

"If we run that, we'll lose half our subscribers," Grimes said sternly, pointing to the paper that still lay on the table.

"Why?" Kilgore asked.

"Oh, God!" Grimes said. "Don't start, Barney, don't start with that goddamn 'why' of yours. You know as well as I do that if we endorse integration, we'll need a third shift to process the subscription cancellations."

"So?" Kilgore persisted.

"I hate it when you get like Thomas Paine arguing the rights of man. We're a business paper, goddammit, not some liberal pink sheet! Let the *New York Times* do it," said Grimes, the mole on his right cheek now bright red.

"Henry's right," Kerby interjected.

Still smiling, Kilgore turned to Royster and said, "You want to say something?"

Pointing to the editorial, Royster said, "I already have."

"You're as cute as he is," Grimes shouted.

"Roy, I'd like to hear why you wrote it," Kilgore persisted.

"It's hard to say, really," Royster said. "Several reasons come to mind, and perhaps a few I'm not even aware of—"

"Oh, Jesus Christ!" Grimes shouted.

"Let him finish," Kilgore snapped.

Still staring at his hands, Royster continued. "Who knows? There may be some guilt. I'm a fourth-generation southerner, and all that. But I keep thinking, This is the law of the land. We either abide by it or anarchy reigns," Royster said. "Besides, we're always saying the *Journal* stands for free markets and free men. What could be more freeing than *Brown v. Board of Education?*"

Kilgore raised his eyebrows as if to say, Roy's right. But before he actually said anything, Grimes had left the room.

Not until the next day, May 20, 1954, when it appeared in the *Journal*, did Kilgore get to read Royster's editorial entitled "Society and the Law."

The Warren Court has spoken.

Separate but equal educational facilities for our children are a thing of the past, if they ever existed in the first place.

The philosophy of racial distinction under the law could not have forever survived, in any event, because it does not comport with the majority view of the equity of government.

When referring to the Declaration of Independence's provision that all men are created equal, we no longer have to add asterisks when referring to classrooms and school busses.

Now, as they say, comes the hard part. How and when to implement this decision?

The Court anticipated this difficult question and wisely postponed answering it. It is clear the days of segregation are coming to an end, but the end will not come immediately.

The Supreme Court's delay is indeed unusual.

But there is no simple way to put an end to an old order before society is ready to create a new one.

Delay or no delay, segregation is dead in the mind, if not yet in the body politic.

It's the law of the land.

Over the years, *Journal* editorials have aroused such controversy that the editorial page has become an institution separate and apart from the rest of the newspaper. Some people, usually older, long-time subscribers, find the *Journal* commentary brilliant. But other subscribers, just as loyal, seldom turn to the page, dismissing it as just so much prehistoric nonsense.

Rarely is there a middle ground for reaction, partly because the

Journal's editorial tone can range from studied reason to smug hysteria, depending on how each essay's subject squares with the *Journal's* secret of life: All things can and should be reduced to striving for "free men and free markets." Various subthemes of this credo include: Finance and business will save the country; both government spending and regulation are intrinsically evil; the United States should stay clear of other countries' problems.

But *Journal* editorials are also provocative because their conclusions often are inconsistent with what most people expect from an archconservative, pro-business publication. Besides endorsing the U.S. Supreme Court's decision on integration, for example, the *Journal* has supported turn-of-the-century coal miners on strike, Theodore Roosevelt's trust-busting measures, the creation of the Securities and Exchange Commission, and U.S. withdrawal from Vietnam from February 1968 onward. *Journal* editorials have also supported Michael Milken and South Korea's military dictator, Roh Tae Woo, and blamed the '92 Los Angeles riots on the sexual promiscuity of the city's black women. Also surprisingly, in recent years the *Journal* has published liberal authors, including Arthur Schlesinger, Jr., and Alexander Cockburn, in an admirable and successful attempt to present the other side. Finally, though its strong Republican preference always shows, the *Journal* has refrained from political endorsements.

More predictably, again over time, the *Journal* has opposed John Maynard Keynes, the New Deal, Truman's seizing the steel mills, and Nixon's price-and-wage controls while lavishly praising Ronald Reagan, supply-side economics, and the 1980s.

The *Journal's* editorials appear under the headline "Review and Outlook," a title Charles Dow created in 1893 when he wrote the paper's first editorial. For the next ten years, Dow was an enthusiastic but irregular essayist, always reflecting his eighteenth-century beliefs temperately.

In 1902, the year Dow sold the paper to Jessie Barron, Thomas Woodlock, a classics graduate of Dublin's Trinity University, took over the "Review and Outlook" column full-time. Woodlock adored Theodore Roosevelt, Jessie Barron did not, and Woodlock was fired after three years on the post. He was succeeded by William Hamilton, a protégé of Charles Dow's. Hamilton was the *Journal's* editorial-page editor for twenty-four years. Among his many triumphs, Hamilton predicted the 1929 stock market crash three days before it happened. He also managed to share the *Journal's* editorial-writing chore with Clarence Barron for seventeen years without getting fired.

After Barron's death in 1929, it was safe again for Thomas Woodlock to return to the *Journal* and establish a new column, "Thinking Things Over," which regularly appeared alongside "Review and Outlook." It was Woodlock who authored the *Journal's* modern creed of "free men and free markets," a refinement of the eighteenth-century monarchic beliefs that guided Charles Dow.

After Woodlock and Hamilton, the next notable editorial writer was Henry Grimes. In 1947 he won a Pulitzer for general editorial excellence—the *Journal's* first. Some said this single two-sentence editorial won him the prize: "Henry Wallace has become the editor of the *New Republic*. We suggest both deserve each other." Whatever the truth of the allegation, the Pulitzer Prize represented acknowledgment by the newspaper industry that the *Journal* had come of age, that Kilgore's resurrection had been a success.

When Grimes's protégé, Vermont Connecticut Royster, an extraordinary writer, took over the page in the fifties, the page lost some of its shrillness to a tone of scholarly elegance. Also under Royster, as a point of honor, the *Journal* maintained strict separation between its news and editorial departments, a division that collapsed under his successor, Robert Bartley.

Royster joined the *Journal's* Washington bureau in 1935 at the age of twenty-one, three months after graduating from the University of North Carolina with a degree in classical languages and literature. At Chapel Hill, since he was already fluent in Latin and Greek, he spent most of his time on the student newspaper. Before he was ten, his father, a law professor, had taught him these languages as one might teach a boy baseball.

But rather than boast about his prodigious erudition, Royster loved to poke fun at it. "In the depression years of the mid-1930s," Royster once wrote, "this educational background was itself a bit out of date. A nodding acquaintance with Euripides proved not a very marketable commodity. For a young man so inadequately prepared for life, there was no recourse but journalism."[1]

Of modest height and frame, with a baby face enhanced by curious, amused eyes, Royster's first job required him to take dictation from the senior *Journal* reporters. But Royster's exceptional writing skills were noticed, and his bosses directed him to do complete rewrites, as well. "'Touching up' is how they would put it. As in, 'Hey, kid, take this down and while you're at it, touch it up, will you?'" Royster later said.

As more and more classical allusions crept into the bureau's copy, Grimes realized it was Royster, not the staff, who was improving. He promoted the young man, now barely twenty-two, to a full-time beat, the Agriculture Department.

But there were problems between the two.

"Roy was a natural writer, smooth, graceful, succinct," Grimes said. "But we had terrible fights because he always wanted to cite the *Iliad* when doing a piece on butter and eggs."

When Kilgore took over the bureau in August 1936, he promoted Royster again, this time to the congressional beat, where the young man's cracker-barrel personality helped him develop sources never before available to the *Journal*. Soon his byline, along with Kilgore's and Kerby's, made the *Journal's* Washington bureau every bit as strong as the *New York Times's*. Like his predecessor, Kilgore admired Royster greatly except for his unbreakable habit of injecting opinion into hard-news stories. Finally, Kilgore solved the problem by permitting Royster to contribute an occasional editorial while still a Washington reporter.

Royster left the *Journal* from 1942 to 1946 to serve as a commander on a destroyer escort in both the Pacific and the Atlantic. After the war, he returned to Washington as the *Journal's* chief correspondent. But within months, he moved to New York to work full-time on editorials as Grimes's assistant.

In his writing, as in his conversation, Royster was always interesting, never pretentious. Though his columns and editorials were replete with bookish references, he conveyed them with such understatement—such southern gentlemanliness—that the sting of not knowing them was invariably nullified. For example, in an editorial entitled "The Theology of Change," he wrote:

> Nobody—well, hardly anybody—reads St. Thomas Aquinas any more. Mostly he wrote about man's relationship to God, a subject lately fallen into disfavor if indeed it's not unconstitutional. Moreover he liked to look at the long-range effects of the moment's pragmatic decisions, which is not only unfashionable but today considered downright tiresome. Yet the young nephew of Frederick Barbarossa was no recluse from worldly affairs. Tucked away in his great *Summa Theologica* are many

shrewd thoughts about such secular matters as man's relationship to man and such practical problems as the mundane laws of
the state. In fact, in different times, the good St. Thomas would
have made an excellent lawyer, or even an editorial writer.[2]

Royster shared with Grimes the same basic Republican beliefs.
But where Grimes was terse and harsh, Royster was soothing and
flowing; where Grimes was myopically introspective, Royster was
munificent in sweep; where Grimes was predictable, Royster was
surprising.

Royster loved to use these gifts to prick the ego balloons of
politicians.

BACK TO BRYAN

I only remember William Jennings Bryan as an old man
wrestling the devil and Clarence Darrow. I wish I could have
known him in the days of his glory, when as editor of the *Omaha
World Herald* he was wrestling with the crown of golden thorns,
the horns of William McKinley, and the shades of Adam Smith.
For it always struck me that Bryan had the simplest, most
straightforward, and logically irrefutable diagnosis of poverty I
ever heard of. Poverty, Bryan argued, is when people don't have
enough money—an observation that surely ranks in acuteness
with Cal Coolidge's remark that unemployment arises when
people don't have jobs.[3]

Royster also criticized Congress for its flagrant procrastination.

TOMORROW ALWAYS COMES

It was Scarlett O'Hara, that scatterbrained minx, who com-
pressed in a phrase an enduring bit of philosophy. As Rhett
Butler walked off into the sunset, the little lady gently wiped
away a tear and remarked to no one in particular, "I'll think
about that tomorrow."* Over the years that cheerful thought has
done yeoman service for all those to whom the realities of the
world are sometimes too harsh for contemplation, which includes all of us at one time or another. But it is the especial
motto of adolescents and politicians.[4]

---

* Scarlett actually said, "Tomorrow is another day."

But in 1950 Kilgore inadvertently hurt Royster. After several years of trial and error, Kilgore came to the conclusion that Buren McCormack, a DePauw graduate who had succeeded Bill Kerby as the *Journal*'s managing editor, was "not working out." Not wishing to fire his fellow alumnus outright, Kilgore created a job for McCormack in the *Journal*'s editorial department. Though Kilgore made it clear to both Grimes and Royster that McCormack would exercise absolutely no authority in this contrived position, the kindhearted Kilgore neglected to inform McCormack of this restriction. On the first day McCormack reported to the editorial department Grimes was away. Trying to establish himself immediately in what he thought was a real job, McCormack called Royster into his office and proceeded to edit a Royster editorial in such a way as to reveal why he had not succeeded as managing editor.

Rather than argue, as he often did with Grimes, Royster walked out of the office without saying a word and took the elevator up to Kilgore's penthouse suite.

In a move reminiscent of Kilgore himself, Royster strode into Kilgore's office, waving his violated editorial. "Barney," Royster said, "I've just had a run-in with that guy who went to the same Methodist high school in Indiana as you did. In your own immortal words, 'Either this runs as is, or you can reach me at the *New York Times* tomorrow.'"

The next day, Barney Kilgore circulated this organizational memo: "I take a very keen pleasure in announcing Buren McCormack's promotion to Dow Jones's business manager, a position he is uniquely qualified for....."

8

Barney Falters

By the late fifties, the United States was exceeding even the fondest expectations of the American Dream. In December 1958, the Dow Jones averages stood at 572, 120 points higher than what they were in February 1957. Every suburban garage had a car, every suburban child a college. The reincarnation of the middle class in the form of corporate middle management became the biggest spoil of war. The Depression was now only the dread of grandparents; the Korean "police action" had ended; Eisenhower, everybody's father, was in the White House. The United States assumed a quiet, acquiescent posture, ideal conditions for the surge of Big Business. Even the nation's worry over Sputnik would result in economic growth.

And what was good for the country's economy proved excellent for the *Wall Street Journal*. The *Journal's* ad revenues for 1958 were $37 million, double what they were at the end of 1951. Circulation had increased to 570,000, and as one of Feemster's promotional ads boasted, the *Journal's* readership increased seventeen times in seventeen years. The average net worth of the *Journal's* subscribers was $75,000. And by 1958 the *Journal* had more subscribers in California than it had in New York, proof that the paper had finally become the country's only national daily newspaper.

Overnight, the *Journal* had achieved the status of an institution. It also seemed like Barney Kilgore's finest hour. From 1958 through 1960, he won virtually every journalism prize awarded. But despite the public acclaim, it was a painful period for him. Ironically, Kilgore's dilemma was caused by the prosperity he himself had created. A newfound security drifted through the halls of the *Journal* and Dow Jones. Everyone smiled. The staff became protective of all it had wrought, as if to say, We have the formula. It works brilliantly. Why change?

In these calm seas, Kerby, as Kilgore's second-in-command, became Dow Jones's gauge reader. In the rare instance something or someone at the *Journal* drifted astray, Kerby would consult Kilgore, who would set the course right again. But it was not enough.

Barney's eldest son, James Kilgore, said, "Not many people realized it, because he rarely expressed what he truly felt, but my father was not happy in the late fifties. He wanted the excitement of rescuing the *Journal*, not maintaining it."[1]

As a symptom of his disquiet, Kilgore took to criticizing Bill Kerby's evolving management-by-committee, "an operating style replete with minutes, memos, and no decisions."

Kerby had expanded and formalized the kaffeeklatsch, conferring upon the group the title Dow Jones Management Committee. It met twice a month to set operating policy. Kilgore once confided in Bill McSherry, his assistant, "It [management committee] sounded good in theory. Bill would preside while everyone made speeches at him. But nothing happened. The only action ever taken was to set the date for the next nonmeeting."

Kilgore could not even seek satisfaction in journalism despite once being the author of the *Journal*'s well-regarded "Dear George" column. "Barney rejected the notion of doing his column again because he knew no one can edit the chairman of the board," Bill McSherry said.

Instead, Kilgore began to search out possible acquisitions to dilute the company's dependence on the *Journal*. And in 1960, Kilgore suggested the company begin its acquisition program by buying *Newsweek* magazine, a poor contender to *Time* back then.

After the Bancroft family, who still owned 80 percent of Dow Jones, rejected his recommendation, Kilgore bought his hometown newspaper, the *Princeton Packet*, for himself. "At first," said James Kilgore, "my father viewed it as an investment. But it was apparent that the *Packet*, at least for a while, was giving him an outlet that Dow Jones wasn't. After working in New York all day as CEO, Dad would get off the train most nights and come to the *Packet*'s office for fun. Often he'd stay until midnight, writing stories, repairing equipment, and doing whatever else was needed to get the paper out."[2]

But soon the *Packet*'s challenges, like the *Journal*'s, proved too tame. Never one to remain idle or bored, Kilgore, forty-three, called a meeting of his close Dow Jones associates in August 1961 to discuss an idea he had.

Contrary to what most people imagine, the Beden's Brook Country Club in Princeton, New Jersey, is not some ivy-covered Georgian mansion with liveried servants swooning over the paunchy elite. It is actually made up of several one-story buildings strung together haphazardly, reminiscent of a good suburban motel more than anything else. And the folks who are members are just like its buildings: prosaic.

Barney Kilgore loved Beden's Brook. In fact, it was such a special place for Kilgore that he rarely did business there. That's why Bill Kerby, forty-three, and Bob Feemster, forty, knew something was up when Kilgore invited them to luncheon there.

Neither Kerby nor Feemster had seen much of Kilgore in the previous year. Both men were busy trying to manage the *Journal*'s success. Record numbers of readers and advertisers were beginning to regard the *Journal* as their guide to power and money.

On this humid day, Kilgore wore his usual chinos and white short-sleeved shirt. Kerby looked much smarter in dark slacks and pale green golfing shirt that complimented his lean, muscular body. Only Feemster drew wondering glances from the Biden's Brook members as his stomach billowed over his white belt. Kilgore ordered a beer, a Schaefer's, while Kerby and Feemster both asked for their favorite, a double Johnny Walker Black Label scotch, no ice.

Never one to mince words, Kilgore was unusually loquacious in his small talk over drinks. After the second drink, Kerby and Feemster began to perspire noticeably. Then Kilgore broached the reason for the lunch.

"Though the company's making a ton of money now, I'm concerned we're too dependent on the *Journal*. What if the paper ever got hit by a truck," he said, grinning.

Both men nodded. Ninety-five percent of Dow Jones's revenues, or $39 million, came from the *Wall Street Journal*.

Kilgore then reviewed his recent attempt to acquire *Newsweek* and how, at the very last moment, the Bancrofts had rejected the idea when informed they would have to take out a bank loan to finance the purchase.

"And so for the past six months or so," Kilgore continued, "I've been trying to figure out how to diversify without upsetting the Bancrofts."

Both listeners put down their drinks.

"And then Laurence Lombard [the Bancrofts' attorney] gave me an idea when he suggested we turn *Barron's* into a newsweekly."

"Brilliant," said Feemster, shaking his head scornfully.

"I didn't like it either," Kilgore continued, "but what Laurence was trying to tell me was, 'You can do anything, just don't borrow to pay for it.'"

So what? Feemster gestured with a shrug.

"Then it came to me while shaving the other day. We should start our own publication," Kilgore said, beaming.

"A junior *Wall Street Journal*? Another *Barron's*? What?" Feemster asked impatiently.

"A national Sunday newspaper," Kilgore said.

"A what?" Feemster asked.

"A Sunday newspaper for the entire country."

There was a pause. Both Kerby and Feemster were clearly stunned.

And then Feemster said, "Most people can't get through their Sunday paper now. Why would they want another?"

"It would be for people who don't have a newspaper yet. Young people, people who grew up on television," Kilgore replied.

Now Kerby looked as shocked as Feemster did.

Kilgore repeated the concept, adding that the new publication would be completely separate from the *Journal*.

"Does it have a name?" Feemster asked.

"The *National Observer*."

Both men looked at Kilgore with dismay.

"Well, we can work on that," conceded Kilgore. "But other than that, what d'you think?"

"Well, it's certainly something to—" Kerby said, searching for just the right words.

But Feemster cut him off. "It's a disaster, a goddamn disaster. I can just see the pitch now. 'Yes, Mr. Ford. The *Observer* is a national Sunday newspaper for young people who don't read. Oh, and they'll get it on Mondays!'" Feemster said. "Let's be honest here. This is a bad idea. There's nothing to it. No concept, no reason for being."

Kilgore stared at Feemster, stung by his opinion.

"What do you think, Bill?" Kilgore asked Kerby expectantly.

"Well, I don't know yet," Kerby said. "How would you staff it?"

"We'd take a few good writers from the *Journal*, and maybe Bill Giles as editor," Kilgore answered.

"And advertising and circulation?" Feemster asked.

"Ted Callis and Buren McCormack," Kilgore said. A DePauw graduate, Ted Callis was a journeyman ad salesperson at the time; Buren McCormack, also a DePauw graduate, had been serving as the *Journal's* business manager since running afoul of Vermont Royster a decade before.

"Great!" Feemster shot back. "With the exception of Giles, we'll have mediocre people for a mediocre idea."

"Don't be insulting," snapped Kilgore.

"Barney, listen to me, please. This is a bad idea," Feemster implored.

Obviously turning to Kerby for some sort of relief, Kilgore said, "Bill?"

"Well, it's interesting," Kerby said halfheartedly.

"For once in your life, say what the fuck's on your mind, Bill," Feemster shouted.

An embarrassed Kilgore looked around the dining room to see if anyone had heard Feemster. But his tolerance for the ad man's candor was so great, he did not reprimand Feemster.

"I simply haven't heard enough to make up my mind one way or another," Kerby said to Feemster acidly. Then, turning to Kilgore, Kerby continued, "Though I did get concerned when you said you want to take writers from the *Journal*."

"Would you be willing to let Giles go?" Kilgore asked.

"Well...yes...of course...though we'd certainly miss him," Kerby replied. Secretly, Kerby was relieved Kilgore wanted Giles. He was far too independent for Kerby's taste.

"I'm going to say this just once more," Feemster said. "Barney, this is a bad fuckin' idea. You're trying to replicate 1941, when you resurrected the *Journal*. It's different now. The *Journal* succeeded because it has a finite audience, business people. The *Observer* has no rationale, nothing you can hang on to. For people who don't read? C'mon. The *Journal* is a 'must read.' People can't do their jobs without it. It's unique. It has no competition. That's why, with all the television and all the other distractions, people still read the *Journal*. But they do it defensively, out of fear, out of fear of embarrassment. Someone at work will know something they don't. They'll be able to impress the boss or make the right decision. Those are powerful motivations, powerful enough to break through the inertia, to get people to read it. But the *Observer* has none of those advantages. Why should people read it? For its good writing? If that were so, then let's excerpt the classics. Those television babies would love reading *Moby Dick* and *The Brothers Karamazov* in serial form. Also, the *Observer* would have to compete with *Time*, the *New Yorker*, *Harper's*, all of those fuckin' thought books which are being eaten up by television.

"The world doesn't need another periodical, no matter how well written it is. If this were England, a nation of readers, then it might have a chance. But it's not. It's the United States, where television is turning everyone, most of all the people you want this thing to go to, into idiots."

Despite Robert Feemster's warnings, the *National Observer* was born on February 4, 1962.

To keep expenses low, Kilgore chose a printing plant in White Oaks, Maryland, an industrial park in suburban Washington, D.C., as the *Observer's* editorial headquarters. It was a fatefully bad decision. Rather than work in the stimulating environs of New York City or Washington, D.C., the *Observer* journalists were relegated to what looked like an airplane hanger sinking in dreary Maryland red clay. The editorial staff, eighteen in total, drawn mostly from the *Journal*, sat in a vast open space, at sturdy steel desks, the type purchasing agents might use, under enormous fluorescent lamps that imbued every face with a jaundiced, stultifying glow. It was clear from this ambience that the *Observer*, and those who worked for it, were second-class citizens.

Rather than fulfill a genuine reader need, the *Observer* was created as an elaborate means for Barney Kilgore to escape the bureaucracy Bill Kerby was so painstakingly and so innocently creating in New York.

The *National Observer* eventually grew to nearly 500,000 in circulation. But rather than become a young person's Sunday newspaper, the *National Observer*, filled with helpful and literate features, evolved into a newsweekly for people who disliked the smugness of *Time* and *Newsweek*.

The paper did not lack for individual journalistic talent. Jude Wanniski, who would later be a cofounder of supply-side economics, Nina Totenberg, later a public-radio star, and *Journal* stars James

Perry, Bill Giles, and Henry Gemmill, all wrote brilliantly for the *Observer* at one time or another. Even Vermont Royster wrote occasionally for the *Observer*. But all these people exhibited no real passion for the publication. The staff sensed on some level, just as their office environment suggested, that the *National Observer* lacked a legitimate reason for being. The *National Observer* was simply a niche in the rock, a temporary resting place, for people either climbing up or falling down from the *Journal*. No one cared about the niche itself.

Tom Dillon, chairman of BBDO, the giant New York advertising agency, said, "Publications are organic. They're far more human than we might think. And when they are under stress, which the *National Observer* was right from the start, advertisers sense that and shy away from them."³ Compared to television's hundreds of millions of viewers, the *Observer's* audience was minuscule. Compared to *Time's* readers, the *Observer's* audience was decidedly down-market. Madison Avenue shunned anyone over fifty years old.

Once it became apparent the *Observer* was not going to succeed, which was as early as 1965, the people of Dow Jones shifted their allegiance from Kilgore to Bill Kerby. More accurately put, people began to emulate Kerby and his more cautious ways, still revering Kilgore, the legend, but from afar. Risk takers were out, compliers were in. Mortgages and tuitions had to be paid. Outside, in the real world, the sixties were erupting. But within Dow Jones, it was still the Eisenhower years, the era of the Silent Generation. Though personal goals began to outweigh the company's, the sense of the individual was diminished. People did their jobs, collected their paychecks, and said very little.

With the *Journal*, and therefore Dow Jones, running smoothly, there was little need for innovation, which meant that Kilgore spent all of his time trying to make the *Observer* work. While he did that in White Oak, Maryland, the *Observer's* headquarters, Kerby remained in New York, maintaining the status quo.

In effect, in the early sixties, Kerby became Dow Jones's new leader. He had the responsibility of Dow Jones's chief executive officer but not the title, similar to how Kilgore shadowed Hogate twenty years before.

Kerby began to assemble his own management team, and his first appointment was as fateful as it was controversial. He promoted his favorite, Warren Phillips, to the company's second-most-critical post, managing editor of the *Wall Street Journal*.

Phillips's promotion riled many veteran staffers.

What upset them the most was Kerby's perceived failure to see through Phillips's politicking. Fred Taylor, a high-ranking *Journal* editor, cited how Phillips, when he returned to New York from a London assignment in the early fifties, "moved next door to Kerby in Brooklyn Heights so as to kiss the old man's ass better. Phillips was about twenty-five then and at least eight rungs below Kerby on the corporate ladder. Every morning, they would ride to work together in Kerby's limousine. How Phillips could afford the neighborhood, and why Kerby stood for it, I'll never know."[4]

But William Kerby did not champion everyone, and he was not above revenge.

In 1963, Kerby convinced Kilgore that Robert Feemster, Dow Jones's top marketing executive, had outlived his usefulness. Still smarting from Feemster's recent negative reaction to the *National Observer*, Kilgore failed to defend his old DePauw schoolmate this time. And so, what appeared as a resignation was in fact Kerby jettisoning someone he could not abide, irrespective of how good he was at his job. Robert Feemster retired to Florida to pursue personal interests, which included operating the motel he owned and learning to fly an airplane.

The loss of Feemster would not be felt for decades, such was the success of the *Wall Street Journal* back in the early sixties. Advertisers flocked to the *Journal*. Since there was no dip in sales after Feemster retired, no one at the *Journal* missed him. The man who succeeded him, Don Macdonald, would later prove to be inferior. But Macdonald's ascent at the time coincided with booming *Journal* sales which obfuscated his shortcomings.

And then, in the summer of 1966, Barney Kilgore was diagnosed with cancer. He died in November 1967. A few days before he died, Bill Kerby paid him a visit at the Kilgore home in Princeton, New Jersey.

It was one of those mornings that presage winter, when everyone and everything look cold and gray. Kerby's chauffeur, Eddie Schamp, said, "Mr. Kerby was definitely sad that morning. I figured he knew it might be one of the last times he'd ever see Mr. Kilgore alive."

Kerby trudged up the Kilgores' long driveway and was greeted at the front door by Mary Lou Kilgore, who smiled sadly at Kerby as he walked the last ten yards to the door. Still handsome and stylish at fifty-seven, Mary Louise Kilgore had known Bill Kerby since 1933, the year she graduated from DePauw. They had grown up and grown rich together.

Kerby hugged her warmly and asked how she was holding up.

"Okay...thanks," she replied, grateful he asked, grateful he had come.

"All the kids here yet?"

"Yes. James was the last. He made it home last night."

The Kilgores had three children: Katherine, twenty-three, a free-lance writer; John, twenty-two, who worked in a New York art gallery; and James, nineteen, a freshman at Stanford University.

"How is he today?" Kerby asked.

"Good. His old self, really," she said.

Kerby climbed the winding staircase, a replica of the one in Jefferson's Monticello, and walked down the long hallway past the floor-to-ceiling bookshelves containing Twain, Tolstoy, Trollope, Lawrence, Joyce, Yeats, Ovid, and many other classics.

Kilgore lay in his bed, slack and sallow like the newspapers that surrounded him. In contrast, Kerby looked flushed with health, as if he had just had a shave in the next room.

"You look great, Barney...just great," Kerby said.

"You were always a bad liar, Bill. A damn bad liar," Kilgore murmured, brightening the moment he saw his old friend.

Kerby reddened and looked away, confused more by Kilgore's condition than his comment. Then, knowing the subject would cause a reaction, he asked, "What'd you think of today's issue?"

"Great! Just great," said Kilgore with surprising energy. "I especially liked the leader on the Vietnam hospital."

That morning, November 2, 1967, the *Journal* had run a front-page story, column one, dealing with the suffering in a remote Vietnamese hospital manned by American medical personnel. It was written by Peter Kann, twenty-four, who had been appointed the *Journal's* Far East correspondent two weeks before.

"I hated it," Kerby said glumly.

"Why?" Kilgore asked, surprised.

"The front page is drifting too far away from business stories," Kerby said.

Kilgore laughed. "You sound like Henry Grimes thirty years ago when he had just been named managing editor," he added.

Kerby smiled sheepishly.

"But it irritates me," Kerby said. "If we're not going to do a business leader, then we should at least do the war better. Hubert Humphrey, the sitting vice president, toured Vietnam battle sites this week. Do we read about it in the *Journal*? No! Where's our guy, that kid, Kann? Off in the boonies, covering some civilian hospital."

Kilgore was gleeful now. Kerby's exasperation always amused him.

"I suspect Kann gave us a clearer picture of Vietnam than had he followed Humphrey around on that phony tour. Those generals were probably up all night, staging dummy battles so Hubert could tell Lyndon everything was fine." said Kilgore. "Incidentally, do you know Kann?"

"No. Do you?"

"Yeah. He grew up here in Princeton. Worked for me at the *Packet* one summer," Kilgore said.

"He seems soft to me. Too much touchy, feely," Kerby said.

Kilgore drifted off for a moment. Then he asked, "How're Phillips and Cony getting along these days?"

Warren Phillips, the *Journal's* executive editor, had been quietly but intently feuding with his immediate subordinate, Ed Cony, the *Journal's* managing editor. Cony favored nonbusiness page-one stories, whereas Phillips, trying to please Kerby, insisted on more business coverage.

"Better. But Cony's temper..." Kerby said, shaking his head in disapproval.

"Difficult, isn't he," agreed Kilgore. "Of course, he is a Pulitzer. And his people do love him," he added.

"But you know...sometimes I get the feeling Cony doesn't like business," Kerby said. "Take the other day. I suggested to Warren we do a story on box manufacturers, since they're somewhat of a measurement of the economy. Other manufacturers use boxes to ship things in, that sort of thing. Warren liked the idea and took it to Cony. But Cony bitched. Called it...how did he put it?...'one of Kerby's stupid barometric box story ideas.'"

Kilgore laughed uncontrollably. Even Kerby grinned.

"You're too tough on him," Kilgore said, wiping his eyes. "Remember you and me in Washington? Hell, we were always fighting with Grimes over the same thing."

Kilgore turned and stared out the window. Kerby let the silence pass.

Then Kilgore asked matter-of-factly, "How's Warren doing?"

"Well...very well."

"You've always liked him, haven't you?" Kilgore asked.

"It's not hard. He's brilliant, just brilliant," Kerby said.

Kilgore cast a skeptical glance at Kerby, as if he accepted, but disagreed with, Kerby's sentiment.

"Brilliant might be a stretch, Bill. Extremely competent, and loyal. Warren's always been loyal, especially to you."

"Do I sense a 'yes, but' in there somewhere?"

"Well, it's just that when it comes to a successor, too much harmony can be a danger."

"You have someone in mind?"

"I'm not advocating any one individual as much as I'm suggesting you broaden your criteria," Kilgore said pleasantly.

"Warren follows our formula perfectly. He's dogged. And because he is, the *Journal* has prospered unbelievably. What's wrong with wanting to preserve that?" Kerby asked.

"Nothing. But someday the *Journal* might need to change again. And your successor should be able to do that, " Kilgore said softly, sensing Kerby's defensiveness.

"Warren is quite capable of that," Kerby said. "In my humble opinion," he added.

"And that's all that counts, Bill."

Sounding more like a son than a successor, Kerby replied: "Don't worry about Warren. He'll do fine, just fine. Besides, I'm looking over his shoulder all the time."

"That's what worries me!" Kilgore said, cackling at his own humor.

"All kidding aside for a moment. What does worry me, Bill, will my baby make it?" Kilgore asked earnestly.

"As long as I'm CEO, it will," Kerby answered.

The reply seemed to comfort Kilgore. He nodded his thanks, turned over, and drifted off to sleep, leaving his friend to carry on.

Two weeks later, Barney Kilgore, fifty-nine, died.

The *Journal's* editorial, written by Vermont Royster, summed up his life.

He was, strangely enough for a dynamic leader, the gentlest of men. There were those who have worked with him a lifetime, and who bear witness to his stubbornness with an idea, who have never seen him lose his temper or make those flamboyant gestures which make for legends. By the nature of his work— from reporter to prominent publisher—he walked with the peers of his time, and he was known and respected by all. Yet he always walked with them shyly, just as he was shy with those who worked with him.

Somehow among those gifts given him was the boon of self-containment, if not always self-content. There was a demon in him about what he wanted to create; his pride in his newspaper was as great as that of a composer for his symphony, and so was his jealousy for it. Yet he had not the slightest need for self-aggrandizement or personal publicity to nourish an uncertain age.

Thus, his work is more famous than himself. If you ask what he did, you need only to look at this newspaper you are reading.

Ironically, throughout the sixties and the seventies, people at Dow Jones rarely mentioned Kilgore's name. Perhaps wanting to prove their own worth, or wanting to prove they could carry on without him, Dow Jones people seemed to say, "The King is dead. Long live Kerby."

But in the eighties, Dow Jones old-timers invoked Kilgore's memory often, especially when recalling how he had shaped the *Journal*'s culture, which was changing radically then.

Kerby kept his deathbed promise, and the *Observer* remained open until 1977, when Kerby retired. His successor, Warren Phillips, wisely terminated the publication in July of that year, after it had accumulated some $17 million in losses. The *National Observer* failed in part because it lacked Kilgore to bring it along. No one else at Dow Jones shared his enthusiasm for it. No one cared about it, really.

Significantly, corporate pride has never allowed Dow Jones to mourn the *Observer*. As a result, the company still lives with the shame of its failure, always fearful it will occur again in some other form, some other venture. That's why, even today, Dow Jones avoids risk and suppresses innovation. It's afraid to fail again.

By the late sixties, after several years of burgeoning dividends, the Bancroft family became more open to the idea of lessening Dow Jones's dependence on the *Journal*. With Phillips running The *Journal* day-to-day, Kerby became a financier, a job he had no training for, to hunt for possible merger or acquisition candidates.

After two years of trying to acquire the likes of Gannett, Whitney Communications (*International Herald Tribune*, Corinthian Broadcasting), and several other respected companies, Kerby purchased Ottaway Community Newspapers for $36 million in Dow Jones stock. This purchase price—twenty-four times earnings—seemed high, considering Ottaway consisted of only nine dailies in markets such as Middletown and Plattsburgh, New York. The average newspaper earned less than $200,000 per year; the average circulation was 12,300.

When the Ottaway deal was consummated in 1970, Dow Jones's gross revenues were $96 million and its profits, $19 million. Ottaway's were $8.1 million and $1.7 million, respectively.

Some Dow Jones staffers were disappointed with the transaction.

"Small potatoes," snorted Buren McCormack, who was now retired from heading circulation. "Ottaway represents less than five percent of our revenues. It will do nothing to broaden our base."

McCormack went on to explain why this deal went through: "After several years of trying, Kerby got desperate and bought the first thing that came along. It happened to be from his friend, Jim Ottaway, Sr., during a round of golf in Buck Hills Falls [Pennsylvania],"[5] McCormack said.

When measured against its acquisition objective, that is, to diminish the *Journal's* shadow on Dow Jones, Kerby's purchase was a curious choice.

One wonders what the Bancroft sisters, or J. Paul Austin, CEO of Coca-Cola, or William McChesney Martin, former chairman of the Federal Reserve Board, all members of the Dow Jones board of directors, were thinking of when they approved Kerby's acquisition of Ottaway in July 1970.

Perhaps they, like Kerby and the outside world, were too thrilled with recent *Journal* accomplishments to care. That summer a Harris Poll revealed the *Wall Street Journal* was America's most trusted newspaper.

9

The Ultimate Follower:
Warren Phillips, Publisher
(1975–91)

In the newspaper business, the publisher is the ultimate boss, the *capo di tutti capi*, over every aspect of the publication, including news, editorial, advertising, circulation, finance, and production. Standing before his publisher, even the most truculent editor or ad sales director turns into a respectful child, anxious to smile and please. The world, though not familiar with many publishers, still can imagine the ideal as a broad-shouldered, white-haired man, partial to dark blue suits, French cuffs, and Monte Cristo cigars, who displays humor, magnetism, and decisiveness appropriately. When people imagine what the publisher of the *Wall Street Journal* looks and acts like, they assume he is the Zeus of the management Pantheon. How else, they reason, could the *Journal* write so convincingly about corporate management?

But Warren H. Phillips, the *Journal's* publisher from 1975 to 1991, as well as Dow Jones chief executive officer during this period, lacked most of these traits and attitudes.[1] Tall and pipe-thin, Warren Phillips usually wore a wincing, pained expression which illustrated his extreme awkwardness with people.

The chance meeting with Phillips on the elevator was cause for nervous exhaustion. While Phillips and a subordinate would shift uneasily from one foot to another for eight to ten seconds, the subordinate would try and put him at ease by asking a casual question or two. His answer would usually sound inane, a draining effect created by his own discomfort. But when he got off the elevator, Phillips and the subordinate would pretend the interchange was perfectly relaxed and free flowing, a pretense which lasted forty-six years, the length of Warren Phillips's career at Dow Jones. It was not that Phillips was a misanthrope; he was just naturally uncomfortable with himself and therefore with everyone else around him.

Ironically, it was Phillips's deficiencies which allowed the *Journal's* transformation from a small, highly personal newspaper dominated by Kilgore's clear-cut values into a $1.7 billion corporate bureaucracy whose values became as expedient as Phillips is shy. But throughout much of Phillips's reign, Wall Street viewed Dow Jones's metamorphosis in sanguine fashion because the company's surface indicators—for example, quarterly earnings—were robust. But these enviable short-term earnings, the result of a good economy and the questionable strategy of selling off assets, began to plummet in the late eighties. By 1991, Dow Jones's revenues remained at $1.7 billion for the third consecutive year, while profits, 71¢ per share, hit an all-time low.

After World War II, many young men like Warren Phillips entered corporate America and thirty years later ended up chief executive officers of their companies. In fact, the story of how Phillips became Dow Jones's chief executive officer explains why once-great companies like IBM and General Motors are in such trouble today.[2] Protected by a booming economy, young managers who could follow the innovative formulas created by previous management generations were in great demand. Implementing, not innovating, was the way to get ahead in corporate America from 1945 through 1985. And Phillips, like Kerby before him, was the perfect follower.

But Phillips was a superb copy editor, for one thing. Had Mies Van der Rohe known Phillips, he would have certainly changed his well-known quote to read: "God and Warren Phillips are in the details." Phillips would calmly and precisely keep track of the various rewrite stages of twelve different stories in his head, a miraculous talent whenever the newsroom scrambled to meet a 6:30 P.M. deadline.

And on occasion, Phillips could be warm. Michael Gartner, a former *Journal* page-one editor and president of NBC-TV News, said, "Warren Phillips is the kindest man I know."

The manner in which Phillips handled John McWethy, the *Journal's* Chicago bureau chief, demonstrates Gartner's point. In 1971, while driving to the University of Missouri on a recruiting expedition, McWethy fell asleep at the wheel. His car rolled over three times and landed in a storm ditch, wheels up. McWethy broke his neck and became a quadriplegic.

At first, McWethy, fifty-eight, did not want to go on living. But Phillips, forty-five, then Dow Jones's number two behind Kerby, sent McWethy a letter instructing him to master a new means of typing and to return to work in a wheelchair. "After all, John, we don't pay you to hop, skip and jump," wrote Phillips. McWethy worked for the *Journal* for another seven years before retiring. He died in 1988, seventeen years after the accident. "Countless times from 1971 onwards, Warren visited my father in Chicago and in Sun City, Arizona, where he retired. Every time he did, Dad would be on cloud nine for days,"[3] said John McWethy, Jr., an ABC News State Department correspondent. "Warren Phillips saved my father's life."

Nevertheless, most people, upon first meeting Phillips, would wonder not unkindly, How did this man get this job?

An incident that occurred when Phillips was still young and green answers the question. It was Monday, May 23, 1954, at 7:43 A.M., and Eddie Schamp, Bill Kerby's chauffeur, had the motor idling as the Dow Jones limousine waited outside 11 Columbia Terrace, a place that looks like an elegant London or Georgetown street which somehow ended up in Brooklyn. Studded with stately town houses, Columbia Terrace enjoys spectacular views of Wall Street, the Statue of Liberty, Ellis Island, and the Staten Island ferry. Norman Mailer lives here, three doors past Bill Kerby, four past Warren Phillips. Nearby is the Brooklyn Heights Casino, the squash retreat for famous Wall Streeters. Around the corner is the once grand St. George Hotel.

A raven-haired young man, his knees practically puncturing his chest, sat in the backseat, lost in that day's *Journal*. Then the curbside rear door opened, and Bill Kerby, forty-six, president of Dow Jones, jumped in, saying, "Mornin', Eddie, mornin', Warren."

Warren Phillips, twenty-five, foreign editor of the *Wall Street Journal*, squirmed over a few inches and tersely returned the greeting. Then Kerby said, "That was some party Friday night, Warren."

"Thanks."

"Did I drink all of New York's Johnny Walker Black Label or what?"

Kerby asked, chuckling to himself. At the time, Kerby was Kilgore's number two, while Phillips had hardly attained the maturity or the success to be Kerby's next door neighbor much less host parties for him.

The limousine turned the corner and snaked by John Sylvester, a *Journal* reporter since 1928, walking to work. Kerby and Phillips pretended not to see him. A few minutes passed quietly as both men read their newspapers. Then, gesturing toward the *Journal*, Kerby asked, "You got anything in there today?"

"I was hoping Vickers's piece on Dien Bien Phu would make it. But it didn't," Phillips said.

"What are you gonna do? Barney's such an isolationist," Kerby said, smiling.

Under the Kilgore regime, the *Journal* accorded international news a very low priority. If an ad dropped out at the last minute, then a story from Phillips's desk might be published.

A few more minutes were spent with the *Journal*, and then Kerby said, "By the way, how do you and Barbara like Chicago?"

"I don't know. We've never been there," Phillips responded.

"Hmmm," Kerby murmured.

"Why do you ask?"

"No reason, other than I was just thinking. The other day, that crazy Gemmill [Henry Gemmill, the *Journal*'s managing editor at the time] came in and asked Barney and me to 'liberate him' from his job. Says he wants to be a reporter again, in Europe. Says we robbed him of his boyhood by making him managing editor when he was so young. So we're going to pull [Robert] Bottorff in from Chicago to replace Henry and I was thinking of you to take Bottorff's place [Chicago bureau chief]."

Phillips sat there, mute. Then he said, "I'm stunned."

"Don't worry. You can do it," Kerby said.

"Who in Chicago thinks he should get the job?"

"I don't know, really. Maybe McWethy, John McWethy. He's a holdover from the *Commerce* people," Kerby answered.

"What are the problems out there?"

"Not too many, really. A few of the old *Journal of Commerce* reporters still have a tendency to sell ads, the office is too cramped, and, of course, there's the view of the whorehouse next door."

"What?"

"The view. Next door. A whorehouse," Kerby said, grinning broadly. "I'm not kidding. It's true."

Phillips looked dismayed.[4]

In 1951, as part of his quest to make the *Journal* a national newspaper, Kilgore bought the Chicago edition of the *Journal of Commerce*, a business newspaper, which he immediately merged with the *Wall Street Journal*. The *Journal of Commerce*'s office and printing plant offered a clear view of its next-door neighbor, the Grand Street Hotel, a haunt of prostitutes. Down on its luck, the hotel could not afford blinds or shades for the windows.

Thus, Warren Phillips, by dint of his address and his wife's party-giving ability, received his first significant promotion, a promotion which launched him on a career trajectory that went straight up. After three years as the *Journal*'s Midwest managing editor, Phillips would move back to New York as the *Journal*'s overall managing editor, a Boswell to Bill Kerby, who in the late fifties was taking over more and more of Dow Jones from a bored Barney Kilgore.

Later, when Phillips succeeded Kerby as the company's chief executive officer, Phillips's obedient spirit seemed adequate for the job until extraordinary economic circumstances forced him to make critical decisions. Then, unused to these situations and too set in his ways to learn from others, Phillips would display egregiously poor judgment. His record for selecting the wrong people for key Dow Jones and *Journal* posts, for example, was only exceeded by his record for selecting the wrong companies to acquire at the wrong prices.[5]

The first time a vacancy occurred on the Dow Jones board of directors during his stewardship, Phillips selected William Agee, the Bendix executive who denied having an affair with a young subordinate, Mary Cunningham, to six hundred employees in the Bendix cafeteria. Six months later, Agee divorced his wife and married Cunningham, an about-face which the nation's headlines revealed. Readers seemed to share the media's glee in exposing Agee, whom they depicted as an arrogant Harvard Business School know-it-all. Certainly Agee was hardly the appropriate successor to Dow Jones director William McChesney Martin, the venerable former chairman of the Federal Reserve Board whom Kilgore had appointed.

Phillips's next board selection was Rand Araskog, chairman of ITT, infamous for earning $11.1 million in 1991 while ITT's share price languished. Graef S. Crystal, the man *Fortune* regards as "America's foremost expert on executive compensation," wrote about Araskog's pay-performance disparity in his newsletter, the *Crystal Report*. The financial press, with the exception of the *Journal*, picked up the story, and a flood of unfavorable Araskog publicity followed. Dow Jones was further embarrassed when it became known that Araskog was the prime mover behind awarding Warren Phillips a special $1 million bonus in 1989, the year Dow Jones laid off seventy-eight employees to reduce expenses because of poor profits.[6]

But what Phillips may lack in judgment, he makes up for in determination, a trait he inherited from both his parents. Abraham Phillips, a garment manufacturer, sought a better life for his wife, Juliette, and his only child, Warren, in 1938 by moving from Manhattan's Lower East Side to a two-bedroom apartment in Briarwood, Queens, which lay in the shadow of the World's Fair Grounds.

Abraham Phillips looked like a circus ringmaster: dark, tall, handsome, and slim. But he was too dignified and too shy to achieve anything of note in New York's competitive garment industry. An introspective man, Abraham was happiest when lost in a vapor of questions that no one else could see. For an uneducated man, he was something of an intellectual.

Unlike Tecumseh Kilgore and Frederick Kerby, Abraham Phillips did not play a big role in his son's youth. Juliette Phillips represented the pivotal authority. Still alive today at the age of ninety-three, Juliette Phillips possesses the strength of personality to match her physical constitution.

An administrator in a junior high school when Warren was growing up, Juliette Phillips fervently believed that education would fulfill the high ambitions she held for her son. And each day, while driving Warren to school, she reminded him of this belief.

Warren Phillips graduated from Franklin K. Lane High School in June 1941, two weeks shy of his fifteenth birthday, an achievement he views much less admiringly than his mother did. Smiling at the reminder of how adoring his mother was, Phillips recently recalled, "Contrary to my dear mother who, you must understand, is a typical Jewish mother, I was not a child prodigy. The New York City Board of Education wanted to get as many kids through the system as possible before the war broke out."[7]

In July 1941, Abraham Phillips, forty-seven, suddenly died of a heart attack. But the death did not interfere with Juliette's plan to board Warren at the Horace Mann School, a boys' prep school in the Bronx, for a year of postgraduate study. "It was," Phillips said, "my chance to see how the upper class lived."[8]

Horace Mann's 1942 yearbook describes Phillips as "this thin man from Queens who breezed into Horace Mann's sixth form and never said a word for the entire year."

Among Phillips's Horace Mann schoolmates were billionaire Marvin Davis, theater critic John Simon, author James Salter, and Anthony Lewis, the *New York Times's* Pulitzer Prize–winning columnist. When asked how he remembered Warren Phillips, Anthony Lewis replied: "Of course, I know who Warren Phillips is. But I did not know he attended Horace Mann when I was there."[9]

Phillips did not like Horace Mann. "It was a very uncaring place," he said. "It's why I've never been back nor given the school any money," Phillips admits. His grades reflected his disillusionment.

Nevertheless, Phillips applied to three colleges—Cornell was his first choice—but only Oberlin College in Ohio and Queens College in New York City accepted him.

In September 1942, Phillips entered Queens College, a former reform school that had been converted into a community college four years before. "Since my father just died, I chose Queens so that I could be with my mother," Phillips explained.

Known as "the people's college," Queens reflected the sentiments of public colleges of the day. Its students were liberal and the children of Italian, Irish, and Eastern European immigrants. After attending Queens for only a few months, Phillips enlisted in the army air corps and spent two years in Texas and San Francisco as a military policeman. Ed Cony, a *Journal* managing editor, once asked, "Can you imagine Warren as an MP? All six-foot-two and a hundred forty pounds of him?"

After the war, Phillips returned to his mother's home, fired with ambition. He reentered Queens and completed three years of work in nine months to graduate cum laude in June 1947. Like most professional newspeople, Phillips worked on the school's newspaper. He also served as campus stringer for the *New York Times*, though there is no evidence he ever filed a byline story. In the spring of 1947, while searching for a career, Phillips sustained a series of rejections which would have crushed a less persistent person. After deciding journalism would be his life's work, each of New York City's twelve daily newspapers rejected him. Undismayed, Phillips then applied to the Columbia School of Journalism. It, too, rejected him. "No one thought much of Queens College back then,"[10] Phillips explained later.

Finally, despite his lack of interest in business, Phillips applied to the *Journal* and found himself explaining to Bill Kerby, the managing editor, why he was a socialist. Kerby hired Phillips as a proofreader on the spot. "I wanted two socialists to work for the *Wall Street Journal*," Kerby later joked.

Proofreader was the perfect job for Phillips. Because he never failed to ferret out a split infinitive, he was promoted to the copydesk in three months. As a deskman, Phillips made sure all stories filed by the bureaus conformed with the *Journal's* style book, which had been recently revamped by Kilgore and Kerby. Frustration erupted as the nineteen-year-old Phillips altered story after story to comply with the new system. Though it is true all reporters rail against the copydesk, *Journal* reporters reacted to Phillips with a singular rancor. But as much as the reporters disliked Phillips's intervention, Kerby loved it. By heeding the style book's criteria so uncompromisingly, Phillips offered Kerby iron control of the bureaus. It was no small accomplishment for a young man with less than six months' experience.

"Warren was remarkable. He was a stickler. Everything had to be perfect. He was only nineteen, yet he stood up to reporters three times his age,"[11] added Kit Melick, an editorial assistant at the time.

Four months later, in January 1948, Phillips was again promoted, this time to the World News desk, where he rewrote wire copy. It was Phillips's first writing assignment, and, contrary to many predictions, he did well. "Phillips did a beautiful job on the Worldwide column,"[12] said Henry Gemmill, a *Journal* editor then.

After eight months on the World News desk, Phillips grew restless. Seeking actual reporting experience, and wanting to see a part of the world he had never seen, Phillips asked to be posted in Europe as the *Journal's* correspondent. Kerby turned him down flat. Shocked and disappointed, Phillips tendered his resignation and joined the *Stars and Stripe's* copydesk in Barmstadt, Germany. "Kerby tried to talk me out of going," Phillips said, "but I was adamant."

Once overseas, Phillips quickly proved himself with his new employer. "He was the best slotman* I'd seen in a long time,"[13] said Nathan Margolin, news editor of *Stars and Stripes*.

Phillips worked from 3:00 P.M. to 11:00 P.M. for *Stars and Stripes*, leaving him ample time for moonlighting. And though he harbored deep resentments of certain people at the *Journal*, he was not above

---

* Newspaper jargon for the chief of the copy desk, which is shaped like a horseshoe or U. The slot man sits in the horseshoe, hence slot, and controls the flow of work as well as supervising it.

sending them free-lance pieces. Phillips's articles, dealing mostly with Germany's reconstruction, required much doctoring before they could be published by the *Journal*. "His initial stories were thoroughly reported, but poorly written," Gemmill said. "Betty Donnelley, our page-one person, had to rewrite most of them." Undeterred by the heavy editing, Phillips continued to submit an avalanche of stories. Soon it became cheaper to rehire him. Gemmill said, "Phillips was filing so many stories that I justified taking him back by proving his salary would be less than his by-the-piece freelance fees."

In January 1950, Phillips moved to London to join four other *Journal* reporters in covering the Atlee-Churchill elections and Britain's deficiencies in the postwar era. "It was horrible," Phillips said later. "People had no food. That's when I learned Socialism did not work."[14] Phillips also covered the spy scandal that tarnished the British Foreign Office when it was learned that Guy Burgess and Donald MacLean had passed secrets to the Soviet Union.

In June 1950, George Ormsby, the *Journal's* veteran London bureau chief, suddenly died and Phillips was promoted over several senior newsmen to replace him. "Ormsby's death was the second luckiest break in my career," Phillips said. Not everyone in the bureau was pleased, however. Frank Linge, a veteran correspondent, quit in disgust when Phillips became his boss. Linge thought he should have received the promotion.

As bureau chief, it fell upon Phillips to entertain Dow Jones officials from New York, many of whom were visiting Europe for the first time. In 1948, Phillips hosted such a splendid banquet to honor editorial-page editor William Henry Grimes on his maiden visit that thereafter Grimes returned almost monthly to visit "the whiz in London." Mrs. Jessie Cox, the hard-drinking owner of the *Wall Street Journal*, relished her frequent trips to London so she might spend evenings dancing with Phillips.

Back in New York, Kerby and Kilgore started to hear good things about their London bureau chief. Warren Phillips, the shy, awkward native of Queens, blossomed somewhat in London. Pygmalion-like, the city imparted to him a surface sophistication, for example, a predilection for dark blue Savile Row suits (Gieves & Hawkes). During his time in London, Phillips divorced his first wife and married Barbara Ann Thomas, an attractive, blond-haired Daughter of the American Revolution from Cape Charles, Virginia.

Then, in December 1951, Kerby called Phillips, twenty-five, back to New York to become the foreign editor. The New York newsroom was incredulous. Just three years before, staffers remembered, Phillips had been little more than a twenty-two-year-old who quit because he failed to become a foreign correspondent. Now he was returning from London as a *Journal* editor, to live right next door to Bill Kerby.

But London had not cured Phillips of all his social ills. He was still extremely awkward around peers and subordinates, a weakness which manifested itself in an inability to remember people's names. Convinced that a new sociability would be his if he could only correct this failing, Phillips was forever devising ways to improve his memory. But sometimes these mechanical aids, always doggedly followed, backfired.

Phillips's return from London to the New York newsroom was one such occasion. Eager to show how much he had changed for the good, Phillips believed that if he could enter the newsroom and greet each former colleague by name, his homecoming would be a success. Scheduled to report to work on a Monday, Phillips stole into the newsroom late on the preceding Sunday evening, when no one was there, and made up a seating chart.

The next day, he timed his arrival to the hour when all the reporters would most likely be at their desks. At the appointed hour, Phillips, in a crisply starched Trumbull & Asser shirt, stood at the entrance to the newsroom and stole one last look at the chart. He then entered the room and walked briskly up to the first desk, which belonged to Amos Smithers.

Unfortunately, Smithers was in the men's room, an unanticipated event that flustered Phillips. He stood before the empty desk for a moment before he proceeded to the second desk, where Fred Taylor sat, observing the whole scene. Upon seeing Taylor, Phillips stuck out his hand and said, quite mechanically, "Amos, it's so good to see you." Phillips then proceeded down the row, greeting each of twelve reporters by the wrong name—off by one desk. "The crazy part," Taylor recalled, "is that Warren knew damn well who I was. He knew I wasn't Amos Smithers."[15]

Inevitably, some people believed Phillips's return to New York sprang from his rejection of his Jewishness so he might better blend in with the all-Protestant Dow Jones. "To get ahead, Phillips changed his name, his religion, and his wife," said Taylor. "And he would have changed his birthplace and alma mater, if he could."

But Taylor's assertions, which have been widely seconded for forty years, are groundless. Family records, most notably Abraham's 1918 army discharge papers, all bear the surname Phillips. The occasion for Phillips to "change" his first wife, Judy, had nothing to do with his career. An eyewitness to the marriage, Nate Margolin, Phillips's boss at *Stars and Stripes*, reveals what had to be one of the most painful experiences in Phillips's life. Margolin recalled, "In August 1949, my wife and I were vacationing on a small Danish island in the North Sea when Warren's first wife at the time, Judy, a dazzling blonde, showed up with a tall, rugged Marine."[16]

Phillips did in fact join the Unitarian Church in 1951, but only in deference to his wife, Barbara, a lifelong member of that church.

After spending three years supervising the foreign desk, Phillips became the Chicago bureau chief in June 1954 at the age of twenty-six, replacing Robert Bottorff, who was promoted to New York. Phillips spent the first weeks of his new job silently walking about the office, black notebook in hand, noting in minute detail the bureau's myriad operations. "At first, Warren was as laconic as a Chicago winter, preoccupied with the many things he didn't know,"[17] said Bill Clabby, a Chicago reporter. "But he soon mastered the job and became successful, quite successful."

While in Chicago, Phillips demonstrated his determination and toughness, qualities which surprised certain recalcitrant staff members. Two veteran reporters, mistaking Phillips's shyness for weakness, ignored his repeated warnings to improve. When it became apparent they were flouting his authority, Phillips surprised the entire staff by summarily firing the two reporters. Despite his reticence, Warren Phillips never lacked for determination, toughness, or ambition.

In fact, in most respects, Warren Phillips was the quintessential post–World War II corporate manager. Provided he had pre-established directives, policies, and tradition to follow, Phillips could supervise others capably. And his lack of judgment and creativity, not much needed in corporate middle-management bureaucracies to begin with, was offset by an obsession for detail.

In August 1957, Phillips was called back to New York by Bill Kerby to become the *Journal's* overall managing editor. It would have been an unusual promotion for anyone barely thirty-one years old; it was an astonishing promotion for a young man who was, at best, a mediocre writer and reporter.[18] It revealed just how much Kerby valued someone who followed orders unswervingly. But similar promotions were happening all over corporate America at the time; the less secure the boss, the more obsequious the subordinate.

But a month into his new job, Phillips surprised everyone, most of all Kerby, by making a courageous decision to cover a story that carried little relevance to the *Journal's* business-oriented readership.

On September 4, 1957, a front-page photograph of a battalion of Arkansas national guardsmen barring a teenage black boy from Little Rock's Central High School galvanized the nation. The country understood at a glance that the photograph presaged the first and possibly the most pivotal battle that *Brown* v. *Board of Education* would face. It would help determine if integration would be a real or fictional social policy of the United States.

Earlier that summer, a federal district court had ordered Little Rock's Central High School integrated. But when school opened in September, Orvil Faubus, Arkansas' governor, who was in the midst of a tough reelection campaign, enlisted the Arkansas National Guard in an attempt to defy the court order. Eventually, President Eisenhower furloughed the Arkansas National Guard and deployed a thousand army paratroopers to escort nine black teenagers through the doors of Central High School.

As riveting as Little Rock was, it was not a traditional *Journal* news story. But Phillips decided to cover it anyway. "I wanted to debunk the myth that segregation was a problem only in the South," said Phillips. He dispatched the *Journal's* two best reporters, Henry Gemmill and Joe Guilfoyle, to Little Rock. Though unfamiliar with the territory and the issue, the *Journal* performed most creditably, particularly in comparison with the other national print media. "Henry and Joe got the story!" beamed Bill Clabby, then a young *Journal* reporter in the Chicago bureau and now a Dow Jones news vice president. "They reported Faubus was manipulating the event to get reelected. Other national newspapers, whose correspondents covered that territory day to day and should have known better, were still mired in the surface facts. Gemmill and Guilfoyle beat them at their own game. I know the *Times* [the *New York Times*], for example, could never have done the same thing to us at the New York Stock Exchange."

In addition to bolstering the newsroom's pride, the coverage of Little Rock marked the beginning of a liberal trend among the *Journal* news personnel which, though never evident to its readers, caused great internal strife over the next fifteen years.

But after Little Rock, Phillips reverted to form. His obsession with detail got the better of him and any number of subordinates. Jim Soderlind, a Phillips aide for forty years, recently recalled, "Precision was Warren's passion. Everything, especially stories on page one, had to be perfect. Like the page- one story on the Catholic Church."[19]

In the 1960 presidential campaign, beginning with the Democratic primaries, Kennedy's Roman Catholicism worried America. Non-Catholics feared that if Kennedy became president they would have to eat fish on Fridays and publicly confess their transgressions.

The media were vexed by Kennedy's religion, too. If they covered it openly, were they fanning prejudice? If they avoided it, were they being irresponsible? But Ray Vickers, a distinguished correspondent in the *Journal*'s London bureau, suggested a novel approach. Do a page-one leader on the Roman Catholic Church, as if it were an ordinary company like General Motors. Phillips approved the idea with some trepidation. He did not want to offend anyone: the Church, Kennedy, Humphrey, or anyone else at risk from the situation.

Vickers spent weeks in the Vatican interviewing an impressive number of church officials and researching how the church functions. After that, he spent several more weeks writing a 10,000-word story, an exhaustive length, which then passed through the scrutiny of three editors: Alan Otten, London bureau chief; Jim Soderlind; a page-one rewrite editor; and Lindley Clark, page-one editor. Something of a prima donna, Vickers responded calmly to the many questions raised and changes requested by these men.

"Ray thought the worst was over, " Soderlind said with a chuckle. "He forgot how Warren could be."

Phillips, as a matter of practice, scrutinized all page-one leaders more carefully than any of his predecessors ever had, including Kilgore. Paul Lancaster, a former page-one editor, said, "After Warren got finished with a page one leader, it would have to be rewritten or polished at least ten more times. And, mind you, that was after it had already passed through the page-one department."[20]

Vickers's frank examination of the Roman Catholic church made Phillips apprehensive. And usually, whenever a situation made Phillips nervous, he would try to control it by mastering every fact, no matter how small. Does the pope have a limousine and driver? How many nuns serve the pope breakfast? Where does he eat it? Finally, Vickers snapped.

"When Warren called Vickers in London and asked, What is the pope's salary? Ray hung up in his ear,"[21] said Soderlind, laughing. Jim Soderlind, at Phillips's direction, ended up rewriting a much-watered-down version of Vickers's piece.

Vickers was not the only staffer who bridled under Phillips's insensitivity. Shortly after the Vatican piece appeared, Phillips paid the *Journal*'s Atlanta bureau "a morale visit" which two reporters still remember.

Phillips started these visits in the late fifties after reading a how-to book for corporate managers. Among many things, it urged managers to venture forth among the workers to gain perspective on what was going on in the workplace. This high-level venturing also improved morale, the consultant suggested, because the little people could speak their mind.

This particular trip to Atlanta occurred at a time when that city's male establishment still retreated every day to the Capitol Club, seeking relief from the effects of the Warren Court and the carpet-baggers who were turning Peachtree Street into a shopping mall.

The club occupied a plain white stucco building which the ordinary world walked by every day without noticing. Its interior, however, was dazzling. A brilliant crystal chandelier glittered a greeting to all members and guests as they entered the red-carpeted, brass-fixtured foyer dotted with huge tropical palms.

A white-haired black man, dressed in a charcoal morning coat, stood at the entrance, the perfect blend of deference and vigilance, making sure all members and guests were properly accounted for. The dining room was even more solemn, shrouded in Irish linen, Philippine mahogany, and sterling silver service. Gangs of black men in white gloves roamed about, dispensing popovers or the club's very own mineral water. Three men in seersucker suits sat at a table waiting for Phillips.

Just as one of them was about to order a martini, a tall, improbably thin man with shoe-polish-black hair and mustache entered the dining room carrying a briefcase. He was dressed in a double-breasted navy blue pinstriped suit.

The man was immediately accosted by the maître d'. "Briefcases are prohibited in the dining room, sir!" he said. Briefcase still in hand and smiling vaguely, the smartly dressed visitor proceeded to the table where the three men waited chastely.

Burt Schorr, the *Wall Street Journal*'s Atlanta bureau chief, who was the member and who witnessed the scene, stood up and greeted his boss. "Hello, Warren. The maître d' was trying to explain the club doesn't allow papers into the dining room. It's a silly rule, but—"

"Yes, I know," said Warren Phillips as he took the fourth seat at the table. "Sorry I'm late. The usual Monday morning at La Guardia. Did you order yet?"

All four men sat over their mineral water making small talk, until a waiter asked, "More water?"

Phillips jolted upright and said sternly, "Speaking of water," at which time he placed the briefcase on the table, opened it, and pulled out a sheaf of letters.

Addressing Schorr, Phillips said, "Do you remember that A-hed you did on the Windjammer Cruise a while back?" (An A-hed is *Journalese* for the column-four story on page one. It is named after the type of headline always used for these pieces.)

Schorr, already embarrassed by Phillips's flouting the briefcase rule, turned ashen.

The other two men, intuiting something unpleasant was about to occur, glanced around the room in search of a place to hide.

"What about it?" Schorr asked.

"It was awful," replied Phillips, waving a handful of letters at Schorr. "Based on your glowing piece, hundreds of readers took the cruise themselves. But they hated it. Said it was nothing like you depicted it. One man said it was so bad, he wonders if you ever took the cruise yourself at all. Did you?"

Schorr was dumbfounded. His two subordinates, reporters Neil Maxwell and Dick Leger, stared into their dessert plates. "How could Warren embarrass our boss right in front of us?" Maxwell wondered.

"In those days, a bureau chief was a powerful person," Leger later said. "We were mortified that Phillips emasculated Schorr in front of us."[22]

The luncheon ended in awkwardness, with the three Atlanta men commiserating silently with one another. But Phillips, though subdued, did not seem to realize what he had done, Leger recalled.

Phillips did not leave well enough alone. Several weeks later he called the Atlanta bureau, asking for Schorr. Leger explained to Phillips that Schorr had just left to go to the hospital to have his testicular varicose veins removed.

"Upon hearing where Burt was," Leger said, "Warren asked for the name of the hospital."

Leger subsequently learned that Phillips had located Schorr right before going into surgery and demoted him over the telephone.

"Schorr was literally and figuratively deballed that morning," Leger said. "They didn't call Warren 'Snake' for nothing."[23]

By 1964, the *Journal's* circulation had leaped to 805,000, which was a function of the country's growing interest in business and the efficacy of the *Journal's* TV ads suggesting the paper was "for men who want to get ahead." In fact, the *Journal's* image began to exceed its reality; it became America's symbol of power and money, an enviable status for any financial publication to enjoy. But Kilgore, Kerby, and, to a lesser extent, Phillips were too parochial to recognize, much less exploit, the country's exaggerated view of the *Journal.* They continued to live in the anonymous suburbs, eschewing New York's power circles, content to work at making the *Journal* better and stronger.

In June 1964, Kerby used some of the *Journal's* profits to lease an IBM 360 computer system to automate the servicing and billing of the *Journal's* 800,000 customers. A year before, Kerby had consolidated many of Dow Jones's various branches and departments— *Barron's*, the ticker facilities, advertising sales and circulation departments—into one building for the first time. It was located at 30 Broad Street, in the heart of Wall Street.

By 1965, it was evident to everyone at Dow Jones what Kerby had long ago decided: Warren Phillips would be his successor. Kerby promoted Phillips to executive editor, a position that removed him more from day-to-day operations. Edward Cony, a swashbuckling Pulitzer Prize winner, replaced Phillips as managing editor at the behest of Barney Kilgore. Though near death at the time, Kilgore was still involved in the major decisions of the company. "Barney insisted on Cony as a counterbalance to Phillips whom he never admired as much as Kerby did,"[24] Fred Taylor said, a former *Journal* managing editor.

Kerby and Phillips disliked Cony intensely, and the feeling was reciprocated, though all three men always hid their discord from others. In Cony's view, the *Journal's* first responsibility was to act as the watchdog of, not a cheerleader for, business. Kerby, and thus Phillips, believed in reporting the successes of business, not its failures.

Cony won a Pulitzer in 1961, only the *Journal's* third, for revealing how the Georgia Pacific Company had enabled one of its directors,

Carrol Shanks, the president of Prudential Insurance Company, to deduct $400,000 in trumped-up interest expenses from his personal income tax return. In the next several years, inspired by Cony, four more *Journal* reporters won Pulitzers: Norman C. "Mike" Miller in 1964, for uncovering the salad-oil swindle; Louis Kohlmeier in 1965, for revealing how Lady Bird Johnson parlayed $400,000 into a multi-million dollar broadcasting empire; and Stanley Penn and Monroe "Bud" Karmen in 1967, for uncovering a former Wall Street financier turned crook in the Bahamas.

But Phillips and Kerby, who by then was Dow Jones's chief executive officer, were concerned that these stories, irrespective of the Pulitzers, contradicted the *Journal's* mission in life. "Phillips and Kerby believed," said Fred Taylor, "that the *Journal* should support free enterprise, a rough-and-tumble system which occasionally and inadvertently spawned excess."[25]

Cony kept pushing for more offbeat pieces, while Phillips, growing more conservative as he ascended the Dow Jones ladder, kept pushing for what Cony derisively referred to as "Kerby's glamorous grease or frisky furniture stories."

After graduating from Oregon's Reed College and Stanford University's Graduate School of Journalism, Ed Cony joined the *Journal's* San Francisco bureau in 1953. There he demonstrated, according to Fred Taylor, a *Journal* contemporary, "the soul of a poet and the pursuit of a Doberman."

After managing bureaus in Los Angeles, Jacksonville, and San Francisco, Cony succeeded Phillips as managing editor in 1965. Following Cony's promotion, seven or eight reporters, all Cony's protégés, formed a group known as "the Green Berets." The Berets led the *Journal's* liberal movement, which eventually threatened the paper's objectivity.

Fred Taylor recalled, "Stan Sesser, who is now at Berkeley's Graduate School of Journalism, Don Moffitt [who eventually headed the *Journal's* investigative unit], Paul Lancaster [future page-one editor], and four other reporters were so liberal we had to break them up. They fed on each other."[26]

The newsroom's liberal-versus-conservative struggle, which focused on Vietnam, came to a head in the fall of 1969. First, thirty-three antiwar reporters wanted Dow Jones to suspend the ticker for one minute to protest the United States' involvement in Vietnam and coincide with Wall Street's demonstration against Vietnam, which

was staged in November 1969. Then, when Phillips, as executive
editor, denied the ticker-suspension request, the dissident reporters
marched in the demonstration under the banner "Wall Street
Jounalists." Later, Phillips sent Cony a scathing memo, stating
reporters should be writing about, not participating in, the Vietnam
protests.

In addition to the *Journal's* liberal and investigative reporting era,
Cony also sponsored the *Journal's* age of good literature when stories
that appeared on the front page, column four, rivaled the *New
Yorker's* for humor, originality, and writing brilliance.

One example is "The Monastic Life" by Roger Ricklefs. Set in
Elgin, Scotland, the story began:

> It is 4:30 in the morning and I am shivering in my cell. The old
> monk in a hooded white robe knocks on the door, peers in to
> make sure I'm awake and chants softly, "Benedicamus Dom-
> ino"—bless the Lord.
> I'm supposed to say "Deo gratias"—God be thanked—but I
> forget and mumble, "Okay, thanks." Feeling foolish, I rise from
> my cot.

What followed was a first-person account of what it was like to live
in a thirteenth-century Benedictine monastery in northern Scotland.
The page-one editor, Paul Lancaster, felt particularly good about the
piece. It served as the perfect antidote, he thought, to the nuts-and-
bolts business stories that the brass increasingly insisted he run.

Several weeks later, while at lunch with Ed Cony and Bill Kerby,
the appropriateness of certain types of page-one stories was raised.
Kerby, "a meat and potatoes type of guy," felt the *Journal* should
greatly restrict whimsy. Using a recent page-one leader on a burlesque star as an example of what he detested, Kerby expressed his
views so strongly as to exceed a simple admonishment.[27] Lancaster,
feeling unduly attacked, began to defend himself. A squirming Cony,
wishing desperately that Phillips was there to help ward off Kerby,
tried unsuccessfully to placate both Kerby, his boss's boss, and
Lancaster, his subordinate.

Finally, after much back and forth, Lancaster said to Kerby: "Well,
surely you thought Ricklefs's piece about the Scottish monks was
good."[28]

"I disliked it even more than the burlesque star piece," Kerby
scowled.

Then, with an obvious sense of triumph, Lancaster offered up what he thought would be compelling evidence to win the day with Kerby. "Well, our reader survey showed that 85 percent of those who saw the front page last week read that story and liked it very much."

To which Kerby replied: "I don't care. Never run a story like that again."

Cony sat in stony silence, uncomfortable that his boss, Phillips, was not there to help ward off Kerby.

Lancaster later speculated: "On occasion I've wondered if Phillips may have stayed away from that luncheon so that Cony and I would have to face Kerby's fire unprotected."[29]

Lancaster added, "It was ironic that Phillips was now disavowing the trend he himself started. It seemed that as Phillips's chances of becoming Dow Jones's CEO increased, so did his reluctance to antagonize Kerby."

When this event occurred in 1970, Phillips was second only to Kerby in the Dow Jones pecking order. Both men had risen to Dow Jones's highest position—chief executive officer and chief operating officer—with absolutely no business experience. At the time, Dow Jones's success made this deficiency seem trivial. Only later, in the next decade, when Dow Jones became a complicated multinational, corporation, would this lack of business experience become apparent. Only later would it become evident that neither Kerby nor Phillips was equipped to create and then follow a strategy for future growth. Moreover, both editors-turned-executive were at the mercy of their business staff. Neither man could tell competence from fraud. For example, as long as the numbers were good, Kerby and Phillips could not have cared less about the details of advertising sales or circulation.

10

The Second Huckster

By the late sixties, Dow Jones had become a very comfortable company indeed. The *Journal's* postwar growth had produced enough dividends to persuade the Bancrofts, who owned 80 percent of Dow Jones's stock, to loosen the purse strings so that employees might enjoy some of the spoils of Kilgore's formula.

Appropriately, the person who benefited most from the Bancrofts' newfound generosity was Barney Kilgore himself. Almost a year before he died, when he retired from Dow Jones at the age of fifty-eight, Kilgore sold his options on 150,000 shares of Dow Jones stock for $3.5 million. That was a small price to repay the man who had rescued the company twenty-five years before and whose methods would continue to generate unprecedented profits for the next fifteen years.

The rank-and-file *Journal* employee benefited, too. People began to dress better, take more interesting vacations, and send their children to more prestigious schools.

Yet, with all this largesse, Dow Jones and the *Journal* were still small enough so that everyone was considered family. Everyone knew what kind of behavior was expected of them, which made for a cohesive work environment and a remarkable newspaper.

Also, the company was still small enough to make the process of managing it quite simple. All Kerby and Phillips had to do was second-guess the decisions made each day by Ed Cony, the *Journal's* managing editor at the time. Everything else—finance, production, and especially advertising and circulation—seemed to fall into place.

And the stronger the *Journal* got editorially, the more demand it stimulated, until finally it reached that wonderful point where it no longer had to be sold. Subscribers and advertisers were happy to buy with little or no persuasion.

But neither Kerby nor Phillips realized this rare advantage because they remained ignorant of the *Journal's* selling process. Following Kilgore's example, Kerby and Phillips delegated sales to Donald A. Macdonald, Feemster's successor. Both editors-turned-executive were satisfied with their dependence on Macdonald because sales were extremely good. And what was even more reassuring. Macdonald acted exactly as Feemster had, crazily and unpredictably.[1] Neither man knew, nor cared, that increased ad sales were due to the country's increased interest in business, not to Macdonald's abilities. Though Macdonald may have acted like Feemster, he never sold like him, a critical difference that advertiser and reader demand for the *Journal* masked until the late eighties. For thirty years, while rising to Dow Jones vice chairman, Macdonald dominated the Dow Jones and *Journal* sales functions completely.

When Kerby ousted Feemster in the early sixties, possibly one of the most destructive decisions in Dow Jones history, Ted Callis, a nice, quiet man of no particular zeal and given to no obstreperous behavior, replaced Feemster for a brief period. But Macdonald was too ambitious and too much of a street fighter to be satisfied with second-in-command for long. In 1963, after a series of daring and effective "internal sales," Macdonald, age forty-four, replaced Callis as Dow Jones's top sales and marketing executive. Like legions of other managers in corporate America, Macdonald was far more adept at selling his bosses than he was at selling his customers.

To be fair, in his early days on the *Journal's* sales force, Macdonald proved to be a good and sometimes outstanding sales person. Macdonald's great failure occurred after he became head of the *Journal's* advertising sales department in 1963. The quest for more power caused him to stop selling outside prospects in order to concentrate solely on forging internal alliances that would help him reach Dow Jones's highest levels. Macdonald's inside sales activities took him away from the real business world so completely that he never regained his initial competence the few times he tried to reenter that world.

Macdonald failed, for example, to revive the *National Observer*, as he did with *Book Digest* magazine.[2] And yet he was always able to

talk his way out of things, claiming he was a "media genius." And
since neither Kerby nor Phillips knew enough to refute this claim,
Macdonald was able to avoid responsiblity for his failures.

Even Phillips, toward the end of the seventies, started to realize
Macdonald was not all that he advertised himself to be. But by that
time, Macdonald had become barnacle-close to Bill Cox, Jr., scion of
the Bancroft family, and Peter Kann, Phillips's protégé. These two
relationships rendered Macdonald all but invulnerable.

Macdonald's rise in the organization began at the Downtown
Athletic Club, a forlorn, orange-brick building overlooking the
Hudson River in lower Manhattan. As one of New York City's more
venerated institutions, each year the club sponsors the Heisman
Trophy and hosts the *Wall Street Journal* sales conventions.

On this particular morning, August 12, 1955,[3] a distinctive odor
pervaded the conference room as ethyl alcohol vaporized through the
pores of thirty-three men seated at two long tables covered with
green felt. With eyes squinting to ward off the ambient cigarette
smoke, most cradled their heads trying to stay awake. Half-full
ashtrays, foam coffee cups, and yellow pads containing one or two
lines of notes followed by aimless doodles were strewn about.

"Well, looking around the room it looks like a few of us were
overserved last night," said Feemster as he stood before the group in
shirtsleeves, unabashed that his belly stretched his suspenders into
skimpy rubber bands. A master of timing, Feemster paused to let the
laughter subside. His formal title at the time was chairman of the
executive committee, Dow Jones; it was, in fact, a position Kilgore
had trumped up to impress advertisers.

Then, with a leer, Feemster added, "We either have to stop serving
booze or stop inviting the secretaries."

The room went wild.

"Now... let's get serious, goddammit!" he shouted as he stubbed
out his cigarette. "Ever since Milton Berle and Howdy Doody came
into our lives, all anybody in our business thinks about these days is
television. Nothin' else. Nothin' but Neilsen ratings and those fuckin'
audience numbers.

"Take the other day. I made a call on J. Walter Thompson for
Kodak. This was a courtesy call. To keep the agency informed
because I'd already sold Kodak six pages in Rochester the week
before. We meet this fuckin' Ivy Leaguer, skinny guy, little gold
buttons on his jacket, a management supervisor, sounds foreign or

something. At any rate, I really pitched him. Gave him the whole nine yards. At the end, I sat back, pleased. I thought I had the sale. Ready to talk ad position with him. But you know what this son of a bitch says? 'Where are your data corroborating your audience?' he says. And he ripped off the word 'datah' as if he were a British mathematician. I almost shit."

Feemster paused deliberately to take a sip of water before resuming.

"Ted tried to shut me up, but... 'Do you know who you're talkin' to?' I said. 'We're the *Wall Street Journal*, the best newspaper in the world. I then told him we're running six pages for Kodak whether he likes it or not, 'datah' or not."

The audience began to stir, grinning at Feemster's accurate portrayal of the arrogant ad agency executive, a type they ran across frequently.

"The little weasel turned red, white and blue. He probably would have thrown us out, but we got up and left before he could. So the moral of this story is," Feemster said, his fist cocked and raised in the air, "if you don't get thrown out of at least one ad agency every week, you're not doin' the fuckin' job!"

The men whistled and stomped their feet. But much to Feemster's continuing dismay, not all *Wall Street Journal* salesmen were as swashbuckling as their enthusiasm suggested. Most, in fact, were like Ted Callis, Feemster's assistant and DePauw classmate, who seemed perfectly content to sit back and let advertisers come to him.

Feemster continued: "The other moral of my little story is that the *Journal* is a client sell. Always see the client first... the president.

"Okay, it's time to hear from someone else. Who's first?" Feemster said, his voice dropping, reluctant to relinquish the dais.

Donald A. Macdonald bounded up with too much energy, too much expectation, causing a commotion as he placed two large pads on easels flanking the podium.

Feemster stared intently at this new and unknown salesman. Unlike the others, who were relieved to remain out of the line of fire, Macdonald seemed eager to catch Feemster's eye.

Turning from the easels, Macdonald pulled out a Marlboro, flicked open and shut his Ronson lighter with a shuddering click, sucked a deep draught, and started to speak, smoke tumbling from his mouth and nose. He looked like Zeus.

"My name is Don Macdonald. I'll be thirty-six soon. I'm older than most of you. I've got four kids and one on the way. I told Ruth this morning—she's my wife—that today's the day. Today's going to change our lives. You see, I was born in Union City, New Jersey, in the shadow of St. Michael Monastery. You can see it right out that window." Macdonald paused and pointed out the window to a spot on the horizon.

No one looked. They were too entranced with the boldness, the rawness of this man, with his stream-of-consciousness bombast and his grating New York City accent. One hand was in his trouser pocket, while the other, the one holding the cigarette, rested comfortably on the podium. They were thick, huge farmhand hands, connected by thirty-seven-inch sleeves to broad shoulders, sloped by generations of ancestors carrying Scottish hods.

Occasionally, as Macdonald spoke, his resting arm with the smoking cigarette would shoot out, back and forth, like an automatic weapon, echoing the rapid-fire cadence of his speech. Smoke and heat enveloped him.

"If it weren't for the war, I would have been a juvenile delinquent or worse. I enlisted in the army, went to O.C.S., was commissioned a lieutenant, saw action at Monte Cassino, wounded at Anzio. When I came back, I decided to go to college on the G.I. bill. Went to NYU. I've got my B.A. and M.B.A. Took me four years, goin' days and nights. I recently came to the *Journal*, late in life. I hate accounting. Love to sell. I'm a natural," said Macdonald, giving off another peculiar little laugh.

Had someone else related these things, he would have been appallingly boring. But this roomful of hung-over men found Macdonald's egocentrism riveting.

"All my life, I've been motivated by achievement. And I love structure, a ladder with clearly defined rungs. And selling gives me structure, something to shoot for. I also have the creativity to come up with ideas and the courage to see the president. I have that knack. It's a gift, really. The guts to be good, I call it. That's me.

"I've sold most of the savings and loan associations throughout the Northeast in the last six months. That's why I said to Ruth this morning, it will never be the same. I'm going to be wearing a Rolex as big as a mace when I come back tonight," said Macdonald, his arm now working feverishly.

The audience squirmed. Was there some prize or something? A Rolex? As usual, no one had told them.

"Last year," Macdonald continued, "we ran an A-hed about savings and loan associations, about how twenty-two percent of their depositors accounted for seventy-eight percent of their deposits. Remember?"

Macdonald then moved to the easel on his right, withdrew a Magic Marker from his suit-jacket pocket, and scrawled on the pad: "22 = 78." Moving to one side, he turned back to the audience, gave another little laugh, and continued.

"Well, I took the article to the president of the Bowery Savings here in New York, Mr. Christopher Little. And I said, 'When you advertise in the *Times* or the *Daily News*, the inquiries or leads generated from these ads are worth $100. If you advertise with the *Journal*, the leads will be worth $1,000," Macdonald said, whacking the pad with the back of his huge hand.

"The guy bought seven 480-line ads, to run in the Northeast edition every Tuesday for seven weeks. And it worked exactly as I predicted. Then I went back and asked him for a letter telling about the Bowery's success. I took it throughout New England, showing it to other presidents of savings and loans. So far, out of the thirty-three savings and loans I've called on, twenty-seven have come in with us."

Two weeks later, a smoking jacket from Rogers Peet, an exclusive haberdashery, arrived at Macdonald's home in Rumson, New Jersey. The card said, "Sorry, it's not a Rolex. Robert Feemster." One month later, Don Macdonald was promoted to New England and Canadian sales manager, based in Boston.

Macdonald's rise at the *Journal* coincided with the dawning of television and the metamorphosis it wrought. In the early fifties, in a matter of months, television swept across America, forever changing its cultural landscape. People stayed home, mesmerized by a ten-inch screen with a ghastly glow. Reading became restricted to school and the job. And the world of advertising turned upside down. Consumer-goods advertisers, in particular, pursued television with a shameless ardor, forsaking radio and giving print only the scantest regard. And soon such daily diversions as the Lone Ranger, Fred Allen, Jack Benny, the *Saturday Evening Post*, *Collier's* and *Look* switched off their microphones or closed their pages.

Procter & Gamble, for example, discovered that an Ivory soap TV commercial aired on the "Philco Playhouse" sold a thousand times more Ivory bars than a full-page, four-color ad in the *Saturday Evening Post*. Fifty million households watched the "Philco Playhouse"; only 2 million read the *Saturday Evening Post*. Moreover, the impact of a television commercial on viewers was infinitely more lasting and memorable.

If television turned corporate America's head, it stole Madison Avenue's ego. The challenge of molding television's sight, sound, and motion into a thirty-second film selling soap became as important as making a movie. No longer were copywriters and art directors limited to the preparation of one-dimensional print ads or radio commercials. They exchanged typewriters and brushes for director's chairs. The noun "creative" became the most exalted word on Madison Avenue. Even the newest "creative" exhibited a demeanor in attitude, dress, and office decor that suggested he had apprenticed for Sandro Botticelli. And the superstars, people like David Ogilvy, Mary Wells Lawrence, and Jerry Della Femina, believed they were on a par with John Huston and Frank Capra. They might well have been, for all the money they made.

Moreover, in addition to creating commercials, Madison Avenue regularly oversaw the conceptualization, casting, filming, editing, and distribution of the actual television programs themselves. Batten, Barton, Durstine & Osborn, for instance, created the "General Electric Theater," right down to hiring an out-of-work actor, Ronald Reagan, to host the show. Television also affected Madison Avenue's other, less glamorous disciplines. Even the media department, the people who analyzed and bought media for the client, exchanged their green eyeshades for sunglasses.

Besides being more hip, television made the media buyer's job infinitely more secure, every adman's dream. Unlike the thousands of controversial options which had to be scrutinized when buying print and radio advertising, television presented the media buyer with only three: CBS, ABC, and NBC. To make the process of buying television even more secure, the networks offered quantitative evidence of the size and characteristics of their audiences through the Nielsen ratings. Therefore, whenever questioned as to why they made a particular buy, the buyer could point to a Neilsen rating, an indisputable number that confirmed their decision.

In contrast, when buying print and radio, decisions were made based on far more debatable factors. Various Neilsen indices—gross rating points, reach percentages, frequency ratios—replaced opinion, intuition, and personal experience. Each number was considered absolutely incontrovertible proof why, say, CBS's "Sid Caesar

Show" should receive the lion's share of Procter & Gamble's advertising budget.

Too busy preening over its newfound authority, Madison Avenue never stopped to question the Neilsen premise: that the viewing habits of twelve hundred households, the size of the Neilsen sample, were identical to the viewing habits of 80 million households, the number of U.S. homes in 1960 having television sets.

Trying desperately to stay alive, publications with the most to lose from television's incursions—large general-interest publications such as *Reader's Digest, Saturday Evening Post, Life,* and *Look*—took to employing bright, bold salesmen who sold their publications ingeniously.

Following the axiom that people like to do business with people they like, print salesmen went to any lengths to develop warm and enduring relationships with advertisers. The *Saturday Evening Post,* for example, spared no expense, no resource, in pursuing Philip Morris, an advertiser with hundreds of millions of advertising dollars to spend. There are those who swear Jim Thompson, vice president of advertising for Philip Morris, and his agency counterpart at Leo Burnett played golf all over the world, fifty-two weeks out of the year, as the guests of the *Post's* sales staff.

But the *Wall Street Journal* never resorted to such tactics. Its specialized audience, over a million businesspeople, could not be duplicated by television's. Nor could television match the *Journal's* news coverage of business and finance. These advantages, plus the midwestern rectitude of Barney Kilgore, enabled the paper to stand above the fray.

"We're the *Journal.* We don't do that," became Feemster's oft-repeated boast.

The *Journal's* refusal to curry favor with advertisers enhanced, rather than diminished, its reputation. The fact that the *Journal* had no competitors contributed to its righteousness. From the mid-fifties onward, the *Journal* became a much sought after advertising medium. Like television, this advantage greatly reduced the need for strong personal advertising sales efforts. In fact, the *Journal* sold itself. Anyone could do it. All he needed was a phone and an order pad.

As a result, the *Journal's* advertising sales department had no need to employ commercial warriors. In fact, unlike the editorial department, the *Journal's* advertising sales department required compliance and obedience, not individual brilliance. The salesperson who succeeded at the *Journal* wanted security, not stimulation, from his job. He relished the *Journal's* prestige, not its challenges.

Like Feemster before him, Donald A. Macdonald was a notable exception. As he had told the salesmen that day, Macdonald was born in Union City, New Jersey, a grimy industrial enclave separated from New York City by the Hudson River. Macdonald's father, Angus, was a comparatively successful man during the Depression. He had a job in insurance. Macdonald's mother, Emily, died when he was a freshman in high school. Several years later, rather than move to Elizabeth with his father when he remarried, Macdonald, at the age of fifteen, dropped out of high school and became fully self-supporting.

Macdonald recalled, "After my mother died, my father started to drink a lot, which I guess my own kids could say about me. At any rate, I moved into the YMCA and got a job. It was no big deal. I wanted to stay in Union City to be near Ruth."[4]

Ruth is Ruth Moran, Macdonald's wife of fifty years, whom he met at the age of thirteen.

After working for a year as a clerk for the Royal Exchange Insurance Company, Macdonald came to realize the value of an education. He returned to school, attending the William L. Dickerson High School by night while continuing to work at the insurance company by day. He graduated from Dickerson in 1939, at the age of twenty. He then went to work for Pacific Insurance, clerking.

Then, in 1941, after the war broke out, Macdonald went to work for the Bendix Corporation, where he labored on twelve-hour shifts, seven days a week. Because of his own temperament and the shortage of men, within months he received several significant promotions, making $100 per week, an unheard-of sum for someone in his circumstance before the war. Buoyed by this newfound success, Macdonald married Ruth, his childhood sweetheart. Three months later, he was drafted by the army. Conditioned by his experience at Bendix, Macdonald applied to officers' training school. After receiving a commission, he served in combat with valor in North Africa and Italy for three years.

In June 1944, after herniating both his legs at Anzio, the result of scrambling about under a heavy combat pack, Capt. Donald A. Macdonald underwent a battlefront operation; through a transplant of the fascia from his hip, his legs were restored. No longer suited for combat, he was then assigned to the 3300 Quartermaster Corps and stationed in Marseilles. In February 1946, Macdonald returned to the United States with vaulting ambitions. Using the GI Bill, he graduated from NYU with a B.A. in two and a half years, and then obtained his M.B.A., a rare degree back in 1950. During and after his graduate studies, Macdonald worked at Olson Electric Company as an accountant, intending to become a certified public accountant. From 1950 to 1952, he passed three of the required four C.P.A. examinations. It was during this period that he made an important discovery.

"Between my job at Olson and my C.P.A. studies, I realized I hated accounting. I didn't want to do it the rest of my life," Macdonald later explained, emphasizing the negative by pounding his fist on a table. "Most people make a mistake by doing what they think they want to do. I looked at it differently. I eliminated what I did not want to do, and that's why I loved every day at Dow Jones."

Responding to an ad, Macdonald, thirty-three, was interviewed by Robert Feemster, forty-one, for a sales job at the *Journal* in late 1952.

"That little fat fuck [Feemster] thought he was Napoleon. Mr. five-by-five was arrogant, difficult. During the interview, he gave me a hard time. Asked why an old guy like me, without any sales experience, was applying for the job. But I told him I had the guts to call on company presidents and that I was smart. I could come up with new ways to sell for the *Journal*. Finally, he offered me a job, though I was pissed it wasn't an executive's position. Christ, I was thirty-two and had an M.B.A. But I took it anyway," Macdonald said, grinning at the memory.

It was in 1955, after impressing Feemster at the Downtown Athletic Club, that Macdonald was promoted to the Boston office. one of the *Journal's* thirteen advertising sales offices throughout the country. During the next three years, he performed some notable sales feats in New England. Macdonald once persuaded Jane Bancroft Cook, one of the owners of Dow Jones, to secure an appointment for him with her friend, Chubb Peabody, the governor of Massachusetts, who was in the midst of a difficult reelection campaign. On the appointed day, Macdonald buoyantly ascended the statehouse steps, two at a time, and strode into Governor Peabody's office as if he had been a trusted aide for years.

Among friends and *Journal* colleagues, Macdonald often started, terminated, or resumed conversations in mid-sentence, a mode of speaking that rendered even the most insignificant encounters bewildering. But whenever Macdonald was in front of a prospect, he could be cogent and succinct. After shaking hands with the governor, rather than accept the offered seat, he remained standing and said: "I know how you can be reelected."

Without waiting for a reply, Macdonald continued. "Your problem is the bad economy resulting from the textile mills moving south. You should take out a full-page ad in the *Journal*, advertising the tax incentives you'll give the first hundred out-of-state companies which relocate to Massachusetts."

No sooner had Peabody agreed to buy the ad than Macdonald was on his way to see the governors of Maine, New Hampshire, and Rhode Island, who, not to be outdone, readily agreed to buy the same ad program. A few days after the last of these state ads ran, Averell Harriman, then the governor of New York State, called Macdonald, incensed. "Why wasn't I given the same opportunity?" Harriman demanded.

In 1958, Feemster moved Macdonald back to New York to become the *Journal's* Eastern Edition advertising manager, a substantial promotion. Taking a page from Warren Phillips's book, Macdonald and his burgeoning family—he and Ruth now had five children—moved to Short Hills, New Jersey, a few houses down from Bill Kerby, who had just relocated there as well. When asked if this wasn't an obviously curious place to live, Macdonald laughed and said, "Hell, I didn't pursue Kerby. He pursued me. He was the guy who would be at my house most afternoons, drinking Scotch."[5]

Just as Phillips had before him, Macdonald rode into work with Kerby every day. Vulnerable to praise, Kerby formed a close relationship with his flattering, scotch-serving neighbor. In fact, Kerby stepped up his efforts to get rid of his corporate enemy, Robert Feemster, believing Macdonald would be a perfect successor to head advertising.

By 1962, after Kerby forced Feemster to retire, Macdonald had been promoted to *Journal* advertising director. He ostensibly reported to Ted Callis, who had been moved up to vice president. In actual fact, Macdonald reported to Kerby in the limousine every morning, an arrangement that made Callis hate Macdonald. One day, after a particularly painful confrontation with Callis in front of others, Macdonald stormed back into Callis's office, shut the door, and said: "You don't like me. I don't like you. Let's resolve it one way or another. If we can't, I'm resigning." That night, after many drinks at

Delmonico's, Callis became Macdonald's lifelong friend. Later, in the eighties, whenever tension developed between Macdonald and a subordinate, Macdonald would relate the Callis anecdote, suggesting that should a similar conflict arise with him, it could be resolved in the same straightforward fashion.

By 1963, the year Macdonald took over the advertising sales and circulation departments, the *Wall Street Journal* was well on its way to being one of America's most powerful and expensive advertising mediums despite the incursions of television. The *Journal's* 1963 ad revenue, $178 million, was 22 percent greater than it had been in 1962 and 18 percent greater than 1961.

The *Journal's* advertising came from three main sources: financial institutions such as stock brokerage firms; classified ads; and corporations wanting to enhance their image with any or all of the following audiences: Wall Street, individual investors, federal and state governments, customers, and their own employees, distributors, and suppliers. These advertisers, whose audiences were too specialized to be reached through television efficiently, flocked to the *Journal* because it was the country's only national daily business newspaper.

In 1963, after gaining Dow Jones's top advertising job, Macdonald stopped selling outside prospects altogether. He spent the ensuing years concentrating solely on "selling" others within the company who could help him achieve his next promotion. Since he had already conquered Kerby, and therefore Phillips, Macdonald's next sales targets were the owners of Dow Jones, the Bancrofts. He concentrated on William Coburn Cox, Jr., son of Jessie Bancroft Cox, and step-great-grandson of Clarence Barron himself. Macdonald, when he wished, could be a masterful salesman. His technique, which sometimes could be fully effective, was to approach other males, usually younger, and present himself as an affectionate, caring father figure. A pivotal meeting with Bill Cox, Jr., illustrates Macdonald's considerable but misdirected abilities.

The meeting took place at the *Wall Street Journal* Circulation Center in Chicopee, Massachusetts in February 1970.[6] Through the center the *Journal* services its 2 million subscribers, an administrative task of Herculean proportions. Each week, it mails 10 million computer-generated letters to current, potential, and former subscribers explaining how to order, renew, cancel, pay for, or give to a friend a subscription to the *Wall Street Journal*. Another series requests, duns, or thanks subscribers for their payment. This process, supervised by engineers and accomplished through computers, laser scanners, and high-speed printers, requires only a few clerks to operate. The work force, then, is composed of several men in white shirts and a scattering of immensely overweight housewives trying to make ends meet.

On this particular day, Macdonald flew from New York City to Chicopee on the Dow Jones helicopter. When the aircraft landed on the lawn, yards from the center's main entrance, a crowd of staffers gathered in the lobby to gawk at Macdonald as he burst through the front doors. The people were accustomed to visitors and helicopters; it was Macdonald's bright orange hair, like a circus clown's, that stunned them. Two weeks before, Macdonald, 52, had tried to dye the grayness out of his hair. The chemical reaction had backfired, producing this ghastly Day-Glo hue instead.

Macdonald pushed his way through the lobby's double doors into a gigantic room filled with a battalion of silent steel-gray desks and beige computers whirring randomly. Cigarette smoke billowed out of Macdonald's nose and mouth as he stalked a man on the far side of the room. The man—broad, smiling face, untucked shirt, a twinkly innocence about him—stared out the streaked window like a teenage boy trying to escape algebra.

"Hey, son!" Macdonald shouted.

Startled, the man spun around to see Macdonald, arms akimbo, bearing down on him.

"Hey, Don," the man cried back, pronouncing the name like a Bostoner: D-A-W-N.

"What are you doin', sittin' on your ass, staring out the window?" Macdonald asked gruffly.

The man laughed good-naturedly, comfortably.

"How's Marty?" Macdonald asked, referring to the man's wife. Without waiting for a reply, Macdonald said: "I came all the way up here to see you."

Flattered, the man reddened and asked why.

"Because I want you to work for me in ad sales in Detroit!"

"Me?" Flabbergasted, the man shook his head and then asked, "How do you know I can sell?"

"Well, if you can't, I'll bury you back here."

"Why Detroit?"

"Because that's where I'm sending you."

"But, Don, I don't want to go anywhere."

"You're bored, but won't admit it."

The man shook his head dubiously. "I don't know. ... I'll have to talk it over with Marty."

"I'll call in several days, tell you when to move," Macdonald said as he turned and hurried out of the building. Macdonald had just promoted William Coburn Cox, Jr., scion of the Bancroft family, which owned 66 million shares of Dow Jones stock, worth $3.3 billion. His dividend income on his Dow Jones stock alone that year amounted to $50 million.

As these staggering figures indicate, Bill Cox, Jr., has lived a life of splendid riches. But he has paid dearly for it. Like his father and his grandfather, Hugh Bancroft, before him, Cox has been a lifelong victim of the family curse: No male member of the Bancroft clan may ever achieve more than the patriarch, Clarence Barron. And this curse has made managing Dow Jones one of the most unusual experiences in corporate America. Kilgore, Kerby, Phillips, and others have had to contend with Bancroft family members, whether serving on the Dow Jones board of directors or working at menial jobs at the *Journal*, in the knowledge that at any moment one of these family members can exercise the power of an autocrat by virtue of his enormous stock holdings. Neither Cox nor any other member has ever exercised this enormous power. But for Kerby and Phillips, it was like constantly tiptoeing around a sleeping lion, wondering if that would be the day it would wake up and attack.

Bill Cox, Jr., grew up in Clarence Barron's sumptuous oceanside estate in Cohasset, Massachusetts, ten miles south of Boston. Bill's father, William, a bookish, amiable man, had come from a modest background. His fortunes changed when he went to Harvard.

Bill Cox, Jr., explained, "My father worked his way through Harvard tutoring. My mother [Jessie Bancroft] hired Dad to tutor my uncle Hugh [Bancroft, Jr., Jessie's younger brother]."[7]

William Cox possessed the ideal temperament to be Jessie Bancroft's husband. He was a Harvard man; and he harbored no desire to manage the *Wall Street Journal*. In fact, William Cox never held a job. Simply as a matter of legal form, William Cox was elected to the Dow Jones board in 1930, the same year Bill, Jr., was born. Back then, as today, the Dow Jones board wielded little power and less influence in the operation of the *Journal*. Hugh Bancroft and Casey Hogate ran the newspaper by themselves.

Just as he became the family's favorite uncle, William Cox proved to be the ideal board member—supportive and unquestioning. "He was kindhearted, gregarious, always inviting us down to Cohassett for a drink," Macdonald said. "But he never meddled in the business."[8]

Bill, Jr.'s mother, Jessie, grew up in Cohassett as well. The favorite step-grandchild, she accompanied Clarence Barron on his European tours, while her father and mother, Hugh and Jane Bancroft, lived in New York, operating the *Wall Street Journal*. To the world, Clarence Barron appeared ruthless, willful. But to Jessie Bancroft, he was a doting grandparent. "My mother loved Clarence Barron deeply. He was the dominant force in her life," Bill Cox, Jr., said. "She tried to be like him in every respect. Drink like him, love horses like him."

Perhaps the strongest dynamic of their relationship was the struggle Clarence Barron waged against Hugh Bancroft for the affections of Jessie. An intensely competitive, unrestrained man, Barron rarely hid his contempt for Hugh Bancroft and his management abilities.

As a result, Jessie developed an aversion to getting involved in the management of Dow Jones, an aversion that she expected her husband, William, to share. "Clarence Barron made my mother ashamed of how my grandfather [Hugh] ran Dow Jones. She didn't want to repeat his mistakes," said Bill, Jr.

But William Cox's compliance made Jessie increasingly strident. Never a handsome woman, Jessie Cox's face would become drawn and hawklike whenever she had to contend with William Cox for long. In fact, she began to react to her husband in much the same way Clarence Barron had reacted to Hugh Bancroft. As a result, William and Jessie Cox became estranged, and she sought diversion in the avocations of the wealthy. In doing so, she also withdrew from her son, Bill, Jr. "My mother was always off with her horses," Cox said. "I used to fight like hell with her. So I spent a lot of time with my father as a boy."

Through this relationship, Bill, Jr., developed an unusually genial nature. All his life, Cox's Gaelic face, lilting voice, and ready laugh has made him an unusually affable, if not naive, man. He still refers to others in trusting, boyish terms. Almost everyone he meets is "a helluva a good guy."

But unlike his father, Bill, Jr., did not do well at school. At the age of twelve, Cox was sent away to Westminster School, a second-tier boarding school. Handicapped by a learning disability, which he did not detect until much later, Cox barely managed to graduate. In fact, his classroom record was so bad he never went to college, "a source of great embarrassment to Bill,"[9] said Kevin McGarry, a former *Journal* sales executive who once was close to Cox in Detroit throughout the seventies.

Bill, Jr., bolstered his self-esteem with athletics. At Westminister, he was a superb ice hockey player and a scratch golfer. In fact, to this day, golf remains a cornerstone in Bill, Jr's life. His love for the game has opened many doors which, otherwise, he would never have ventured through. And his modesty makes him a welcome partner throughout the world.

After graduating from Westminister, Cox spent four years in the air force. Then, at the behest of his father, he worked for a liquor wholesaler and the New Haven Railroad, mostly in clerical positions.

In 1951, Cox called a girl at Walnut Hill, a New England finishing school, for a last-minute date. She wasn't available, but her room-mate, Martha Whiting, was. "I fell in love with her immediately," Cox revealed. "Marty had this direct, no-nonsense way about her." Two years later, Cox married Martha Whiting, a native of Wilton, New Hampshire, who could have passed for Jessie Cox's daughter, the two were so similar. "Marty says it like it is, just like her mother-in-law did. She even resembled Jessie in that same sturdy New England way," said Kevin McGarry.

To this day, Cox speaks of Marty, his wife of thirty-eight years, with wonder. "Boy! She's some lady, some partner," Cox exclaims. Most people who know the couple agree with Kevin McGarry's assessment: "Marty is terrific, very outspoken and the boss in that family."

In 1960, William Cox advised Bill, Jr., then thirty, to join Dow Jones. "He told me I should start preparing for the day I'd succeed him on the board," Cox explained.

What to do with the owner of Dow Jones who demonstrated no great talent for business? John McCarthy, then Dow Jones's chief financial officer, suggested to Barney Kilgore that Bill, Jr., work in Circulation Service in Chicopee. "It was close to Boston, and he couldn't get in much trouble,"[10] McCarthy once told a colleague.

Bill, Jr., made sure subscribers received at least six reminders to renew their *Journal* subscriptions, a job he performed daily for ten years until the day Macdonald spirited him away. Though neither

Bill, Jr., nor his mother ever saw through Macdonald's actions, others did. "Mac clearly created a sinecure for Bill when he promoted him into ad sales in Detroit,"[11] said Kevin McGarry.

Since the early fifties, beginning when he was the Boston ad sales manager, Don Macdonald has maintained close and separate relationships with William and Jessie Cox. "My father liked Don because he would come down to Cohassett and drink with him. And my mother, who was always very interested in men, adored Don Macdonald because he reminded her of Clarence Barron," Cox said.

But the family member who liked Macdonald the most was Bill, Jr., himself. "From 1969 on, the year my dad died, Don became my mentor," Cox recalled. "He taught me everything I know about this business."

In 1969, Bill, Jr., went to work for Macdonald temporarily, trying to salvage the ill-fated Dow Jones Golf Tournament in Montclair, New Jersey. They failed at their task but remained fast friends thereafter, drawn together by their mutual dislike for the tournament's director, Ed Roll, head of Dow Jones Circulation, who was Macdonald's archrival at the time.

Ten months after Macdonald transferred young Cox to Detroit, the Dow Jones board of directors made Macdonald a senior vice president, the company's fifth-highest-ranking executive.

11

The First Dauphin

By 1971, Bill Kerby, Dow Jones's CEO, was content to sit back and watch his surrogate son, Warren Phillips, then executive vice president and general manager, maintain the *Journal's* momentum. The paper's circulation had reached 1.3 million; and it contributed 81 percent of Dow Jones's total 1971 revenues, which were $156 million.

Throughout this time, Kerby and Phillips appeared untouched by Vietnam and the upheavals of the sixties. Unlike the editors of the *New York Times* and *Washington Post*, Kerby and Phillips preferred to withdraw from the country's general news events and fine-tune the *Journal*, ever careful not to stray far from the Kilgore formula. In the previous decade Phillips had gone against Kerby by initiating the *Journal's* coverage of Little Rock, but he was now anxious to implement his planned succession to the Dow Jones throne. This meant doing Kerby's bidding completely, covering business at the expense of the social concerns of the day, which were benignly neglected. On a typical front page in the early seventies, the *Journal* would run a piece that chronicled IBM's remarkable process of automating the world. There would be scant mention of America's campus unrest or the effects of its drug culture.

Kerby and Phillips's insularity explains why the *Journal* struck out on the Watergate scandal.

Despite having three reporters in the Washington bureau who had recently won Pulitzer Prizes for investigative reporting, backed up by an executive editor in New York, Ed Cony, who had won a Pulitzer Prize in the same category, the *Journal* inexplicably sat back and allowed the *Washington Post* and, later, the *Los Angeles Times* and the *New York Times* to report the story. There was gossip Warren Phillips was being considered for an ambassadorship, most likely to China, and thus did not want to embarrass Nixon. But Fred Taylor, who had succeeded Cony as the *Journal's* managing editor, rejected these rumors. Taylor explained, "We just blew that story from the very beginning. We were two steps behind everyone else, and we never were motivated to catch up."[1]

To pursue the Watergate story meant, of course, pursuing the most powerful man on earth, a task that required the extraordinary courage of Woodward and Bernstein. But the people who exhibited even more courage were Ben Bradlee, the *Washington Post's* editor, and Katherine Graham, the newspaper's owner. Had Woodward and Bernstein been wrong, they were young enough to have outlived the mistake. But Bradlee and Graham risked much more by standing behind their reporters. Bradlee would certainly not have survived the backlash, and it's doubtful the *Washington Post* would have, either. Investigating incumbent presidents is a dangerous activity; and the *Washington Post* was prepared to accept the consequences if their two young reporters failed, a courageous act of management support that rightly earned the newspaper a Pulitzer Prize in 1973 for meritorious public service.

But Kerby and Phillips had succeeded at the *Journal* by avoiding the very risks that Graham and Bradlee took. And Kerby and Phillips conveyed their aversion through several critical acts: by promoting Ed Cony, the fiery managing editor, to a meaningless job; by criticizing daring literary stories such as Roger Ricklefs's piece on the Scottish monastery; and by stating bluntly at a 1970 Cape Cod editors' conference that the *Journal* would concentrate on business and finance, not general news. Fred Taylor, Alan Otten, a respected *Journal* veteran, and several others who attended that conference protested vigorously. But it was a hollow gesture. Once back in New York, Phillips forced Taylor to run "frisky furniture"* stories more than ever.

There were exceptions to the *Journal's* harsh swing back to

---

* "Frisky furniture" story is a term coined by Ed Cony to refer to profiles of manufacturers of furniture or boxes or some other basic commodity, whose sales were an indicator of the health of the U.S. economy. Kerby championed these stories, while Cony thought they were "dull, inelegant, and stupid."

business news; the most notable emanated from Hong Kong, where the *Journal*'s Far East correspondent, Peter Kann, resided.

As another demonstration of Kerby and Phillips's insularity, Kann had covered Vietnam single-handedly since the fall of 1967, which meant the *Journal* reported the war through the eyes of a twenty-seven-year-old man who had never been a foreign correspondent before flying to Saigon from Los Angeles, where he had covered Hollywood. Certainly no other major daily would have entrusted its total Vietnam coverage to such a tyro.

According to Taylor, "Kerby and, thus, Phillips did not like Vietnam. It was not patriotically rousing, as World War II. It did nothing for the economy; and there were a lot of wild-eyed demonstrators, some of whom worked for us, who were getting in Kerby's face over it."[2]

But Kann turned Kerby and Phillips's neglect of Vietnam into an advantage. He was allowed total freedom to roam about Vietnam, and he wrote about whatever pleased him in a voice that broke all *Journal* traditions.

"I gave up trying to coerce Peter into doing it our way," said Fred Taylor, the *Journal*'s managing editor. "He was halfway across the world. What could I do? Besides, he was a phenomenal writer."[3]

As the following story illustrates, Kann's writing ability is only exceeded by his charm, a trait that borders on magical, which he used to particularly good advantage in the early seventies when *Journal* executives began to explore the Far East after Nixon normalized relations with China.

It was September 12, 1971, and Peter Kann and his wife, Francesca, were hosting an outing on their Chinese junk, *Low Profile*, in Hong Kong's Deep Bay.[4] The guests included Donald A. Macdonald and Ed Cony, Dow Jones vice presidents for business and editorial, respectively. Lt. Col. Bill Sorenson and his wife, Martha, Francesca's sister, were along for balance and ballast.

The *Low Profile* had just sailed beyond the smell and plea of Victoria Harbor's poverty. Ahead, off the bow, lay Macao; off the stern, rising up from the harbor like a dangling bracelet, was Hong Kong.

"This is as good a time as any to break out the scotch," called Kann, twenty-nine, a handsome young man with liquid brown eyes. "We want to be well fortified when we reach Hanoi," he added with a laugh.

Still grinning broadly, Kann and the sprightly Francesca distributed Johnny Walker Black to their four American guests while he directed their attention to the starboard side of the junk. Kann said, "That's Stonecutter's Island off to the right. And beyond that is mainland China, the province of Guangdung to be specific. Warren's there now with Keatley."

Macdonald and Cony both perked up at the mention of Warren Phillips's name.

"Did he pass through here?" Macdonald tried to be casual.

"Yes," replied Kann matter-of-factly.

Cony and Macdonald glanced at one another. The two senior men were impressed that Phillips had spent time with Kann.

"And that's Green Island on the near left," Kann continued. "In the 1830s, the British used Green Island as a stronghold in the Opium Wars. It was hard to tell who was dealing, the Chinese or the Brits."

Everyone laughed.

Kann had a slow and easy way about him, never threatening, never pedantic. Macdonald once said, "Kann's the only guy I know who entered Harvard saying 'incredulous' and came out saying 'bullshit.'"

Just then, Francie spoke Mandarin Chinese to the boatman, who, following her instructions, steered the junk into the wind and dropped anchor. Ed Cony, impressed, said, "Where d'you learn that?"

Francie blushed and Kann said proudly, "University of Washington, where she got her master's."

Martha, her sister, added, "You should hear her play the piano."

Francie put her hands to her ears in mock modesty and said, "Stop it. Both of you. Let's have another drink, for God's sake!"

Peter Robert Kann and Francesca Mayer were an idyllic couple. One would never have guessed they came from totally different backgrounds, a difference blurred by Kann's humility and Francie's intelligence.

Francie's father, Arthur A. Mayer, was a sweeper with the F. W. Peevy Milling Company. Peter's father, Dr. Robert A. Kann, was a world authority on the Hapsburg Empire. Francie's mother, Dorothy Flynn Mayer, was a housewife. Peter's mother, Marie Breuer Kann, was a lawyer in her native Vienna.

While pouring more scotch, Francie said, "Why don't you take your ties off and roll up your sleeves, you two."

Macdonald, more so than Cony, had been acting as if he had been to Hong Kong many times before. But it was obvious from his dress—white shirt and somber, unstylish tie—that he was not prepared for the hot, humid climate. Everyone else wore Bermudas and cotton polo shirts.

As the party stood on the afterdeck, gazing back at the city, Martha exclaimed, "This is paradise! You would never know there's a war in Vietnam going on."

"You can feel the excitement, see it in the streets, smell it," Cony said. "It's like Paris after World War II."

"The whole Pacific Basin's like this," Peter said calmly. "Communism may be prevailing in 'Nam, but capitalism has taken over everywhere else."

Despite the war in Vietnam four hundred miles to the west, by the early seventies Hong Kong had begun to evince the rewards and hysteria of a gold rush. The city's unfettered commerce hatched millionaires by the hour. For every rotting raft that housed generations of beggars, there was a brand-new, gleaming two-hundred-foot yacht bought with a few hours' profits from textiles, pineapples, rice, plastics, jewelry, money, land, and dreams.

"This is our story. We own it," said Cony enthusiastically.

"That's why there ought to be an *Asian Wall Street Journal*," Francie said.

"Easy," Macdonald warned. "Before anyone walks off into the sunset, know that the advertisers don't give a fuck that we own this story!" He had spent much of the previous three weeks touring the Far East, gauging advertiser reaction to a mock-up of an *Asian Wall Street Journal* that looked identical to the domestic *Journal*.

Tactfully, Francie changed the subject. "Enough business. Let's eat." She proceeded to pass out wicker plates filled with fried chicken, potato salad, and cole slaw, Macdonald's favorite meal.

Then, trying to draw out her other guests, Francie asked pleasantly, "Bill, what's the latest from the air force?"

Lt. Col. William Sorenson was responsible for a wing of flying boxcars that provided much of the U.S. troop supplies and matériel in Vietnam. He and Martha were in Hong Kong on leave, staying with Peter and Francie.

"Damned if I know," Sorenson replied amiably. "You're the one with the high-level contacts."

In June 1967, immediately after obtaining her master's in Asian Studies from the University of Washington, Francesca Mayer, twenty-two, and her older sister, Martha, went to Saigon to help the war effort. A registered nurse, Martha joined the medical division of the U.S. State Department as a heart specialist, while Francie went to work for an international volunteer association. Later, she was employed by the Stanford Research Institute to do classified studies for Gen. William Westmoreland.

"No more. Peter's the one," Francie said.

Smiling, Peter Kann gazed down at an imaginary spot three inches in front of his right foot. Right then he looked vulnerable and particularly appealing.

"Yeah! What's goin' on, Peter?" yelled Cony, fired up by the scotch.

Peter grinned. Then he said, "I've not been in Saigon for three months. Spending all my time in Dacca, covering the war [Indo-Pakistani War]."

"C'mon! Tell us where you stand," Cony persisted.

"Well...I guess...somewhere to the left of Harrison Salisbury," Peter replied with a chortle.

In 1967, after becoming the first U.S. journalist to enter North Vietnam, Salisbury reported that many civilians had been killed by bombings that the Johnson administration had strictly insisted were dropped on military targets. Salisbury failed to make clear that his sources were all North Vietnamese Communists. Though what Salisbury reported was true, he was roundly criticized by the Johnson administration and those journalists sympathetic to Johnson.

"That's revealing!" Cony said. "Christ! That could mean anything."

"Exactly," Francie said, laughing. "Peter's the world's best strad-dler. Just when you think you've got him pegged, he does the opposite. I had a devil of a time getting him to marry me until I saw his Harvard class book. Then I figured out how to do it."

"How?" Macdonald asked with genuine interest.

Francie paused for a moment. "Well, there was his picture. He looked serious, earnest, very sincere. And then I noticed he was a member of the Harvard Young Republicans, the Harvard Young Democrats, the Harvard Conservatives, and the Harvard World Federalists. I figured anyone who belonged to all those disparate groups at once can't make his mind up about anything. So I asked him!"

Everyone roared, Peter, twenty-nine, most of all. Francie, twenty-six, was a gifted hostess: charming, smart, radiant. The group had hung on every word.

"But you're letting him get off the hook!" Cony yelled at Francie. Turning to Peter, Cony persisted: "What do you think? Did Nixon's Vietnamization work? Are we out of Cambodia? Is Kissinger accomplishing anything in Paris?"

"Am I on trial or what?" Peter asked, smiling. "Before I answer that barrage of questions, let me ask you one: Why did Ellsberg only leak the *Pentagon Papers* to the *Times* and the *Post*? What happened to our bureau? I thought Otten [Alan Otten, a veteran reporter] owned Washington."

"Hey! I've got a question," Macdonald blurted, apropos of nothing.

"Shhhh," Francie shushed as she put her finger to her lips. "Don's got a question." Everyone laughed.

"I need someone to write a little travel article for a Far East travel special section I'm trying to put together for the *Journal*. Will you do it?"

"Sure!" Peter answered swiftly.

"I mean will you do it for free?" Macdonald asked.

"No problem," Kann replied. "What do you want it on? Hong Kong? Japan? Or the whole Far East?"

Macdonald sidled up to Peter and, in a fatherly fashion, put his arm around him and said, "You know, you're all right!"

Peter looked down at his toes again.

"You know," Macdonald continued, now turning to Francie, "I could teach your husband how not to be an asshole. If he'd listen to me, he could go all the way."

"Are you saying he's an asshole now, Don?" Francie asked with mock, wide-eyed innocence.

Again, everyone howled. And again, Peter laughed the hardest. "I'm not kiddin'. I mean, he could go all the way. Become CEO even," Macdonald said, making an expansive sweep with his right arm, as if he were bequeathing the Dow Jones kingdom to Peter, his new best friend, whom he had met for the first time three days before.

"You're drunk, Macdonald," Cony giggled.

"Not that drunk, Eddie," Macdonald replied. "Not that drunk."

It took the *Low Profile*'s young owner less than twenty years to prove Macdonald right. In July 1991, Dow Jones's board of directors elected Peter Robert Kann the company's chief executive officer. Along the way, Kann bewitched everyone with whom he came in contact, especially Warren Phillips. In fact, the two became so close that the Macdonald-Cox friendship seemed tepid by comparison. But unlike Macdonald and Cox, Kann always had the upper hand with Phillips despite their sixteen-year age difference. It always struck observers that Phillips lived through Kann vicariously, compensating for his many deficiencies, beginning with his childhood.

Peter Robert Kann was born on December 13, 1942, to Robert Abraham and Marie Breuer Kann, people whose high achievements were made all the more remarkable because of the hardship they overcame. Both Peter's father and mother had been successful attorneys in their native Vienna. But in March 1938, the Kanns had to abandon their high stations and flee Austria disguised as peasants to avoid the advancing German occupation.

Forsaking relatives, friends, and possessions at a moment's notice, Robert and Marie Kann smuggled themselves westward across Austria, traveling only the most remote thoroughfares by night. Trusting no one, they slept by day in caves burrowed in the melting snow, stealing whatever food they could along the way. Sixty-three days later, affecting the dress and manner of diplomats, the Kanns quite literally talked themselves past an awed German border guard to walk into Switzerland. They then flew from Zurich to London. Like other escapees of Nazism in the late thirties, the Kanns found London bleak. Robert Kann could find no employment, and Marie Kann took to cleaning houses in Belgravia.

In June 1939, as part of the U.S. government's program to expatriate distinguished Europeans fleeing Hitler, Robert Kann was admitted to the United States and given a position with Princeton's Institute for Advanced Studies, working on a classified intelligence project that required a knowledge of Austrian law.

Impressed with the comfort of academic life, in September 1942 Robert Kann entered Columbia University to prepare himself for a career of teaching at the university level. Four years later, while still working full-time for the government, Kann had obtained a Ph.D. in history at the age of forty. His widely acclaimed thesis was entitled "The Intellectual History of Austria."

After Columbia, Kann became a lecturer at Rutgers University's Graduate School of Arts and Sciences. He remained there for forty years, rising to full professor and becoming a world authority on Austria and the Hapsburg Empire. To this day, in fact, most encyclopedias and reference works cite Kann's *Multinational Empire* as the seminal history of Austria. Some of his other books, also highly acclaimed, include *The Hapsburg Empire* and *The Problem of Restoration.*

When Kann joined the Rutger's faculty, he and Marie were able to salvage and then liquidate some of their Vienna assets from the Austrian provisional government. The proceeds allowed them to purchase a beautiful eighteenth-century Colonial farmhouse in Princeton, New Jersey, a mile north of the university.

Located forty miles southwest of New York City, Princeton is a three-hundred-year-old idyll, reflecting the beauty and magic of a great university. It is not surprising Albert Einstein spent the last twenty years of his life there. Settled in the late 1600s, Princeton served as a colonial social and cultural center before the Presbyterians founded the College of New Jersey, Princeton's predecessor, in 1746. Princeton was also the site of a pivotal revolutionary war battle. It was there, in 1777, George Washington attacked and defeated a much superior British force, headed by Gen. Hugh Mercer.

Princeton provided Peter and his sister, Marilyn, with many of the advantages that his parents had enjoyed growing up in Vienna. Opting not to resume her law career, Marie Kann channeled her considerable energies into raising Peter and Marilyn. When Peter was twelve, for example, he and his mother published and distributed "The Jefferson Street Snooper," a neighborhood gossip sheet.

By the time Peter entered the local public high school, he had already developed into a fine athlete, excelling in soccer, tennis, and squash, and an excellent, if not always compliant, student. "Peter always looked so innocent, so cooperative, sitting in the classroom. But actually, he was headstrong. He did exactly what he wanted to do,"[5] said Mrs. Sommers, Kann's eleventh-grade homeroom teacher. "This manifested itself in his choice of colleges. Here he was, a local boy. His father was a visiting professor at Princeton. But what does Peter do? He goes off to Harvard! It was like he sided with the enemy."

In 1962, during the summer following his graduation from Princeton High School, Kann worked for the *Princeton Packet*, where he soon caught the eye of Barney Kilgore. From there, he moved on to intern at the *Journal* during his college summers under Kilgore's sponsorship. But while at the *Packet*, despite Kilgore's enthusiastic endorsement, Kann did not distinguish himself as a journalist. When asked what kind of performance he had turned in, general manager

Roslyn Denard said: "I don't know. He wasn't here long enough to do anything. He was just passing through, getting to know Barney."[6]

Cambridge, Massachusetts, is very similar to Princeton in historical, cultural, and educational significance. And life revolves around Harvard, where Peter was one of 1,200 students accepted out of 5,400 applicants for the class of 1964. Harvard College comprises a number of residential houses which, at any other university, would be called dormitories. Freshmen live in Harvard Yard, presumably under the watchful bronze eye of John Harvard. From his sophomore year on, Peter was a member of Dunster House, which occupies a Georgian mansion on the banks of the Charles River near the Weeks Memorial Bridge and the Harvard Business School, which lies on the other side of the river.

Peter entered Harvard as a history major, but in his sophomore year, he switched to government. The highlight of his four years at Harvard was the time he spent on the *Crimson*, the university's daily newspaper. The *Crimson* is to journalism what Harvard is to higher education. It is simply the best collegiate newspaper in the world. Founded in 1873, the *Crimson* is published every morning Monday through Saturday from September to May except during school holidays. When warranted, the *Crimson* publishes extra editions, as it did on the afternoon President Kennedy was assassinated. It is not uncommon for a student to exit Harvard stadium after a football game with a rival school and be handed a copy of the *Crimson* covering the game just ended. Occupying an ancient building at 14 Plympton Street, the *Crimson* owns two Mergenthaler linotypes, which it keeps in the basement.

The paper's content is a surprisingly sophisticated balance of state, city, municipal, and university news provided by its own student staff of reporters, editors, photographers, and editorial writers. The *Crimson* relies on the Associated Press for national and international news, as well.

To work on the *Crimson* is to give your life to it. David McClintick, bestselling author and former *Crimson* board member, said, "When I was on the *Crimson*, I worked on it seven days a week, sixteen hours per day. At first, I tried to juggle between the paper, lectures, and sleep. Then it was the paper and sleep. And finally, the paper prevailed. I don't know how I graduated."[7]

In the spring of 1963, the second semester of his junior year, Peter Kann was named the *Crimson's* city editor, a beat which entailed covering how the university interacted with the state and Boston and

Cambridge. His more prominent stories included the antics of Timothy Leary, a lecturer on clinical psychology who gained notoriety through his experiments with the mood-altering drug psilocybin.

In one article, Kann revealed how the nearby city of Newton had sued Leary and an associate, Richard Alpert, and ten other adults for living in a one-family residence. Prompted by "15 cars coming and going at 2 and 3 A.M.," the suit was answered by Leary, who insisted he and his eleven friends comprised one housekeeping unit and had therefore complied with Newtown's zoning regulations.

Though Kann wrote serious articles as well—he once interviewed Sen. John Sherman Cooper on his stance to blockade Cuba—he was happiest reporting the offbeat story filled with memorable quotes.

Kann's stint on the *Crimson* board exposed him to many Harvard classmates who went on to distinguished careers in publishing. According to David Halberstam, "Peter's *Crimson* board was very powerful. Donnie Graham [publisher, the *Washington Post*] and Michael Crichton [bestselling novelist] were on it with him. Every ten years or so, a board like that comes along which produces future Pulitzers."[8]

In June 1964, Peter graduated from Harvard College cum laude, as did half his classmates. As an outgrowth of his internship, Kann went to work at the *Wall Street Journal* in Pittsburgh as a reporter.

Curiously, years later, at his twenty-fifth class reunion, Peter Kann began his autobiographical essay in the program commemorating the event by writing: "My first career after Harvard was as a bulldozer operator in the Cambridge city dump. My ambition was to earn enough money to get to Asia as a free-lance writer. I failed. So I went to work for the *Wall Street Journal* as a reporter." Classmates who knew Peter smiled at his poetic license, realizing that once again he was making a good story even better. Peter was no more a failed bulldozer operator, they chuckled, than they were.

Any other reporter starting out would have been thrilled to report how Alcoa was replacing United States Steel, National Steel, and Jones & Laughlin. But Pittsburgh's foundries and smelting processes, and the people who manned them, bored Peter. His copy was adequate, but nothing special.

"Peter was too romantic for Pittsburgh,"[9] said Bernie Flanagan, a *Journal* salesman who shared the Pittsburgh office with Kann in 1964. "He was far more interested in what I was doing than what he was supposed to do."

Eighteen months later, Peter was transferred to the *Journal*'s Los

Angeles bureau, where, it was hoped, the film and aerospace industries would prove more stimulating. But even Hollywood failed to inspire Kann. By mid-1966, two years after he had joined the *Journal*, many of Peter's supporters from his intern days were becoming disenchanted. Ed Cony once observed, "Peter couldn't write a 'frisky.' His mind went blank. And that's all there were in Pittsburgh and Los Angeles."

Rather than master the dull but important business stories, Kann found salvation on a completely unrelated front. In May 1967, Fred Taylor, the *Journal's* diplomatic correspondent, toured Vietnam as part of Secretary Robert MacNamara's press retinue. When Taylor returned to Washington, he urged Cony, managing editor at the time, to appoint a full-time Vietnam correspondent. "The story was too important, and our coverage was too inadequate," Taylor explained.

David Halberstam observed, "When I was in Vietnam [1961–64], the *Journal* had someone in Tokyo who would fly into Saigon and do an occasional story. His stuff was very soft. It was incredible that a newspaper the size and reputation of the *Journal* would not have at least one full-time correspondent in Saigon then."

Taylor was successful in convincing Cony to appoint a full-time correspondent to Saigon. But Phillips, then executive editor, rejected Cony's nominees for the post and installed his own choice. Most newsroom people were shocked when the October 1967 "Dowcomm" announced the appointment of Peter R. Kann as the *Journal's* new Far East correspondent. Taylor said, "It came out of left field. Kann had no foreign experience and his domestic record was at best lackluster."

Kann opened the first full-time *Journal* bureau in Saigon, which consisted of a corner of a friend's desk in the Associated Press office.

Despite its horror, Saigon inspired Peter. His first story movingly conveyed the effects of the war from the perspective of its most innocent victims, Vietnam civilians—women and children—ravaged by the cross fire.

But Bill Kerby was unnerved by this story. "He [Kerby] thought Peter should be covering the battle of Khesanh, not some civilian hospital off in the boondocks," Taylor explained.

Taylor and Cony passed this criticism on to Peter via teletype. But he ignored it. "The damn teletype, so he said, was always breaking down," Taylor said chuckling. "We could never get to him, but he could always get to us. Peter never did one thing Ed and I asked him to do. Finally, we gave up and let him cover 'Nam the way he wanted to."

Kann's approach differed markedly from that used by other daily news media. The newspaper wire services and the television networks reported the daily facts of Vietnam gathered by large teams of correspondents and camera people who accompanied the troops into actual combat. Other news-media correspondents would fly into Saigon for a week at a time. Their news items added depth and analysis to the stories already reported by television and the wire services.

Kann, however, took a different tack. Not restricted by daily deadlines, he was free to wander about, reporting the war from the perspective of its victims, the Vietnamese people themselves. Kann's stories amounted to parables, passion plays. They told stories within stories which, with devastating simplicity and subtlety, conveyed the courage, the inanity, the humanity of the people trapped in the war.

One such piece, entitled "Value and Price in Battle of Dak To," was replete with quotes from U.S. military officials assessing the strategic importance of the battle of Dak To. Here is how Kann ended it.

Much analysis has been written and will be written on the battle of Dak To.

But Richard Cremer, a young medic, was sitting in the dust on top of Hill 873, surrounded by bomb-blackened remains of trees, caved-in bunkers, and the littered fragments and shreds of equipment, and of men. "Is this battle a big thing back in the States? Will my kids read about this hill someday?" he asks sardonically.

And down on the Dak To airstrip helicopters were unloading the equipment of the dead and wounded. The helmets, weapons, and packs mounted in little pyramids along the runway. Resting on top of one such pile was a tattered paperback copy of "How to Prepare for College."

Unlike other journalists in Vietnam, Peter rarely had to persuade or argue with his editors over the veracity of his reports. On the contrary, the page-one staff paid him the ultimate compliment. The operator had instructions to fetch Mike Gartner, the page-one editor, whenever the New York teletype machine signaled that copy from Saigon was about to be transmitted. As a service to his colleagues,

Gartner would transmit Peter's raw copy to the *Journal*'s forty-four bureaus scattered throughout the world before even processing it for publication.

"It was like reading a Dickens serialization in a magazine. We thought it was brilliant. We were all mesmerized," said Gartner. "None of us, me least of all, ever stopped to think it was being written by a twenty-seven-year-old kid who, six months before, was in Los Angeles getting his ass chewed out because he couldn't spell."[10]

Kann's instant success in Vietnam spawned many corporate fathers. Editors who at best had been lukewarm about his appointment were now lavishing praise on him. Fred Taylor said: "In Vietnam, Peter became one of the three best writers the *Journal* has ever had."

Kann's coverage was brilliant; yet it was strictly apolitical. He achieved an ideal that every journalism school professor puts forth daily. His copy was balanced: Conservatives like Bill Kerby and liberals like Ed Cony loved it in equal measure.

But Kann had a detractor or two. A. Kent Macdougall,[11] then a *Journal* reporter and now a professor at UC-Berkeley's graduate school of journalism, said recently, "How good was Peter Kann, really? He had a great eye and a great ear, to be sure. But he was too young and he didn't know anything about Asia. His grasp of the situation there, his knowledge of the history and the culture was too cursory. He had no sweep of history. He was too facile to be a great reporter on Vietnam like, say, I. F. Stone was."

David Halberstam, the *New York Times*'s Pulitzer Prize–winning Vietnam correspondent, is also critical of Kann. "Virtually every correspondent except Peter Kann emerged from Vietnam highly skeptical of the government and its role in the war. But Peter was unaffected by it. That's because he really never covered Vietnam. He did not spend a lot of time there. I never heard any members of the primary club of Vietnam correspondents—Neil Sheehan, Peter Arnett, Charley Moore, or Ward Just—ever mention Kann's name,"[12] said Halberstam.

When asked if he agreed with this assessment, another Pulitzer Prize–winning Vietnam correspondent, Peter Arnett, laughed and said, "That's David! He's tough on everyone." Then Arnett grew serious and added: "I knew Peter in 'Nam, too. He had a great knack for the unusual story and the colorful quote. But the thing I remember the most about him is, he risked his life many times to do his job."[13]

In February 1968, a group of civilians who had been admiring Saigon's skyline from the roof of the Imperial Hotel were trapped by the unexpected bombings that marked the beginning of the Tet Offensive. Peter, who had witnessed the attack from a café across the street, was the first person to reach the roof, where he administered first aid to several of the wounded before escorting everyone to safety. A romance quickly developed between Peter and Francesca R. Mayer, twenty-one, a civilian assigned to General Westmoreland's staff who was on the roof that night.

Seth Lipsky, a Harvard and *Journal* colleague of Peter's, once speculated, "Peter must have been irresistible to Francie. This swashbuckling correspondent, this knight in shining armor, rescuing her in the moonlight."

Besides her professional accomplishments, Francie was a pretty, bright, and dynamic woman who, together with Peter, "made a golden couple. She was so outgoing, so hospitable, so excited to be in Peter's life," said Martha Sorenson, Francie's sister.

In January 1969, after spending fifteen months in Saigon, Peter was ordered to move to Hong Kong so that he might better cover the entire Far East, now that Laos, Cambodia, and the India-Pakistan conflict were beginning to heat up. Curiously, Kerby and Phillips still refused to hire more correspondents, though they were content to maintain five news bureaus and seventeen reporters in Europe. "Ed and I could never persuade Kerby and Warren that this was an unwise use of personnel," Fred Taylor said. "The news was in the Far East, especially the business news."

Francie Mayer accompanied Peter to Hong Kong, where they lived together, working out of a two-bedroom apartment that had a spectacular view from the Peak of the harbor and Kowloon. Three months after the move, Peter and Francesca were married. Sen. Mike Mansfield was among their wedding guests.

Francesca Kann played such an integral role in Peter's life that, together, they were the *Journal's* Far East correspondent. Both shared their impressive talents modestly and considerately with others. And their home became a salon for the celebrities of Hong Kong. "Everyone from Chinese bankers, British diplomats, American politicians, even the head of Jardine Matheson, would come to their beautiful apartment. Francie played the piano magnificently. And we would all sing and drink until we dropped," Seth Lipsky recounted.

The comparative luxury of Hong Kong after Saigon did not hinder Peter's work. He continued to pursue the difficult story and state things that other newspapers avoided. Once, for example, in a piece about Laos, Peter revealed that the U.S. government had spent more money and effort rescuing an elephant, a gift from Cambodian prime minister Lon Nol to American admiral John S. McCain, Jr., than it had trying to repel the North Vietnam army's attack on Phnom Penh.

In April 1972, at the age of twenty-nine, Peter Kann won a Pulitzer Prize for international reporting. The Pulitzer Prize committee recognized Peter's first-person account of the Indo-Pakistani War, which he wrote on December 18, 1971.

Some artists believe that certain geographic areas have positive effects on their work. It is no accident, they maintain, that Italy, for example, has produced great art down through the ages. If there is any truth to this observation, then Vietnam proved to be Peter Kann's Italy. From the moment he set foot in Saigon, he became a journalistic poet of sorts. Peter Arnett said, "Peter wrote very few pieces, but they were brilliant."[14]

12

The Second Dauphin

When Peter Kann, barely thirty, returned to New York in May 1972 after having won the Pulitzer Prize the month before, he suggested to Warren Phillips, who was much taken by the award, that the *Journal* launch an Asian edition. Kann's argument was simple. Although capitalism might be losing in Vietnam, it was winning convincingly throughout the rest of the Far East. And this economic victory, which would only grow more decisive with time, was the perfect story for the *Wall Street Journal*. Yet, because this boom would last for generations, it required a separate edition, not a lone correspondent, to be covered properly.

Overriding the objections of Don Macdonald, who believed an Asian edition could not generate enough advertising revenues to make a worthwhile profit, Phillips authorized the launching of the *Asian Wall Street Journal* and installed Peter Kann as its founding publisher and editor.

It was one of Phillips's more questionable decisions. Instituting an Asian edition made sense, but promoting Kann from frontline reporter to publisher and editor in one fell swoop was unprecedented. Though Kann was a brilliant Vietnam correspondent, it did not necessarily follow he would make a competent business and editorial executive. Yet, no doubt because Kerby and Phillips had risen to the top of Dow Jones without business experience, Phillips thought Kann, whom he now admired inordinately, could do the job easily.

Kann's elevation was symptomatic of a problem besetting much of postwar corporate America in the early seventies. But the problem's consequences would not be felt until the late eighties, when the recession unveiled a multitude of bad decisions, not the least of which was the promotion of the wrong people for the wrong reasons.

After World War II, when the modern corporation—Dow Jones, IBM, General Motors, Sears, and the like—became the prime employer of America's white-collar work force, a major curse of the industrial revolution was born. Every college graduate wanted to be a boss, to sit in an enclosed office with a title on the door and a secretary hovering nearby, to watch subordinates do what he used to do. Few could resist this pull to the top of the hierarchy. There was little glory or power or money in frontline jobs, no matter how satisfying or productive they might be.

At Dow Jones, for example, talented reporters aspired to be editors for the sake of added recognition and money. But all too often these talented reporters became untalented editors. Engineers at General Motors, retail sales clerks at Sears, and salesmen at IBM fell into the same trap. Frontline jobs became "entry-level positions for professionals," corporatese for relegating once-critical posts to young, inexperienced college graduates who used them to achieve their own ends, the ascent up the corporate ladder.

Though it seemed like the American way, climbing this ladder carried pitfalls that the booming postwar economy masked. Since young, inexperienced college graduates regarded entry-level positions as mere career way stations, no one bothered to master these jobs. Salesman became sales managers without ever learning how to sell; reporters became editors without ever learning how to write; editors became chairmen without ever learning how to preside.

Corporate America became a nation of poseurs, not doers, which produced a fundamental shift in performance criteria. Form triumphed over substance. Appearance, education, where one lived, whom one knew, golf handicaps, and a million other frivolous considerations were emphasized unduly as like-minded males bonded. Usually, subordinates assumed the traits of their superiors, but sometimes this process was reversed.

Perhaps Dow Jones's most prominent promotion based on form, not substance, occurred in the early fifties when Warren Phillips attached himself to Kerby through a shared gene. Both men followed orders to the letter. And at that time, Dow Jones needed Kerby and Phillips to follow Kilgore's orders perfectly.

Then, twenty-five years later, Phillips needed a different set of genes, so he thought, to lead Dow Jones. He obtained these new credentials in an inverted fashion when he promoted Kann to head the *Asian Journal*. Because of, or as a result of, this decision, Kann became like a son to Phillips, which in turn permitted Phillips to lay vicarious claim to Kann's charm, Harvard education, and Pulitzer Prize—writing abilities.[1] Such was sway the Kann held over Phillips.

Five thousand miles separated *Journal* headquarters from Hong Kong. And once again Kann reveled in the freedom. In setting up the *Asian Journal*, there were no policy manuals, stylebooks, prying editors, or detail-obsessed Phillipses to heed.

Once again, following only his own instincts, Kann was buoyant twenty-four hours a day. Ably assisted by his wife, Francie, he was living out a journalist's dream: starting a newspaper with all of the resources, but none of the hassle, of Dow Jones behind him.

Seth Lipsky, a young Harvard graduate who was the *Asian Journal*'s first reporter, recalled, "I can't think of a more romantic time than the launching of the *Asian Wall Street Journal* in the mid-seventies. Led by Peter, we worked day and night. It was one big party. We simply never left the office, such as it was."[2]

Kann believed people who socialize well together work well together. In his own demonstration of form over substance, Kann was forever throwing a party. Once, when the carpenters hired to renovate office space for the *Asian Journal* were behind schedule, Kann's solution was to give them a lavish, on-site party. But the party delayed the work further because the carpenters, unused to the champagne Kann provided, suffered violent hangovers.

Being cautious, Phillips had insisted that the *Asian Journal* start out as a joint venture, and an alliance was forged with the *South China Morning Post*, Hong Kong's largest English-speaking newspaper. The *Morning Post* was owned by the same family that manufactured Tiger Balm, a popular ointment that had enabled it to earn billions and build, among many things, a theme park that features dragons and other Oriental monsters. The *Asian Journal*'s first offices were in a forgotten portion of the *Post*'s warehouse.

Unhappy with their progress, Kann finally fired the carpenters.

Then he and his staff, five people, ripped up moldy carpeting, tore down the cheapest type of wallboard, and built new offices from scratch themselves.

Frequently during the construction, with sawdust obliterating his glasses, Lipsky would shout, "Well, we're a long way from Hunza," referring to one of Kann's most famous stories. In the early seventies, as a break from the Vietnamese, Cambodian, and the Indo-Pakistani wars, Kann had traveled to Hunza, a village-state hidden in the highest Himalayas surrounded by Afghanistan, China, and Kashmir. There Kann filed an A-hed whose lead paragraph featured a Hunza chieftain demonstrating the importance of his country by drawing a map in the sand and saying, "Here's the U.S.A., Russia, Europe, and, in the center of this world, Hunza."

The first issue of the *Asian Wall Street Journal* appeared on September 1, 1976, with 70 percent of its news stories lifted from the domestic *Wall Street Journal*. But good luck caused the balance between Asian- and U.S.-originated news to shift almost immediately because, on September 10, 1976, Mao Zedong died, and the *Journal* was the only news organization in the world that had a reporter in China at the time. Bob Bartley, a *Journal* editorial writer, happened to be in Beijing with James Schlesinger, then U.S. secretary of defense. Bartley calmly walked to the nearest public telephone, called Kann in Hong Kong, and dictated a world scoop of the country's first shocked reaction to Mao's death.

Kann's right-hand man in Hong Kong was Norman Pearlstine, *Asian Journal* managing editor, who was two years younger than his boss. The pair epitomized corporate America's male-bonding phenomenon. Though Pearlstine was noticeably more insecure and in need of recognition than Kann, the two men shared a common privileged childhood and education, ambition, and talent. In fact, if ever two men loved each other fraternally, Kann and Pearlstine did as they launched the *Asian Wall Street Journal* together.

Kann and Pearlstine only stayed with the *Asian Journal* for eighteen months. When both men left Hong Kong in 1978, Kann to New York, as Phillips's assistant, and Pearlstine to Los Angeles, as an executive editor for *Forbes* magazine, the *Asian Journal* had only achieved a circulation of 12,000, with each issue averaging a scant eight pages of news and ads.

In the opinions of some, Kann and Pearlstine accomplished very little in Hong Kong. William Dunn, a former Dow Jones executive vice president and defeated rival of Kann's, said, "To this day, the *Asian Wall Street Journal* has never turned a profit. But in the seventies, you would have thought Kann and Pearlstine invented frozen pizza with the way Phillips and others would carry on. It was like a high school paper, and neither Pearlstine nor Kann stayed in Hong Kong that long to see it through anyway."

Fred Taylor, the *Journal's* managing editor at the time, was even harsher than Dunn. Taylor recalled, "Norman Pearlstine quit as managing editor of the *Asian Wall Street Journal* because he thought it was going to fail. He solicited *Forbes* for a job, and then, while still the *Asian Journal's* managing editor, he went throughout the Far East passing out his *Forbes* business cards."[3]

Taylor added, "Pearlstine's timing was interesting. He shows up in New York to resign. I was on the West Coast, Cony [the *Journal's* executive editor at the time] was someplace else. Warren was the only person Norman could resign to. Surprise, surprise! When Norman cried on Warren's shoulder, Warren then wanted to save Pearlstine."

But Phillips's idea of transferring Pearlstine back to the West Coast as a super bureau chief for San Francisco and Los Angeles never worked out. Pearlstine's shift to *Forbes*, according to friends, was his means to circumvent the many people who were ahead of him at the *Journal*. Pam Hollie, Pearlstine's friend, said, "It was a clever move. It moved his career along faster than ordinary. Norm is a pretty political guy."

Though working for competitors, the two men stayed in constant contact over the next several years as Kann, in 1980, became the *Journal's* associate publisher and Pearlstine prospered under Malcolm Forbes. Then, in 1981, Kann wanted to nudge aside the veteran spot-news editor, Bill Kreger, so that Pearlstine could return to the *Journal*. But when Taylor objected, Kann said, "Why are you so mad, Fred? Norman quit on me, not you."[4]

Eventually, Phillips intervened. "Warren said to me, 'You will rehire Norman.' It was the only ultimatum Warren ever gave me," Taylor said.

In 1981, despite Taylor's protests, Pearlstine returned to the *Journal* as something of a prodigal son, a perception engineered by Kann and endorsed by Phillips. For the next ten years, Kann and Pearlstine reshaped the *Journal* almost as drastically as Kilgore had forty years before, but not necessarily for the better.

Pearlstine had originally joined the *Journal* in June 1967 as a reporter in its Dallas bureau. He had just fled the *New York Times*, after only three months, unable to endure the traditions that the *Times* thrusts upon all new news assistants.[5]

At six feet two and broad-shouldered, Pearlstine had reported for work at the *Times's* squalid West 43d Street building, preoccupied by his status. With his articulate drawl, dark suit, and air of entitlement, Pearlstine looked like he should be attending the four o'clock news conference to help Clifton Daniel, managing editor, decide what the next day's lead was to be.

To his near fatal chagrin, Norman Pearlstine, twenty-four, soon discovered he would start at the *Times* the way every other news assistant did, "schlepping copy."

Copyboys did the bidding of editors and reporters. Those grateful for the opportunity, and most were at the *New York Times*, took their jackets off, filled paste pots, delivered copy, picked up dry cleaning, and developed mentors through flattery, humor, and hustle. These aspirants, most of whom held graduate degrees in journalism, did not recoil when an editor, never looking up, would summon them with "Boy!"

But Norman Pearlstine did.

"It was a most painful period for Norman," said Barry Newman, veteran *Journal* reporter who was a peer at the *Times* with Pearlstine. "Here he was, a lawyer. He had also been a reporter in Pennsylvania. And what did he do? In starched white shirt and rep tie, Norman kept circling around all day in that bizarre newsroom, pain and misery etched in his face, delivering copy."[6]

Perhaps this demeanor accounts for what a *Times* editor said to Pearlstine during his first week on the job: "You will never make it here."[7]

In June 1967, after only three months on the job, he fled to a smaller pond, the *Wall Street Journal*, where he was made most welcome by Warren Phillips and Peter Kann.

Pearlstine arrived at the *Journal* when Phillips, anticipating the day when he would succeed Kerby, had begun to select his future corporate team. And because he was re-creating himself instead of choosing people out of the Kilgore tradition, the diffident Phillips was partial to urbane Ivy Leaguers. And Pearlstine epitomized Phillips's vision.

Pearlstine had enjoyed an ideal childhood under the watchful and loving eyes of Raymond and Gladys Pearlstine in Collegeville, Pennsylvania, a suburb of Norristown. His father, Raymond, a lifelong native of Collegeville, was a successful Norristown lawyer specializing in bankruptcies and estate planning.

After graduating from the Hill School, an exclusive preparatory school, Pearlstine went to Haverford College, a highly selective Quaker school on Philadelphia's Main Line, where he won the school's Freshman of the Year Award in 1960–61. The award recognized his grades and athletic triumphs—varsity wrestling and football—and involvement with student publications. He was on the staff of the yearbook and served as news editor for the *Haverford News*, the student newspaper. In his senior year, Pearlstine cocaptained the wrestling team and served as editor in chief of the newspaper, for which he wrote one to three editorials an issue.

Slated to attend Columbia Journalism School, at the last minute Pearlstine changed his mind and entered the University of Pennsylvania Law School. Law school, he explained to his parents, would better prepare him for any number of careers, including journalism. His father, of course, hoped Norman would join his law firm. During the summers, Pearlstine worked as a *Wall Street Journal*-sponsored trainee at the *Allentown Globe Chronicle*. Pearlstine graduated from Penn Law in May 1967, passed the Washington, D.C., bar, and went to work for the *New York Times*, all in a matter of months.

When Pearlstine applied to the *Journal* for an opening in its Dallas bureau, he stood out from the hundreds of people who sought the job. According to Herb Lawson, the Dallas bureau chief who hired him, "Norman had prepared for the interview as if he were arguing a case before the Supreme Court. He knew things about the *Journal* you'd expect only a veteran to know, the personalities, the politics, things like that. And his enthusiasm to work for the *Journal*, not his writing samples, impressed me the most."[8]

Unlike his experience with the *Times*, Pearlstine's salad days with the *Journal* turned into a conquest. From the start, he discarded whatever pretensions he may have displayed at the *Times* and demonstrated an unusual ability to get on with all manner and class of sources.

One of his first stories involved a New Orleans teamster official whom the police had arrested for an alleged bribery scheme connected with the laying of Louisiana's oil pipelines. Because the official was close to Jimmy Hoffa, a pack of journalists, Pearlstine included, descended on New Orleans. Lawson recalled, "Norm befriended this character's bodyguards, got them to reveal their boss's scheme, and then filed an exclusive before anyone else wrote a word."

Sometimes Pearlstine could get too close to sources. Again,

according to Dallas bureau chief Lawson: "Once, Norman drove into the New Mexico desert to do a story on the hippie idol of the sixties, Wavy Gravy. Within hours of his entering the commune, Gravy's followers borrowed Norm's rental car and made a dope run to the border."

Besides building his professional reputation, Pearlstine also began contributing to his legend of being a bon vivant. "Norm loved to eat, drink, and have fun. He had a little house in Dallas which became a great party center," Lawson said, who admitted going there many times himself.

It was evident to his Dallas bureau colleagues that Pearlstine came from a well-to-do and caring family. "A Journal reporter's salary could hardly pay for the house and the brand-new Volvo he drove," Lawson said.

Not long after Pearlstine joined the paper, both Raymond and Gladys Pearlstine appeared at the Dallas bureau, unannounced. After inspecting the premises carefully, evaluating whether it "was good enough for their son, Norman's father took the entire bureau out to dinner. It was the first and last time I ever experienced such generosity from a reporter's parents," added Lawson.

Three years later, Pearlstine grew restless with Dallas and requested a transfer to Detroit, a bureau abounding in smokestacks and "frisky furniture" stories. When Pearlstine arrived in Detroit, he was a full-fledged professional. In fact, Larry O'Donnell, the bureau chief, said: "Norman was the best reporter I ever had in the bureau."[9]

Pearlstine himself recounted an anecdote which illustrates how even Detroit's celebrities came to acknowledge, if not actually accept, him. "When I moved to Detroit in 1970, I bought a Datsun 240-Z," Pearlstine said, smiling at the memory. "I drove it to my first big social event, a Ford preview dinner. As luck would have it, who sees me and my date getting out of the car but Lee Iacocca. He rushes up to me and says right in my face, 'Where the fuck did you get that piece of shit!' Iacocca then gives me the cold shoulder for the next several hours, cozying up to all the other reporters. But then a light goes on in his wife's head, and she whispers something in Lee's ear. After that, he could not have been nicer, especially to my date. You see, his wife finally recognized that my date taught their daughter French. It also helped that the kid was flunking the class."[10]

Back in Pearlstine's early days with the Journal, the job of reporter was divided into two unequal parts: gathering facts and writing.

Since the *Journal* maintained a phalanx of rewrite editors, reporters rarely were motivated to develop their writing skills to their own satisfaction. By and large, with the exception of Kann and Barry Newman, Dennis Farney, Jim Gannon, and a few others, reporters felt their writing abilities were lacking. Pearlstine, while in Detroit, was no exception.

Pearlstine recalled, "Writing has always been so painful for me. But I made up for it by developing good relationships with sources. That's why, for instance, I gained twenty-five pounds in Detroit, eating pizza and drinking beer with union officials."[11]

But as the following excerpt reveals, Pearlstine is being modest.

Dearborn, Michigan—Many of his credentials are neither impressive nor conducive to advancement in the conservative industry that he is in.

Caught with a ghost-written paper at Yale, he never graduated. Attracting reams of copy in the tabloids, he divorced his Establishment wife of many years and promptly married an international beauty and jet-setter. He is chronicly late for work; "Everybody else here starts up at 8 a.m., but I can't get up that early," he confides.

And a product he pushed several years ago was such a roaring flop that its name has become synonym for failure and the very mention of it is sure to get any comedian a big laugh.

Yet this mod man in a straight industry rules his company with an iron hand and will never be replaced except by choice. "He is the final approving body in this company," says a vice president. And another underling says, "If he makes a casual suggestion in conversation, we break our necks to please him without questioning whether the suggestion makes any sense." Except for his brothers, not even the highest executive in his company dares call him by his first name, which is Henry.

His last name is Ford.[12]

Pearlstine distinguished himself and the *Journal* with stories on James Roche, then chairman of General Motors; the United Auto Workers; and the collapse of Detroit's Bank of the Commonwealth. After Pearlstine interviewed Roche for the *Journal* profile, the General Motors public relations staff used the videotape of the proceedings to teach other GM executives how not to react in a press interview. Pearlstine was flawless in his handling of one of the world's most powerful industrialists.

Another Pearlstine classic, according to Larry O'Donnell, was a two-part series on General Motors and Isuzu that explained how "Japan, Inc." would come to dominate this country's economy.

But after eighteen months in Detroit, the flamboyant Pearlstine, then twenty-seven, became bored again, and in the summer of 1971 he requested another transfer to the more pleasant and exciting Los Angeles bureau. Pearlstine was following the example set by Kann four years before.

Pearlstine's transfer request upset the New York editors. Fred Taylor, managing editor, recalled, "After his success in Detroit, Norman became a problem. Every six months he wanted to move someplace else. For the rest of us, the *Journal* came first. But for Norman, it started to be the other way around."[13]

Up until then, the *Journal* simply did not allow anyone to become a star. Scornful of celebrity newspeople, the culture believed what Barney Kilgore had articulated twenty-five years before: "A journalist should observe and chronicle the news, not be part of it. With fame and recognition comes the tendency for reporters and editors to believe they, not their publication, are the stars."[14]

For this reason, *Journal* staffers were not allowed to appear on television, author books, or engage in any activity that might lead to individual glory. There were, of course, exceptions to this rule. Years of writing brilliant columns and editorials, and winning two Pulitzers, made Vermont Royster a celebrity despite Kilgore's edicts. And to Royster's credit, he never abused his special status.

Besides keeping staffers humble, the *Journal*'s anti–star system vested New York editors—as opposed to bureau chiefs or reporters—with power. Again, there were exceptions, most notably the Washington bureau chief. But, overall, the editors in New York, especially the managing editor, ruled the *Journal* without question.

One manifestation of the New York editors' power was the chesslike manner in which they moved reporters from one bureau to another. These editor-engineered moves always satisfied the organizational needs of the *Journal*, not the preferences of the individuals involved.

However, like Peter Kann, Pearlstine was different. Taylor had little choice but to accede to Pearlstine's wish because Warren Phillips stood in the wings, ready to intervene. "Norm's request caused a big problem,"[15] Taylor said. "Phillips's indulgence of Pearlstine marked the beginning of the *Journal*'s current two-tier system: stars and workers. Stars write the features and workers do the scut work."

Phillips played the role of an indulgent father by countermanding Taylor and permitting Pearlstine to transfer to Los Angeles. It marked the beginning of a politicized environment at the *Journal*.

Just as Pearlstine demonstrated a disregard for convention by driving a Japanese sports car in Detroit, he continued to exude independence when he moved to Los Angeles. Most *Journal* staffers back then tended to lead unobtrusive lives in quiet suburbs. Even the New York brass, with the exception of Phillips, preferred to live namelessly in Short Hills or Princeton, shunning the high-profile life of New York City. But Pearlstine demonstrated a sense of style and attachment to good living by renting a small but lovely beachfront apartment in Malibu.

"Norman always made the right friends, lived in the right places. That's why he moved to Malibu," said Pamela Hollie, a former *Journal* reporter.

Malibu was where Pearlstine first met James Brooks, the movie director whose credits include *Starting Over* with Peter Sellars and *Terms of Endearment* with Jack Nicholson. Malibu also allowed Pearlstine to indulge in another interest, physical fitness. An enthusiastic runner, he ran most days either on the beach or in the Santa Monica mountains. While running, he met his second wife, Adele Wilson, a five-foot-ten-inch teacher from Boston who liked to stay in shape, too. Wilson went back to school and became a banker, demonstrating an ambition that Pearlstine admired. Hollie said, "Norman always liked career women, women who did something. They had to be intelligent and interesting. Beauty was secondary."

While Pearlstine's transfer to Los Angeles irritated Taylor, William Blundell, the Los Angeles bureau chief, welcomed him. Blundell said, "It did not take a genius to see that Norman Pearlstine had a red tag tied around his neck that said Future Managing Editor."[16]

Though Pearlstine was destined for greater things, he still developed close ties with his peers. "Norman was a wild man. He was wonderful, fun,"[17] said Hollie. Every Thursday night, the entire Los Angeles bureau, led by "scoutmaster" Blundell, would go to Olympics Auditorium and watch the fights. The most vociferous fan was Pearlstine. "It was magic the way Norman kept us together like a family," said another member of the bureau.[18] Often the group would repair after the fights to Pearlstine's Malibu house, where he could hold his guests spellbound peeling a banana with his toes.

The LA bureau was a *Journal* training grounds because Blundell, a superb writer, was adept at teaching others how to write front-page stories. Once, when Pearlstine was doing a piece on Howard Hughes, Blundell joined Pearlstine in Las Vegas for the final interviews. Blundell then insisted they fly to a Santa Fe resort, where Pearlstine wrote and Blundell rewrote the definitive account of Howard Hughes's demise. "It was one of the highlights of my career," Blundell said. "He was an exciting guy to be around, to work with."[19]

After covering the activities of Lockheed, McDonnell Douglas, North American Rockwell, and the aerospace labor unions for eighteen months, Pearlstine wanted to gain experience as a foreign correspondent. Inspired by its success with automobiles, Japan was now conquering the worldwide consumer electronics market. As a consequence, the Far East was where Pearlstine wanted to be posted.

In March 1973, Norman Pearlstine became the *Journal*'s Tokyo bureau chief. Again, his affability and talent served him well. Though the incumbent bureau chief, Bill Hartley, was shunted to Singapore to make room for Pearlstine, Hartley liked his successor. "I could not help myself. I was fond of Norman the moment I met him. He also wrote some great stuff off my beat, some truly great stuff."[20]

As a foreign correspondent, Pearlstine no longer had the help of the *Journal*'s vaunted rewrite or copydesk. "In the States," he recalled, "we always had so much help that I never fully developed as a writer. But in Tokyo, I started writing for the paper, not some editor, for the first time."[21]

But foreign correspondents serving in Japan in the mid-seventies were severely restricted by the government, which was anxious to control the foreign press. Foreign reporters could not ask questions at press conferences, for example. In the spring of 1974, Lee Iacocca, who was visiting Tokyo for the first time, held a press conference. While the Japanese press swarmed about him, Iacocca noticed Pearlstine standing in the background. Startled by his shyness, Iacocca asked Pearlstine, "What's wrong, Norman?" An interpreter quickly explained the gag rule to the honored guest. "But you don't understand," replied Iacocca. "If I don't talk to him, they'll [the *Journal*] kill me back in the States."

Perhaps the most memorable story Pearlstine wrote while stationed in Tokyo dealt with the psychological problems that sprang from the extraordinary congestion of the city. The lead related, twenty years before people recognized the adverse effects of noise pollution, how one man had died from the noise.

In the meanwhile, the domestic *Wall Street Journal* was fast becoming one of America's largest and most influential newspapers. By the end of 1977, its daily circulation was nearing 1.6 million. More important, because of the paper's huge pass-along readership, the *Journal* was now being read by over 4.3 million people each day.

In record numbers, doctors, lawyers, retirees, schoolteachers, politicians, and other nonbusiness people gladly paid $79 for a year's subscription to the *Wall Street Journal*. It was worth it. No other news medium could tell them how best to invest their money. Besides, business was interesting now, and the *Journal's* writing was superb.

And advertisers, in record numbers, too, rushed to tell these same *Journal* readers how they should spend or invest their money. A page of advertising in the *Journal* cost $78,000 in 1977, up from $53,000 in 1974, and advertisers were still waiting patiently for the *Journal* ad salesperson to tell them when they could run their ad.

The roots of the *Journal's* prosperity sprang from the conglomeration of corporate America, a term used to describe a big corporation becoming even bigger by acquiring a number of smaller and often dissimilar corporations. Whenever ITT or LTV or General Electric, or a whole host of other companies, acquired another entity, the economy was stimulated. Hundreds of millions of dollars' worth of purchase loans were made, new plants and production techniques were financed, and people kept their jobs. There were days even when Wall Street's bulls predicted the Dow might one day exceed two thousand.

The buoyant news of conglomerates replaced the enervating news of Watergate, Vietnam, and the 1974 recession. And, of course, no one segment of the population was more interested in this news than the readership of the *Journal*; and no one medium could report this story better than the *Journal*. There were times when the Cox family, which still owned 80 percent of Dow Jones, "thought some higher power permitted Clarence Barron and Barney Kilgore to return and write the perfect ending to their lifework."[22]

Aside from the Cox family's good fortune, 1977 was also the perfect time for Warren Phillips to emerge as Dow Jones's CEO. Bill Kerby, who had lingered for four years beyond Dow Jones's mandatory retirement age so that his stock options might be worth more, was finally preparing to retire at the end of the year.

Buoyed by Kerby's impending exit and the size of Dow Jones's profits, Warren Phillips shut down the *National Observer* in the summer of 1977, plugging a $10 million annual profit drain. Other than its loyal readers, the rest of the world hardly blinked. Most people thought the *Observer* had been dead for years. But the people of Dow Jones reacted curiously. Rather than sadness, relief was the prevailing sentiment. "Finally, someone was doing something about that damned *Observer*," exclaimed a staffer. "It was killing my profit sharing."

No one expressed concern that even when the vaunted resources of the *Wall Street Journal* were brought to bear on the situation, the *Observer* still failed. Instead of acknowledging and learning from this failure, everyone hid behind the *Journal*'s burgeoning success. Despite widely proclaimed plans to diversify and introduce new publications, Dow Jones grew even more dependent on the *Journal*.

Within months of closing the *Observer*, Phillips also tried to settle an old score in the *Journal*'s editorial department, one that had begun back in January 1970 when Phillips promoted a friend, Sterling E. "Jim" Soderlind, to replace Ed Cony as the *Journal*'s managing editor. A former Rhodes scholar, the diffident Soderlind had blossomed into a capable page-one editor under Phillips's watchful eye. But within weeks of assuming the managing editorship, Soderlind's troubles surfaced. "No one knew Soderlind was an alcoholic until he became managing editor,"[23] said Fred Taylor, who was then the assistant managing editor.

Reluctant to admit he had made a mistake, Phillips tried to ignore the situation. But finally Soderlind's erratic behavior became so egregious that Kerby himself had to intercede. With great haste, Kerby replaced Soderlind with Fred Taylor, then forty-two, as managing editor. Taylor, who had recently come to New York from San Francisco, recalled, "It was clear Soderlind could not function. So while he was on vacation, Kerby told me to take his job. I felt terrible, awful."[24]

Both Kerby and Phillips preferred to take a chance with Taylor, who was respected but light on managerial experience, rather than bring Cony back from his seven-month-long exile. What Taylor

lacked in command experience, he made up for in intellect, cama-
raderie, and accessibility.

Taylor's closest friend then, Michael G. Gartner, former *Journal*
page-one editor and now president of NBC News, said: "Taylor's desk
was right on the floor. You could always talk to him. He was very
relaxed and there was little bureaucracy. He had great integrity and
great instincts. He was a wonderful managing editor."[25]

But others saw a more human side of Taylor. "I loved Fred Taylor,"
said Mary Bralove, one of the first women reporters at the modern
Journal. "He was a very bright, well-read man who trusted you. He
did not meddle, which takes a lot of courage for an editor. But, and
this pains me to admit, he was also lazy. He realized there was a life
outside the *Journal* and he just didn't work as hard as the others."[26]

Others likened Taylor to a character out of *Front Page*. His
seemingly gruff exterior hid a decent, warm human being. Of the
eight men who had held the post of managing editor since Kilgore,
Taylor, after Cony, was the most beloved. But the trait that explained
his popularity also explained his downfall. Like Cony before him,
Taylor had a penchant for defending his subordinates. And also like
Cony, Taylor eventually paid the price for it.

At Taylor's first bureau chief meeting as managing editor, held in
September 1970 at a Cape Cod resort, Taylor ran true to character.
Though it was in the first weeks of his new job, his reactions affected
his career greatly.

"With Kerby in the audience," Taylor recalled, "Phillips started in
on the business stories. Not enough of them, too much soft, liberal
stuff. The same old crap. Alan Otten and others refuted him. They
got into a great row. It was a god-awful session. I was brand-new, and
I didn't know what to do. Finally, I leaped to my feet and announced
that we would not change page one's direction, which of course
contradicted what Phillips wanted. He never said a word, only
glowered."[27]

While Taylor ran the domestic news department, the *Asian Wall
Street Journal* became Cony's temporary refuge. At first, in the early
seventies, Cony performed a legitimate function, traveling back and
forth between Hong Kong and New York, serving as Kann's eager, if
not unwitting, courier. With wondrous tales of Peter and Southeast
Asia, Cony kept the idea of the *Asian Wall Street Journal* alive in New
York until the paper was launched in September 1976.

Thereafter, his talents no longer relevant, abandoned by both

Kann and Macdonald, Ed Cony—Pulitzer Prize winner and once the passionate leader of the *Journal's* newsroom—fell asleep in the corporate snow. For the next ten years, he roamed the halls, his once-flaming blue eyes dulled.

Years later, Phillips was asked if Cony was the father of the *Journal's* golden age of writing. Phillips responded with strong emotion. "Cony was not as good as everyone thinks. Certainly the *Journal's* golden age of writing, or the peak of its prowess, did not exist under him. If there was a golden age, and I don't like that concept, Norman Pearlstine, not Ed Cony, created it."[28]

While Cony faded in the Dow Jones bureaucracy, Fred Taylor kept distancing himself from the day-to-day news operation. Anxious to correct this defect, in 1976 the administrative-minded Phillips appointed Lawrence O'Donnell, then Taylor's assistant, to replace Taylor as the *Journal's* managing editor.[29]

Following Ed Cony and Fred Taylor, O'Donnell was the third managing editor to serve under Phillips since 1965. He was a journeyman blue-collar editor who clung to the rules rigidly to compensate for his own lack of vision and creativity.[30] Though O'Donnell held the post for seven years, his reign can be summarized through the experience of David McClintick, a well-regarded *Journal* reporter in the late seventies.

In the fall of 1977, several months before O'Donnell was named managing editor, McClintick suddenly discovered why the top executives of Columbia Pictures, subjects of a page-one profile he had been preparing, had seemed so preoccupied and troubled for the past several months. Through an ambiguous press release which provoked more questions than it answered, Columbia announced that David Begelman, its studio head, would take a leave of absence while Columbia's board of directors investigated "certain unauthorized financial transactions between Begelman and the company."

Everyone shared McClintick's astonishment that David Begelman, one of Hollywood's crown princes who earned upward of $300,000, could be involved in scandal. Just four years before, Wall Street financier Herbert Allen, Jr., and Ray Stark, producer of *Funny Girl* and other megahits, had recruited Begelman to save the floundering studio. By promoting such films as *Funny Girl*, *Shampoo*, and *Close Encounters of the Third Kind*, Begelman improved Columbia's fortunes beyond even Allen's and Stark's demanding expectations.

Like every other reporter covering the film industry, McClintick set about to discover the exact nature of Begelman's "unauthorized financial transactions."

Aided by the fact he was a reporter for the *Wall Street Journal,* and by his soft-spoken yet diligent manner, McClintick induced certain sources within Columbia to reveal to him what they flatly refused to divulge to other journalists. And so, for much of October and November 1977, McClintick ferried between New York and the Beverly Hills Hotel, at last to discover that what Columbia's board had labeled "unauthorized financial transactions" were three separate embezzlements.

To ferret out these facts required considerable skill, since there was an all but impenetrable wall of silence around Columbia Pictures and David Begelman.

But McClintick persisted. He learned that Begelman's most astonishing act, and the one that had caused his undoing, involved the actor Cliff Robertson. Unbeknownst to Robertson, Begelman had authorized Columbia to make out a $10,000 check to the Oscar winner for bogus travel expenses. The check was delivered directly to Begelman, who then forged Robertson's endorsing signature, cashed it, and pocketed the $10,000. Eight months later, after he received a tax form that indicated Columbia had paid him this sum during the previous year, Robertson complained to the studio. An investigation followed, and it revealed that Begelman had used Robertson and two other unsuspecting people as straw parties to embezzle his employer.

McClintick was about to write a page-one story exposing these derelictions when, on Saturday, December 17, 1977, he received a tip that was even more startling. Rather than prosecute Begelman for grand theft, the Columbia board of directors, led by Herbert Allen and Ray Stark, was going to reinstate Begelman the following Monday. Irrespective of ethical considerations, Allen and Stark wanted to keep Begelman on the job simply because he could make them, Columbia's largest shareholders, more money, McClintick's source said.

The actual press release announcing Begelman's reinstatement, the source added, contained an extraordinary admission. It would read as follows:

New York (December 19, 1977)—Columbia Pictures Industries Inc. announced today that David Begelman has been reinstated as President of its Motion Pictures and Television Divisions. Mr.

Begelman has been on leave of absence since September 30, 1977, pending an investigation by the Audit Committee of the Board of Directors into a number of unauthorized financial transactions involving Mr. Begelman and the Company. The investigation established that in a number of separate and unrelated transactions from January 1975 to May 1977, Mr. Begelman obtained through improper means corporate funds in the amount of $61,008 for his personal benefit, and that the emotional problems prompting these acts, coupled with ongoing therapy, will not impair his continuing effectiveness as an executive.

The next morning, Sunday, December 18, McClintick went in to work and proposed to Mack Solomon, deputy page-one editor, that the *Journal* run his version of the Begelman saga the next day as a counterpoint to Columbia's press announcement. His story, McClintick promised, would reveal for the first time the exact nature of Begelman's crimes. It would also show Herb Allen and Ray Stark attempting to convince Wall Street, Hollywood, the SEC, Columbia's employees, shareholders, and suppliers, and the public in general how twelve visits to a Hollywood psychiatrist had cured David Begelman of his felonious urges. Besides, McClintick added, his story would be breaking news, something O'Donnell was brought in to do.

Known as an inspired editor, Solomon accepted McClintick's story pending the managing editor's final approval, though Solomon was "concerned I could crash such a long and legally complicated story through the system on a Sunday afternoon."[31]

While McClintick set about finishing the piece, Solomon called Lawrence O'Donnell. Three weeks into his new job as managing editor, O'Donnell was at home that Sunday morning, preparing to attend a Dow Jones Christmas party that afternoon. When told that McClintick's scoop would replace the column-six feature he had previously approved, O'Donnell balked.

Hollywood was not McClintick's usual beat, and this story would cause territorial problems with the Los Angeles bureau, which covered the movie industry, O'Donnell protested. Besides, he added, "McClintick was supposed to be working on a profile of Columbia Pictures, not Begelman. I was also bothered by the piece alluding to Begelman's psychiatric care. The whole issue of privacy was different then."[32]

Later that day, over the telephone, McClintock asked O'Donnell why he was unwilling to run his piece. O'Donnell replied that in addition to considering the story unimportant, he wanted to see Columbia's press announcement himself before refuting it on the *Journal's* front page.

His explanation, curtly conveyed, upset McClintick even more. "Larry did not understand the story. He had just been named managing editor after eight years in Detroit, where he covered nothing but mortar and brick. He was used to things you could drive; he thought Hollywood was flighty. But what really got me was when he said, 'We better wait for the announcement,' as if I were not capable of handling the story. It was not what O'Donnell said, it was the way he said it ... as if he were saying, 'I'm the managing editor and you're just the reporter and you have no right to question my authority.'"[33]

On Monday, December 19, Columbia called a press conference to distribute the release announcing Begelman's reinstatement. The release was exactly what McClintick had said it would be. On Tuesday, December 20, in the "Who's News" column, a three-paragraph item told of Begelman's return to Columbia despite his crimes, which were listed, including the Cliff Robertson forgery.

Even though it failed to appear on the *Journal's* front page, McClintick's story was a major scoop. To make up for lost ground, rival media, led by the *Washington Post*, pursued the Begelman affair with a fury that obliterated McClintick's advantage. Most of the news accounts concentrated on the Cliff Robertson forgery and failed to emphasize Columbia's tacit endorsement of Begelman's crimes, which was even more astonishing.

For the next two weeks, McClintick updated his page-one feature, which, as a compromise, O'Donnell agreed to run once he saw that the Begelman affair was in fact a major news story. Though McClintick turned in the expanded piece on January 19, O'Donnell stalled publishing it for another ten days. By that time "the *Journal* was no longer ahead of the pack," McClintick lamented.

Now agitated by O'Donnell's cavalier treatment of him, McClintick wrote a memo to O'Donnell airing his grievances. Five weeks later, O'Donnell, McClintick, and McClintick's immediate boss, Stew Pinkerton, New York bureau chief, met to discuss the contents of the memo. According to McClintick, O'Donnell truculently said: "You have no right to question my decisions. I'm the boss, and you do what I say."

A year and a half later, McClintick resigned from the *Journal* to write a book on the Begelman affair entitled *Indecent Exposure*. It sold 150,000 hardcover copies and 800,000 paperback copies, netting McClintick an estimated $2 million. It was nominated for a Pulitzer Prize and a National Book Award, and *Business Week* deemed it one of the ten best business books ever published. Perhaps more important, by adapting certain techniques first used by Truman Capote in *In Cold Blood* and then by Norman Mailer in *The Executioner's Song*, McClintick created a whole new genre for nonfiction business books. Through reconstructed dialogue and re-created scenes, McClintick wrote the Begelman story in such intimate detail that people invariably describe a fly-on-the-wall feeling when reading *Indecent Exposure*.

Looking back, McClintick summarized what many other *Journal* staffers who worked for O'Donnell from 1977 to 1983 thought: "O'Donnell was interested in the price of newsprint, not the big story,"[34] he said.

Ironically, though Phillips ousted O'Donnell in September 1983, O'Donnell was a Phillips-type editor through and through. In fact, O'Donnell did to McClintick what Phillips had done to Cony ten years before—discouraged journalists from investigating business irregularities. Eventually, this deterrence would explain in part why the *Journal* failed to investigate Michael Milken, Ivan Boesky, and the savings-and-loan scandal's most prominent felon, Charles Keating, Jr., until it no longer mattered.

13

Book Digest: Compounding Disaster

In 1977, while Kann and Pearlstine were busy launching the *Asian Wall Street Journal* in Hong Kong, Warren Phillips began to smile openly for the first time in his career. The nation's appetite for news about Wall Street and corporate America continued to increase, driving hordes of advertisers and subscribers to the only national daily business newspaper. As a result, Dow Jones's 1977 revenues had reached $317 million, double what they were in 1970. And forecasts for the future proclaimed this figure would triple again in the next seven years, such was the power of the supply-and-demand forces working on the *Journal's* behalf.

Phillips also was smiling because Bill Kerby, at sixty-nine, had finally retired as CEO at the end of that year, an event a long time coming. Kerby had lingered four years beyond the company's mandatory retirement age so he might sell his Dow Jones stock options at their peak. He was the only employee allowed to delay retirement. As an added incentive to leave, Phillips had granted Kerby a three-year consultancy for $126,000, with no assignments. After nearly five decades with the company, few staffers marked Kerby's exit with any emotion other than casual relief. As one indication of how Kerby was regarded, two months after he retired, Dow Jones senior vice president Don Macdonald, who had benefited greatly from living next door to Kerby in Short Hills, moved back to Rumson, another New Jersey suburb, fifty miles away.

With Kerby gone, Phillips was finally the company's sole leader. And his string of titles, longer than the Sultan of Brunei's, demonstrated that Dow Jones, once small and entrepreneurial, had become a full-fledged member of corporate America overnight. His titles—chairman of the board, chief executive officer, president, and publisher of the *Wall Street Journal*—also indicated that Phillips could no longer function as a mere supereditor. Ideally, he would operate as a true general executive, concerned with quarterly earnings, Wall Street analysts, the Securities and Exchange Commission, where the next printing plant should be located, and most important, how to reduce Dow Jones's reliance on the *Wall Street Journal*. That year, 1977, the *Journal* had contributed 84 percent of Dow Jones's revenue and 93 percent of its profits. But with no business experience, Phillips was unprepared for these challenges, a fact his ego, titles, and *Journal* profits prevented him from acknowledging.

Despite his shy and awkward appearance, Phillips possessed an ego inflated far beyond normal size by years of being deferred to as the publisher of the *Wall Street Journal*. As a result, Phillips believed that it was he, not the economic principle of supply and demand, that had produced the *Journal*'s burgeoning profits. The truth, however, was that the postwar corporatization of America created a need for more and more daily business news, and the *Wall Street Journal* was the nation's only source for it. But Phillips would never admit this fact, nor would the people at Dow Jones.

The sixteen-member Dow Jones board of directors, for example, seemed downright fawning. William McChesney Martin, Jr., the distinguished former chairman of the Federal Reserve Board and Dow Jones director, once admitted to *Dun's Review*, "Who am I to tell Warren Phillips, publisher of the *Wall Street Journal*, how to run the *Journal!*"

Besides William McChesney Martin, other outside directors like James Riordan, senior vice president for Mobil, and J. Paul Austin, chairman of Coca-Cola, were happy to sit back, enjoy their association with a prestigious publication, and ask, "If the toy is not broken, why fix it?"

The owners of Dow Jones, the Bancroft family, were even more loath to interfere. In 1974, the Bancroft family's Dow Jones stock was worth $350 million; in 1978, it had swelled to $2.2 billion. Their dividend income averaged $36 million a year in those four years.

But Phillips's shortcomings were never so evident as when he attempted to reduce Dow Jones's dangerous dependence on the *Journal*. On the surface, the solution seemed simple enough: Broaden Dow Jones's revenue base by launching new publications and effecting acquisitions.

But creating a new publications requires institutional verve, which, for Dow Jones, had been bled dry by the recent death of the *National Observer*. The fear of failure was so great that creating another newspaper or publication on any worthwhile scale was not an option.

The acquisition of other companies, then, was the only diversification alternative open to Phillips. Since 1945, Dow Jones had made two acquisitions, the Ottaway Community Newspapers in 1970 and the Richard D. Irwin Textbook Publishing Company five years later. Both deals illustrated Kerby and Phillips's lack of judgment in determining which companies to acquire, at what price, and how to manage them once they were acquired.

Kerby acquired Ottaway Newspapers, for example, during a round of golf at his Pocono Mountain retreat.[1] On this particular day, while waiting to tee off, Kerby lamented to his friend, Jim Ottaway, how difficult it was to find suitable companies for Dow Jones to acquire, a remark prompted by Kerby's recent rejection of Gannett Newspapers because it lacked Dow Jones's "blue chip quality."

By the fourth tee, Ottaway had suggested Kerby might want to look at his own company, Ottaway Community Newspapers, a chain of thirteen small-town publications, mostly weeklies, whose average circulation was 14,000. By the ninth tee, Kerby and Ottaway had struck a deal. Dow Jones would pay the Ottaways $36 million in Dow Jones stock for the company, a price equivalent to twenty-four times earnings, exactly twice the going rate in 1977. Jim Ottaway also secured from Kerby the assurance he would continue to operate the newspapers autonomously, as if there were no Dow Jones. Yet he and a family member would always be represented on the Dow Jones board to protect their holdings.

Since the company's earnings were only $1.7 million, tiny in comparison to Dow Jones's, the acquisition of Ottaway did little to lessen Dow Jones's dependence on the *Journal*. Yet the Ottaways became one of the most powerful families in the newspaper industry. Today the Ottaway family owns 5.1 million shares of Dow Jones stock worth $150 million, which, next to Clarence Barron's descendants, makes it the second largest Dow Jones shareholder.

Dow Jones's next acquisition—the purchase of the Richard D. Irwin Company, college textbook publishers—took ten years to complete. In 1965, Phillips approached Irwin, and a deal soon appeared imminent. But problems developed over the right purchase price that took a decade to resolve. Finally, in 1975, the deal went through. But again, like the Ottaway acquisition, Irwin's revenues were so small—$24 million—it made no difference to Dow Jones. Like Kerby before him, Phillips had trouble thinking on a large scale. In 1988, after thirteen years of disappointment, Phillips sold Richard D. Irwin back to its management, realizing a $142 million gain from the sale. Had Phillips put the equivalent of the Irwin original purchase price in 7 percent Treasury bills in 1977, the gain would have been $212 million by 1988.

While Kerby and Phillips were buying Ottaway and Richard D. Irwin and closing down the *National Observer*, William Dunn, head of Dow Jones's technology, had begun to create several projects which, in theory, appeared exciting. In reality, though, they were a long way from being actualized. Dunn, an economist by education, had become interested in technology when he took over the *Journal's* printing and distribution department in the early seventies. The only newspaper to do so, the *Journal* used satellite technology to print the paper in eighteen plants throughout the country simultaneously.

Partial to jeans, the Dow Jones helicopter, and the word "fuck," Dunn's greatest skill consisted of trumpeting the inventions of subordinates to the press, newspaper industry groups, and, most of all, Phillips and the Dow Jones board of directors. Sometimes Dunn even remembered the inventors' names.

Dunn did suggest one proposition to Phillips in the mid seventies which, had it been accepted, would have forever changed Dow Jones. In 1975, two young Californians came to Dunn in search of funds to manufacture and distribute a new, easier-to-use personal computer. But Phillips declined the opportunity believing, according to Dunn, "that friends of Warren's at IBM told him the future of computers lies with mainframes, not with those little ones you stick on your desk."[2] Steven Jobs and Robert Wojniak, cofounders of Apple Computers, had to look elsewhere for their financing.

Because Phillips had trouble acknowledging his mistakes, he always repeated them. Nothing demonstrates this observation more convincingly than Dow Jones's acquisition of *Book Digest* magazine in 1978 for $10.1 million.

One January day in 1978, Warren Phillips accepted Dr. Frank Stanton's invitation to have lunch at the River Club. Stanton was the chairman of the American Red Cross, a position he assumed after retiring from CBS, where he had been president and William Paley's right-hand man for thirty-five years. The invitation signaled a thrilling moment for Phillips.

The River Club is considerably tonier than the University Club, to which Phillips belonged at the time. Located on East 52 Street, hard by the East River, the River Club is a social, residential, and sporting enclave of America's elite. Virtually every member is a diplomatic or corporate world figure. Henry and Nancy Kissinger eat in the club's dining room at least three times a week; Gene Scott, former Davis Cup player, plays tennis in the club's clay court, while John Prescott Bush swims in the club's indoor swimming pool.

Frank Stanton was the ideal member. Successful and close-mouthed, he was not about to reveal to *Vanity Fair* what prominent member had been suspended for nonpayment of dues. Stanton, a septuagenarian, displayed certain vanities unusual for any age. He blow-dried his hair in an era when that practice had not yet come into vogue; he also sported the widest French cuffs on any shirtsleeve in the city of New York. They looked like crisp, white mortarboard—the perfect foil for the blue-and-gold presidential cuff links that Stanton wore everywhere.

Though Stanton had received a Ph.D. from Ohio State in clinical psychology and was a licensed therapist in the state of New York, it was difficult imagining him conducting one-on-one therapy with a patient. He was not garrulous, and when he did talk, words tumbled out of his mouth in angry little bursts. Most of the time, he stared at people icily, which made all but the most confident feel diminished. But the day Stanton hosted Phillips for lunch, he was positively ebullient. He had something to sell: *Book Digest* magazine.

In 1973, Stanton retired involuntarily from CBS after William Paley, CBS's founder, recruited Arthur Taylor, an outsider, to be CBS's next CEO. Shattered, Stanton understood he would not realize the ambition that had enabled him to endure Paley all those years. He did what so many other spurned executives do. He fell under the spell of the first person who saved his ego, John Veronis, cofounder of *Book Digest* magazine.

Without quite realizing he was doing it, Frank Stanton joined other celebrity investors, for example, the late Steve Ross of Time

Warner, and invested $2 million in Veronis's *Book Digest*, a new magazine that excerpted the latest quality fiction and nonfiction for people who lacked the time to read most books through. *Book Digest*, Veronis often said to prospective investors and advertisers, was the upscale *Reader's Digest*, the country's most successful magazine at the time, with a circulation nearing 20 million. As magazine concepts go, *Book Digest*'s was quite ingenious. *Book Digest* fulfilled a need among people who would rather do anything but read a book.

Several years after Stanton's investment, *Book Digest*'s circulation leaped to over one million, a most unusual level for a magazine with an upscale audience. Also, *Book Digest*'s advertising sales department, headed by John Veronis's brother, Peter, sold a number of national advertisers who normally would have shunned such a specialized magazine.

After learning about these feats, Phillips accepted Stanton's invitation to meet Veronis for further talks. Having been raised in the sheltered world of Dow Jones and the *Journal*, Phillips was unprepared for John Veronis, a charismatic, hypnotic man. Within minutes of their introduction, Veronis had swept Stanton aside and sold Phillips the entire magazine, not just Stanton's portion, for $10.1 million.

The team Phillips assembled to study the deal—Don Macdonald for advertising, Ken Burenga for circulation, and Fred Harris for finance—conducted a cursory examination of *Book Digest*, knowing full well that in Phillips's mind the acquisition was already a fait accompli. Only one man, Joe Perrone, the person most responsible for the *Journal*'s circulation climb from 1.43 million in 1973 to 1.91 million in 1977, advised against the acquisition. Perrone's premonition was confirmed when Burenga informed him of the results of an audit of *Book Digest*'s circulation file.

According to Perrone, "Kenny could only come up with 700,000 paid customers, not the million Veronis said he had. But Kenny never blew the whistle. He didn't want to rain on Warren's parade."[3]

With great fanfare, Dow Jones announced its acquisition of *Book Digest* magazine in August 1978. In the heralding press release, Phillips innocently revealed that Burenga had never informed him of the circulation shortfall. Phillips was quoted as saying, "*Book Digest* is filling a growing need. The magazine's appeal was underlined when it passed the one million mark in circulation earlier this year. Only three other magazines founded since 1970 have achieved this popular acceptance."[4]

Shortly after the sale, Phillips confirmed his infatuation with John Veronis by naming him a Dow Jones vice president. Thereafter, Phillips viewed Veronis as the one manager at Dow Jones with the entrepreneurial flair and experience necessary to start new products and businesses.

Charming, bright, witty, and persuasive, John Veronis was, and still is, a force in the world of commerce. Anyone could readily see why he captivated the likes of Frank Stanton and Warren Phillips, two men sheltered from entrepreneurs like Veronis by CBS and Dow Jones's corporate bureaucracies.

The president of Curtis Publishing before he was forty, Veronis established a company with the curious name Communications/ Research/Machinery in 1967, which, in turn, founded *Psychology Today*, a magazine that discovered an instant readership in the "Me Too" generation of the late sixties. Leveraging the success of *Psychology Today* enabled Veronis to acquire the venerable *Saturday Review*, which he attempted to revitalize by splitting it into four separate magazines. His partners in these ventures included his saturnine brother, Peter, and Martin Gross, an editor of boundless, and at times uncontrollable, energy and confidence.

During John Veronis's first year with Dow Jones, he met with Phillips frequently to map out bold, imaginative, and diversified strategies for the future. Both Veronis and Phillips acted as if it were a foregone conclusion that *Book Digest* would be a howling success. Twice during the first year, Veronis interrupted his strategic planning long enough to ask Phillips for $1.3 million, each time to finance a direct-mail solicitation campaign for *Book Digest*. Both requests were granted without question, though Fred Harris, Dow Jones's chief financial officer, began to wonder why it cost so much to maintain the magazine's one million circulation level.

But rather than confront Veronis directly and run the risk of offending Phillips, Harris placed one of his trusted lieutenants in *Book Digest*; Leonard Dougherty became vice president of finance, replacing a Veronis appointee, Jack Reinhardt. A seemingly affable Irishman, Dougherty quickly became a friend of Veronis's. Veronis who never realized that at the end of each day Dougherty would compile a written report of that day's activities to send to Harris.[5] Soon Dougherty had the best of both worlds: Veronis trusted him, as did Harris. Neither man ever realized the compromises Dougherty effected to gain the complete trust of both camps.

At first, the money spent to finance *Book Digest's* direct-mail campaigns baffled Dougherty. He was unaccustomed to funding promotions, such as sweepstakes contests for vacation trips to China, to induce prospective subscribers. Dougherty belonged to the *Journal* school of circulation marketing and promotion best characterized by Don Macdonald: "You deliver a stack of *Journals* to a newsstand, come back twenty minutes later, and they're all gone."

As 1978 came to a close, the differences between *Book Digest's* actual performance and the optimistic projections Veronis had prepared were alarming. By year's end, responding to Harris's warnings, Phillips had begun to cool toward Veronis. Possibly because of his self-confidence, Veronis never sensed the change. By the spring of 1979, it had become apparent that something drastic had to be done with "the *Book Digest* situation." Even John Veronis began to wonder out loud, "Why doesn't Warren return my calls?"

Book Digest's problem was pretty apparent: It required massive amounts of money to fund the direct-mail campaigns necessary to build the magazine's circulation level to one million copies. In essence, *Book Digest* was buying—and some believed, bribing—new subscribers, an accepted practice in the competitive world of consumer magazines. If Dow Jones refused to invest money for direct mail, *Book Digest's* volume of new subscriptions would fall, reducing its circulation level commensurately. Should this happen, then *Book Digest* would be in default of its "rate base" guarantee, the promise made to advertisers that each issue of the magazine would be distributed to a million subscribers and newsstand buyers. Should this occur, then a far more serious problem would develop: Madison Avenue would lose faith in *Book Digest*, and advertisers would abandon the publication in droves.

Like most consumer-magazine publishers at the time, Veronis willingly lost money acquiring and maintaining *Book Digest's* circulation. The expanded circulation was expected to generate enough advertising revenue to make up for the loss and post an overall profit. Veronis also charged minimal amounts for *Book Digest* subscriptions, $8 for twelve issues, to attract as many people as possible.

This concept pervaded the world of consumer magazines because the competition for the ever-dwindling reading universe was so fierce. But it had no currency with the Dow Jones folks who expected readers to pay a substantial price for a *Journal* subscription or a single copy off the newsstand. The *Journal* never had to regard its circulation as a loss leader to attract advertisers. In fact, the notion of offering promotional inducements and discounts to prospective subscribers—and advertisers, for that matter—was anathema to *Journal* people.

This difference in attitude between the *Journal* and the more competitive world of consumer magazines created a huge obstacle for the inexperienced Warren Phillips. Neither he nor his senior editors-turned-executive could comprehend the environment within which *Book Digest* operated.

This attitudinal difference, and Veronis's final decline, became apparent in October 1979 when an ashen Robert Potter, Dow Jones's patrician counsel, informed Phillips that the state of California was suing Dow Jones for $100 million. *Book Digest* had conducted a sweepstakes contest for potential California subscribers, and the state's Department of Consumer Affairs had deemed it illegal.

All chances of a meaningful career for John Veronis at Dow Jones evaporated as a legion of aides and lawyers scrambled to calm Phillips's wrath. What enraged Phillips the most was that, several weeks before, the *Journal* had run a column castigating Ralph Nader for using the exact same type of sweepstakes offer to raise funds for one of his organizations.

When informed of the situation, Veronis responded with a characteristic shrug. "Some politician in California is just trying to make a name for himself."

Within two weeks, Robert Sack, Potter's capable assistant, had negotiated a consent decree with California providing that *Book Digest* promise never to mail to the state again.

A week later, Veronis was fired, though he never admitted it, just as he never admitted there was a problem with *Book Digest*. Veronis went on to become a hugely successful media investment banker. In a typical deal, his firm, Veronis & Suhler, arranged the $3 billion sale of *TV Guide* to Rupert Murdoch.

As a result of the consent decree, Dow Jones quite properly insisted that *Book Digest* should completely cease mailing the offensive direct mail. This commitment presented *Book Digest* with yet another problem. Though *Book Digest's* sweepstakes offer may have been illegal, it did induce record volumes of people to subscribe—four to five times more than other, more proper offers. But now, faced with the same need to add ever more new subscribers, *Book Digest* had been deprived of its most effective tool to acquire them.

With John Veronis gone, Phillips tapped Don Macdonald in June 1979 to lead *Book Digest* out of these straits. Macdonald was not pleased with the *Book Digest* challenge. "I hate to retire like this," Macdonald lamented. "I guess I'm in Phillips's shithouse."

Macdonald, at best, was a peculiar choice for the job. *Book Digest* needed someone steeped in consumer magazine circulation marketing. The only prior circulation experience Macdonald had had— running the *Journal*'s circulation department in the early seventies— had ended badly.[6] The *Book Digest* job also required an executive with an appreciation of good literature who possessed enough sensitivity and restraint to supervise the magazine's bright but explosive editor, Martin Gross. Besides having never supervised an editor of any temperament before, Macdonald openly boasted that he never read books. This remark would be followed by one of his frequent non sequiturs: His favorite author was Louis L'Amour.

In August 1979, Macdonald assembled *Book Digest*'s remaining management team in the bar of the University Club, which was conveniently located several blocks south of *Book Digest*'s rather expensive address at Fifth Avenue and 57th Street.[7] Leonard Dougherty, Peter Veronis, John's older brother, who was still with the magazine, and Martin Gross were joined by two other newly appointed department heads recruited from the *Wall Street Journal*. Like Macdonald and Dougherty, they, too, lacked consumer-magazine experience.

Five men sat around a table staring at their diet Cokes, waiting for Macdonald to begin the meeting. What followed was a garbled message due, in no small part, to Macdonald's habit of speaking in streams of consciousness. His purpose, no doubt, was to motivate the staff. But the only memorable or intelligible thing he said was: "From now on, I'm the chairman of *Book Digest*. But any one of you could be president in six months."

Each of the five men, believing he would make the best president, started running for the post that very moment. Martin Gross, Peter Veronis, and Leonard Dougherty were especially aggressive in their campaigning, understandably, having stood in John Veronis's shadow the longest.

Macdonald then excused Gross and Veronis and proceeded to belittle John Veronis with a rare viciousness. "That Veronis is a crook, a fuck," Macdonald fairly screamed in the grill of the sedate University Club, where John Veronis was also a member. "That fuck sold us an empty bag, and now I've got to clean it up."

But rather than sit in John Veronis's corner office on Fifth Avenue and manage *Book Digest* day by day, thereby harnessing the fiery competition he had stirred up, Macdonald remained at Dow Jones corporate headquarters at 22 Cortlandt Street. In his absence, each of the five men did whatever he pleased, rarely conferring, much less coordinating, with one another.

The next time any of the five heard from Macdonald was three weeks later. Upon returning from Hong Kong, Macdonald telephoned one of the department heads and proceeded to blame him in profane and abusive terms for a litany of sins perpetrated by the other four.

Already disenchanted, the general manager screamed back into the telephone: "Had you not created this chaos yourself by saying any one of us could be president, these things might not have happened."

The offices of *Book Digest* became the scene of many such confrontations, but the worst always occurred between the magazine's editor, Martin Gross, and Macdonald.

Extremely bright and hyperactive, Martin Gross would arrive at work no later than noon each day, and the entire operation had to stop as he went from office to office offering up whatever was on his mind at the moment. On any given day, a listener could be subjected to Gross's lecture on Alexis de Tocqueville's theory on political democracy or how best to control the flow of traffic on Fifth Avenue during Christmas rush hours.

Sometimes, perhaps unwittingly, Gross wielded his loquacity like a weapon. Brighter than virtually everyone else around him, a fact he never failed to bring up, Gross could launch into a monologue that left a listener exhausted, bewildered, and searching for any means of escape.

A former *Book Digest* associate said this of Martin Gross: "Once Martin came into your office and uttered the frightening 'Got a minute?' it was best to sit back, resign yourself to listening for at least the next twenty minutes, and smile and nod your head periodically throughout his remarks. It was not necessary, however, to listen. In fact, if you did, if you actually tried to follow what he was saying, this inevitably led to trouble. His mind just worked three times faster than yours and you were defeated before you began." Undaunted by any man or institution, except John Veronis, Gross thought he should run *Book Digest* once Veronis was unseated. But despite his eccentricities, Gross was an especially shrewd and intelligent editor who perhaps fancied himself a bit too much like Harold Ross, the

legendary editor of the *New Yorker.* Regardless, Gross was the one
who had devised *Book Digest's* rather ingenius concept, which sprang
from an earlier creation of his, *Intellectual Digest.*

One memorable morning, on one of Macdonald's rare visits to
Book Digest, Macdonald was sitting in a department head's office
about to leave for lunch at the University Club when Gross arrived for
work.[8] At that time, Gross, who assumed he would be named
president of *Book Digest* imminently, wanted to get to know his new
boss better. Smartly attired in a gray flannel suit, Martin, coffee and
bagel in hand, walked right into the office as if it were his own and
uttered the frightening "Got a minute?"

Macdonald, momentarily stunned by Gross's impertinence, asked
rather harshly: "Are you just getting to work, Gross?"

Martin, who had a habit of ignoring any remark that did not fit into
his notion of how a conversation should go, answered, "So, Don, what
kind of advertising campaign are you going to do for the magazine?"

Accustomed to being fawned over, a vivid red flush swept over
Macdonald's face. That would have been an obvious danger signal to
anyone else, but Martin Gross was accustomed to asking rhetorical
questions, never expecting, or wanting, a reply. Consequently, Gross
sailed right into his next thought without noticing Macdonald's florid
complexion.

"I, of course, have some thoughts on the matter. You see, Don,
Book Digest, as I conceived it..."

For another three minutes, Gross reviewed the brilliance of his
magazine and why it was necessary for the advertising to be equally
brilliant. Not surprisingly, Gross then declared, "I, and no one else,
should create the advertising."

This is when Macdonald exploded.

"Wait a fuckin' moment!" he roared, cigarette smoke tumbling out
of his mouth and nose, waving his huge hand and equally huge Rolex
like a mace.

Even Gross was startled and became quiet for a moment.

"I'm a fuckin' media genius, and if any advertising is goin' to be
done around here, I'm the one who's goin' to do it," Macdonald
bellowed.

"Really!" Gross screamed. "Then what are you going to do?"

Both men were now on their feet, staring menacingly at one
another. Gross came up to Macdonald's chest.

For a split second, Macdonald searched the ceiling for an answer to
Gross's taunt.

"I've got it! I've got it!" Macdonald suddenly cried.

Looking down at Gross, Macdonald held his two hands in the air in a framing gesture, coddling a precious thought.

"What? What is it?" Gross screamed.

"It's what we call in the business a testimonial ad," Macdonald explained enthusiastically. "*Book Digest* needs a series of ads from intellectuals talkin' about how great the magazine is, how it satisfies their curiosity ... all that sort of crap."

"Brilliant, Don, brilliant!" Gross yelled sarcastically. "Who are you thinking of?"

Again Macdonald looked to the ceiling. And again he exploded as an epiphany bubbled up from his depths.

"Einstein! What about that guy Einstein? Is he still alive?" Macdonald asked.

Book Digest did not see Macdonald for another month, until his secretary called and summoned the four operating heads to a meeting in the Dow Jones boardroom for the following Monday. Gross was purposely excluded because, as Macdonald later explained, "he would talk too much."

On the appointed day, the four *Book Digest* people walked into a convivial gathering already in session. Representing Dow Jones were Warren Phillips, Don Macdonald, Ray Shaw, executive vice president, and Peter Kann, then Phillips's special assistant. Also present were Frank Stanton, who was still a member of *Book Digest*'s board of directors, and three men from *Reader's Digest*, who introduced themselves in military fashion by smartly giving their full names and precise titles: "John O'Hara, CEO," "Richard McLoughlin, vice chairman," and "Ron Cole, vice president of circulation."

Macdonald then explained to the *Book Digest* contingent that Dow Jones and *Reader's Digest* had just minutes before entered into a historic joint venture whereby both "publishing houses would share certain strengths with one another. In exchange for Dow Jones's minority interest in *South China Morning Post*, *Reader's Digest* would take over the circulation marketing of *Book Digest*. Also, both companies would purchase together a data-base company known as the Source.

There was an awkward silence as the *Book Digest* contingent tried to grasp this radical news. Jim Rigier, recruited by Macdonald just two months before to head *Book Digest*'s circulation, looked particularly stunned, realizing the move would put him out of a job.

On the surface, the venture appeared a stroke of genius. *Reader's*

Digest could become a part of the exploding Far East market without investing a dime. And *Book Digest* could avail itself of the best circulation/marketing minds in the business, Macdonald explained. Self-satisfaction permeated the room. Even Stanton seemed pleased with himself.

After waiting for Macdonald to conclude his remarks, Jim Rigier pointedly asked: "Could you give us an example of how *Reader's Digest* might help us?"

There was a moment of awkward shuffling as it became apparent no one from Dow Jones had thought to ask this question before. Stanton looked at the table, apparently absorbed in the pad he had been writing on for the last fifteen minutes.

Finally, John O'Hara, chairman of *Reader's Digest* and a great bear of a man, smiled disingenuously and said, "Let me take a stab at that."

Both McLoughlin and Cole shifted uneasily.

"We're going to position *Book Digest* like one of our new products, a condensed version of the Bible," said O'Hara enthusiastically.

No one but the *Book Digest* people seemed the least bit shocked that the Bible was being abbreviated. Nor did anyone question whether there was a need for such a product.

"We're going to search our data base ... the most extensive in the world, I might add ... and mail to all those people who have bought a religious book in the last five years," O'Hara continued, obviously pleased with the *Reader's Digest's* vaunted system for such things.

Smiling appreciatively now, *Book Digest's* circulation director then asked: "And could you tell us a little about the type of direct-mail package you will be mailing for *Book Digest*?"

McLoughlin interrupted and said protectively, "Maybe Ron should answer that, John."

Relieved, O'Hara nodded his head.

Ron Cole, the *Reader's Digest* circulation director, who looked like an acolyte in the Mormon church, did not miss a beat. "A sweepstakes package, of course," said Cole. Phillips's and Macdonald's heads snapped.

"Sweepstakes?" Macdonald asked incredulously.

Macdonald then explained that Dow Jones, having just been cited by the state of California for a sweepstakes package, had vowed never to use that promotional device again. Now eloquent, Macdonald used such phrases as "the need to protect our integrity and our editorial reputation," implying, of course, that *Reader's Digest*, being a lowbrow publication, never concerned itself with such issues.

The fiery McLoughlin, the *Reader's Digest* vice chairman, took umbrage at Macdonald's inference, and the meeting quickly deteriorated. Jim Rigier was the only person whose spirits actually improved. As a face-saving gesture, Phillips suggested to O'Hara that another meeting be called in several weeks to discuss the matter further. A good ten minutes passed while everyone sought to agree on a date. During this discussion, Stanton passed around the sheet which had required so much of his attention throughout the meeting.

Using a Mont Blanc pen, Stanton had painstakenly drawn a calendar for the next two months; he had then proceeded to fill in each day with a circle. Some circles were blank, others only half shaded, while still others were completely black. Off on the lower right-hand side, he had scrawled: "Key: when a circle's lower half is shaded, it means my morning is filled; upper half shaded means my afternoon is filled; the entire circle shaded means my whole day is filled, and blank circle means my whole day is free."

In the months to follow, Dow Jones and *Reader's Digest* proceeded with their joint venture. Rigier did lose his job, but only after Macdonald discovered he had been floating his résumé around town. *Reader's Digest* installed its own man, Roger Miller, as *Book Digest's* circulation director. After four months, during which time Miller showed up for work a total of six days, he, too, was fired.[9]

A bigger source of friction between the *Reader's Digest* and Dow Jones was the direct-mail package used to solicit the all-important new subscribers. *Reader's Digest* finally persuaded Macdonald and Phillips to use "a sanitized sweepstakes package." Unfortunately, though Dow Jones in principle agreed to the compromise, the Dow Jones lawyers, Bob Potter and Bob Stack, rejected every specific *Reader's Digest* sweepstakes proposal. In the meanwhile, *Book Digest's* circulation began to dip perilously because of a lack of direct-mail solicitations.

Several months later, a discreetly worded press release announced the dissolution of the Dow Jones/*Reader's Digest*/*Book Digest* joint venture. Over the next year, Macdonald went to Hong Kong more frequently and stayed much longer than he had in the past. *Book Digest* began to falter badly. Martin Gross finally quit, and Macdonald replaced him with Raymond Sokolov, an old friend of Peter Kann's from the *Harvard Crimson*.

One of Sokolov's first acts was to commission the magazine's art director, Carolyn Bowers, to redesign *Book Digest* completely. Sokolov then improved the magazine's editorial contents by bringing in such authors as Tom Wolfe, John Irving, David Halberstam, John Steinbeck, and John Updike.

But Sokolov's improvements were for naught because *Book Digest* still suffered from hemorrhaging circulation. Because of the legal restrictions imposed by Dow Jones, more and more money was needed to harvest fewer and fewer subscriptions.

Finally, in a move that many industry experts found curious, Macdonald reduced *Book Digest*'s circulation from one million to 400,000. The rationale, which Madison Avenue never understood, much less bought, was that *Book Digest*'s remaining audience was more selective and thus more responsive to advertisers. Macdonald, of course, was only trying to eliminate those costly mailings. But his cover story was essentially correct. By reducing the circulation 60 percent, Macdonald eliminated most of the people who had subscribed to *Book Digest* not to read it but to participate in the $100,000 sweepstakes. "*Book Digest* had one million gamblers, not readers," Joe Perrone used to joke.

Several months later, another item in the *Wall Street Journal* alarmed the staff. The board of directors wrote down $9.2 million of the original $10.1 million purchase price for *Book Digest*. It was Perrone again who explained this baffling move. "Originally, Warren paid Veronis and Stanton $7 million too much for *Book Digest*. Now he was saying that in the eighteen months Macdonald took over from Veronis, he had run the magazine into the ground to the tune of another $2.2 million."

On March 24, 1982, the *Wall Street Journal* reported: "Dow Jones & Co. is exploring the possible sale of *Book Digest* magazine which it acquired in 1978 for $10.1 million."

On April 29, 1982, another *Journal* article reported:"Dow Jones & Co. will cease publication of *Book Digest* magazine because of inability to find a buyer of the publication; the magazine employed 38 people."

Don Macdonald, who had recently been named vice chairman and president of Dow Jones's international and magazine divisions, was in Hong Kong on the day of the announcement.

Book Digest represented a classic case of the blind leading the blind. Warren Phillips allowed Frank Stanton and John Veronis to hoodwink him into buying *Book Digest* for $10 million, at least $7 million more than it was worth. Then, at the first sign of trouble, Phillips turned to Macdonald for help. When Macdonald failed, Phillips turned to the *Reader's Digest* for help. When *Reader's Digest* failed, Phillips gave up and closed the publication down.

High Tech and a Rodeo
for Suits

A *Book Digest* employee once remarked, "Being acquired by Dow Jones is like becoming a stepchild. I feel barely tolerated."

Regardless of the validity of the comparison, the remark expressed the way many people, consciously or otherwise, view their place of work, namely, as a substitute family, a venue where people relate to fellow employees, or acquired companies, in the same way they related to their families as children. Superiors become fathers, subordinates become sons and daughters, and peers become siblings—all in an unconscious replay of the search for recognition, love, and assurance.

There may be little truth in this metaphor, but if there is, Dow Jones has spawned many colorful and interesting family leaders down through the years, all male, reflecting the bias of business. Certainly Clarence Barron was the quintessential patriarch, a Ulysses in the world of commerce who provided for his hearth through fearless adventure. Then there was Barney Kilgore, the ideal father, the sensitive redeemer who saved his family from certain ruin without exacting worship in return. Bill Kerby was more the classic bachelor uncle, not especially able or outstanding, yet respected because of age and tenure. Then there was Warren Phillips, the scrawny, inner-city cousin who came to visit one summer and never left, who gained the head of the table through obedience and good study habits rather than inspiration or accomplishment.

All these men became ultimate father figures by demonstrating a talent or an interest in journalism, a subject so consuming at Dow Jones as to separate, often cruelly, the favored sons and daughters from the tolerated stepchildren. At Dow Jones, to be a journalist is to be loved; to be a salesperson or a lawyer is be endured.

With Warren Phillips, the obsession for journalism was even more pronounced because he felt so uncertain about his own talents, an insecurity he tried to bolster vicariously by fathering Kann, the ultimate journalist, the Pulitzer. That's why Dow Jones sales or production people always felt lonely around Phillips. They had nothing to offer him, and, as a result, Phillips turned his back on them to favor Kann and, to a lesser degree, Norman Pearlstine and editorial-page editor Robert Bartley. Everyone else was a stepchild, someone to do the chores.

In 1979, Phillips announced that Peter Kann, founding editor and publisher of the *Asian Wall Street Journal*, would be returning to New York to serve as his special assistant. No doubt it was Phillips's special feeling for Kann that caused him to secure for Kann a Dow Jones $100,000 loan at 2 percent interest so that Peter and his wife, Francie, could buy a home in Princeton, New Jersey.

It was a most unusual gesture for the man who always operated by the book, especially when no other employee could merit such an arrangement. Executive editor Fred Taylor described the loan as "shockingly bad judgment. Of course, many of us lined up for the same thing, to find the till was only open to Kann."[1]

The company's chairman had never had a special assistant before. It was an untimely move, some staffers thought, because the *Asian Wall Street Journal*, less than three years old, had just begun to solve its many difficulties.

Still other staffers were baffled by Peter's appointment.

"I didn't know what the hell it meant," Fred Taylor admitted. Naively, the paper's executive editor approached Phillips to suggest that Peter become the *Journal's* answer to Charles Kuralt and travel around the country writing front-page leaders on whatever struck his fancy. "Warren looked at me like I was crazy," Taylor said. "Now I see why. A year later, Peter became my boss."[2]

But William L. Dunn, head of Dow Jones's Information Group, a division comprising various product lines that published business news electronically, sensed that Phillips might be previewing the choice of his successor. To combat this eventuality, Dunn reasoned that if he could launch a new publication that would be more successful than Kann's *Asian Wall Street Journal*, he would be the first noneditor to reach the top at Dow Jones.

A charismatic Dow Jones executive, Dunn revealed his vaulting ambition at a July 1979 meeting at which he opened up "preliminary discussions" for launching a European *Wall Street Journal*.[3] The meeting was held at Dow Jones's complex in South Brunswick, New Jersey, ten miles north of Princeton on Route 9. The installation was built in the mid-sixties for the convenience of Barney Kilgore, a nearby Princeton resident.

On this particular sunny morning, ten men sat around a blond oak table, listening to Bill Dunn begin the meeting with his idiosyncratic rhetoric. Looking like a fit high school soccer coach, Dunn sat at the front of the table, in a yellow short-sleeved shirt, western string tie, and jeans.

"Thanks for coming down, you New York ad guys," Dunn said as he nodded in the direction of two *Journal* ad sales executives. "It's always nice to have you city slickers visit us here," he added with a wry smile.

One of the admen, Victor Webb, head of Dow Jones's International Sales, grinned and nodded back. But Lee Heffner, the *Journal's* advertising sales director, kept his eyes down.

Just then the double doors to the conference room burst open, and in strode Senior Vice President Don Macdonald, hand in trousers, smoking as usual. From the tension that seeped into the room, it was obvious Macdonald and Dunn had little use for one another. Reluctant to acknowledge Macdonald's late entrance, Dunn continued matter-of-factly. "There has been a global change in the way people receive information. People understand MTV [Music Television], but they don't read newspapers. Everything is changing except newspapers. TV is failing; newspapers are failing. George Gilder [a leading economist] said it best when he said: 'I'm continually amazed at man's inability to understand the fundamental change brought on by siliconization which has forever disturbed basic economic transactions.'"

Bill Dunn was Dow Jones's evangelist, and he spoke in corporate tongues. Often his listeners had no idea what he was saying, but they were still inspired by a 220-volt delivery fueled by anger.

Charles Dow. Together with Edward Jones and Charles Bergstresser, Dow founded the *Wall Street Journal*, the Dow Jones ticker, and devised the Dow Jones averages. After quarreling with his partners, Dow sold the *Journal* to Clarence Barron's wife in 1902.

Clarence Barron, publisher of the *Wall Street Journal*, 1912-1928. After becoming Boston's most successful financial journalist, Barron then moved to New York and rescued the *Wall Street Journal* from his wife and son-in-law. A man of gargantuan appetites and confidence, Barron overcame his "shanty Irish" background to become the crony of kings, presidents, and tycoons. His descendants still control the company.

Bernard Kilgore, Dow Jones president, 1946-1966. Despite being the *Journal*'s patron saint, Kilgore made two huge mistakes in his otherwise superb career, creating the *National Observer* and choosing William Kerby as his successor.

Vermont Connecticut Royster, *Journal* editorial page editor, 1953-1971. Winner of two Pulitzers, Royster was the *Journal*'s most graceful and courageous commentator. A Southerner, he was the first to endorse the *Brown v. Board of Education* decision.

Warren Phillips, Dow Jones chief executive officer, 1976-1991. Remote and shy, Phillips presided over the *Journal* during its most prosperous years. But in the end, his flaws in selecting people and companies to acquire caught up with him.

I. Norman Pearlstine, former *Journal* executive editor, 1983-1992. A gifted reporter, once he became editor Pearlstine "sullied the *Journal*'s reputation, that great halo," by maintaining completely inappropriate friendships for a journalist.

To the shame of many *Journal* reporters, *New York* magazine chronicled how Norman Pearlstine and his wife, Nancy Friday, were taken for a ride, literally and figuratively, by Donald Trump in his helicopter.

The floor of the New York Stock Exchange on Black Monday, October 19, 1987. Norman Pearlstine chose to remain in Paris to attend a party that evening with Nancy Friday instead of returning to supervise the *Journal*'s coverage of Wall Street's biggest news in fifty years. As a result, the *New York Times* reported the story far more comprehensively.

Peter Kann, present Dow Jones CEO. Once a Pulitzer Prize-winning Vietnam correspondent, Kann lacks the judgment to run Dow Jones, a $1.7 billion corporation. Kann allows, for example, his wife, Karen Elliott House, to run roughshod over the *Journal*'s staff.

Karen Elliott House, present Dow Jones vice president, international. For the past ten years, the *Journal* newsroom has asked: Did House win her vice presidency because of her talent or because of Peter Kann?

Journal columnist R. Foster Winans (left), with his gay partner, David Carpenter. In 1984, the financial world was shocked to read in a *Journal* front-page story that Winans had been selling his stock-touting column "Heard on the Street" in advance of publication. The story's editor, Norman Pearlstine, emphasized Winans's homosexuality so much that people forgot to ask why Winans, an inexperienced, $30,000-per-year reporter, was assigned the column in the first place.

James B. Stewart, former *Journal* Page One editor. Author of the acclaimed *Den of Thieves*, Stewart became a millionaire reporting on Michael Milken five years after the facts of the case.

Stephen Pizzo, former editor of California's
Russian River News (circulation 5,200). After the
Journal ignored his tips, Pizzo and two colleagues
wrote *Inside Job*, the book which eventually
exposed the savings and loan scandal two years
later. Famed *Journal* reporter Jonathan Kwitny
admitted that had Norman Pearlstine and others
listened to Pizzo, the *Journal* could have saved
the country a lot of money. (Courtesy Stephen P.
Pizzo)

Charles Keating, Jr. With the help of $50 million in junk bonds from
Michael Milken, Keating acquired Lincoln Savings of Irvine, California.
By 1986, Keating had become the industry's number-one felon,
unnoticed by the *Journal*'s Los Angeles bureau, where the newspaper's
S&L expert resided. Keating here arrives for a court appearance in Los
Angeles. He had been charged in a 42-count fraud indictment.

Ivan Boesky (second from left). A month after billionaire Boesky incriminated Michael Milken in November 1986, the *Journal* ran a largely complimentary story about Milken and his firm, Drexel Burnham. Here Boesky leaves a New York court after receiving a three-year prison sentence for masterminding the biggest insider trading scandal in Wall Street history.

Michael Milken (second from right). Milken became Wall Street's biggest crook of the century, undetected by the *Journal*. Then, after Milken was convicted, fined, and sentenced, the *Journal*'s editorial pages praised him. Here he leaves Federal Court in New York after agreeing to set aside $600 million of his assets in government accounts to guarantee payment if he is convicted of fraud and racketeering in the government's largest ever securities trial.

"Few people can see the future in the present chaos. But that has always been the case. When twelve-masted ships were toppling over in their bid to go faster, everyone ignored the steamship that was chugging up the Thames twice as fast. People simply refused to see it.

"The teeter-totter that separates the *Journal* and the Information Services Group is beginning to totter, and it will totter forever when we launch the European edition of the *Wall Street Journal*."

While Dunn paused for a breath, Macdonald took an angry drag on his cigarette, quelling an impulse to scream: "Shut the fuck up."

"We're goin' to surprise some people in this motherfuckin' company, I tell you that," Dunn continued, clenching his fist in the air. "We're goin' to launch a newspaper, not some piss-ass, piddling little shopper like they got over in Asia. We're goin' to do it right, do it big, if we're goin' to do it at all!"

Dunn was referring to the *Asian Wall Street Journal* and the size of its circulation, which, after three years, had only just reached 29,000.

Quietly, Carl Valenti, Dunn's lieutenant, leaned over and said, "Huh, Bill ... perhaps it's time we get to why we're all here."

Dunn grinned and said, "How can I ever fail with fuckin' Keemasawbees like Valenti here?" Accustomed to Dunn's bantering, Valenti chuckled.

"Let him go on," said Victor Webb, the bulky Brit who considered himself Macdonald's protégé. "I actually was inspired, as if we were all about to go off in battle together."

"What the fuck do you know about battle, Victor?" Dunn asked sharply. "I do not spend a lot of time on the eighth floor [Dow Jones's executive floor in New York] politicking for this job, Victor. I don't have a lot of internal buddies and I say 'fuck' a lot. But these things make me unworthy? Not this motherfucker. No, sir!" Webb tried to stammer out an apology.

"Just shut up, Victor," Macdonald snapped.

Attempting to reduce the tension, Lee Heffner, the former but still quintessential Time Incer, looked up and asked curtly, "How can we help, Bill?"

Dunn turned to face Heffner, grinned, and said, "Well, I want you to tell me how many ads you're goin' to sell for Europe."

There was no particular edge to the question, but it still caught Heffner off guard. Reddening, Heffner squared his pad with some imaginary line and adjusted his tie before replying. In the publishing business, advertising sales is a form of alchemy whose success depends on how much the buyer likes the seller. This determinant defies quantitative prediction, of course, which explains why Dunn's question ruffled Heffner so.

"Well, I can't put my name to any forecasts before knowing what the publication will be like," Heffner finally said. "Who's the target? What's the editorial? What's the circulation going to be? Subscription or newsstand?"

It was obvious that Dunn had never considered these questions. Then he said: "Well, Lee ... most people fall in the water. They are not balanced enough to step from the old to the new without getting their balls, or the female equivalent, wet."

The meeting ended when Victor Webb suggested that he and Lee Heffner confer in New York and then get back to Dunn with three years' worth of ad projections.

In October 1979, Dunn submitted a sixty-page proposal to Phillips entitled "Europe: The Next Beachhead." Dunn had no compunction posing as the proposal's author, though it had been a group effort. The proposal laid out how best to establish a European *Wall Street Journal*. Weeks passed without a response from Phillips. Once, when one of the proposal's coauthors asked Dunn what Phillips's reaction had been, Dunn replied, "Silence is the opposite of love."

Three months later, in December 1979, Dunn and his colleagues were elated after receiving a handwritten note from Peter Kann in his familiar black-felt-tip-pen scrawl. "Thanks for this. It's the most comprehensive plan I've ever seen. It will be invaluable. The best, Peter."

Still nothing happened.

Later when asked again about the status of the European proposal, Dunn had an enigmatic response: "Beware of princes from the Far East bearing gifts of praise."

Finally, four years later, long after Dunn had gone on to other things, Warren Phillips announced in November 1983 the birth of the *Journal*'s European edition as another "link in the *Wall Street Journal* becoming a global newspaper." In the same release, Phillips named Norman Pearlstine as the edition's editor and publisher, reporting to Peter Kann, the associate publisher of the *Wall Street Journal*. In launching the edition, Kann and Pearlstine did not follow a single suggestion contained in the Dunn proposal. In fact, Pearlstine did not know it existed.

By denying Dunn any involvement in Europe, Phillips once more sent a clear signal to the organization: Critical projects such as the launch of a *Journal* edition would only be entrusted to journalists. It was the same prejudice that had injured Charles Bergstresser, one of the founders of Dow Jones, in the 1890s and Joe Ackell, head of engineering, in the 1940s. At Dow Jones, no matter how great their contributions, technical people, like advertising people, are second-class citizens. But the enormousness of Dunn's contribution—harnessing satellite transmission technology to make the *Journal's* nationwide printing and distribution system state-of-the-art—was so great, so revolutionary, that Dunn thought he would be an exception to the rule.

William L. Dunn grew up on a farm seven miles outside of Waterloo, Iowa. His was a forlorn, isolated childhood.

"I was raised by an uneducated mother who became bewildered when my father died when I was five. As a result, I was very lonely,"[4] Dunn said.

When he was seven, his mother remarried a sixty-five-year-old man. "He did not want a young stepson around," admitted Dunn, with lots of hurt and anger still apparent.

Dunn survived his uncaring stepfather by immersing himself in books and acquiring recognition in school. An honors student in high school, he was awarded a full scholarship to Drake University in Des Moines, Iowa. When Dunn entered Drake, he was afraid he would flunk out in his first semester. Instead, he compiled a 3.9 grade point average in his freshman year and was elected to Phi Beta Kappa two years later.

Dunn graduated from Drake as an economics major and joined Dow Jones in 1961 as a production assistant in the Chicoppee, Massachusetts, printing plant. "I wanted to get as far away from Iowa as possible. Dow Jones was the first company that offered me a job, and western Massachusetts seemed as good as place as any," Dunn said.

Within two years, George Flynn, Dow Jones's vice president of operations, became Dunn's first and only mentor. Flynn, a quiet, self-effacing native of Elizabethtown, Illinois, admired Dunn for his fire. "Bill has this maniacal will to accomplish things," Flynn said of Dunn. "But if you cross him, he can go crazy."

Flynn had inherited the company's technology mantle from Buren McCormack, who had inherited it from Joe Ackell. All three men quietly devoted their careers to making sure the *Journal's* technology was the most advanced in the newspaper industry. Flynn was fond of saying, "It's not the *Journal*'s editorial that keeps the *Trib* or the *Times* from competing with us. It's our technology. It would be just too big an investment for them to catch up with us now."

Dunn's career opportunity came in 1975, when Flynn asked him to develop a quicker, less expensive method of transmitting the *Journal* master copy to Dow Jones's thirteen plants for printing and distribution. At the time, Dow Jones was using telephone lines, paying standard long-distance rates. It was a slow and costly process.

Dunn tackled the project with the energy and frenzy of a workaholic. He assembled a small team of production engineers, and they worked around the clock for seven months, devising and refining a system that used microwaves and a satellite 23,000 miles above the earth to replace AT&T's longlines.

Each evening at 7:30 P.M., with the aid of laser beams, Chicopee would convert the next day's *Journal* into a microwave edition and send it to the Westar satellite, which in turn would redistribute this electronic master to the *Journal*'s regional plants for printing and distribution.

Dunn's satellite replaced the more expensive method of relaying data via long-distance telephone lines. Dow Jones's daily transmission expense was reduced from $3,500 per day to $90; each plant's productivity increased from 25,000 copies per hour to 70,000 copies. And success encouraged Dow Jones to build five more printing plants over the next five years.

Because of this remarkable achievement, Dunn became Dow Jones's architect of the future. Dunn and his team had perfected the satellite transmission system in July 1975. He then convinced Flynn and Phillips to hold the November meeting of the Dow Jones board of directors in Orlando so that the board could witness, firsthand, what satellite transmission was all about.

On the evening of November 19, Bill Dunn, in shirtsleeves and grinning broadly, stood alongside Bill Kerby, Warren Phillips, and seven other board members who seemed not to notice the pristine cleanliness of the brand-new pressroom. At the appointed time, a red light signaled receipt of the microwave edition from Westar, which was transformed into silver plates corresponding to each page of the *Journal*. These plates were then affixed to the drums of the presses, and within sixty minutes, 70,000 copies of the next day's *Journal* lay on the docks, neatly bundled, ready for delivery. The board looked as if they had just witnessed a miracle. Champagne flowed, and everyone remained smiling throughout Dunn's usual controversial and turgid speech.

"I'm an economist, not a techie, so I know about models and about life. And, tonight, we have all witnessed a fundamental change in the model and life of this great newspaper known as the *Wall Street Journal*," said Dunn, pausing to take a sip of champagne and bowing to the applause his opening remark prompted.

"Things at the *Journal* will never be the same again, and they shouldn't be, which is what Heraclitus was trying to say at the river. The conventional newspaper model must face the ugly realities of ever-increasing labor and ground-transport expenses. Because of satellite technology, not only will the *Journal* never meet the grim reaper of rising manufacturing costs, but we will defeat him at his own motherfuckin' game," Dunn continued, his voice rising toward the end of the last sentence.

Cheers, shrill cowboy whistles, and the cry "Tell 'em, Billy-bob" rang out from Dunn's loyal staff, some of whom had been drinking since lunch. Caught up in the moment, the board, led by William McChesney Martin, joined in the celebration.

The next day, one Orlando newspaper described the occasion as "a rodeo for suits from New York, and just as wild."

It was the day Bill Dunn formally announced his candidacy for Dow Jones CEO. Over the next five years, though he would try with Videotext, Dow Jones News Retrieval, Dow Jones Interactive Cable, and other technological communication advances, Dunn would never again replicate the miracle of his satellite invention or reap the glory of its celebration.

Throughout this same period, Dunn remained addicted to the limelight, as if he didn't trust the normal forces to give him his due. As a consequence, he hired a *Journal* reporter to create a four-color press kit to herald the Information Services Group's accomplishments, real or imagined.

Dunn's penchant for celebrations continued unchecked, as well. In fact, Dunn's conduct increasingly became a problem, one no doubt exacerbated by his prodigious drinking.

Several years later, at a *Wall Street Journal* sales convention held in Florida, after many hours at the bar, Dunn and a salesperson, Joe Maddox, found themselves in the middle of a dance floor trying to dance with the same woman. An argument ensued. Dunn fired off the first remark, but Maddox fired off the first punch. The next day, Dunn reveled in telling everyone about how he was "coldcocked." It added to his legend, he explained.

But what Dunn accomplished during this period—which no one, including himself, ever acknowledged—was possibly more valuable even than his satellite coup. He was a true leader.

Throughout the seventies and much of the eighties, Dunn represented a rare bird in the conformist corporate world—he was fearless, profane, iconoclastic. And subordinates worshiped him. Men like Carl Valenti, a Lower East Side dropout who eventually rose to great heights at Dow Jones, followed Dunn around day and night. These cronies never went home. Eventually, they were all divorced by their wives, Dunn included.[5] And the bonds only strengthened then, as if they were corporate desperadoes.

Once after dinner, Dunn and his followers sat in a South Brunswick bar preparing to return to work that evening. Dunn stood up on the table, took a swig from his long-necked Budweiser, and said, "I live my life in visions, not words. That's why I'm quixotic, always tilting at windmills. That's why those motherfuckers in New York don't understand me."

Bill Dunn never fit in at Dow Jones, a difference he tried to exploit as an indication of the independence needed to lead Dow Jones into new territories, as Kilgore once had. By assuming such a posture, Dunn bet he could defeat the reckoning that every bureaucracy eventually imposes on eccentrics. But in the end, corporations are not venues where people get the chance to revisit their childhoods and work out their deprivations. It's a simple matter of raw power, and at Dow Jones that meant the supremacy of journalists.

15

Ascent of the First Dauphin: Peter Kann, Publisher (1991–Present)

In the first quarter of 1981, despite *Book Digest*'s difficulties, Dow Jones had much to celebrate. Its revenues had reached $531 million, up 21 percent from the previous year; earnings per share had tripled from $1.19 in 1976 to $3.69 in 1979. And the very embodiment of the *Wall Street Journal*, Ronald Reagan, had just assumed the presidency through the promise of unrivaled prosperity, a welcome relief from the economically hapless Carter administration.

A trade publication, the *Wall Street Transcript*, had just named Warren Phillips the newspaper publisher of the year, edging out Arthur Sulzberger of the *New York Times*, Katherine Graham of the *Washington Post*, Robert Erburu of the *Los Angeles Times*, and Allen Neuharth of Gannett. But perhaps the development that made Warren Phillips and Peter Kann, in particular, happiest was a study just completed by McKinsey & Company, the prestigious management consulting firm, which recommended how Dow Jones might reconfigure itself for the eighties.

At the time, corporate America and Wall Street were absorbing the first torrent of M.B.A.s, bright young men who had obtained master's degrees in business administration from the nation's best-known universities. By hiring M.B.A.s, the world of business was trying to duplicate the professionalism heretofore enjoyed only by law and medicine. But unlike law-school and medical-school graduates, who undergo a long and arduous apprenticeship before anyone takes them seriously, corporate America and Wall Street received these young M.B.A.s right off the campuses of Harvard, Stanford, Wharton, Chicago, Northwestern, and MIT as if they were wise and experienced beyond their years.

It was not unusual, for example, for an M.B.A. to enter corporate America as assistant to the chairman at a salary equivalent to what a middle manager might earn after twenty years with the company. Once hired, the M.B.A. would introduce a whole new vocabulary, which included such phrases as "running the numbers," "strategic alliances," "long-range plans," and other buzzwords that bolstered their confidence and intimidated everyone else.

When Phillips and Kann learned of the M.B.A. phenomenon, it made them uncomfortable. They wanted to be up to date in management sciences, but their deep-rooted aversion to business-people precluded them from recruiting any meaningful number of M.B.A.s. So Kann convinced Phillips to do the next best thing—commission a management consulting firm to study Dow Jones.

In the world of the M.B.A., the Harvard Graduate School of Business Administration is widely regarded as the Pantheon of business schools. For this reason, years ago when the M.B.A. phenomenon was first gaining currency, McKinsey and Company made a "strategic marketing decision" to recruit only Harvard Business School's Baker scholars. Baker scholars are the top 5 percent in each year's graduating class of approximately eight hundred M.B.A.s. Though McKinsey has reduced its standards somewhat in recent years to meet its manpower needs, the firm still enjoys a superior image gained through its Baker scholars.

Considering the obvious—Phillips's fascination for all things Harvard—it was no surprise when McKinsey received the assignment in June 1979 to study and upgrade, if necessary, the management practices and structure of Dow Jones. For the next six months, a legion of young, confident M.B.A.s, who all seemed to wear the same designer spectacles and suspenders, swept through the Dow Jones ranks interviewing everyone from security guards to Phillips himself several times over. Recording each response verbatim on legal-sized yellow pads, the young consultants began each interview with the simple question: "What do you do?"

From the hundreds of answers to this question came McKinsey's findings, which Phillips accepted and announced in January 1980. The core recommendation was for Dow Jones to create seven operating groups corresponding to the company's various product lines. McKinsey also suggested that five presidents be named to head these operating groups. In communicating the changes to Dow Jones personnel, Phillips wrote, "We are streamlining our management structure to organize the company more effectively for growth."

Commenting on the organization's changes, Bill Clabby, the *Journal* news veteran, said, "How can you streamline something by making five guys presidents?" Many other staffers felt let down, too. After months of anticipating suggestions from McKinsey for imaginative and much-needed change, the recommendation was a disappointment. The consulting firm merely formalized how Dow Jones had been organized informally for years.

But three men in particular were thrilled with the findings.

Instead of being forced to retire, as he had suspected, Don Macdonald, sixty-three, found himself president of the International and Magazine groups. He was now responsible for *Book Digest*, *Barron's*, and the Asian and European editions of the *Journal*. Despite his difficulties with *Book Digest*, Macdonald continued to rise in the hierarchy principally because of his relationships with Kann and Bill Cox, Jr.

William L. Dunn, forty-one, Dow Jones's firebrand technocrat, was named president of the Information Services and Operations groups, which, he thought, put him in the running with Peter Kann to succeed Phillips as Dow Jones chief executive officer.

But the person made happiest by McKinsey was Peter Kann, thirty-eight, whom the firm recommended to head the *Wall Street Journal*. Instead of president, Phillips gave Kann the title of associate publisher and made him responsible for the *Journal's* news, advertising, circulation, finance, and production departments. With no other publishing experience save eighteen months with the *Asian Wall Street Journal*, circulation 12,000, Kann would now oversee one of the country's top three newspapers with a circulation of nearly 2 million.

Peter Kann's self-deprecating manner served him well as he went about learning his new responsibilities. In fact, he was brilliant at winning people over, especially the *Journal's* advertising sales staff. Despite ever-increasing revenues, the *Journal's* advertising sales department had suffered from management upheaval throughout the seventies. Two of Macdonald's handpicked protégés, John Orr and

William Henry Marx, failed to succeed him as advertising sales director. But in both instances, it became apparent Macdonald was not good at grooming successors. Macdonald explained, "John Orr had a love-hate relationship with me, and eventually he left to go to another newspaper, the *Manhattan Transfer*, which folded almost immediately."[1]

Orr was succeeded by Henry Marx, who was "smart enough" but not beloved, Macdonald added.[2]

In 1977, Ray Shaw, a former *Journal* bureau chief and now president of Dow Jones, appointed Lee Heffner, former ad director of *Fortune* and president of Time-Life Films, as head of *Journal* ad sales. A bull-necked man who spoke gruffly and infrequently, Lee Heffner would sit in his office at 420 Lexington Avenue for days on end, seeing and speaking to no one except his secretary. Twice a month, Heffner would trundle down to Wall Street to give Ray Shaw a glowing report on the *Journal's* ad sales. Neither Shaw nor Heffner had any idea why sales were doing so well, but each had enough sense to remain modest and ride the boom.

In fact, Shaw and Heffner were alike in many respects. Underneath their harsh exteriors, they could be nice, even sensitive. Both desperately sought mentors, fearing that their lack of a college degree would eventually get them fired. The more amiable Shaw found his protector in Warren Phillips. The more prickly Heffner experienced a series of disasters, first with Henry Marx and then with Don Macdonald.

"The trouble with Heffner," Macdonald later said, "was he did not grow up selling the *Journal*. Nobody knew him, nobody liked him."

More so than perhaps most corporations, Dow Jones remains to this day a culture dominated by men, all of whom—whether a reporter, an advertising salesperson, or an accountant—joined the company right out of college. Ray Shaw took a huge risk in appointing Heffner, an outsider, head of advertising sales. But Shaw's courage did not hold out. Once he put Heffner in the job, Shaw never stood up for him again. Perhaps because he was too preoccupied with his own standing, Shaw left Heffner to fend for himself.

Heffner endured this isolation for four years, either too proud or too afraid to resign. His state of continual uneasiness was exacerbated by Don Macdonald, who would periodically swoop down and criticize him savagely. In 1979, at a sales convention held in the Poconos, while a hundred sales people and assorted industry guests were finishing their dinner, Macdonald commandeered the after-dinner speaker's microphone. Waving ads he had ripped out of competitive publications minutes beforehand, Macdonald kept roaring, "Why don't we have this one?" At first the audience laughed nervously, thinking it was Macdonald's peculiar idea of a joke. But as Macdonald became increasingly abusive toward Heffner, the audience became commensurately mortified.

No one tried to stop Macdonald, however, even when he switched his attention from berating Heffner to dragging Ingrid Berentsen, circulation director of the European *Wall Street Journal*, onstage against her will. Underestimating the sophistication of the audience, Berentsen was wearing a see-through dress that evening that aroused Macdonald greatly. Later, Kann tried to attribute Macdonald's loutish behavior to alcohol. But Heffner remained humiliated, not by Macdonald's words but by his audacity.[3]

From 1975 through 1983, irrespective of who served as the ad sales director, substantial yearly sales gains became an expected part of life. The intrinsic appeal of reading about the country's increasing prosperity put the *Journal* at the head of virtually every major advertiser's list. And in a startling reversal of the selling relationship, advertisers would wait patiently until their salesperson told them they could run their advertisements. *Journal* salespeople did not so much sell as broker space.

This aberration lasted only from June 1977 to June 1984, but it was long enough to give Peter Kann a false sense of what type of person was needed to sell advertising for the *Journal*. Innocently, Kann believed the best salespeople were those who were most amiable toward him.

In June 1980, Kann named Paul Atkinson, twenty-seven, his assistant. A crisp and recent graduate of Princeton University, Atkinson had served with Kann in Hong Kong, doing various odd jobs, including part-time sales. Appointed to be Kann's eyes and ears in the advertising sales department, it did not take long for Atkinson to realize that if he confirmed the negative things Macdonald was saying about Heffner, he would be helping his own ambitions. In August 1980, in the middle of the Hudson River. Macdonald, Atkinson, and Kann were together on a cruise that *Barron's*, the *Journal's* sister publication, was hosting for advertisers. Macdonald and Atkinson were articulating Heffner's many failings when, unexpectedly, Kann interrupted and asked, "Who should replace him?"

For a split second, Atkinson fell silent, thinking Macdonald might nominate him. Even though he was only twenty-seven and had no real selling experience, Atkinson fervently believed that he was more than capable of taking over the *Journal's* complicated $300 million ad sales department that very moment.

Instead, Macdonald scanned the deck of the cruise ship for a moment. Then his eyes brightened as he pointed to a cherubic, red-faced Irishman and shouted, "Flanagan." Atkinson's normally impassive face froze with fury. A fourth-generation patrician, Paul Atkinson loathed Bernie Flanagan, a loud, beer-bellied near graduate of St. John's University's night school.

The following week, Bernard T. Flanagan, former publisher of *Barron's*, was named vice president, marketing, for the *Wall Street Journal*. Lee Heffner, the announcement said, would report to Flanagan. Later, Kann assured Heffner that his door would always remain open to him and that Lee would benefit greatly from the increased attention Bernie would be giving him. Kann had just fired Heffner, *Journal*-style.

In his new job, Peter Kann did not limit his energies to the business side. On the day Kann became associate publisher, Fred Taylor, the *Journal's* executive editor, was called to Warren Phillips's office, where he was told that Kann was his new boss.

"I was stunned," Taylor remembered. "Hell, I had recommended him for 'Nam just a dozen years before and now he was going to be my boss!"

Phillips went on to explain to Taylor that O'Donnell, the *Journal's* managing editor, would report directly to Kann, too. He had been reporting to Taylor since 1977. "That pissed me off, and I said so," Taylor recalled. "In effect, Warren stripped me of my line job. Warren gave me some story, like it was going to shorten the lines of communication. But I didn't believe it."

Soon Taylor found himself immersed in the same type of aimless projects that had wasted Cony ten years before—television and a *Journal* business magazine.

Larry O'Donnell did not greet Taylor's demise with the same equanimity as Atkinson had showed when Heffner was demoted. In fact, the more exposure O'Donnell had to Peter Kann, the less he liked him. A chain-of-command editor, O'Donnell became incensed when Kann started to wander down to the news floor in shirtsleeves, smoking his Schimmelpfennigs, talking and joking with reporters.

Fred Taylor confirmed this assessment. "Larry O'Donnell was of the old *Wall Street Journal* school. Kann, on the other hand, wanted an informal structure, one that would allow him to wander the news floor and have direct input with the reporters. Peter wanted to run the *Wall Street Journal* as he ran the Asian *Wall Street Journal*. This bothered me, but it really bothered O'Donnell. Larry viewed Peter as the associate publisher who also was a business guy, an advertising guy. Both of us clearly conveyed to Peter that we thought his attempts to get involved in editorial were inappropriate. We also said it was difficult to run a large, complex organization like the *Journal* if he were going to pass on story ideas without going through the managing editor.

"It got so bad that O'Donnell started to lecture Peter. Larry would actually take Peter by the arm, lead him into his office, and say, 'We don't do things like that around here. They have one boss. Me.' Peter would nod amiably, leave his office, only to return the next day with another idea or comment."

Though few realized it at the time, Peter Kann's visits marked the beginning of a change in the *Journal's* culture, the profoundest since Barney Kilgore had taken over in 1941. By going directly to the reporters, Kann contradicted Kilgore's insistence that the integrity of the news department's chain of command be maintained. No matter how peripatetic Kilgore was, no matter how many times he dined, sang, and cavorted with the beat reporters, he never undermined the middle men.

By bypassing O'Donnell so conspicuously, Kann was preparing the way for his friend, Norman Pearlstine, who was still at *Forbes,* to replace O'Donnell. Kann also signaled the beginning of the cult of the individual at the *Journal.* Despite the company's ability to tolerate zany individuals, every person had a sublime respect for the company. As ambitious and rambunctious as, say, Don Macdonald appeared, his first worry was always the *Journal* rather than his own career.

With a genius that rivaled Kilgore's, Kann introduced his message of change in an unassailable manner. His charm lulled everyone, a lull that he used to implement change with little to no resistance. "Who could fault his nice-guy attitude," Taylor said. "Rather than bitch, I complied at first, thinking maybe his new way of looking at things was best for the organization."

Taylor's dilemma was shared by virtually the entire news staff, who felt themselves caught between O'Donnell, their direct boss, and Peter Kann, the obvious savior. But O'Donnell did not make it easy on himself. He became more and more resentful of Kann in the months to follow, a resentment he expressed indirectly in his increased rigidity with the staff and, on occasion, in his own bizarre conduct.

"After Kann became associate publisher, O'Donnell started acting weird," said Norman Pearlstine, executive editor at *Forbes* at the time. "*Journal* friends would tell me Larry started to wear women's hats and jump off file cabinets."

Just as advertising swept in over the transoms regardless of who was managing the *Journal's* ad sales department, the same relentless success applied to the news department. Irrespective of O'Donnell's troubles or Kann's meddlings, every issue of the *Journal* continued to rank among the world's best journalistic endeavors—the Kilgore formula was still that good.

While Kann developed new muscles as the *Journal's* de facto president, his boss, Ray Shaw, tried to flex his as well. A grim-looking man from the Oklahoma panhandle, Ray Shaw was burdened with a shocking lack of self-confidence that he tried to obscure by taking himself and his job far too seriously. [5]

Once, an enterprising *Journal* reporter broke through the computer code of the Dow Jones payroll system and obtained the salaries of the news department. The next day, many of them appeared on page six (the gossip section) of the *New York Post*. Rather than let the incident pass without comment to minimize the attention such events arouse, Ray Shaw became indignant. In a memo he wrote to the staff, he declared:

> While a handful of people might look on this as harmless high jinks, we consider the matter a grave breach of the trust we put in Dow Jones people....
>
> We believe that an unauthorized individual somehow took the information from one of our computer systems.
>
> We have asked our internal audit and legal departments to look into the matter because it represents theft of corporate information and is an unjust intrusion on personal privacy.
>
> We're saddened by what has taken place. One can only question the motives of those who engage in such practices.

Of course, Shaw's memo appeared in the *Post* the very next day. "You would think Ray, a newsman for thirty years, would have known better," said Shaw's close friend, Bill Clabby. But the incident was indicative of Shaw's trusting, if not naive, nature, a quality which caused him to stand by Warren Phillips's side for thirty-five years, doing his bidding without complaint.

Shaw first assumed this patient stance in 1966, when Warren Phillips plucked him out of the Dallas bureau and named him the head of a new joint venture with the Associated Press called AP–Dow Jones, a syndicated news service operating mainly in Europe and Asia. By dint of hard work and attention to detail, Shaw made the enterprise a resounding success. In fact, twenty-five years later, AP–Dow Jones still ranks as one of the *Journal's* most successful divisions.

From AP–Dow Jones, Shaw went to South Brunswick, New Jersey, to create the framework for what would later become Bill Dunn's barony, the Information Services Group. In 1976, Phillips bought Shaw to New York and appointed him Dow Jones's general manager. As such, he inherited many of Don Macdonald's duties, including the *Journal's* floundering circulation department. Shaw's first act was to appoint Ken Burenga and Joe Perrone co-marketing directors of the circulation department, a most unusual management structure.

To the surprise of everyone, two of the most dissimilar men in the world, Joe Perrone and Ken Burenga, took the *Journal's* stagnating circulation from 1.4 million to nearly 2 million in less than three years, making it the largest newspaper in America.

Even back in 1976, both Perrone and Burenga had already exceeded their parents' fondest dreams. Perrone, who quit high school and started with Dow Jones as a messenger when he was sixteen, looked and acted like a gang member of a secret society— tough talking, daring, and frighteningly bright. But Perrone had two saving graces: In the conflicts he inevitably provoked, he was usually right; and he had a ready, infectious smile for everyone. One could not help but admire Joe Perrone, even after being corrected by his thick Brooklyn accent.

Burenga was the quintessential accountant, respectful, quiet, loyal, discreet, and obedient. He could add and subtract quickly in his head, a facility most journalists, especially Shaw, attributed to a high IQ. Burenga could always be found in the office, either his own in South Brunswick or Ray Shaw's in New York, poring over statistics that tracked the circulation progress produced by Perrone's innovations. On the other hand, Perrone could never be found. He was always roaming the country with his young assistant, Mary Waters, the first female M.B.A. to work for Dow Jones, implementing schemes to increase the *Journal*'s circulation.

During his first six months in circulation, Perrone came across an advertising agency known as Lawrence Butner and Associates, Inc. Occupying a netherworld niche in advertising, Larry Butner specialized in direct-response television, the commercials that feature, for example, a smiling Oriental chef slicing up mountains of carrots with a magical implement known as a Ginsu knife, which can be purchased by any viewer for $19.95 if he telephones the flashing 800 telephone number immediately.

In direct-response television, an advertiser buys what is known as "remnant time," those spots that appear in the middle of the night which normal advertisers shun. Rather than pay cash for a remnant spot, the direct-response advertiser shares a portion of the proceeds of each sale with the station. In this example, for every pair of Ginsu knives sold through WABC-TV, the Ginsu knife manufacturer gives the station $10 and keeps the remainder of the sale price.

When executed properly, direct response is a boon for everyone. The advertiser lays out cash only when he makes a sale, and the station sells spots which otherwise go begging. After hearing Butner's explanation of direct-response advertising, Perrone saw immediately how it could help the *Journal*'s circulation efforts.

Overnight, by producing tasteful commercials and offering a $78 subscription deal which gave television stations three times their usual direct-response split, Perrone and Larry Butner virtually cornered the country's inventory of the best remnant time. Over the next three years, direct-response television generated 548,000 *Journal* subscriptions, which represented 90 percent of the *Journal*'s circulation gain during this period.

From 1978 onward, Perrone became more and more self-assured, and Burenga became more and more compliant, attitude shifts that eventually produced a predictable result on their boss.

"Shaw always wanted me to cross every T," Perrone explained. "I couldn't and Kenny could. Finally, I dreaded coming to work, and I jumped at the first offer that came along."[4]

Perrone left Dow Jones in January 1980 to join Lebhar-Friedman, a trade publisher, as vice president, circulation. Later, when asked why Perrone left, Shaw said, "You know, I really don't know. I've often wondered why myself."[5]

Perrone's departure preceded Kann's promotion to associate publisher by a few weeks. Like Shaw, Kann did not know enough about circulation to appreciate Perrone's contributions. In 1970, the *Journal* charged $19,000 for a page of advertising; in 1978, because of the circulation increases gained through Perrone's television ads, that same page of advertising cost advertisers $49,000. And those who did realize the magnitude of Perrone's contributions, people like Ken Burenga and Don Macdonald, remained silent, pleased that another rival had departed. Like the news and the advertising departments, it was a period in the *Journal*'s life when it didn't matter who was running circulation. The subscriptions kept sweeping through the transom in tidal waves.

Another trait Shaw shared equally with Warren Phillips was attention to detail. Once, after *Book Digest* had enlarged its format and revamped its graphics, the staff waited anxiously for weeks while Phillips formulated his reaction to the radical transformation. With each passing day, the staff embellished its fantasy of Phillips delivering sweeping and helpful comments on the magazine's new direction.

On the appointed day, before the magazine's assembled and anxious department heads, Phillips opened up his ubiquitous black notebook and read out seven specific comments, each exactly like the following in tone, content, and conceptual sweep. "On page twenty-six, in the caption, you used six-point type. Perhaps it would be better to go with ten-point next time," Phillips said.

Phillips's criticisms, as anticlimactic as McKinsey's study, were no more uninspiring than Ray Shaw's reaction to the *Journal*'s 1979 long-range plan, which contained several strategic recommendations worthy of response, such as building three more plants. Three weeks after the plan was submitted, Shaw returned it through the interoffice mail. His reaction was contained in a single handwritten note: "Please! Nothing annoys me more than the incorrect use of 'their' for 'its.'"

When Peter Kann assumed Shaw's direct duties for the *Journal*, Shaw turned to internal diversification as one means to occupy his time. Within a matter of months, Shaw unveiled the *Journal*'s

"Employment Weekly," a rehash of the classified want ads that first appeared in the *Journal*. After its first year on the newsstand, *Employment Weekly* sold, on average, 6,000 copies each week—sales that were hardly worth the effort.

While Shaw was proudly inventing his new product, Phillips was deeply involved in trying to solve a problem other publishers only dream about. The *Journal* had too much advertising. In January 1977, the *Journal's* ad lineage stood at 1.4 million lines, a yearly growth rate of 8 percent. By January 1979, the lineage had vaulted to 1.89 million, a yearly growth rate of 20 percent. Considering that the *Journal* was charging advertisers nearly $49,000 a page, a rate second only to the *Reader's Digest's* these gains were incredible.

The increase in advertising produced several results, not all of them positive. Besides making the *Journal's* sales force smug and mediocre, the ad wave lulled Phillips, Shaw, and Kann into believing these increases would last forever, just like the growth in circulation.

But the most negative effect of *Journal* advertising demand exceeding supply affected advertisers. In January 1978, IBM placed an order for twelve full-page ads to run on various specific dates throughout the year. Following procedure, Thomas O'Mara, the salesman, immediately reserved the twelve full-page positions with the advertising production department in Chicopee, Massachusetts. The first eleven ads ran as scheduled.

The last ad, the most critical, was to serve as the cornerstone for IBM's plan announcing a new personal computer. A series of other ads asked IBM customers and personnel worldwide to consult the October 15 issue of the *Wall Street Journal* for an exciting announcement.

On Monday, October 15, as O'Mara, the *Journal's* salesman in charge of the IBM account, commuted by bus into New York City from his suburban New Jersey apartment, he casually scanned the pages of the *Journal* in search of the IBM ad. O'Mara was not alarmed at first when he could not locate it. But after several more forays through the issue, he realized the IBM ad had not run, at least in his issue.

Twenty minutes later, O'Mara rushed to a phone booth in the Port Authority Terminal, only to learn that the *Journal's* advertising production department had accidentally lost the IBM ad in a flood of full-page requests that had swamped the department over the weekend.

O'Mara said later, "What enraged IBM was when I had to tell them that the nearest date we could run the ad was Thursday, October 25."[6]

Though resentful, IBM, like many other national advertisers, refused to boycott the *Journal* simply because there were no alternatives. No other publication—not *Business Week, Forbes, Fortune, Dun's Review,* or the *New York Times*—could match the *Journal's* 6 million affluent daily readers.

Fortunately, a newsprint shortage occurred in 1979 which forced Phillips to examine the supply and demand for *Journal* advertising space from a different perspective. It resulted in Phillips's finest hour in his fourteen-year reign as Dow Jones's chief executive officer. Though the threat of the newsprint shortage never materialized, it did cause Phillips to reexamine the *Journal's* ratio for allocating newsprint between editorial and advertising. He decided to expand the number of pages in each issue so that the *Journal* could offer, first, more news to readers, and, only secondarily, more space to advertisers.

To the uninitiated, Phillips's decision seemed simple enough. Had he been an accountant, he would have been sorely tempted to keep the *Journal* at its present page size, reduce the space allocated for news to accommodate more advertising, and thereby increase the revenues and profits of each *Journal* issue by a quantum amount. For example, in 1978, the *Journal* could not exceed a 32-page issue because of the restrictions imposed by its printing presses. This meant that each issue carried 16 pages of news and 16 pages of advertising at $50,000 per page, or a total ad-revenue-per-issue figure of $800,000.

Had Phillips been more profit minded, he could easily have decided to keep the present page capacity at 32, reduce the news pages to, say, 12, thereby increasing the ad pages to 20 and the ad-revenue-per-issue figure to $1 million. Since it would cost no more to print and distribute the same 32-page issue, this advertiser-favored ratio could have resulted in a yearly increment to Dow Jones's profits of $50 million.

But Phillips, remembering how Kilgore had solved a similar dilemma in the early forties, opted for a reader-oriented solution. He increased the *Journal* page capacity per issue to 48 and increased the news pages to 26, which left advertising with 22 pages. To increase the page capacity to 48, Phillips had to replace the *Journal's* network of printing presses at a capital expense of $250 million. He was willing to risk this substantial amount of money to preserve the Kilgore tradition: the reader comes first, advertisers follow. It was a decision seldom made in corporations, then and now—sacrificing a sure short-term gain for the benefit of the customer. It paid off handsomely for Phillips in the long run, but there was no way of knowing that in 1979.

Once this critical decision had been made, Phillips was faced with a far less significant question: What is the best format for a 48-page issue? Keep the present single section or divide it in two? Phillips headed the project to answer these questions himself, with Fred Taylor and Fred Zimmerman, a page-one editor in the Washington bureau, assisting him.

A single-section, 48-page *Journal* issue would be too bulky for either the *Journal's* distribution system or the average reader to handle easily. Thus, the decision to create a second section of 16 pages became obvious. With the major format decisions made, namely, dividing the *Journal* into two sections and increasing page capacity of the printing presses to 48, Phillips became worried about the easiest part of the job: The layout for the front page of the second section.

"Warren was extremely nervous about the second section,"[7] Zimmerman said. "He breathed down our necks all the time. He did a lot of heavy editing."

Remembering how it was fifteen years earlier working with Phillips on a new page-one column, Taylor assumed a different stance from Zimmerman's. "I stayed in the background because I knew how Warren could get. Poor Freddy was so eager to make a name for himself that he almost allowed Warren to drive him mad,"[8] Taylor chuckled.

On June 23, 1980, after a year in the making, the *Journal* published its first 48-page, two-section issue. Aside from adding international coverage, the new section cannily resembled the old *Journal* in tone and look. The event passed largely unnoticed, precisely the response Phillips had hoped for. Had there been more of a reaction, either positive or negative, it could have meant problems, because what pleases one group of readers usually displeases another.

On June 24, 1980, a bureau chief happened to ride a Dow Jones elevator with Phillips. During the brief ride together, the chief congratulated Phillips on the second section. As he got off the elevator, Phillips turned and said, "Thanks. Peter and I worked very hard on that." It was the first time anyone knew that Peter Kann had been involved.

A week later, the *Journal* news department throughout the world was rocked by an interoffice announcement from Peter Kann. "I take particular delight in announcing that Norman Pearlstine, former editor of the *Asian Wall Street Journal*, will be returning home shortly as national news editor."

Since 1979, Pearlstine had been an executive editor for *Forbes* magazine, covering the Far East. The memo also said that Bill Krieger, the incumbent national news editor, would be shifted to "special projects. Please join me then in welcoming back Norm and wishing Bill success in his new assignment."

When Fred Taylor, the *Journal's* executive editor, first heard rumors that Pearlstine was returning, he confronted Kann directly. "No way!" Taylor screamed.

Peter grinned and asked, "Why are you so mad, Fred? He quit on me."

Still angry, Taylor stormed into Phillips's office across the hall. "Warren said to me, 'You will rehire Norman.' It was the only ultimatum he ever gave me," Taylor said sorrowfully.

Rehiring Pearlstine was a means for Phillips and Kann to express their discontent with the Kilgore tradition, the status quo. Fred Taylor lamented, "By taking Norman back they were saying to us, 'Your old ways are not successful.' But we were successful. The *Journal* was at its peak, and not because of Kann's writing or Phillips's editing, either. I couldn't figure out why they were dissatisfied." [9]

Certainly O'Donnell was giving Phillips and Kann reason to consider a change. "But they could have replaced him with an insider, with one of us," Taylor said.

Instead, Phillips and Kann "summarily discarded a truly beloved and respected thirty-year *Journal* veteran, Bill Krieger, to make way for Pearlstine, whom I and others viewed as a traitor," Taylor said, making no bones about the threat to Kilgore's tenet of placing the *Journal* in front of individual career considerations.

"I have this theory that the whole affair with Pearlstine—going to *Forbes* and then coming back in a higher position—was planned by Peter and Norman years before in Hong Kong," he continued.

Pam Hollie, a friend of Pearlstine's and former *Journal* reporter, confirmed Taylor's suspicion. "Let's just say that Pearlstine was a smart, ambitious guy who sold himself to his friend, Malcolm Forbes, so the *Journal* would eventually realize how much they lost."[10]

The newsroom reacted strongly, pro and con, to Pearlstine's return; people sensed it meant change, welcome for some, gut wrenching for others. The old order, the Kilgore tradition of self-effacement for the good of the *Journal* that Larry O'Donnell had personified, was being preempted by a new order, the cult of the individual, which Pearlstine personified.

Many welcomed the change Pearlstine represented. "Norman was a visionary, one of the best journalists in the country,"[11] said Nancy Cardwell, a former assistant managing editor. "We felt bad about Krieger. But it marked the beginning of a different culture. The *Journal* had been a small, paternalistic company. About the time Norm returned, the *Journal* had started to become big and depersonalized. It had to survive its own phenomenal growth."

With Pearlstine's return also came a change in attitude marked by backbiting and fierce office politics. "Larry's [O'Donnell's] fate was sealed the day Norman became national news editor. He would spend hours on the phone with Peter, bitching about Larry," Taylor said.

But Pearlstine's return certainly had a favorable effect on Peter Kann. A comrade in arms was once more by his side, someone to whom Kann could relate. For that reason, he seemed to enjoy visiting the newsroom more, and not just New York's.

Kann, then thirty-eight, became noticeably friendly toward one person in particular, Karen Elliott House, then thirty-two, a beautiful Veronica Lake look-alike who covered the State Department for the *Journal*, the Washington bureau's most coveted beat.

"By 1981, it was evident the associate publisher and Karen were having an affair," said Fred Zimmerman, her mentor in the late seventies. "Both were still married at the time."[12]

Shortly after Francesca Kann returned from Hong Kong with Peter in 1979, a widely circulated rumor around Dow Jones had it that she suffered from a severe drinking problem and that she and Peter had separated.

In June 1982, Karen Elliott House accompanied Peter on a business trip to Europe. Fred Taylor recalled, "In London, Peter and Karen took the bureau out to dinner and Karen proceeded to tell the group how to do their jobs. Everyone was infuriated."[13]

When the pair returned from Europe, Peter took Fred Taylor aside and admitted he and Karen Elliott House had struck up a relation-ship. "We've become friends, good close friends," Kann told Taylor.

Kann also said that his relationship with House should pose no difficulty for Taylor or anyone else at the *Journal* because "Karen does not report to me."

Bullshit! thought Taylor to himself. Why does Warren tolerate this?

At the time, Karen Elliott House was married to Arthur House, whom Zimmerman described as "another dull blue blood from Connecticut. We nicknamed him Do-do. It seemed like whenever Peter was in town, Do-do would call, asking where Karen was. It was pathetic."

Karen Elliott House and Arthur House were divorced in Septem-ber 1983. Francesca Meyer Kann died on July 3, 1983, the victim of a cirrhotic liver. Peter Kann and Karen Elliott House were married a year later, a union that galvanized the news department. A powerful minority, led by Warren Phillips, approved of the marriage, believing it presented no difficulty whatsoever for Kann, House, or their superiors, peers, and subordinates.

The vast majority, however, disagreed. They argued that any sensible person would perceive Karen Elliott House not as who she was but as who she was married to, namely, the *Journal*'s associate publisher. Alan Otten, senior reporter in the *Journal*'s Washington bureau, said, "It was a disgrace. Warren should never have allowed it to happen. Karen should have left the company when she married Peter. How can anyone relate honestly to her knowing she sleeps with the boss?"[14]

Since becoming engaged to and then marrying the *Journal*'s associate publisher, House has received the *Journal*'s nomination for, and then won, a Pulitzer. She has also received several significant promotions. In a matter of three years, from 1984 to 1987, House went from diplomatic correspondent to foreign editor to vice president, international, a post equivalent to being the publisher of the *Journal*'s Asian and European editions and the *Far East Economic Review*, another Dow Jones publication. Like Phillips and Kann, before becoming the publisher of these foreign publications, House had no business experience whatsoever.

Though Phillips dismisses the controversy as the workings of small, envious minds, ten years later the Kann-House marriage continues to sap the strength and integrity of the *Journal* news operation.

16

Mr. Peepers, the Zany
Editorialist

Throughout the late seventies, as Peter Kann began to realize his personal and professional ambitions under the paternal eye of Warren Phillips, another Dow Jones prince, Robert L. Bartley, began to realize his ambitions under the eye of Vermont Royster, then the Pulitzer Prize–winning editor of the *Journal's* editorial page. No one doubted both men would soon achieve their separate and compatible ambitions—Kann, to head of one of the world's most influential corporations, Bartley, to head one of the world's most influential editorial pages.

Kann's eventual sovereignty was management, where he sought and gained acclaim from subordinates. His strength lay inward, within Dow Jones. Bartley's eventual sovereignty was journalism, where he sought and gained acclaim on the basis of his words. His strength lay outwards, among readers. Kann ostensibly reports to the board of directors, but in reality reports to no one. Bartley ostensibly reports to Kann, but in reality reports to himself. But Bartley is not entirely independent, nor is he apolitical.

Kann gained acceptance from his *Journal* colleagues because he looked like a dauphin and acted like Mr. Peepers. Bartley gained acceptance from his colleagues because he looked like Mr. Peepers and wrote like a dauphin. Wearing eyeglasses as big as windshields, victim of a middle-aged cowlick, Bob Bartley hardly resembles the go-for-the-jugular essayist most readers imagine him to be. In his twangy Iowa drawl, Bartley explained, "I'm a continuation, really, of Barney Kilgore. Personally conservative, reserved, trained from childhood not to toot your own horn."[1]

If there is truth in the saying that most men play their lives as they play their games, then one of the weekly tennis matches held throughout the eighties at the Wall Street Racquet Club may provide insight into Kann's and Bartley's characters.[2] Used as the set for the tennis date between Woody Allen and Diane Keaton in *Annie Hall*, the Wall Street Racquet Club is a converted pier jutting out into the East River in Lower Manhattan. Despite its celebrity players, the club's atmosphere is something like that of a British public school: spartan and stoic. The lounge, for instance, consists of one stained upholstered love seat and a vending machine for juices that has never worked.

In the winter, each of the club's six courts is encased in a dirigiblelike balloon, held aloft by streams of hot air blasting out of four compressors positioned around its perimeter. Each court's clay surface is marred by a rash of sandy anthills, which makes for erratic bounces.

On this particular Wednesday, exactly at 12:55 P.M., four men approached the club's synthetic grass threshold, lost in an amiable, work-related conversation. Once inside the club, they became sober and intense, especially Peter Kann, associate publisher of the *Journal*, and Bob Bartley, the *Journal's* editorial-page editor. Made nervous by the abrupt silence, the other two players, Tom Bray, an assistant to Bartley, and Tom Herman, a *Journal* reporter, affected a false joviality.

First to dress and to be on the court ready for play, Kann loosened up by swinging his racket back and forth ferociously a hundred times. As the other three men walked on the court, Kann, Bray, and Herman looked reasonably comfortable, if not graceful and attractive, in their tennis attire. Despite expensive and matching sweater, shorts, and shirt, Bartley still looked like a small, frail boy.

Bartley asked, "Whose got the balls?"

Smiling slightly, Bray produced four new yellow balls, one more than usual to save time retrieving them between points, a requirement imposed by both Kann and Bartley.

Then, looking at Tom Herman, Bray asked, "How should we do this today?"

"Why don't I play with Bob," said Herman quickly.

A certain tension began to rise on the court. Since Kann and Bartley despised losing, especially to one another, Bray and Herman felt all too keenly the pressure not to make mistakes. Each considered himself responsible for protecting his boss's pride.

After the teams were determined, a few minutes of warm-up—casual, low-key ground strokes and volleys—followed. Peter signaled the match was about to begin when he walked to the service line. He always liked to serve first because service was the best part of his game. Kann swung so violently at the ball it made a terrible "thwack" on contact. When his serve went in, he usually won the point straightaway. When it "wasn't going in," unlike virtually anyone else, including the pros, Kann never took power off his second serve to play it safe and get the ball in play. It was all or nothing for Peter, a curious lack of restraint for someone who, in all other situations, looked and acted as if he were unflappable.

On this particular Wednesday, eight "thwacks" reverberated throughout the bubble in rapid succession, indicating that Peter had served four double faults in a row to lose the game. His partner, Tom Bray, stared at the ground as if to say, It's going to be a long afternoon. Bartley smiled.

For the second game, Tom Herman, Bartley's partner, served first and won the point off Bray, who netted his return. When Herman served to Peter in the backhand court for the next point, Kann, a lefty, purposely swung late and drilled the ball 90 miles per hour directly at Bartley, who was standing three feet from the net, unaware. Peter's return hit Bartley squarely in the chest, and he staggered backward several feet. Herman and Bray exchanged glances.

Bartley, roused, injected himself into the game with an energy that infected his partner, Tom Herman, as well. Though Bartley lacked Peter's grace and fluidity, he turned into a human backboard. Nothing got by him. The next fifty minutes were marked by ferocious exchanges, each lasting four to five volleys, with Kann and Bray hammering Bartley at the net. Just as relentlessly, Bartley managed to keep the ball in play, allowing Herman to creep into the exchange for an occasional kill.

Perhaps it was the heat of the battle, but with each point Bartley got better, more confident, a change that Kann and Bray failed to notice. At exactly 1:58 P.M., with less than two minutes remaining before they would have to relinquish the court, the score was advantage Bartley and Tom Herman, which meant they needed only one more point to win.

Herman was serving to Peter, with Bartley standing practically on top of the net, he was so eager for the fray. The serve was a medium-paced ball that twisted away toward the sideline. Peter deftly took one step sideways and strenuously began his backswing as if, once more, he was going to drill the ball right at Bartley's chest. Sensing another exchange at net, Herman rushed in from the service line to protect his side of the court.

But right at the very last second, for the first time in the match, Kann altered the course of his racket and delicately lobbed the ball over Bartley's head. At first, both Bartley and Herman stood rooted to their spots, stunned. But then Bartley came alive. He took three half-steps backward and leapt in the air. At that instant, this strange-looking little man turned into a bird in flight. As Bartley rose to the apex of his jump, he simultaneously brought his racket back and then, when gravity started his descent, he swung with all his might, racket and ball meeting in one explosive grunt. All that was heard was a thwack reminiscent of one of Peter Kann's serves.

And then, as if shot, Kann staggered to the ground and rocked painfully back and forth, eyes tearing, knees up, clutching his crotch. It was a good five minutes before Kann could hobble off the court hanging on the shoulders of Bray and Herman. Bartley, in the meantime, had gathered his belongings and made for the locker as if nothing had happened.

Bartley's violence is not restricted to the tennis court. Certainly Sen. Edward Kennedy could never have anticipated the editorial "Chappaquiddick and Credibilty," which appeared in the *Journal* on Thursday, November 6, 1979. The piece was prompted by a prime-time CBS news show aired the previous Sunday evening that had featured an interview between Roger Mudd and Kennedy. Kennedy, who was considering a run for the presidency, had agreed to do this high-profile interview to see if Chappaquiddick still haunted him. By noon the next day, Monday, it was evident that it did. That morning, front pages everywhere had convinced even the senator's staunchest supporters that his response to Chappaquiddick had been pitiful. It was obvious the senator could not and would not run.

It was especially surprising, then, four days later, to find "Chappaquiddick and Credibility" on the *Journal*'s editorial page. Even more surprising was how Bartley had chosen to present his views. "Chappaquiddick and Credibility" was less an editorial than a violent Bartley tantrum.

The piece covered two columns of the page, three times the usual length. Even more startling were the four photographs embedded in the text. No one had ever seen a *Journal* editorial with photographs before. Running alongside the editorial was another article, incorrectly and perhaps misleadingly headlined "A Judge's Remarks on Chappaquiddick," which occupied an entire column as well. It contained verbatim excerpts of a report made by James A. Boyle, the justice of the peace—not a judge—who had presided over the inquest into the death of Mary Jo Kopechne.

The editorial and the justice's excerpt were redolent with confusing facts, diagrams, inferences, observations, and explanations which readers had pored over ten years before. No one was surpised by, nor did many disagree with, Bartley's conclusion: "Edward M. Kennedy operated his motor vehicle negligently ... and ... such operation appears to have contributed to the death of Mary Jo Kopechne."[3]

But more than a few readers were surprised, shocked even, by Bartley's excess. It was as if, somehow, Kennedy had personally offended him. Bartley's piece was hardly reminescent of his esteemed predecessor, Vermont Royster, whose often controversial opinions were always presented soberly and magnanimously. Instead, the Kennedy editorial reminded veteran newswatchers of William Loeb, the reactionary and fanatical owner of the *Manchester (N.H.) Union-Leader*.

The fury of "Chappaquiddick and Credibility" called into question Bartley's own credibility as well as Warren Phillips's. "I don't see how Warren could ever have allowed such a thing to run," said a *Journal* staffer at the time.

When asked if he had shown Phillips "Chappaquiddick and Credibility" before it ran, Bartley answered, "In twenty years, I've only shown Warren two or three editorials beforehand. The Kennedy piece wasn't one of them."[4]

Bartley is not so much arrogant as he is self-assured, the result of the praise he has received from men like Vermont Royster, Warren Phillips, and Peter Kann for more than half his adult life. Bartley's self-assurance also grew when, in the early eighties, he and fellow *Journal* staffers George Melloan, Jude Wanniski, and Paul Craig

Roberts, together with Prof. Arthur Laffer, served as Ronald Reagan's chief economic adviser and created supply-side economics.

But today a more mature Bartley downplays this association. "I only met with the President three or four times to discuss supply-side economics,"[5] Bartley insists.

Even though he appeared to have the upper hand with the president, there is mounting evidence Bartley was persuaded by Reagan to fight some highly questionable battles. Take the case of El Salvador. Throughout the eighties, Bartley's editorials defended the Reagan adminstration's $6 billion support of that country's military junta, despite allegations the junta regularly resorted to atrocities to maintain control over political opponents. When the 1993 UN Truth Commission found that Bartley's and Reagan's heroes, political leader Roberto d'Aubuisson and defense minister Gen. Rene Emilie Ponce, had ordered the assassination of the archbishop of San Salvador, the ambush and murder of three American nuns and a lay church worker, and the execution of six Jesuit priests, Bartley condemned "the United Nations and the fashionable media" (that is, the *New York Times* and the *Washington Post*) for revisiting decade-old events which should best be forgotten because the Salvadoran economy "is today growing at a healthy [but unspecified] rate."

Bartley's relationships with world leaders do not affect him. Recently, his assistant, Pat Broderick, without ostentation admitted to a visitor, "We've had a busy week—Thatcher for tea, Salinas [president of Mexico] for breakfast, and Roh Tae Woo [president of the Republic of South Korea] for lunch."[6] Despite his celebrity entertaining, Bartley came across to the visitor as the same appealing, self-effacing Iowan he's always been.

In fact, Bartley's modesty, reminiscent of Kann's but of a quirkier texture, explains why his *Journal* colleagues admire him so much. Robert Bartley does not threaten people; no one has to gird himself around Bartley; no one is going to lose his job to him.

With Vermont Royster, his mentor and first boss, he was the ideal editorial apprentice—bright, tough, impertinent perhaps, but only in his writing. Not that he could, but Bartley never attempted to upstage Royster or any of his other bosses. With Warren Phillips, Bartley never brandished his superior erudition and writing ability. He gladly allowed Phillips to be chief executive officer, and Phillips gladly allowed Bartley to run his own show.

With Peter Kann, his new boss, Bartley has forged a strong

fraternal relationship. "Bartley is simply the best,"[7] volunteered Peter Kann when asked to name outstanding *Journal* newsmen. Kann, more so than Phillips, is thankful that Bartley has never used his position or relationships to endanger Kann's own ambitions. In turn, Bartley allows Kann to contribute an occasional review or editorial, an urge all other Dow Jones CEOs except Clarence Barron have always resisted. "If Peter wants to write something, I let him do it." Bartley shrugged, smiling. "He's not bad, you know."

In a cracker barrel–like atmosphere that contradicts the mahogany formality of the editorial department, Bartley supervises a large staff of thirty-four professionals which includes the *Journal's* leisure- and arts-page people. The department's day-to-day boss is Dan Henninger, Bartley's loyal and faceless assistant. Henninger is assisted by an array of homegrown talent, including Paul Gigot, George Melloan, Melanie Kirkpatrick, Raymond Sokolov, and, until recently, Suzanne Garment and Gordon Crovitz. Bartley takes great pride in these people.

"The *Journal's* editorial-staff page has far more 'ferment' [read brain power] than the *Times* or the *Post* or the *LA Times*," Bartley said. "Besides, the *Journal's* editorials are eleven hundred to twelve hundred words in length. Those other papers only have seven-fifty to eight hundred. It makes a big difference."

The staff's capable writers also do their own reporting. Rather than be bound to their desks by the breathtaking view of the Statue of Liberty, the editorial writers, like their news-department counterparts, "actually go out and gather their own facts,"[8] Kann said, beaming.

Out of every hundred editorials, Bartley usually writes five or six himself. The rest are parceled out by Henninger in what Bartley describes as "a chaotic manner." Bartley took glee in remembering how David Shaw, when researching his book *Press Watch*, was permitted to be a fly on the wall in the *Journal's* editorial department for a day. After watching the staff and Dan Henninger in particular walk aimlessly around for hours, Shaw gently asked *Journal* columnist George Melloan, "When do you have your editorial meeting?" Surprised by the question, Melloan gestured to the perambulating Henninger and replied, "You're looking at it."

Bartley is not shy about what he views as the positive effects of *Journal* editorials, whose central themes, he says, "are always advocating free markets and free men." Bartley cited Dan Henninger's news-breaking crusade against Prozac, an antidepressant drug which, many allege, can cause neurotic and psychotic side effects. According to Bartley, "Henninger scooped everyone, including our own news department, when he revealed in a series of editorials that it was the country's tort lawyers, intent on litigating the many lawsuits that stemmed from taking this controversial drug, who lobbied to keep Prozac on the market so long."[9]

The *Journal's* archconservative editorials, of course, thrive on controversy. "They give the *Journal* a personality, especially when they contradict what our own reporters sometimes write,"[10] said Norman Pearlstine, the *Journal's* managing editor.

Several years ago, for example, a *Journal* news item reported that the worsening of New York City's telephone service was due to "AT&T's decision to cut costs and reduce service levels to boost profits." A day later, a *Journal* editorial on the same subject blamed the deteriorating service on "AT&T's policy of hiring slum dwellers who were less educated and less skilled to do the jobs properly."

The disparity between the *Journal's* news and editorial departments can be traced back to Clarence Barron, who allowed reporters to codify the facts in the front of the paper if he could interpret them in the back. Today, like Phillips before him, Kann encourages a certain degree of editorial-news contradiction to keep the paper interesting.

Sometimes conflicts among the famous and powerful editorial staff make news, too. Suzanne Garment, Washington correspondent and spouse of Leonard Garment, Nixon's Watergate counsel, recently lost her job quite unexpectedly. Garment learned of her dismissal by reading about it in the *National Review.* Some believe Garment fell from favor when she lavishly praised one of her husband's clients in a column.

Bartley downplayed the affair, claiming that Garment had informed Henninger of the possible conflict beforehand. But Bartley added, "It's true I wanted to replace her. But Suzanne quit before I could. But we still gave her a good jacket blurb for her latest book."[11]

Bartley became a first-time author himself in the spring of 1992 when he published *The Seven Fat Years*, a defense of Reagan, prosperity, and supply-side economics. Written during the day in his office, it took Bartley only six months, from April to September 1991, to complete the manuscript. Rather than his signature rock-'em-sock-'em-no-nonsense prose, Bartley relied upon a deus ex machina to convey his belief that the prosperity of the eighties, due solely to Reagan and supply-side economics, can and should return in the nineties, if only everyone will stop complaining and start counting their blessings.

Bartley's deus ex machina was the Man from Mars who lands in a Kankakee, Illinois, shopping mall and proceeds to note the many signs of affluence (e.g., $100 sneakers) all around him. Much to his relief, these observations contradict "the poormouthing" about junk bonds, the savings-and-loan scandal, unemployment, homelessness, and other economic woes America has only imagined it is experiencing. Moreover, through constant repetition, the Man from Mars learns Bartley's most familiar refrain: "The United States is the wealthiest society on earth, indeed the wealthiest society in the history of mankind."

That Bartley wrote a book about finance and economics surprised no one. It was long overdue. But excerpting it in the *Journal* raised some eyebrows. On May 5, 1992, a week before the book went on sale, two-thirds of the *Journal's* editorial page was devoted to an excerpt of *The Seven Fat Years*, complete with an italicized message that advertised its $22.95 selling price.

Though often of genuine reader interest, *Journal* excerpts of staff-written books raise serious questions of probity, questions which rarely occur to the public. Few realize, for example, that because Bartley could assure the book's publisher that the *Journal* would excerpt *The Seven Fat Years*—in effect, sample it to 6 million of the book's most likely buyers—Bartley sold this priceless exposure, which was not his to sell, for probably a higher advance than he would have otherwise received. Bartley also benefited from the royalties on incremental sales that, without the excerpt, would certainly not have occurred.

Before Bartley became a master at self-promotion, he did more to enliven and broaden the editorial page than any previous *Journal* editor. In the mid-seventies, he created the board of contributors, a forum that enables the *Journal* to give voice to all manner of opinion, not only from the expected Far Right. Patterned after the *New York Times* op ed page, over the last eighteen years *Journal* readers have read the views of archconservative Paul Craig Roberts and liberal columnist Alexander Cockburn on the same day on the same page.

Another Bartley triumph occurred in 1982 when he hired Peter Kann's friend, Raymond Sokolov to be the *Journal's* leisure- and arts-page editor. Prior to Sokolov's arrival, the page consisted of Edmund Wilson's respected but infrequent theater reviews and Frederick Klein's week-old rehashes of the Super Bowl.

A graduate of Harvard College and Oxford University, Sokolov transformed the page into a feared but respected venue for criticism. The last full-time job Sokolov had held before joining Dow Jones was with the *New York Times,* as its food and restaurant critic. Prior to that, he had wandered the fringes of the New York literary scene, writing a biography of A. J. Liebling and a jejune novel.

Abe Rosenthal, then managing editor of the *Times,* took a risk hiring the young and untested Sokolov in the late seventies. Rosenthal was in the midst of creating the *Times* soft-news and features sections, which ultimately revived the paper. At first glance, Sokolov had the class and erudition to be the perfect restaurant critic for the new *New York Times.* But Rosenthal had no way of knowing that Sokolov, back then, had an extremely short attention span. He tired quickly of any routine, including eating at the Four Seasons and La Côte Basque.

The first time Rosenthal had any inkling his new critic could be a problem occurred when Sokolov solemnly reviewed a diner located in the salt marshes next to the New Jersey Turnpike. Believing that most people still followed the forties fable "Eat where the truck-drivers eat," Sokolov felt he was performing an admirable service by alerting readers to the diner's tasty Salisbury steak, though he did add that the lavatory needed to be hosed down.

According to Sokolov, Rosenthal was enraged. "You're supposed to review Lutece, not some hole-in-the-wall!" Rosenthal screamed.

Several months later, Sokolov was summarily fired after he reviewed dog food, dry versus canned.[12] But middle-age, a third chance in life, and the *Journal's* enormous power have inspired Sokolov, single-handedly, to lead the *Journal* out of the cultural dark ages. As an indication of how far the *Journal* has come, in 1977, when Ray Shaw, then Phillips's right-hand administrator, was shown a promotional ad featuring the *Journal's* review of a ballet complete with a line drawing of a ballerina, he rejected the ad out of hand, snorting, "The *Journal* will never be known for that kind of crap!"

But today, nothing of note happens in theater, film, books, art, music, dance, television, architecture, sports, or anything else that strikes Sokolov's quirky curiosity without comment from the *Journal.* Knowing this, book authors, for example, will do anything not to jeopardize their chances for a review in the *Journal*. A close friend and former *Journal* reporter flatly refused to be interviewed for this book, explaining, "I want the *Journal* to continue to review my books."

Gay Talese, the celebrated journalist/author, also wants to preserve his ties to the *Journal*'s 6 million potential book buyers. Three times, Talese received letters asking him if he would contribute whatever thoughts he had on the *Journal* and his friend, Norman Pearlstine, for this book. Twice, Talese cordially refused, claiming he knew nothing about the *Journal* or Norman Pearlstine. The author of the acclaimed story of the *New York Times*, *The Kingdom and the Power*, Talese is a recognized expert on newspapers; he also attended Norman Pearlstine's 1986 wedding to Nancy Friday. Talese's latest book, *Unto the Sons*, was reviewed favorably by the *Journal* in February 1992.

And sometimes, with or without Sokolov's knowledge, book reviewers use the enormous power of the *Journal*'s arts page for ulterior motives. On Friday, September 13, 1992, Peter Kann and his wife, Karen Elliott House, a *Journal* vice president, were among the weekend guests of Peter Jennings and his wife, Kati, in the Hamptons. Before the weekend, while admitting she was anxious to make a good impression, House joked to a visitor, "And Peter won't be much help. As usual, he knows none of the other people invited."[13] Among the other guests was Ken Auletta, author of the just-published book *Three Blind Mice*, a nonfiction account of the recent troubles of network television. What better way to make a new friend and to confirm your standing with your weekend host than to review the new friend's book in the *Wall Street Journal*?

In the September 20, 1992, issue of the *Journal*, a week after meeting Auletta, Peter Kann, who has no credentials in television, gave *Three Blind Mice* a rave.

The *Journal* arts page, which is sophisticated and smart, compares most favorably to the often bizarre and reactionary editorial page, whose chief creator, Bob Bartley, started off life in the small town of Ames, Iowa, where the University of Iowa and the State Highway Commission are located.

The only son of a veterinarian who taught at the university, Bartley was born in 1934 and raised in what he regards as idyllic circumstances. Bartley recalled, "I was part of a bunch of kids who were all children of college professors, and we received a remarkable education. It was simply a wonderful life."

Bartley's memories of growing up in Ames are so positive that he tried to reconstruct his youth for his children thirty years later in New York City.

"When Bartley told me his three daughters all went to Brooklyn public schools because he wanted them to experience life as he did, I thought he was crazy," said a former *Journal* reporter and Brooklyn Heights neighbor.

Bartley's naïveté and idealism, along with his rage, racism, and sardonic voice, occasionally creep into his editorials, which is why they are the most controversial in America. Here is a portion of the *Journal*'s commentary, "Heresy on Los Angeles," on the May 1992 riots that occurred after the five L.A. police officers who savagely beat Rodney King were acquitted of any wrongdoing.

> One important root of the drug problem in the lowlands of Los Angeles today, we have not the least doubt, lies in the glorification of drugs centered in the same city's uplands in the pop culture of the 1960s. Similarly, the proliferation of fatherless children by mothers who trace their lineage to Baptist and African Methodist churches is in no small part explained by the casual attitude toward sexuality harbored in and proselytized from the same precincts. Nor is this trend likely to be reversed by an easy line on condoms and abortion, or for that matter by militant feminism or government funding for the Mapplethorpes among us.

Reacting to this editorial, a black *Journal* reporter said: "It's a disgrace. Baptists and African Methodists harbor casual attitude towards sex! . . . How could Peter condone this?"

The editorial raises a more important question, though. Does the *Journal* practice what it preaches? Could Peter Kann, Karen Elliott House, Norman Pearlstine, or Robert Bartley himself stand up to the same moral scrutiny that "Heresy on Los Angeles" directs at the people of Los Angeles?

17

The Column Heard Round
the World

In March 1981, deep in the bowels of the Dow Jones, far from the
glamour of Peter Kann and Norman Pearlstine, Everett Groseclose,
managing editor of the Dow Jones News Ticker, finally convinced his
boss, Bill Clabby, to authorize the hiring of another reporter to
relieve the ticker's overworked staff.

Despite its eighty-seven-year history of providing professional
financiers with instant and invaluable news, within Dow Jones the
ticker was considered a backwater. "It's a place you were banished
to,"[1] said Fred Taylor, a former *Journal* managing editor. "The ticker's
strictly for drones, people who don't mind constant and blinding
deadline pressures, no bylines, and no chance for page-one glory."

After serving as Dow Jones public relations flack for five years,
Groseclose, a former Dallas bureau chief who hated the duplicity of
executive life, was desperate to return to journalism. Since he was
neither a skilled corporate courtier nor an admirer of Peter Kann's,
the lowly ticker job was the only slot open to him. That night,
commuting to his New Jersey home, Groseclose complained to a
neighbor that he had neither the budget nor the time to hire a proper
candidate. Groseclose griped about Clabby's and Dow Jones's par-
simony. "We just had our best year, yet we still pay our people
ridiculously low salaries," Groseclose said.

Dow Jones had just announced that its 1980 revenue and profits were up 20 percent from the previous year, which allowed its largest shareholders, the Bancrofts, to share $58 million in dividend income for the year. But influenced by a management axiom first promulgated by their ancestor Clarence Barron, the Bancrofts did not countenance "frivolously high" salaries. As a result, an average *Journal* reporter earned 25 percent less than his counterpart at the *New York Times*. Nevertheless, Groseclose had a plethora of candidates to choose from, people drawn to one of the finest companies in journalism irrespective of the low pay or the ticker's internal reputation.

Several weeks later, Groseclose hired R. Foster Winans, thirty-two, a trim, unprepossessing young man who had worked for the *Trentonian* for four years and who contributed an occasional free-lance piece to the *New York Times* and the *Philadelphia Daily News*. Had Groseclose had more time and less fear that Clabby would rescind the hire authorization, Groseclose perhaps might have checked Winans's background more closely. Despite its legitimate-sounding name, for example, the *Trentonian*, circulation 67,000, was hardly the type of newspaper from which Dow Jones liked to draw its recruits. Specializing in stories that help people endure supermarket checkout lines, the *Trentonian* had been scorned by a front page *Journal* article as a scurrilous tabloid in April 1979. Winans had been a general-assignment reporter for the *Trentonian*, "rewriting press releases." Prior to working for the *Trentonian*, Winans had driven a cab in New York City for three years. Before that, he had spent four years in his father's tobacco business as a salesman. Winans's education consisted of trying to complete his freshman year at McGill University twice; he left the university in November on his second attempt.

After hearing good things about Winans from a friend at the *New York Times*, Groseclose was happy to hire him at the salary of $379 per week. (In the newspaper business, because of a union mentality, salaries are usually expressed in weekly, not yearly, terms.) Winans himself had mixed feelings about the job change. On the one hand, he was thrilled to join such a prestigious organization, especially in comparison to the *Trentonian*. But the move to Dow Jones meant he would have to take a pay cut. Between his salary and his free-lance fees, Winans averaged $450 per week, which was tolerable for a young man living in Trenton, New Jersey, at that time. Now Winans had to move to New York City and live on less pay, since he could no longer string for the *Times*.

Nevertheless, Winans and David Carpenter, his gay partner since 1974, approached the opportunity with a sense of adventure, eventually finding a place they could afford on a tenement block filled with crack houses on the Lower East Side. Rent for their fifth-floor walk-up was $560 per month, a bargain considering most one-bedroom apartments in the city were going for twice that amount. It was a beginning, just as Winans's job at the ticker might be a start at big-time journalism.

Founded in 1897, the Dow Jones ticker is an electronic or on-line newspaper that provides businesspeople, especially Wall Street people, with news the moment it is reported. Speed and accuracy, not flowing prose, are what make the ticker valuable.

Journal reporters are the primary source of ticker news. Before writing their stories, reporters are required to call the ticker first, a delay most find intrusive and frustrating. When they do call the ticker, reporters convey their news through a headline and an abbreviated summary of the events. A ticker reporter then translates this news into tickerese and passes it on to the ticker's rim editor, who puts it on the wire. When a press release, for example, announces that IBM's 1990 third-quarter earnings of $2.45 per share represent a 12 percent increase over the previous year's third-quarter figure, within seconds a reporter translates this to read: IBM's 3rd qtr, $2.45 eps, up 12%.

When Winans joined the ticker, most of the staff consisted of nonjournalists with little hope of progressing to the *Journal*. The ticker required fast and accurate typing and shorthand, not a mastery of theory taught at journalism school. It also required a strong emotional makeup to withstand the constant pressure. Unlike a beat reporter who experiences peaks and valleys of activity, Winans and his associates were always at the mercy of the telephone and an impatient *Journal* reporter. Between the screams of the ticker rim editor, the constant red winks of the telephone consoles, and the need to coax the *Journal* reporters to be more cogent, working at the ticker could be worse "than Sartre's vision of hell," as a ticker reporter said recently.

Nevertheless, Winans excelled at the job. Despite a slight frame and almost fragile physical appearance, he was capable of tremendous stamina, supported by an appealing manner. Realizing his dependence on reporters, Winans went out of his way to make the experience of calling him as pleasant as possible for them. Whenever he was on the line with a reporter, he would offer up a stream of jokes that the reporters, and Everett Groseclose, soon came to appreciate.

In March 1982, Groseclose promoted Winans to cover the stock market. Lacking any financial experience or education, the next six months were marked by daily humiliations for Winans. Once, when interviewing a *Journal* reporter, Winans had to ask, "What's a P-E ratio?" But again, Winans's sense of humor, together with a quick mind and ready ambition, enabled him to master the job. Used to subordinates who were not as talented or as attractive as Winans, Groseclose became Winans's biggest booster. By the spring of 1982, Winans was earning $489 per week.

As the ticker's stock market person, Winans came in daily contact with the *Journal* stock market reporters. Again, he became friendly with many of his counterparts, particularly with George Anders, a cowriter of "Heard on the Street," which together with "Abreast of the Market" is one of the *Journal's* famed stock-touting columns. A recent graduate of Stanford University, George Anders was one of the *Journal's* new breed of the eighties, a star before he began, one of Norman Pearlstine's protégés. A bureau chief once heard Dick Rustin, Anders's boss, describe Anders as "a smart-assed kid whom Norman is spoiling."

In June 1982, Anders applied for a transfer to London so he might help Pearlstine launch the European *Wall Street Journal.* Realizing he had little say in the matter, anyway, Rustin was relieved to see Anders go. But before he could fill the slot with his own selection, he was informed by his boss, Stew Pinkerton, the New York bureau chief, that R. Foster Winans would be Anders's replacement.

Despite a pugnacious and often embittered nature, Dick Rustin knew how to survive at the *Journal.* He concealed his resentment that a ticker emigrant would shortly be coauthoring one of the country's most influential investment columns. Later, referring to Winans's promotion, Rustin confided to another bureau chief, "This place gets crazier every day."

Other *Journal* veterans were equally amazed and dismayed. Fred Taylor, the *Journal's* executive editor at the time, who carried no authority in the matter, said, "I was stunned. Who ever heard of a wire guy writing 'Heard'? You've got to be kidding?"[2]

On Anders's recommendation, Pinkerton had given Winans the job without so much as discussing it with Rustin, even though Rustin would be Winans's direct supervisor. Rustin also served as the *Journal*'s stock-market expert, having covered it since 1966, and won a Gerald Loeb Achievement Award in 1971 for *House of Cards*, which detailed the collapse of Goodbody & Co., Inc, a large securities firm.

Rustin let the snub pass without comment because he knew Pinkerton, the New York bureau chief, was playing office politics with the Winans promotion. Pinkerton hired Anders's friend so that Anders would speak highly of him to Norman Pearlstine. As a graduate of City College of New York, and therefore as someone whom Pearlstine regarded as unsophisticated, someone he would never have dinner with, Rustin had to compromise many times to remain at the *Journal*.

The move to the *Journal* made Winans compromise, too. Knowing that the other cowriter of the "Heard" column, Gary Putka, made $1,058 per week, Winans expected to receive a healthy raise. On his first day, Winans, dressed in a $28 secondhand blazer and borrowed tie, arrived in Pinkerton's office to be offered a $50-per-week raise, a sum that would boost his weekly salary to $526, exactly half of what Gary Putka made. Stunned by this paltry increase, Winans had a difficult time concentrating on what Pinkerton said after that.

Eighteen months before, in an unrelated development, David Carpenter, Winans's gay partner, had been hired by the *Journal* as a news assistant on the national news desk, working for Norman Pearlstine. That evening, Carpenter, trying to make light of the situation, said: "Please, Foster! No more unbelievable promotions. We can't afford them anymore."

Knowing he had little recourse, Winans decided to accept the situation, temporarily at least. Though he now had almost a year's experience covering the stock market for the ticker, the "Heard" column offered even that much more of a challenge. Again, his indoctrination was painful. Rustin was as remote and mean-spirited with Winans as he had been with Anders.

In fact, Rustin's desk was so close to Winans's he could hear every telephone call his subordinate made. In Winans's first week, Rustin severley chastised him for revealing to a source the subject of a forthcoming column. "You owe these fuckers nothin'," Rustin screamed at Winans the moment he put the phone down. "They're thrilled to get their name in the paper. Don't tell 'em a goddammed thing. You ask the questions, not them!"

Just as he had survived the ticker, Winans survived Rustin by making friends around him, friends who taught him the business. One of his best allies turned out to be his column partner, Gary Putka. It helped that Winans was a graceful writer. "This som'bitch can put some words on the paper," Putka would yell as he reviewed Winans's columns before they were submitted to Rustin. Winans and Putka divided the work load evenly, three columns one week, two the next. Putka had come to the *Journal* from *Business Week*, where he had covered the securities markets for three years. Before that he had been at a securities industry trade publication for four years.

Three times during his first year, Winans committed errors so serious that they required printed corrections, an embarrassment to the *Journal*, especially when related to one of its investment-advisory features. Winans appeared to lack the desire to go to any length to make his column "bulletproof." His errors, and their printed corrections, also indicated that Rustin did not review Winans's columns before they were published.

"Heard on the Street," which was created in 1928 by Casey Hogate and Clarence Barron, provides information, both positive and negative, on stocks. Heard's first author, Oliver Gingold, Hermione's brother, worked for the *Journal* for sixty-five years, retiring in 1965 after amassing a fortune of $3.2 million, following his own advice. The inventor of the phrase "blue chip stock," Gingold served for many years as chairman of the Dow Jones profit-sharing fund and guided its investments. Shortly after Gingold retired from Dow Jones in 1965, the company thought better of the practice of *Journal* reporters benefiting from their own stock advice and prohibited *Journal* news personnel from owning securities which they wrote about. "Heard" was then taken over by a series of high-profile writers, among them Dan Dorfman, who went on to further fame with *New York* magazine, *USA Today*, and cable television.

Always powerful, the "Heard" column took on even greater import in August 1982 as the market started to recover from the economic doldrums of the Carter administration. And Winans's job became more interesting as he began to interview more and more Wall Street people who made millions off his column. As just one example of his power, Winans did a story on Radiation Technology in early January

1983 in which he revealed that, despite the company's claims, the army had not authorized a huge contract for its services and FDA approval was at least a year away. The stock, which had been at $28 the day before the column appeared, plunged to $14 when the story was published.

Resentful of the disparity between his influence and his salary, Foster Winans decided to contradict the Dow Jones conflict-of-interest policy and exploit the "Heard" column to improve his finances. On January 11, 1983, Winans purchased 400 shares of stock in a company called American Surgery for $1,817.17 in the name of David Carpenter. Sometime shortly thereafter, Carpenter asked Nancy Cardwell, then the night news editor, how to look up the stock symbol for American Surgery, explaining, "That's my stock. Foster likes that stock."[3]

Winans then wrote the first of two favorable "Heard" columns on American Surgery which appeared on January 13, 1983. Worried that the first "Heard" was too positive, Rustin toned down the story. "Let's take some of the gushy stuff out," Rustin told Winans.

After USA Today's Dan Dorfman wrote a negative column about American Surgery in April, Winans, with Rustin's approval, called Lynn Singley, American Surgery's chairman, who told him the company had obtained new financing worth $25 million.

Winans, again with Rustin's approval, then wrote another column, the second on American Surgery in sixty days, relating this positive fact while also detailing the stock's slide of the previous day. By May 1983, American Surgery had gone up to $12. Winans/Carpenter cashed in and made $3,000 on their original investment of $1,800. By the end of May, the stock had risen to $15.

Winans sold the 400 shares of American Surgery on May 17, 1983 for $4,673.64, realizing a profit of $2,856.41, or 157 percent, in four months. Similarly, Winans bought 1,000 shares of Institutional Investor stock for Carpenter's account on April 28, 1983. Winans then wrote a column praising Institutional Investor on June 1, 1983, and five days later, on June 6, 1983, Winans sold the Institutional Investors stock for a profit of $497.59 off his investment of $1,237.50.

In May, while writing about American Surgery, a public relations consultant for that company introduced Foster Winans to Peter Brant, a broker with Kidder Peabody worth $20 million. He suggested to Winans that the flamboyant Brant, who had earned $1.8

million in commissions the previous year, might be an interesting subject for a *Journal* front-page feature.

Winans and Brant met in May 1983 and had at least two subsequent meetings at Park Avenue's Racquet and Tennis Club and the 21 Club in June 1983. During all three of these meetings, Brant's fabulous market success and opulent life-style mesmerized Winans. Not surprisingly, Brant's name started appearing in the "Heard" column.

Peter Brant was born Peter Bornstein into a middle-class family in North Buffalo, New York, on December 25, 1953. As a teenager, Bornstein began to create a new identity by affecting the dress and mannerisms of the rich. In 1971, Bornstein entered Babson College, a third-tier college noted for its business courses. There he learned to play the sports of the upper class—squash, fly-fishing, shooting, and polo—and little else. In his junior year, Peter Bornstein changed his name to Peter Brant. A year later, Peter Brant was accepted into the Myopia Hunt Club.

Brant graduated from Babson in June 1976 and joined Kidder Peabody a month later as a sales trainee in the bond department. Within fifteen months, he was earning annual commissions of over $300,000. Handsome, articulate, and fearless, Brant became the quintessential stockbroker, motivated by greed and his own insecurity.

At the end of 1977, through polo, Brant met David Windsor Conger Clark, a blue-blood attorney for Appleton, Rice & Perrin. Clark in turn introduced Brant to many wealthy friends, many of whom became Brant's clients.

Meanwhile, the relationship between Winans and Brant continued uneventfully until Wednesday, October 12, 1983, when they met once more at the Racquet Club for drinks. During the course of conversation, Brant confided to Winans that he had been trading heavily in Apple Computer stock. Then, according to Winans, Brant said: "You know, if I knew beforehand what was going to be in the column ["Heard"], we could make a lot of money."

The next Sunday, October 16, Winans visited Brant at the Meadowbrook Golf Club on the North Shore of Long Island. While accompanying Brant around the golf course, Brant and Winans struck an agreement whereby Winans would leak to Brant the contents of his columns in advance of their publication so that Brant could then trade the securities mentioned in Winans's columns. The pair agreed that Winans would not slant his columns in any way, since the *Journal* readership's natural reaction to the column would provide them with ample profits. Brant and Winans also agreed to split the profits after taxes evenly.

At that same meeting, Winans informed Brant that David Carpenter would participate in his end of the arrangement. Two days later, Brant informed Winans that a Kidder Peabody colleague, Kenneth Felis, plus a client and friend, David W. C. Clark, would participate in his half of the deal.

The next morning, Winans received at his desk on the *Journal* news floor a $15,000 check from Brant, made out to Carpenter, as an advance. Carpenter endorsed the check, and Winans deposited it in their joint checking account. The scheme began later that day, October 17, 1983, when Winans, using a pay telephone off the *Journal* premises and the code name, "Howard Cohen," tipped off Brant that the subject of his column for Tuesday, October 18, 1983, would be a favorable review of several oil drilling companies, including Schlumberger, Ltd. Unfortunately, as often happens, the "Heard" column was bumped for more pressing news, and it did not run until Wednesday, October 19, 1983. The first trade resulted in a loss of $37,914.25 for Felis and a $9,550.53 loss for Brant.

On Friday, October 20, 1983, Brant, accompanied by Felis, met Winans at the Racquet Club for drinks again. There they agreed that "Heard" columns which mentioned only one company, not several, might prove more fruitful. Implementing this strategy in three columns the next week, Brant made $442,409 profit from Commodore Computers, Key Pharmaceutical, and TIE Company. Winans and Carpenter celebrated by spending the weekend with Brant in his home on Long Island.

On November 3, 1983, Kidder Peabody's Compliance Department detected a correlation between the "Heard" columns of the previous week and Brant's trades in the three stocks mentioned in these columns. Suspicious after questioning Brant, Kidder Peabody hired outside counsel Sullivan & Cromwell to investigate if Brant and Felis were being tipped off by the *Wall Street Journal.* Alerted by the same correlation, the American Stock Exchange initiated a separate investigation.

When questioned by Sullivan & Cromwell, Brant and Felis denied knowing anyone at the *Wall Street Journal*. They explained that their previous week's trades in Commodore, Key, and TIE came about because they were merely following the example of Brant's friend, David W. C. Clark. If anyone had an insider at the *Journal*, Brant and Felis said, it was Clark.

The next day, November 4, 1983, Brant and Felis closed their Kidder Peabody account and opened a Swiss banking account under the name of Western Hemisphere Trade Corp., which they used for all subsequent trades with Winans. Sullivan & Cromwell and Kidder Peabody interviewed David W. C. Clark on November 17, 1983, and Clark emphatically denied knowing a tipster at the *Journal*. The next day, Clark moved his account to Bear Stearns.

In a related development, in September 1983, Norman Pearlstine finally replaced the hapless Larry O'Donnell as the *Journal's* managing editor. In his first six months on the job, Pearlstine hired vast numbers of new reporters, editors, and news assistants. The tidal wave of recruits created pandemonium. Consequently, throughout the fall of 1983, while the confused news department reeled from Pearlstine's changes, Winans and Brant carried out their scam undetected. During this period, Rustin was moved to the foreign desk, and Paul Steiger, one of Pearlstine's recruits from the *Los Angeles Times*, became Winans's boss.

Neither the intervention of Kidder Peabody's Compliance Department nor Sullivan & Cromwell's investigation deterred Winans and Brant in the least. In fact, from October 1983 to February 1984, virtually every time Winans wrote a "Heard" column, he leaked it to Brant. All told, the ring netted $690,000 from twenty-seven separate transactions. Winans called Brant so frequently that Brant's secretary, Diane Hackett, soon knew that Howard Cohen was really R. Foster Winans, reporter, the *Wall Street Journal*.

On February 4, 1984, AMEX turned over the findings of its investigation to the SEC, which indicated it was launching its own investigation.

On March 1, 1984, Winans was unexpectedly called to Norman Pearlstine's eighth-floor office. Robert Sack, Dow Jones's counsel, met him there. A few moments later, with both Sack and Pearlstine listening on extensions, Winans was interviewed over the telephone by Joseph Cella of the Securities and Exchange Commission. Winans described this scene in his book *Trading Secrets*.

After conveying Winans's rights, Cella began his questions.

"Do you maintain any brokerage accounts?" Cella asked.
"No."
"Do you know a person by the name of David Clark?"
"No."
"Have you disclosed to anyone prior to publication the subject of your articles?"
Pearlstine shook his head.
"I can't answer that until I have a chance to discuss it with counsel."
"Do you know an individual named Peter Brant?"
"He's a broker at Kidder Peabody," Winans said.
"Have you ever spoken to him?"
"Yes."
"Do you know any of his customers?"
"No."
"Do you recall the last time you spoke to him?"
"No. I was going to do a feature story about him last year but it didn't come to pass."
"Have you ever told Brant about articles that you were writing?"
Winans looked at Pearlstine. "I can't answer that until I have a chance to discuss it with counsel."
"Have you ever received money from Mr. Brant?"
"No."[4]

When the conversation terminated shortly thereafter, Winans was near collapse. But instead of a reprimand or a word expressing concern, Pearlstine said: "Don't worry, Foster. It happens to all of us eventually."

Despite Pearlstine's seemingly casual reaction to the SEC telephone call, Winans was running scared. Convinced it was just a matter of days before he would be exposed, Winans decided to accept a job previously offered him by Standard & Poor's. On Monday, March 5, 1983, Winans informed his boss, Paul Steiger, that he was resigning to accept the S&P offer. Steiger said, "How much are they offering you?" Winans responded, "Forty thousand per year." "Would you stay if I could get you $45,000?" Steiger asked. Winans refused, amazed that Steiger would try to save him after the SEC telephone call.

A week later, on March 14, 1984, Winans and Steiger were called to the office of Stew Pinkerton, then assistant managing editor. Pinkerton informed both men that the SEC had decided to make the investigation formal. On March 16, 1984, Bob Sack called Winans and recommended several lawyers. In the same telephone conversation, Sack told Winans that the *Journal* would help him pay his legal fees.

Throughout this month, Winans continued to write the "Heard" column, although, at Pearlstine's suggestion, he did stay away from any mention of the more controversial companies, Winans's last day at the *Journal* was Friday, March 23. Steiger treated him to a farewell lunch. The next day, Saturday, March 24, Winans and Carpenter, laden with guilt, confessed to their attorney, Don Buchwald. Up until that moment, Winans had always denied any wrongdoing. On the following Tuesday afternoon, March 27, Buchwald met with Dow Jones attorney Bob Sack and revealed the entire Brant/Winans scheme.

News of the scandal swept through the *Journal* newsroom like a fire, scarring everyone. Hardened, cynical reporters were shocked that the *Journal's* impeccable reputation would now be sullied. The staff was at once angry and fearful, worried over how the fallout would affect them.

That evening, while Winans and Carpenter were in Washington confessing to the SEC, Rustin left this message on their home telephone answering machine: "Foster Winans, this is Dick Rustin. All I've got to say to you is I think you are the scum of the earth."

On Thursday, March 29, 1983, Winans and Carpenter confessed to Joseph Cella at the SEC offices in Washington. That same day, March 29, on page three of the *Journal*, this story appeared:

SEC Investigates Charges of Traders
Profiting on Leaks by *Journal* Reporter

The Securities and Exchange Commission is investigating allegations that a ring of securities traders made illicit profits using information leaked to them by a *Wall Street Journal* reporter about articles subsequently published in this newspaper.

The reporter, R. Foster Winans, 35, is understood to have conceded to the SEC through his attorney that, over the past year, he periodically leaked market-sensitive information in advance of publication in the *Journal's* Heard on the Street column to one or more persons. Most of the information concerned columns that Mr. Winans wrote himself, but some involved columns written by other *Wall Street Journal* reporters when Mr. Winans learned their content.

The SEC is examining at least 21 such columns and trading in the stocks and options of the companies involved, to determine the extent to which the information may have allowed participants in the alleged scheme to realize illegal profits.

Mr. Winans, whose employment was terminated yesterday, is understood to have told the SEC through his attorney that no other *Wall Street Journal* staff members were involved in leaking the information.

The story included a statement from Dow Jones CEO Warren Phillips:

> We are saddened and shocked by this betrayal of trust. The *Journal* has stringent policies designed to protect against ethical abuses, including use of inside information. The *Journal*'s staff works day in and day out, year after year, to earn and retain the confidence of our readers. When an individual breaks faith and casts a blot on the paper's reputation, it can only inspire a deep sense of hurt and outrage among all who have labored so hard to build that reputation.

The article went on to declare that, only senior editors supervised and edited the "Heard" column. The story then said:

> After the SEC interview with Mr. Winans, the *Journal* took three steps, Mr. Pearlstine said. It began its own investigation into the security of the Heard on the Street column, seeking to identify procedures that would reduce the risk of information leaking before a column is published.
>
> It temporarily ceased assigning Mr. Winans to stories with great market sensitivity. And it reported, in one of a major group of stories on the problem of insider trading—which, by coincidence, was being published in the next morning's paper—that the SEC was "informally investigating allegations that a stock trader had advance knowledge of certain articles that have appeared in the *Wall Street Journal*."
>
> "In the final analysis," Mr. Pearlstine said, "no matter how strong the ethical codes we issue and how carefully we check a reporter's background before hiring him, the only thing that prevents occurrences like this is the character and sense of

commitment of each of our people. Even in retrospect, it is difficult to imagine what we might have done to avert Mr. Winans's acts. But we will dedicate ourselves to repairing the damage those acts may have done to the reputation for honesty and professionalism of our reporters."

Many people throughout the country were dazed. No one could quite comprehend that the *Wall Street Journal*, one of the most trusted newspapers in the world, was involved in scandal. What had gone wrong?

The article raised more questions than it answered:

Why didn't it mention Peter Brant and Ken Felis?

Why did the *Journal* offer Winans a 50 percent raise on March 5, 1984, when it knew on March 1 about the SEC allegations?

Why did the *Journal* permit Winans to continue with the "Heard" column after March 1?

Why didn't someone at Kidder Peabody, Sullivan & Cromwell, or the American Stock Exchange contact the *Journal* in November 1983 to convey the suspicion that Winans was selling his column?

How did Winans sell twenty-seven columns to Brant without detection?

If three editors reviewed every column, as the *Journal* later stated, why did Dick Rustin permit three columns on American Surgery when even Gary Putka criticized Winans for being overly optimistic and biased toward the company?

Precisely what were the *Journal's* "stringent" policies which Phillips referred to in his press release?

Why was Foster Winans hired for the position in the first place?

The investigation Pearlstine alluded to in this article was conducted by an army of the *Journal's* best reporters and editors. The findings were reported on Monday, April 2, 1984, in the *Journal's* featured column six, page one. The article was accompanied by the single phrase "A Wall Street Journal News Roundup." A byline was no doubt ruled out because it was impractical. So many reporters—and from all over the world—had worked on this piece, it would have run halfway down the page.

One eyewitness, Bob Sack, provides an interesting account of how Pearlstine and his army worked. Sack recalled:

> I remember that all-day session before the page-one piece was published [Sunday, April 1]. It was held in the editorial

conference room; on the north side of the 22 Cortlandt Street building. I walked in and they were all there: [*Journal* reporters] Jim Stewart, Dick Rustin, Monica Langley, Gary Putka, and maybe two dozen others. It was like a war room and Norman was very much in command, talking to George Anders in London through the squawk box or telling [Monica] Langley to call Winans's mother in New England somewhere. No one was better at marshaling the troops than Norman doing a breaking front-page news story. I also remember feeling sorry for Foster. He was all alone; he never knew what hit him"[5]

"The reporters had sifted through what looked like 20,000 pages of Foster's notes. They called everyone he ever worked with and for. Called his relatives, his mother, his father. Called his friends all over the world, including a reporter in Moscow. They did the same for David Carpenter," he added.

Pearlstine appeared to be at once outraged by Winans's crime and stimulated by the need to protect the *Journal*'s good name. Pearlstine also seemed to be enjoying himself. He allowed *Esquire* magazine to observe him running the project, and he likened his role, laughingly, "to someone who has to perform an appendectomy on himself."

The results of Pearlstine's crusade were contained in this headline on April 2: "SEC's Inquiry Widens as It Questions Broker, Others in *Journal* Case."

The article's meandering lead paragraph implied that the *Journal* editors were too smart to accept Winans's proposal to do a front-page leader on superbroker Peter Brant back in May 1983.

Then, in the fourth paragraph, it got down to cases:

Last week, Mr. Winans was fired by the *Journal* after conceding to the SEC that over the past year he had periodically leaked market-sensitive information.

Investigations by the SEC and by this newspaper are continuing to determine the nature and the extent of this trading network and the identities of the people involved.

The article followed with brief histories of Brant and David W. C. Clark. Then it said:

David J. Carpenter, age 34, a former *Wall Street Journal* news clerk, who has a homosexual relationship with Mr. Winans, is a key figure in the SEC's investigation.

Pearlstine approached this story with scorching vengeance. Later, for example, the piece needlessly returned to Winans's homosexuality, which must have given pause to at least two *Journal* reporters in the war room that Sunday afternoon who were themselves homosexuals.

> ... investigating Winans's relationship with Carpenter. The two are lovers. Winans recommended Carpenter for employment at the *Wall Street Journal*. They live together and Winans wears a gold ring given to him by Carpenter. . . .

The article went on to detail that Carpenter, a onetime leukemia victim, "'constantly seemed to need money,' says one of his brothers. Carpenter called his brother often, asking 'for $1,000 to $1,500 at a time,' the brother recalls."

The piece then delved into Winans's prior employment:

> Both Wilson Barto, the *Trentonian's* city editor, and a reporter at that paper allege that Winans made use of other colleagues' notes in stories that he sold to other newspapers.
> The *Trentonian* incidents didn't come to the attention of Dow Jones when Winans was hired. Everett Groseclose, the manging editor of the Dow Jones News Service, where Winans was initially employed, doesn't recall checking references at the *Trentonian*.

Pearlstine convicted Winans on the front page of the *Journal* before Winans ever went to trial. With a fury rarely exhibited by a professional journalist, Pearlstine disassociated Winans from the *Journal*. As a result, the public viewed R. Foster Winans as a felon, but not as a *Wall Street Journal* felon.

By emphasizing the issue of homosexuality as vividly and as often as the article did, the *Journal* also established new guidelines for deciding what was acceptable to publish about the personal lives of news subjects.

Some readers praised the story, others decried it.

Elna R. Tymen from Palo Alto, California, wrote:

> Your article on R. Foster Winans [page one, April 2] afforded the nation a rare look at what happens when the *Wall Street Journal* gets caught with its hand in the cookie jar. It overreacts. Like a kid blaming his actions on an imaginary friend who led

him astray, your story goes into elaborate—and importantly, irrelevant—detail to show that Mr. Winans's basic character was flawed, rather than sticking to the facts which are germane to the SEC investigation.

Since when is one's sexual bias, one's salary, the fact that one has a lover or roommate or husband or wife or whatever the arrangement might be and wears a gold wedding ring and whom one lives with—since when are these germane to a news story on a SEC investigation?

What positive steps are [sic] the *Journal* taking to stay within admittedly narrowly defined ethical and legal guidelines?

David Lukes of Kensington, Maryland, wrote:

You have washed your dirty linen with impeccable grace, honor, and class. I'm 38. I'm looking forward to reading every edition of the *Wall Street Journal* for the rest of my life.

Joseph M. deCallick of Monterey, California, wrote:

I commend you on your swift and direct response to the Winans case. Actions such as the ones you have taken to investigate and expose information which is, at the least, embarrassing are a great inspiration to those who believe in ethics in journalism.

Joseph Vaughn of West Newbury, Massachusetts, wrote:

Your self-serving article of April 2 is an outrageous example of the *Journal* covering up its own incompetence. Hanging out a few employees to dry in no way explains your hiring a woefully inept and unqualified person such as Mr. Winans.

The Winans article also marked a historic change internally. It was the first time in recent memory that the *Journal's* editorial page came to the support of the news department, the result of Peter Kann's urging Robert Bartley to help his other friend, Norman Pearlstine. On April 3, the *Journal's* lead editorial, entitled "Dirty Linen," suggested that the best way to handle such an embarrassing and unprecedented scandal was "to explore and expose" every fact. And so, Warren Phillips, CEO, watched as Kann and Pearlstine ripped down the Chinese wall between editorial and news, so long preserved by Hogate, Kilgore, and Kerby.

On April 16, prompted by criticism of the article's improper emphasis on Winans and Carpenter's homosexual relationship, Pearlstine responded with a non sequitur: "It was necessary to bring the nature of their relationship to light since Winans would not submit to an interview himself," he wrote.

A decade later the incident is still remembered by many people throughout the world. No one has ever been the least bit sympathetic toward Foster Winans. But what bothers some people was best expressed by former *Journal* reporter and then ABC business reporter Don Cordtz on Ted Koppel's "Nightline" in May 1984: "The managers of the *Journal* do have more responsibility in this situation than they have been acknowledging so far. They took a very inexperienced man, put him in a highly sensitive job, paid him some thirty thousand dollars a year, and he was an easy mark for temptation."

Peter Brant cooperated with the federal authorities and pleaded guilty to one count of mail, securities, and wire fraud for which he never received a sentence. He paid a fine of $450,000 and lives in West Palm Beach, Florida.

On August 6, 1985, Foster Winans was sentenced to eighteen months in prison, $5,000 in fines, five years' probation, and four hundred hours of community service.

David Carpenter received three years' probation, $1,000 in fines, and two hundred hours of community service.

Ken Felis received six months' imprisonment, to be served on weekends, a $25,000 fine, five years' probation after prison, and five hundred hours of community service.

Winans unsuccessfully appealed his verdict up to the U.S. Supreme Court.

Since the *Journal* established a person's sexual preference and conduct as legitimate news facts, one wonders what Jim Stewart, homosexual, future Pultizer Prize winner, page-one editor, and author of the widely acclaimed book *Den of Thieves*, felt that Sunday, April 1, when he contributed to the Winans story.[6]

Taken for a Ride in the
Trump Helicopter

Through his clamorous front-page attack on Foster Winans, Norman Pearlstine was able to divert the public from asking, Did the *Journal* demonstrate good judgment in assigning an impoverished, untested, unknowledgeable reporter to write an investment advisory column? Had the question been asked, of course, the answer would have been an equally clamorous no.

But judgment was not especially needed once the *Journal* began to ride the postwar boom. The newspaper's considerable progress was determined by an ebbless tide of prosperity, not Phillips's or Kann's ability to make wise decisions.

The Foster Winans scandal marked the start of an era in which the effects of other decisions made with the same dangerous lack of judgment began to surface. By October 1984, for example, the company's stock price had slid $7 from $51 to $44 as Wall Street reacted to the fall of Dow Jones's third-quarter earnings to 10 percent below 1983's level.

Profits were down because Phillips and Kann incorrectly calculated they could pay for managing editor Pearlstine's plans to revamp the news department with advertising- and circulation-revenue gains. But these anticipated gains did not materialize for several reasons, all linked to poor judgment.

First, Ken Burenga, then Dow Jones chief financial officer, had increased the *Journal* subscription price from $92 to $110 at the end of 1983, a decision that provoked subscriber sticker shock. By October 1984, subscriber price resistance was so great that the *Journal's* circulation dipped 3 percent, the first decrease in twenty-two years. At the same time, the *Journal's* advertising also flagged. Expecting the usual 15 or 20 percent advertising-revenues gain, Phillips and Kann were shocked as third-quarter ad lineage posted a one percent decline from the previous year's. Longtime *Journal* advertisers, such as Merrill Lynch, T. Rowe Price Funds, and Fidelity Mutual Funds, were testing competitive publications like *USA Today* and *Investor's Daily.*

And just as these damaging revenue shortfalls occurred, Norman Pearlstine exacerbated the problem. In his enthusiasm to revamp the *Journal,* the new managing editor, who had never supervised a large, complicated department before, allowed his messianic vision to get the better of him. Within ten months of assuming the post, Pearlstine hired 143 new people, increasing the staff from 417 to 560. Since the budget called for only 36 new hires, Pearlstine incurred some $11.4 million in unexpected and unbudgeted payroll expenses. Explaining Pearlstine's lack of restraint, and Kann's lack of governance, would have made for an interesting *Journal* page-one leader. Finally, when the third-quarter earnings dip raised eyebrows on Wall Street, Kann confronted his friend.

"Norman, the budget allows you to hire thirty-six people, but you've hired ninety-six!" Kann exclaimed.

"Actually, Peter, you're a bit out of date. I've now hired one hundred seventeen people over budget,"[1] Pearlstine said, laughing.

With this avalanche of new people, Pearlstine changed the *Journal's* culture overnight. Computers, internal politics, bureaucracy, memos, interminable meetings, and a staggering hierarchy of editors replaced a leaner, albeit more old-fashioned, staff. Before Pearlstine, there were, worldwide, 200 reporters, 62 editors, and 32 bureau chiefs. When Kann finally put an end to Pearlstine's employment delirium, there were 189 reporters, the same number of bureau chiefs, and 136 editors. In one month, March 1984, Pearlstine hired 19 editors for the spot-news desk alone.

Journal editor Don Moffitt said, "Chaos reigned. The *Journal* newsroom's table of organization looked like the U.S. Post Office's. Editors didn't know where the men's room was, much less when the deadlines were."[2]

Moffitt added, "When Taylor was managing editor, his desk was right on the news floor and you could talk to him anytime. Pearlstine's office wasn't even on the same floor, the venetian blinds always drawn, with his assistant, Julie Allen, standing guard like Cerberus."

But some new recruits appeared to justify Pearlstine's lack of restraint. James Stewart, for example, had the good sense to enter the *Journal* newsroom quietly and modestly, resisting the temptation to flaunt his credentials, Harvard Law School and five years as a reporter for the *American Lawyer*. An undergraduate from DePauw, the tall, natty Stewart had just the right blend of education, sophistication, and compliance to thrive in Pearlstine's new-wave culture. Eventually, Stewart won a Pulitzer, become page-one editor, authored the bestseller *Den of Thieves*, and left the *Journal* for a $2 million advance to write a book on Citicorp.

But in September 1984, Pearlstine's confidence was shaken when Peter Kann unwisely promoted his new wife, Karen Elliott House, to foreign editor. According to Fred Taylor and other *Journal* veterans, Pearlstine remarked openly, "How am I supposed to handle her? If she doesn't like the size of her raise, all she has to do is go to my boss, her husband."[3]

Pearlstine's disenchantment with House marked the beginning of a schism between Kann and himself which, although never acknowledged, eventually forced Pearlstine to resign from the *Journal*. Before Karen Elliott House entered Peter's life, no one would have predicted he and Pearlstine would eventually be estranged. About the time of House's promotion, Pearlstine confided to friends his fear of being fired by Peter Kann, either for squabbling with House or for exceeding his budget by an unacceptable amount.

But if Norman Pearlstine was worried, it didn't detract from his social life. Divorced from his second wife, Pearlstine started to be seen around New York with several ladies. The first was *Journal* reporter Laura Landro, a beautiful twenty-six-year-old journalist from *Business Week*, who was hired by Pearlstine in 1981 to work on the *Journal's* second section. Shortly after Landro arrived at the *Journal*, she and Pearlstine started dating. The newsroom viewed the relationship as unwise. Philadelphia bureau chief Frank Allen said: "It compromised the integrity of the newsroom. There were many reports of her sleeping with Norman. She was in his office all the time, and she was the source for all personnel moves."[4]

When asked if her relationship with Pearlstine compromised the integrity of the *Journal* newsroom, Landro said, "That's bullshit! Yes, I did go out with Norm. But who cares? It's nobody's business. It didn't affect my ability to do my job. I didn't get the MCA scoop or the Time Warner scoop because of it."[5]

But Allen disagreed. "As a result of sharing Norm's pillow, Landro knew beforehand who was going to be fired, promoted, and transferred. She often leaked that information. Besides detracting from Norman's credibility, Laura compromised herself. Was she competent, or was Pearlstine making his girlfriend look good?"[6]

Under Pearlstine, the value system of the newsroom changed. Members of the Kilgore tradition, people like Frank Allen and Fred Taylor, thought the change was for the worse. Members of the new wave, people like Laura Landro, couldn't understand what the fuss was all about.

Again, the *Journal's* many publics—its readers, advertisers, sources, Wall Street, Washington—did not know, nor did they care, about these internal conflicts. To them, the *Journal* was doing a brilliant job chronicling the eighties. And this success and its resulting celebrity seemed to change Norman Pearlstine. Stephen Schwarzman, CEO of the Blackstone Group, a prestigious investment banking firm, said, "Pearlstine became a star-fucker."[7]

As Pearlstine settled into his new job, he began to relish the relationships formed with Wall Street celebrity deal makers the likes of Ron Perelman, who acquired Revlon in a hostile takeover, Henry Kravis, of RJR-Nabisco fame, and Joe Flom, the Skadden Arps law-firm partner and perhaps the biggest mergers-and-acquisitions attorney on Wall Street.

Don Moffitt said:

"It was part of Kilgore's tradition that the *Journal* would ignore, and be ignored by, the financial establishment. We had to keep our distance to do our jobs. Pearlstine changed that. He mingled his personal social ambitions with his professional responsibilities to such an extent that Kilgore would have fired Norm. In fact, we used to joke and say, Kilgore's grave is as smooth as a rifle barrel's from all the spinning he's doing watching Pearlstine."[8]

After Laura Landro, Linda Gosden served as Pearlstine's Pallas Athena to New York's black-tie world. Gosden, a beautiful and vivacious Reagan press aide, came to New York in 1983 as senior vice president of corporate affairs for Warner-Amex, the ill-fated cable television venture owned jointly by Warner Brothers and the American Express Company. New York's society columns chronicled Norman Pearlstine and Linda Gosden's dating relationship. Both Phillips and Kann seemed more amused than concerned that Pearlstine was flouting the *Journal's* tradition of anonymity.

Gosden then broke off with Pearlstine to marry James Robinson III, CEO of the American Express Company. Two years later, when American Express sold its interest in Warner-Amex, Linda Robinson reaped a windfall payment of $1.07 million from the sellout. Along with several colleagues, Robinson then established Robinson, Lake, Lerer & Montgomery, a public relations firm that soon boasted an enviable client roster, including her husband's firm, American Express. Within two years, Linda Robinson was mentioned in the same breath with Gershon Kekst, long considered Wall Street's most effective public relations counselor.

Linda Robinson was so successful she became the subject of a *Journal* front-page profile. To readers, it was an interesting, well-balanced account of a beautiful, ambitious, and controversial woman who may or may not be riding her husband's coattails. But to the *Journal* newsroom, the Robinson piece caused quite a stir. Commenting on the Linda Robinson piece, *Journal* veteran Don Moffitt said; "It was a subtle form of corruption. A page-one profile in the *Wall Street Journal* is worth an awful lot of money. It's perhaps the best publicity a PR firm, or anyone else, could hope for."[9]

Bill Paul, a *Journal* reporter in the New York newsroom at the time, said, "We all knew Norman rewrote the piece to make his old girlfriend look good."[10] Some *Journal* reporters admitted it was a struggle to maintain their sense of objectivity and fairness. "When you're doing a piece on one of Norman's friends, it's hard to ignore him looking over your shoulder, even when he's not,"[11] said Laurie Cohen, a *Journal* reporter. Since Pearlstine determined Pulitzer and Nieman nominations and helped enrich several reporters by excerpting their books in the *Journal*, it's not difficult to understand his power.

Linda Gosden Robinson's sway over Norman Pearlstine and over certain reporters who were eager to please Pearlstine can be seen in the *Wall Street Journal's* treatment of her husband, Jim Robinson. In front-page articles and a subsequent book, *The Barbarians at the*

Gate, Journal reporters Bryan Burrough and John Helyar told the riveting story of how Henry Kravis, of Kohlberg, Kravis and Roberts, outsmarted Jim Robinson and others to acquire RJR-Nabisco for nearly $25 billion in January 1989. Throughout their extensive coverage, Burrough and Helyar were exceedingly kind toward Robinson, whose poor judgment had contributed to the loss by American Express and its subsidiary, Shearson-Lehman, of a surefire deal for their client F. Ross Johnson, RJR-Nabisco's CEO at the time.

Burrough and Helyar's bias can be traced to Pearlstine, who had never lost touch with Linda Robinson. In fact, their friendship eventually extended to their respective spouses. Norman Pearlstine and Nancy Friday, who had meanwhile become his third wife, saw Jim and Linda Robinson three to four times a week in New York City or in western Connecticut on weekends. "At one time, we were very close with Jim and Linda,"[12] Pearlstine recalled.

As Burrough and Helyar reported, Linda Robinson maintained an inordinately powerful role throughout the RJR-Nabisco proceedings, ostensibly as Ross Johnson's public relations counsel. A fearless and seductive manipulator of reporters, Linda Robinson struck a deal with Burrough and Helyar. In exchange for access and inside information, she implied, Burrough and Helyar were to protect her husband. Mrs. Robinson also let it be known that this *Journal* protection did not extend to Peter Cohen, head of Shearson-Lehman, an American Express subsidiary. After an eight-year honeymoon, Cohen had fallen out of favor with her husband, who was looking for any excuse to terminate his obstreperous but powerful subordinate.

On January 29, 1990, at 5:45 P.M., the *Wall Street Journal* was hosting a $68,000 book party for Burrough and Helyar's *Barbarians* in the World Financial Center, to which Pearlstine had invited many of the celebrities mentioned in the book. Ironically, at precisely the same time, thirty-three floors above the *Journal* party, Jim Robinson was firing Peter Cohen. Burrough and Helyar's portrayal of Cohen in *Barbarians* had finally given Robinson the ammunition he needed to oust the Shearson head. After terminating Cohen, Robinson joined his wife, Linda, and Burrough, Helyar, Pearlstine, Peter Kann, Warren Phillips, Nancy Friday, and many other guests at the *Journal's* party.

The first person to point out Burrough and Helyar's bias was Connie Bruck, whom Time Inc.'s editor in chief, Jason McManus, once described as "the finest financial journalist there is." Writing in the *New Yorker*, Bruck said, "What is remarkable about *Barbarians* is the degree to which the book vilifies Cohen while taking such pains to exculpate Robinson."[13]

Nothing stabs a journalist of reputation more than reproach from another journalist of even greater reputation. Connie Bruck was the first to expose Michael Milken in her book *The Predator's Ball*. Ever since she scooped the *Journal* and the rest of the financial press on the most important business stories in recent times, Bruck has wielded great influence over Wall Street. After her July 1989 *New Yorker* article appeared, her reputation grew even more authoritative because she was the first journalist to question Jim Robinson's competence in print.

Stung by Bruck, Pearlstine and Burrough needed to prove they no longer were under the thrall of Linda Robinson. There was only one way, Pearlstine and Burrough reasoned, to prove Bruck wrong: Go after James Robinson, hammer and tongs. And if another book like *Barbarians* resulted from the article, so much the better.

The handsome, always smiling, six-foot-two-inch, 220-pound James D. Robinson III, "ol' Jimmy Three-sticks" to his fellow Georgia Tech alumni, represented the quintessential corporate American prince of the eighties. He seemed to have everything, could do everything: one thousand sit-ups and three hundred bicep curls every morning, a beautiful, seductive wife, an M.B.A. from Harvard, and a management support group that included McKinsey & Company's Baker scholar-consultants, New York City's premier financier Felix Rohatyn, and "my highest flying Wall Street legal eagle, Joe Flom."

But despite these remarkable resources, Robinson's failures at American Express, as articulated by Bruck, were both numerous and notorious. These are only the highlights: Robinson's embarrassing hostile-takeover attempt to acquire McGraw-Hill in 1977; his mismanagement of American Express's Fireman's Fund insurance company, which lost $452 million in 1982 and 1983; his humiliating 1983 dissolution of the Warner Amex joint cable venture when Warner's Steve Ross decimated Robinson in the buy-out deal; his 1988 ill-fated acquisition of Kopper's, a Pittsburgh industrial conglomerate, for a Shearson client, a takeover that so vexed Koppers employees they cut up their American Express cards on national television; his January 1989 mishandling of Shearson client Ross Johnson's bid to acquire RJR-Nabisco; his inability to keep his gifted but disillusioned subordinate Lou Gerstner, who, ironically, left American Express in

March 1989 to become the CEO of RJR-Nabisco, working for the man who defeated Robinson, Henry Kravis; and perhaps most humiliating, his July 1989 public apology, accompanied by an $8 million charitable donation, to Edmond Safra, a former colleague, for American Express's worldwide smear campaign of Safra. In short, Jim Robinson presented an all-too-easy target for Burrough to prove how tough he could be.

On September 24, 1990, the *Journal* published Burrough's front-page article which told how American Express orchestrated a smear campaign against Safra. More akin to a criminal indictment than a news story, Burrough had treated Jim Robinson and Harry Freeman, an American Express executive vice president, in much the same manner Pearlstine treated Foster Winans six years before. Entitled "Vendetta," the article went on for thirteen columns, one of the longest pieces ever to appear in the *Journal*. With flourishing diagrams, maps, illustrations, and encyclopedic detail, it recounted American Express's worldwide effort to discredit Safra and his competitive banking activities. Though the reader was asked to believe that Burrough, acting as the *Journal*'s Woodward and Bernstein, had uncovered a major crime, the piece revealed nothing new. In fact, Jim Robinson had publicly admitted and apologized for American Express's wrongdoing a year earlier. The Safra smear campaign made Jim Robinson look asinine, of course. But it was not a felonious act, as an uninformed reader might have surmised from the sensationalistic treatment the *Journal* and Burrough accorded the story.

Regardless, the article enabled Pearlstine and Burrough to achieve their respective ends. Pearlstine would later boast, "Jim and Linda don't talk to me anymore,"[14] implying their enmity proved he was a fearless, objective journalist impervious to manipulation by powerful friends. Burrough redeemed his crusader image and also secured a $1 million advance from HarperCollins to transform the *Journal* article "Vendetta" into book form. As evidenced by the expensive party he gave in honor of Burrough and his coauthor, John Helyar, Pearlstine was immensely proud of the two reporters, especially Burrough, a fact that did not escape the *Journal* editors, any one of whom might have restrained "Vendetta" had it been written by someone else. Burrough figuratively sprang from Pearlstine's thigh, a celebrity, bestselling author created by the pages of the *Wall Street Journal*. The ethical lines between *Wall Street Journal* reporter and bestselling author had become blurred. It was impossible to tell where the *Journal* article left off and the book began.

Normally, Jim Stewart, the *Journal's* page-one editor, would have been the one to bridle such a piece. But Stewart knew, as did everyone else in the newsroom, that to take on Burrough in an editing dispute was to take on Pearlstine as well. Stewart had the stature and the inclination to do so, but at that moment he was negotiating for a contract for his own book, to be entitled *Den of Thieves*, and was hoping Pearlstine would excerpt it in the *Journal* as he had excerpted Burrough's *Barbarians*. To cooperate with Norman Pearlstine could mean much for the right *Journal* reporters and editors.

Later, Harry Freeman, one of the objects of Burrough's *Vendetta*, brought a $50 million libel suit against Dow Jones & Company, Inc., the *Wall Street Journal*, and Bryan Burrough. Mr. Freeman alleged that Burrough defamed him in "Vendetta" and that it "represented a concerted effort by the publication and its editorial staff to obtain a lucrative book contract—at the expense of the facts." The suit was eventually settled out of court. In its press release claiming unequivocal victory, the *Journal* termed the thirty-year-old Burrough "an outstanding reporter," citing his new job "and $600,000 contract" with the magazine *Vanity Fair* as proof of its opinion.

Just as Pearlstine predicted, when the *Journal* published *Vendetta*, the Robinsons stopped talking to him and his wife, Nancy Friday. But by that time, the Robinsons had become expendable because, mainly through Nancy Friday's tireless efforts, Pearlstine's circle of friends had widened enormously. An implacably self-confident woman, Friday introduced Norman to people no former *Journal* editor ever dared, or cared, to meet. Many were the clients of Michael Milken.

Besides being a beauty consultant to Ron Perelman, Nancy Friday has authored six books. Her best book, *My Mother My Self*, explored mother-daughter relationships and made a legitimate contribution to the Women's Movement. But after that, Friday resorted to more tawdry but lucrative subjects. "Nancy now commands an advance of over a million per book," Pearlstine said proudly. Friday's latest book, *Women on Top*, records the sexual fantasies of 150 females who responded to her questionnaire. *Time* magazine didn't like it. "If Friday hadn't padded her pages with psychobabble about women claiming their sexual destiny, and Simon & Schuster hadn't been willing to print anything to make a buck, *Women on Top* would be available only by mail and would arrive in a plain brown paper."

The Pearlstine-Friday relationship proceeded intermittently for seven years[15] until December 1987, when Friday, after a long and bitter struggle, divorced her husband, William Manville. The following July, on a Monday, the only day the couple could rent the lavish Rainbow Room, Norman Pearlstine and Nancy Friday were married before six hundred guests, including Henry Kissinger, Donald Trump, and virtually every other member of the glitterati of the eighties.

Judging from how lovingly Pearlstine speaks of his wife, it is easy to conclude she represents the single most important influence in his life today. "Nancy has emotionally emancipated me," he declared. "She has opened me up to so many other possibilities in life. There's been a real change in me after meeting her. I used to be a workaholic."[16]

Nothing captured Pearlstine's fascination with his wife, or the limelight, better than an article that appeared in *New York* magazine on February 15, 1988. In a typical Trump stunt, Donald and Ivana Trump gave *New York's* Julie Baumgold exclusive access to cover one of their junkets. The Trumps were flying several dozen celebrity guests from New York to Atlantic City in their private helicopter, *Ivana*, to attend the Holmes-Tyson fight staged at Trump Castle.

Mostly by reporting the conversations aboard the helicopter and at ringside, Baumgold captured the vulgarity of the Trumps and their guests. One paragraph caused shame in the *Journal* newsroom:

> "This is the helicopter Fergie wanted to ride in," Donald explains, leaning back on the "Ivana's" beige-pleated leather seats.
>
> "Everything in life is luck," says Donald as the "Ivana" whirls 200 miles per hour through the darkening skies.
>
> Norman Pearlstine, the managing editor of the *Wall Street Journal*, leans across the aisle to Donald.
>
> "Nancy," he says very quietly, nodding at the tall blonde woman with the gold dog-collar necklace across the way, "has had three No. 1 best-sellers. She sold 12 million books."
>
> "Twelve million books," says Donald, and his face goes down as Pearlstine explains who Nancy Friday is.

Bill Paul, veteran *Journal* reporter, said, "Had I done that, I would have, and should have, been fired."[17]

Pearlstine, however, was not the least bit embarrassed. "The Trump helicopter ride?" Pearlstine said. "When I was invited, I went to Warren and Peter. I told them the positives—getting closer to Trump—and the negatives—how it might look to some people. Both Warren and Peter said, 'By all means. You and Nancy go.' The conflict of interest policy states in instances like that, you check with your supervisor. I did. When the CEO and the publisher both say it's okay, then I assume it's okay."

Both Peter Kann and Warren Phillips confirmed they gave Pearlstine permission to accept the Trumps' invitation.

Many other *Journal* newspeople, however, merely smiled at the Trump incident. To them, it was simply "Norman being Norman," a quirk to be tolerated in exchange for what they consider his outstanding contributions to the *Journal*. Perhaps Pearlstine is best known for creating the *Journal*'s third section in the fall of 1988.

Unlike the *Journal*'s second section, which had been instituted seven years earlier to accommodate advertisers' crushing demand for more space, the third section was created strictly with the reader in mind. Pearlstine wanted the *Journal* to cover new beats, such as technology, the environment, law, enterprise, small business, and media and marketing. To accomplish this, he shifted all financial news and statistics to the new third section, freeing up the second section for the new-industry articles and columns. As testimony to the effectiveness of Pearlstine's changes, within a year of establishing the *Journal*'s media and marketing beat, the advertising industry began to regard it as a must read. Previously, the *New York Times*'s equivalent had been the industry's standard for thirty-five years.

Dow Jones CEO Warren Phillips, the chief designer of the second section, said, "Norman Pearlstine is a brilliant editor who, more than anyone else, prepared the *Journal* for the twenty-first century with the third section."[18]

Inevitably, some *Journal* newsmen disagreed. Fred Taylor, former managing editor, said, "In effect, the third section chops up the paper into little newsletters. For example, instead of a red-hot story on an antismoking law ruling appearing on the front page or page three, it can be buried in the legal column on page twenty-three underneath three other stories."[19]

But many other people, in and out of the *Journal*, agreed with Phillips, especially with respect to Pearlstine's competence and contributions. David Halberstam, for example, was highly complimentary. "Under Norman Pearlstine, the *Journal* has made a concerted effort to hire good, aggressive reporters. The paper has a real commitment to good journalism nowadays. I don't know Pearlstine well, but when I do run across a bright young person, I send him or her to Norman rather than to the *Times*. He's the best editor at the *Journal* in a long, long time."[20]

Nodding his head affirmatively when told of Halberstam's opinion, Pearlstine rates himself highly, too. "Malcom Forbes left his deathbed to give me the National Press Foundation's Editor of the Year Award," Pearlstine remarked. "Compared with my immediate predecessors, I am a different person. Ed Cony, though extremely difficult to work for, was the best newsman of the bunch, I guess. But he was no great shakes. Fred Taylor simply never read the paper. He was an average diplomatic reporter, a San Francisco bureau chief and then they brought him in to be Jim Soderlind's assistant. But in the first six months of Jim's reign as managing editor, Jim developed an alcohol problem and the company had to get rid of him. Taylor sort of fell into the job. He was not very good at it. Then there was Bill Kreger who had been the national news editor for eighteen years. A nice guy, but the spot news stories were so loose you could drive a truck through them. Then came O'Donnell, who in the last eighteen months of his tenure developed severe emotional problems. He exhibited notice-able mood swings which made it very difficult to work for him."[21]

Laurie P. Cohen, a *Journal* reporter who researched and reported for Jim Stewart's *Den of Thieves*, is one of many *Journal* newspeople who is extremely fond of Pearlstine personally, but who chafed under him professionally. "When I worked for Dick Rustin [Foster Winans's editor]," Cohen said, "that cretin wanted to fire me. Norman saved me, and I'm grateful to him for that."[22]

But in March 1991, when Cohen turned in a story preapproved by her immediate supervisor, Dan Hertzberg, revealing that hostile raider Eli Jacobs was about to default on $400 million worth of junk bonds, the piece was summarily killed. In explaining why, Hertzberg told Cohen that the *Journal* editorial hierarchy had said, "We can't run that, Jacobs is a good friend of Norm's."[23]

Outraged, Cohen went directly to Pearlstine, who said, "I don't want to alienate one of our good sources. And besides, Eli is not going to default on those bonds."[24]

Later, when asked if Cohen's version of what happened is true, Pearlstine said, "I was not involved at all because I am too close to Eli. You're going to have to talk to [associate managing editor] Paul Steiger and [senior editor] Barney Calame. My recollection, how-

ever, is the story was not strong enough. But that was Barney
Calame's decision. The story contained several unattributed quotes,
and an analyst from a peripheral industry was quoted. It seemed to
me we should not be quoting analysts who are not expert in Eli's
business. I talked to Calame, and I reminded him that Jacobs had
been a good source to the *Journal* over the years. He's always talking
to a number of our reporters, helping them out. I said to Barney: 'You
don't owe him [Eli Jacobs] anything. Just make sure you're
accurate.'"

Assistant Managing Editor Paul Steiger was more indignant but
less illuminating in his disagreement with Cohen's account of this
incident. "That's absolute nonsense," said Steiger. "It just isn't true.
Barney Calame determined the story didn't work."

Why?

"It didn't go anywhere. Just didn't move the ball,"[25] Steiger
responded vaguely.

Although Barney Calame, who considers himself the newsroom's
ethicist, initially refused to speak about why he rejected the Eli
Jacobs story, he eventually explained: "Both Norman and Paul
[Steiger, Calame's immediate boss] were away, and the national news
desk asked me to look at the story because they knew Jacobs was a
friend of Norm's. The story did not add up. I rejected the piece
because Laurie did not specify what Jacobs's consultancy fees specifically were."*

Throughout their lengthy and conflicting explanations, both Pearlstine and Calame referred to Cohen, a ten-year respected veteran, as
if she were a wayward child acting out against her kind and indulgent
older brothers.

But three other unlikely people confirmed Cohen's version of the
story.

The first person to agree with Cohen's version was a $12-million-
per-year Wall Street executive, Stephen A. Schwarzman, president
and chief executive officer of the Blackstone Group, a small but
influential merchant bank. Schwarzman's confirmation occurred in
the middle of a conversation about a *Wall Street Journal* front-page

---

*Calame was referring to the part in Cohen's news story which alluded to fees Eli Jacobs
paid himself as a consultant to his own company. Apparently, Cohen considered these fees
irregular and excessive, though she had not specified them. Presumably, Calame felt that if
Cohen were going to make such an accusation, she should have included the exact sum of
the fees.

article on Blackstone that "made the firm look bad. And me, I looked like a real asshole."

Seated in his private conference room overlooking the Waldorf-Astoria, Schwarzman looked slightly wilted in contrast to a glistening gold-framed oil painting depicting a nineteenth-century naval battle and an impeccable antique Sarouk rug.

Schwarzman continued: "Randy Smith [a *Journal* reporter] called one day and said, 'We are going to do a piece on you, whether you cooperate or not.'"[26]

Though he resented Smith's strong-arm approach, Schwarzman gave Smith complete access after conferring with his partners, who include Peter G. Peterson, Nixon's secretary of commerce. Schwarzman said, "Randy had the run of the place. There was one time even when I told him: 'Look, we're open here. I have nothing to hide, and you'll find out about it anyway. I'm getting a divorce. But please, don't use it.' Randy says, 'Don't worry. I won't cross that line,'" Schwarzman said.

"But then I start getting these calls from friends telling me 'Smith just called me. Wants to know the dirt about you and your divorce.'

"Pissed, I call Randy. 'Hey, fuckhead. What the fuck are you doing? You told me you would not cross that line,'" Schwarzman recalled.

"Randy said, 'Yeah. But I never told you where the line was!'

"Don't ask me how, but I get a copy of Smith's story several days before it ran. I go fucking out of mind. I don't care so much about myself. But I am really pissed about the firm. This is my life. We've got great people here and a great reputation. It's not a job, it's my life, for chrissake. So I call Steve Swartz, a *Journal* editor and a good fucking guy. He and I had been on a few TV shows together.

"Steve agrees to see me. On the morning of our meeting, while shaving, I write on a tissue all that's right with Blackstone and all that's wrong. These are facts, not opinions. I present them to Steve and ask him to evaluate Smith's piece and see if he was being fair. That's all I ask.

"Swartz says to me, 'You're right, Steve. Smith was not fair. I'm not concerned so much about you as I am about the *Journal*. We should get this story right.' So Steve does as much as he can to fix the piece. The first several paragraphs end up being positive about the firm, but then Smith got me back for going to his boss by printing all sorts of negative things about me in the middle of the story.

"So then, through Pete [Peterson, Schwarzman's partner], who plays tennis with Warren Phillips [CEO of Dow Jones at the time], Pearlstine comes up and visits me. I tell him the paper is adrift. It has no compass. It has lost its way. I quote Jack Welch [CEO of GE] who wondered, 'What are they [the *Journal*] trying to do these days?'

"I saw Norman at lunch at the Four Seasons the other day. He called me over and asked, 'Have you noticed a change, Steve? Haven't we been more positive lately?' We all know Norm is a star-fucker and the way to get to him is to take him to lunch.

"Look what happened to Eli Jacobs. Now here's a guy who is a crook, an out-and-out crook, but he's a big buddy of Norm's. About a month ago, Jacobs called Norman up and got a negative story about himself killed. He told Norman that the *Journal* reporter Laurie Cohen's assertion he was in financial trouble was untrue. Norman believed him and killed the story."[27]

The second person to confirm the Jacobs-Cohen-Pearlstine episode was Davis Weinstock, a financial public relations consultant whose clients include IBM and Wasserstein & Perella, a Wall Street investment banking firm as well known and as prestigious as Blackstone.

"It is absolutely true that anyone of public note in the business world can call Norman Pearlstine, either through intermediaries or direct, have dinner with him, and, as a result, get a *Journal* story about them either killed, postponed, or ameliorated. That's what Eli Jacobs just did. We all know that. Pearlstine is, as the street says, 'reachable.'

"The *Wall Street Journal* is a disgrace. How can Norman Pearlstine and Nancy Friday, two social wannabes, hobnob with Jim and Linda Robinson, Joe Flom, the Perelmans, Dick Beattie [Cravath, Swain & Moore attorney], Eli Jacobs, and many others and not compromise the basic integrity of the *Journal*? Pearlstine is an insult to journalism. I find it shocking, absolutely shocking.

"Norman, of course, argues he is free to do whatever he wants, including maintaining a very close friendship with Ronnie Perelman. But that's unethical. As the top editor of the *Journal*, Pearlstine has the responsibility to monitor the financial community as other papers monitor the general community.

"Dick Beattie enjoys absolute interference with Norman Pearlstine over any of Beattie's clients. Sarah Bartlett, in her recent book [*The Money Machine*], also showed how Randy Smith and George Anders [two *Journal* reporters] favor Kravis shamelessly, all because Henry [Kravis] is a pal of Norman's. Let me cite a recent example. I happen to know for a fact that Randy Smith had written a story on Kravis which both he and Paul Steiger [then the *Journal's* assistant managing editor] thought was going to appear on the *Journal's* front page. It talked about Kravis making billions off some deal. Pearlstine interceded because Dick Beattie called him. Pearlstine postponed the story for ten days. Then it appeared in the back of the third section, buried in the stock tables. Worst of all, the story did not have a headline and a certain word, 'fraud,' was excised from it.

"Norman Pearlstine cultivated the worst kind of unhealthy atmosphere for reporters at the *Journal*, sensationalistic. Randy Smith, David Hilder, Bryan Burrough, Jim Stewart, and George Anders create the news for sensationalistic purposes.

"George Anders is a product of Pearlstine's sensationalistic atmosphere. He compromised his objectivity and the *Journal's* integrity to gain access to KKR [Kohlberg, Kravis and Roberts]. The *Journal's* newsroom and other responsible financial journalists laugh at George Anders. Look at the story Anders wrote about Kravis and RJR's refinancing deal with Met Life. He made it appear heroic when in fact it was a horrible bailout for KKR's heinous miscalculations."

[In her book *The Money Machine* Sarah Bartlett reports that George Anders, the *Journal* reporter who covers Henry Kravis and his firm, received a $275,000 advance to write a history of KKR. Bartlett accuses Anders of writing overly flattering and at times misleading accounts of Kravis's activities so that he would continue to enjoy Kravis's confidence to finish his book.][28] Weinstock continued. "Dick Beattie likes to impress potential clients. If they mention they are having a problem with the *Journal*, Beattie inevitably says: 'Norman Pearlstine is a close friend. Let me call Norman and set up a dinner and tell him the *Journal* is killing you. Inevitably, Norman comes to the dinner and just as inevitably, Norman compromises. And I can vouch for this with one of my own clients, Bruce Wasserstein of Wasserstein & Perella [another prestigious Wall Street merchant bank]. For years, the *Journal* was all over Wasserstein. Burrough played him for one of the heavies in *Barbarians at the Gate*. When Bruce became my client, I advised him to ask Joe Flom [partner at Skadden Arps, a law firm] if he would set up a dinner with Norman Pearlstine. At first Bruce thought I was crazy to suggest that. But eventually he did, and guess what? Since the date of that dinner

with Flom and Pearlstine, the *Journal* has not printed one negative
thing about Wasserstein.

"Bruce Wasserstein was depicted by the *Journal* as the symbol of
greed and an unlikable chap. The *Journal* made him the whipping
boy of the eighties. Hilder and Smith [David Hilder and Randall
Smith, two *Journal* reporters] did an update story on Wasserstein,
emphasizing how he slipped in the deal rankings. The irony is that
Wasserstein, like Joe Flom, was still able to manipulate and use the
Journal. Both those guys put companies in play, thereby getting
clients, by saying to Jim Stewart [*Journal* reporter] or some other
[*Journal*] reporter, 'Listen, you should probably know that I hear XYZ
company has compiled a short list of companies to buy and the A,B,
C companies are on it. The reporter in turn would call, say, Company
C and say, 'You're on the short list.' This happened with Campeau,
which happened to be a client of mine. Three days later, a *Journal*
story confirmed all this. It was all part of the deal frenzy of the
eighties. It became a self-fulfilling prophecy. All because of the
Journal."[29]

The third person to confirm Cohen's version of the Eli Jacobs story
was Bob Dallos, a reporter in the New York Bureau of the *Los
Angeles Times* and a former *Journal* staffer. Like Schwarzman, during
an unrelated conversation, Dallos volunteered; "Eli Jacobs got a bad
Journal story about him killed by calling Norman."[30] When asked
how he came by such information, Dallos explained that one of his
Los Angeles Times colleagues in the New York bureau, John Goldman, was a good friend of Jacobs's and that Jacobs had boasted to
Goldman how he got the story killed.

Six weeks later, Memorex, Eli Jacobs's company, defaulted on $400
million worth of junk bonds, just as Cohen had predicted. With no
excuse left, Pearlstine had no choice but to run a story on Jacobs. But
it was not Cohen's original story that finally appeared in the *Journal*.
The second story "was cowritten with a Washington bureau reporter
to water it down considerably,"[31] Cohen said.

Later, when told about these stories and asked to comment if the
Journal's integrity had been compromised by Pearlstine and his
book-publishing reporters, Don Macdonald, vice chairman of Dow
Jones, said, "[Pearlstine] sullied the *Journal*'s reputation, that great
halo. And those guys would never have written books under Kilgore.
It's Warren Phillips's fault. He's the CEO. I'm disappointed Warren
never raised hell with Norman."[32]

19

Black Monday

The one staffer-authored book the *Journal* should have excerpted—but didn't—was Tim Metz's *Black Monday: The Catastrophe of October 19, 1987 and Beyond*. Metz was a twenty-one-year *Journal* veteran and member of the newspaper's Market Group, which consists of senior specialists who cover the financial markets. He reported what many people believe, that the *Journal* failed in its coverage of Black Monday. Moreover, Metz also admits that the *New York Times*, whose business coverage had provoked derisive criticism from readers for years, did a good job.

He wrote:

> There is a scattershot flavor to the *Times's* coverage, but it is immensely dramatic and will galvanize critics of Steiger [the *Journal's* assistant managing editor] and the Market Group. The *Journal's* coverage, these critics will allege, is dull and undramatic, overstocked with numbers and unclear. And while it won't be articulated, there will be a persistent suggestion that the Market Group's stock market coverage has been soft and uncritical...that if the Markets Group had been tougher and more vigilant, the excesses that led to this debacle might have been checked.... Yes, the Markets Group had failed the *Journal*. Steiger had failed."[1]

Metz singled out Paul Steiger, the *Journal's* assistant managing editor, because Steiger ran the *Journal* throughout much of the two-week stock-market crash. Norman Pearlstine, Steiger's boss, was in Frankfurt, Paris, and London from October 11 to October 20, 1987.

Later, though disagreeing with Metz's appraisal, Norman Pearlstine did admit the *Journal*'s coverage was less than adequate. He
said, "Black Monday was a breaking story which does not play to our
strength. And we thought Black Monday was going to be merely a
one-day correction of a hyperactive market."[2] Black Monday was the
day the Dow Jones Industrials fell 508 points, down 22 percent, the
single largest decline in the history of the market.

As Metz implies in his book, Black Monday was years in the
making. It began as a lurking shadow in 1981, when Ronald Reagan
proclaimed that deregulation and supply-side economics, working in
tandem, were the answers to the country's fiscal prayers.

Ronald Reagan was elected largely on his campaign promise that
within four years he would eliminate the $73.8 billion federal budget
deficit, which was up from $2.8 billion in 1970. Reagan and his many
supporters fervently disagreed with Keynesians, who regard deficits
as a necessary evil to prime the nation's economic pump. Reagan
believed the country should be run like a prudent household. The
government should live within its means and only spend in a year
what it earns in a year. And the way to accomplish that, Reagan said,
was through supply-side economics, a theory that Robert Bartley, the
Journal's editorial-page editor, had persuaded Reagan to adopt.

Since 1976, Bartley had repeatedly told Reagan through editorials
and one-on-one conversations that the deficit would be eliminated if
the supplyside of the supply-and-demand economic model was
stimulated by lowering tax rates and increasing defense spending.
Reagan was skeptical at first. The core argument of supply-side
economics—lower tax rates result in higher tax receipts—was difficult for even the most sophisticated intellects to accept.

But after seeing the famed Laffer curve, which proved through its
graphic depiction of quadratic equations that Bartley was correct, and
after being reminded that the new theory also called for increased
defense spending, a holy tenet of archconservatism, Reagan became
Bartley's most impassioned economic disciple. So much so, in fact,
that supply-side economics became Reaganomics. It was the first
time in recent memory that a journalist had held such authority over
an incumbent president, an advantage which pleased Kann and
Phillips but displeased many *Journal* Washington bureau staffers
greatly. Alan Otten, *Journal* Washington veteran, said, "Bartley was
so tight with the President that it reflected badly on our credibility,
our impartiality."[3]

From 1981 to 1986, President Reagan did all that Bartley suggested to make supply-side economics work. The president increased the defense budget 41 percent by funding such military projects as the B-1B bomber ($280 billion), the MX missile ($20.7 billion), and Star Wars ($9.3 billion) while simultaneously reducing taxes 23 percent. But contrary to Bartley's assurances, Reagan's actions had an effect opposite to the one intended on the federal budget deficit. By 1987, it had ballooned to $220.7 billion.

Both Bartley and Reagan blamed Federal Reserve Chairman Paul Volcker, who, ignoring supply-side economics, had increased interest rates to double-digit levels to combat the country's 11.2 percent inflation rate. As a result, rather than spend the largess gained from Reagan's tax rate reductions, consumers kept their money in high-interest savings instruments. By so doing, consumers contradicted the core expectations of Bartley's Reaganomics. By spending less, less tax revenue was generated. Less tax revenue from spending, coupled with lower tax rates, decreased the government's tax receipts appreciably. Then, with fewer tax receipts available to pay for its sharply increased defense spending, the federal budget deficit grew much worse instead of disappearing.

In late 1982, with inflation under control, Volcker did ease interest rates back down, which made the stock market soar. Now overflowing with new capital, Wall Street devised several new debt instruments to soak up the excess. The most famous, the junk bond, spawned the peculiar prosperity of the hostile-takeover mania which raged until Black Monday, October 19, 1987. While perhaps fifty hostile raiders became billionaires, hundreds of thousands of middle managers were imprisoned in their suburban dens, made redundant by these same raiders bent on slashing payroll expenses to help meet their 15 percent junk-bond debt payments. At the same time investment bankers two years out of business school were receiving bonuses of $400,000, hundreds of thousands of assembly-line workers, shipping clerks, and route drivers were losing their homes. But rather than heed the economy's failures, the nation became mesmerized by the economy's successes.

Bartley's editorials romanticized the era. Men like junk-bond king Michael Milken, arbitrageur Ivan Boesky, and billionaire raiders Ron Perelman, Henry Kravis, and Donald Trump became folk heroes, the Wyatt Earps of the eighties. Many people, including those in the *Journal's* newsroom, were lulled into believing corporate America's massive unemployment and other signs of economic failure were merely a "one-day correction of a hyperactive market."

Although the Dow reached its all-time high of 2700 in 1987, several developments occurred that year which signaled all was not well on Wall Street. First, the market experienced several days when the Dow Jones Industrials gyrated wildly, up by 50 points one day, down by 40 the next. Then, in September, Alan Greenspan, Volcker's replacement at the Federal Reserve, increased the federal discount rate from 5.5 to 6 percent, thereby driving up interest rates. Institutional investors prepared to leave the stock market for the bond market in pursuit of the higher yields caused by higher interest rates.

Then, coincidentally, in early October 1987, West Germany increased its interest rates for the third time in four months, slowing down America's much-desired reduction of its trade deficits. On the advice of Treasury Secretary James Baker, the president had switched his deficit-erasing ambitions from the federal budget, which now stood at $227.8 billion, to the trade deficit. Baker believed if more European countries could increase their importation of U.S. goods, the trade deficit would be reduced, putting the economy on a more solid footing. But every time West Germany increased its interest rates, its European neighbors and U.S. customers had to retrench to defend against the stronger deutsche mark. Retrenchment, of course, meant postponement of plans to buy U.S. goods.

On Friday, October 8, the New York Times ran an article that explained Baker's annoyance with the West German Bundesbank and its possible deleterious effect on the U.S. economy.

On Sunday, October 11, 1987, Norman Pearlstine, accompanied by Nancy Friday, flew to Paris for a ten-day visit to see European Journal advertisers. It was more a junket than a legitimate business trip. Fred Taylor said, "Hell, at that time, the European Wall Street Journal barely had any advertisers, much less advertisers who needed or wanted to see Norman."[4]

On Wednesday, October 14, the New York Times reported that Wall Street was rocked by news that the just-announced August trade deficit had not improved as much as had been expected, a direct result of West Germany's increase in interest rates. Accordingly, the Dow Jones Industrials plunged a record 95.48 points.

But Pearlstine continued his visit to friends and advertisers in Paris on October 14, unfazed by the Wall Street turmoil. He could have, for example, gone to Bonn, two hundred miles away, and interviewed officials at the Bundesbank, who might have been eager to tell their side of the interest-rate story to such an influential American journalist as the managing editor of the *Wall Street Journal*.

On Thursday, October 15, the Dow dropped another 57 points, to close at 2355. The drop was caused by lingering reactions to the August trade gap and to a New York bank's raising its prime lending rate from 9.25 percent to 9.75 percent. Pearlstine continued to enjoy Paris.

On Friday, October 16, an Iranian missile hit an American-flagged Kuwaiti tanker in the Persian Gulf, injuring eighteen crew members. Fear of war with Iran caused the Dow to plunge 108 points, another record drop. On Saturday, the *New York Times* predicted an avalanche for Monday's stock market. The *Wall Street Journal* does not publish on Saturdays.

Pearlstine and Friday spent the weekend at a little Left Bank hotel, apparently still unconcerned by what everyone else was predicting would be a debacle on Monday.

On Sunday, October 18, Paul Steiger, one of two *Journal* deputy managing editors, and a full complement of editors reported for work to prepare Monday's edition of the *Journal*, including a page-one leader that soberly reported the stock market turmoil of the previous week. Steiger did not confer with Pearlstine on this decision or on any other aspect of the coverage of the impending crisis. When the last catastrophe had occurred, the previous year's explosion of the *Challenger* space shuttle, Pearlstine had been in France, too.

In a burst of optimism, Steiger softened the story considerably at the last moment. "The market could come back," he explained. Unfortunately, Steiger was wrong. By the end of business, Monday, October 19, the Dow had plunged to 1738.74, a drop of 508 points, or 22 percent, the single largest decline in the history of Wall Street. Norman Pearlstine chose to remain in Paris to attend a party that evening.

All day Monday, as the debacle grew worse, Steiger and his associates, led by John Prestbo, a senior stock-market editor, felt an added pressure. The story did not play to the *Journal's* strength: magazine-type articles that revisit an event after months of research to explain why it happened. On top of everything else, *Journal* reporters kept bumping into their *New York Times* counterparts, which ten years before would have been an unprecedented intrusion.

Working out of the ninth-floor editorial conference room, by 6:30

P.M., Monday evening, Steiger and twenty subeditors had signed off on the *Journal's* reporting efforts of Black Monday, which had included 325 out of the news department's 500 employees, worldwide. Throughout it all, Steiger was his usual calm, undemonstrative self even while settling a raging dispute between Karen Elliott House and Glynn Mapes, the page-one editor, who were old enemies. As the foreign editor, House felt the *Journal* should report on page one how the United States had answered the Iranian missile strike over the weekend. Written by Tim Carrington and Gerald Seib of the Washington Bureau, the three-paragraph story, slated for page twenty-five, reported that U.S. Navy warships had bombarded an abandoned Iranian oil platform late Sunday evening.

House seized the piece and "added any number of assertions which were neither accurate nor responsible to get it on page one,"[5] said Alan Otten of the Washington bureau. "She added all kinds of bullocks as to how the Reagan administration was going to deal with the Ayotollah strongly. Shelling an oil-rig with no one on it was hardly a retaliatory act of war."

Mapes, the page-one editor, had seen Carrington and Seib's original piece. He called the two reporters in Washington and asked them if they were aware that House had hyped their story so it might qualify for page one. They were not, and only after Seib and Carrington insisted their bylines not appear on her exaggerated article did House retract her additions. But she did manage to persuade Steiger to slot the piece for column one in the Tuesday, October 20 issue.

Nevertheless, by 7:00 P.M. on Monday, Steiger and his associates had penetrated Wall Street's hysteria to produce three page-one leaders which reported the facts, if not the causes, of Black Monday. On the first page of the second section, and throughout the inside pages, additional stories explained other aspects of the crash.

The *Journal's* coverage of Black Monday contrasted sharply with how the *New York Times* reported it in both tone and quantity. As Metz had suggested in his book *Black Monday*, the *Journal* reported the debacle in a muted voice. As it had done with the 1929 stock-market crash and the attack on Pearl Harbor, the *Journal* searched desperately for a silver lining and implied, as Pearlstine had admitted, that the Dow would rally by the end of the week.

The *New York Times* devoted its entire front page to Black Monday.

It led with a banner headline, almost as big as its logo, which covered the entire width of the page. But even more dramatic than the text was a large three-column photograph of young Wall Street traders sitting at their desks at the end of the stock-exchange trading day, their faces buried in their hands, trying to forget the psychological earthquake they had just walked through.

Commuters on the New Haven railroad who normally glance at the *Times* first and then study the *Journal* carefully, lingered with their *Times* that morning. Comparing the two papers' issues for Tuesday, the *Times* ran thirty-eight columns on the story versus the *Journal's* seventeen.

Five years before, these same commuters, many of whom worked on Wall Street, would regularly deride the *Times's* Wall Street coverage. But ever since the *Times* had discovered satellite transmission in 1984 and decided to be a national newspaper of sorts, its Business Day section had been improving steadily.

Later, industry experts confirmed what many *Journal* staffers feared that day. On one of the biggest financial stories of the century, the *Journal* had been upstaged by a once-weak competitor. The *Times* had conveyed the trauma, the human toll, of Black Monday convincingly, while the *Journal's* coverage had been clinical, too full of statistics. Moreover, some felt that the *Times* was more critical of some of the suspected causes of the crash, principally large stock portfolios traded on computers.. The *Journal*, on the other hand, seemed to back off criticizing Wall Street, its core readership.

Norman Pearlstine returned to work on Wednesday, October 21. He and Nancy had remained in Paris to attend a party Monday evening hosted by newspaper publisher Jean-Jacques Servan-Schreiber. At any time from the previous Thursday, October 15, onward, Pearlstine could have returned to his responsibilities in New York via a charter or the Concorde within four hours. Later, Pearlstine would admit: "Besides Black Monday, there were three other big stories in the eighties. And I was in Paris or the south of France for all four of them."[6] They were the *Challenger*, the attempted overthrow of Gorbachev, and the Solomon Brothers trading scandal.

Pearlstine's absence revealed his unsteady regard for his responsibilities and Kann and Phillips's unwise tolerance of cavalier and capricious behavior. Moreover, Pearlstine's abandonment of his colleagues in a time of extreme crisis, besides demoralizing the *Journal* newsroom, stood in contrast to the conduct of his *New York Times* counterpart, Abe Rosenthal, who pursued this story as if his reputation rested on the outcome.

But a month later, on November 20, Jim Stewart and Dan Hertzberg redeemed the *Journal's* honor. In a page-one leader entitled "Terrible Tuesday," Stewart and Hertzberg explained how Tuesday, October 20, not Black Monday, was the "most perilous day [on Wall Street] in 50 years." Stewart and Hertzberg offered an hour-by-hour explanation of how the world's financial markets, pegged to the New York stock market, had almost collapsed. They showed how the markets were enlarged by program trading and an across-the-board reluctance by major banks to extend loans to Wall Street's specialists who needed financing to complete their trades. And without the specialists' trades, the market could erupt. Catastrophe had been averted, Stewart and Hertzberg explained, only through the intervention of White House chief of staff Howard Baker and the staged turnaround of the Chicago futures market.

"Terrible Tuesday" offered what people had wanted ever since the market crashed: a rational explanation as to why the Dow dropped seven hundred points in a week. Six months later, Stewart and Hertzberg won the Pulitzer for explanatory journalism for "Terrible Tuesday" and a piece published nine months earlier on Martin Siegel, the investment banker convicted of insider trading with Ivan Boesky. But many other journalists agreed with Tim Metz who wrote: "The *Times*, and certainly Bob Cole's interview with Phelan, president of the New York Stock Exchange which appeared on Tuesday, the twentieth, deserved the Pulitzer more."[7]

Black Monday signaled the end of the prosperous eighties. IBM stock purchased for $1,000 in August 1982 was worth $3,123 on October 12, 1987, and $1,983 on October 20. Less traditional financial instruments, like junk bonds, lost even more as Wall Street became a graveyard for risk arbitrage, mergers and acquisitions, and leveraged buy outs (LBOs) overnight. Following Wall Street's lead, corporate America and hostile raiders defied the promises of the M.B.A. and the personal computer as profits and productivity dropped to record lows. The only solution, so preached the raiders, was to "downsize." It wasn't long before a substantial segment of the middle class— middle managers, many of whom subscribed to the *Journal*—had lost their jobs. Only the fate of corporate America's chief executive officers went against the tide.

Black Monday changed the advertising business as well. In times of economic uncertainty, the first budget to be eliminated and the last to be reinstated is advertising, the heart and soul of a publication's profit-and-loss statement. Overnight again, many national publications went out of business, killed by the loss of advertising revenues.

In November 1987, a month after Black Monday, Geoffrey Meyer, the *Journal's* financial advertising manager, informed his bosses that the *Journal's* financial advertising, which represented one-third of the paper's total advertising volume, was virtually wiped out.

The *Journal* would finish 1987 with its ad lineage down 17.2 percent from 1986, the fourth consecutive year of advertising declines. Said a former *Journal* ad manager, "Many advertisers used it as an excuse to rebel against the high out-of-pocket ad costs [nearly $100,000 per page] and the way the *Journal* had treated them in more prosperous years."

But advertiser retaliation explained only a small part of the *Journal's* advertising drought. Wall Street had virtually no one to sell to, no one to boast to.

The *Journal* ended 1987 with $325 million in advertising revenues, down some $85 million from the year before. More significantly, *Journal* revenues in 1983 had been $478 million.

In a peculiar sense, the *Journal's* advertising management welcomed Black Monday. It allowed them to cover up the *Journal's* advertising declines; which had begun as early as 1984. Though the 1987 advertising losses were more precipitous and more dangerous, Kann and Phillips could now blame the sad state of the *Journal's* advertising on market conditions. And their lack of experience and judgment precluded them from making the right decisions to get out of this dilemma. In January 1987, in a highly unusual move, Peter Kann had named his former assistant, Paul Atkinson, who lacked domestic advertising sales experience completely, to the post of advertising director for the *Wall Street Journal*. Kann had effected this promotion to compensate for the weaknesses of Bernie Flanagan, the *Journal's* vice president of marketing, who lacked strategic marketing ability. "Bernie was more a peddler than a thinker,"[8] remarked Don Macdonald, his former boss.

Compared to the rotund and florid Flanagan, Atkinson appeared to be the model of a business executive, French cuffed, witty, articulate. And so, when the *Journal's* advertising declines began to occur and an absent Flanagan was always to be found on the West Coast,

Atkinson stepped into the void to impress the inexperienced Kann with theories and stratagems which, although untested, sounded plausible.

As mundane as it may seem, the way to sell advertising is to make sales calls; no matter how lofty his title, that was one thing Flanagan always did. Sales calls amount to baptisms of fire where an executive learns firsthand how advertisers regard his product against the competition. Sales executives like Atkinson, who sit behind desks and author strategic sales plans, are severely handicapped without this insight. A rival publisher said: "The *Journal* became so successful in the seventies that it didn't pay attention. It didn't have to. And no one at Dow Jones was the wiser."

To exacerbate the situation, when Kann promoted Atkinson to advertising sales director, he kept Flanagan as the vice president of marketing. Kann believed that Flanagan would be content to travel around the United States as the *Journal's* advertising ambassador while Atkinson remained in New York to do the brainwork.

But Flanagan, for all his Willy Loman–like demeanor, could not bear to be replaced by Atkinson. "Paul has no people skills," Flanagan commented. "And unless he develops them, he'll never make it in this business."[9]

Never close to begin with, Atkinson and Flanagan were soon enemies; each one tried to undermine the other continuously. Atkinson exploited his prior relationship with Kann, constantly circumventing Flanagan to confer directly with him. On the other hand, Flanagan continued to use his contacts on Madison Avenue, but he never introduced Atkinson to anyone.

For all his failings, Flanagan did come up with a scheme that helped answer the biggest advertiser objection to the *Journal*. "The damn thing used to be so expensive,"[10] said Robert Coen, executive vice president of McCann Erickson, a worldwide advertising agency. "When the crunch came, to spend $100,000 for a page in the *Journal* became too big a bite. And then Flanagan created regional editions, an old idea really, but new to the *Journal*."

No longer were companies forced to advertise in the *Journal's* national or regional editions. Instead, Flanagan made it possible for advertisers to specify those portions of the *Journal* audience most relevant to them. Digital Equipment, for example, could run in Flanagan's newly created New York, Dallas, Los Angeles, and Chicago city editions rather than pay more to run in the *Journal's* eastern, midwestern, southwestern, western or national editions.

Though Flanagan's innovation saved the *Journal* from even worse ad declines during the last half of the eighties, it did not help his relationship with Atkinson. Finally, after a sales meeting at which the two men warred openly to the dismay of the sales force, Paul Atkinson was made vice president of advertising, a promotion that took him out from under Flanagan, who was given an imposing title and nothing to do.

Throughout the three years of conflict between Atkinson and Flanagan, the *Journal's* advertising continued to slide. But each year, with circulation remaining flat or declining slightly, the *Journal* was able to ameliorate the ad declines by increasing its advertising rates. Still the all-important volume or lineage decreased on average 10 percent per annum from 1987 through 1991, a total dollar loss of some $225 million. As Atkinson said, "The *Journal* will never regain its former ad lineage level. It's a condition of the business now."[11] As a result, he was not able to do much to reverse this tide.

Other publications, such as *Fortune, Time,* or *Business Week,* began to climb out of their advertising slumps by offering steeper discounts to volume buyers, or, in the case of *Time,* packaged cable television advertising spots with pages in their own magazine.

Atkinson and Kann, however, shunned these steps, still clinging to the notion that, in Kann's words, "when the market comes back, we'll be there, poised, ready to come back with it.[12]

Back in the early eighties, when *USA Today* and *Investor's Daily* were starting up, and when the *New York Times* had just begun to expand its distribution in airports everywhere, Dow Jones president Ray Shaw, and several top-level colleagues would laugh whenever someone cited these publications as potentially harmful competitors. In fact, Dow Jones was so blasé about *USA Today* that when Alan Neuharth, *USA Today's* founder, decided to launch the newspaper, he received invaluable help from Dow Jones which it later regretted.

"The single biggest trick to being a national newspaper," said Neuharth, "is distributing it throughout the country on the same day it's printed. Back when we started out, we had no idea how to do that. But I asked Warren Phillips for help, and he let our technical people go to school on Dow Jones, learning as much as we could about satellite transmission. That's how *USA Today* became the country's second national newspaper."

Since *USA Today* was founded in 1982, the newspaper's circulation has grown steadily to where it now hovers at 1.8 million. In this time period, as its audience grew, *USA Today's* advertising increased as

well, often at the expense of the *Wall Street Journal's*, particularly
with tobacco, spirits, and automotive advertisers. Explained a former
Journal New York ad manager, "What Phillips, Shaw, and Kann
didn't realize was that although *USA Today* was an editorially inferior
newspaper to us in every respect, from an advertising point of view it
was similar. Advertisers could reach a large, national audience more
cheaply through *USA Today* than through the *Journal.*"

USA Today's advertising incursions, coupled with those of the *New
York Times* and *Investor's Daily*, also contributed to the *Journal's*
advertising sales declines.

Although Black Monday had a devastating effect on the *Journal's*
operating results for the year, it could have been worse. Operating
income for 1987 was $162 million, compared to $191 for the previous
year and $224 for 1985. But when Dow Jones melded in the earnings
from its other divisions, especially those of Telerate, a recent partial
acquisition, Dow Jones showed a gain, not a decline, for 1987.
Telerate's earnings per share ratio, for example, was $2.10, 10 percent
greater than the previous year's, an increase which helped mask the
problems of the *Wall Street Journal*. Eventually, Telerate, an electronic publisher of financial data, would represent 45 percent of Dow
Jones's revenues and cost the company a record $1.6 billion to acquire
in total. It would also become another management nightmare for
Phillips and Kann.

But still another nightmare, more personal and more pressing,
plagued the *Journal* in 1987, one that had begun eight years earlier
and shows no sign of abatement even today.

20

Nepotism: Peter Kann and Karen Elliott House

Despite the serious damage to morale it has caused since 1979, one problem continues to plague the newsroom which Peter Kann and Warren Phillips steadfastly refuse to acknowledge, much less solve. It all began in October 1979, when the New York–based Kann, then Phillips's assistant, struck up a relationship with Karen Elliott House, then the *Journal*'s diplomatic correspondent based in Washington. Fred Zimmerman, a member of the page-one staff working out of Washington, said, "I began to notice how much time Peter was spending in Washington, hanging around Karen's desk. They would talk for hours."[1]

Somewhere between 1979 and 1981, the relationship turned into romance, a development which polarized the bureau. Some staff members, like Washington veteran reporter Alan Otten, disapproved. "It wasn't the morality of the thing," Otten said, "it was how it affected working relationships. Karen, who was never shy, started to throw her weight around."[2] But other staffers, like reporter and future Washington bureau chief Al Hunt, supported it openly. Zimmerman said, "Peter and Karen and Al Hunt and his wife, [PBS television's] Judy Woodruff, spent a lot of time together. In fact, Al served as Peter's beard with Karen."[3]

Finally, after bureau reaction to the couple began to boil to the point of distraction, Kann, who by that time had been appointed the associate publisher of the *Journal*, approached his subordinate, Fred Taylor, the *Journal's* executive editor, seeking to explain and legitimize the union. "We've become friends, good, close friends," Peter told Taylor. "And I hope you're happy for me, Fred." Kann added that his relationship with House should pose no management difficulties because "Karen does not report to me."

"Bullshit!" thought Taylor to himself. "Why does Warren [Phillips] tolerate this?"[4] It became a management nightmare, Taylor went on to explain. "How could we supervise House if she was always pulling rank by quoting her boyfriend, who happened to be the associate publisher, which was several ranks above us?" Taylor said.

Back then, the *Journal* culture could tolerate liaisons provided they were handled with discretion and hidden from view. It helped if the romance involved two people with low-level jobs who were separated from everyone else. This way, other staffers could figuratively walk around the situation, assured that their reaction, "It's none of my business. It doesn't affect me," was absolutely true.

But this particular romance fit none of these criteria. Both people held important and visible posts. Moreover, both Kann and House were insensitive to their colleagues: Kann, by pretending nothing was awry; House, by exploiting Kann's station.

Five years later, in June 1984, Kann and House were married. Three months later, House was appointed the *Journal's* foreign editor. Since then, Kann has become Dow Jones CEO, and House is now Dow Jones vice president, international, a critical position.

In corporate America, when an affair ends in marriage, most work-related problems first caused by the relationship are usually eliminated. But in the case of the Kann-House marriage, the problems have only multiplied and become more harmful. In fact, their marriage incites darker emotions today than their affair ever did fourteen years ago, as evidenced by the following questions raised frequently by *Journal* newspeople.[5]

Did Karen Elliott House win a Pulitzer because she slept with Peter Kann?

Why was Karen Elliott House appointed the business and editorial head of the *Asian Wall Street Journal*, the European *Wall Street Journal*, and the Dow Jones–owned *Far Eastern Economic Review* when she had no business experience whatsoever?

Would Karen Elliott House be allowed to terrorize subordinates, as some staffers claim, if she were not married to Peter Kann?

Why is Karen Elliott House allowed to bias the *Journal*'s news coverage of public officials who have performed enormous personal favors for her and her husband?

Is Karen Elliott House the victim of a smear campaign that many women who rise above a certain level in corporate America must endure?

If Karen Elliott House were a man would she be the object of so much criticism?

Why are *Journal* staffers more apt to disparage Karen Elliott House than Peter Kann? After all, didn't Kann seduce Warren Phillips for a Pulitzer nomination and his current position?

Irrespective of the validity of, or the answers to, these questions, the mere fact they are raised explains why prudent members of corporate America simply refused to allow relatives to work together long ago. Through horrific experiences, corporate America learned that nepotism—real or imagined favoritism shown by one relative, lover, or mate, to another—can destroy an organization's morale, with the eventual result of lower profits. These companies have learned that no matter how brilliant the nepotic undividuals are, their singular contributions do not outweigh their combined negative effect on the rest of the staff. Are there instances where nepotism is not a negative? If there are, they exist in small, family-run businesses. They also involve people who are more sensitive than Karen Elliott House and more forthcoming than Peter Kann. Thus, in the case of Dow Jones, two Pulitzers—won respectively by Kann and House— do not justify the end.

Perhaps the most notorious recent case of business nepotism concerned William Agee, CEO of the Bendix Corporation, the aerospace conglomerate, and Mary Cunningham, Bendix's head of strategic planning. Within twelve months of joining Bendix from the Harvard Business School, the twenty-seven-year-old Cunningham, blond, blue-eyed, beautiful, and married, leapfrogged over many senior people to assume her strategic planning post. A rumor soon circulated that Cunningham's amazing progress was due not to her Harvard M.B.A. but to sleeping with the boss, Bill Agee. A thirty-eight-year-old swashbuckling raider with a Harvard M.B.A., Agee was married.

Someone tipped off the media, and a steady stream of newspaper articles reporting the allegation followed. At first, Agee and Cunningham scoffed at the charge. But it would not go away. The media knew this was not an ordinary case of the boss and the secretary, that the Agee-Cunningham affair was a paradigm for many similar instances which were about to occur as a by-product of the M.B.A. phenomenon.

Cunningham embodied the new wave of women entering corporate America. Smart, tough, and ambitious, she was not content to head Bendix's personnel department as her female predecessors had. Mary Cunningham threatened the men of Bendix. A strategic planner, she could run the numbers with the best of Bendix's engineers and middle managers. Moreover, these men were further intimidated because, for the first time, they could see their worst fear, "working for a woman," come true. And finally, because Cunningham was attractive, there was sexual tension in the air everywhere she went.

The story persisted. It hurt morale and Agee's credibility. It also damaged Cunningham's reputation. Finally, Agee called a special meeting of all Bendix headquarter personnel, six hundred strong, in the company cafeteria and declared, "Mary and I are just good friends." *People* magazine and every major daily in the country, including the *Journal*, reported the incident. Still, the rumors persisted until eventually Cunningham resigned, as did Agee a short time later, both tarnished by the episode. Eighteen months later, they married.

The Agee-Cunningham relationship brought into focus a question that had been vexing corporate America ever since the M.B.A. wave introduced young women to business. Like Mary Cunningham, these women could dazzle male peers, subordinates, and superiors alike with their attractiveness and with their knowledge of business theory. How do you handle them? How do you relate to them?

The Agee-Cunningham scandal hit a particular nerve at Dow Jones because William Agee was a member of the Dow Jones board of directors throughout much of the episode. In fact, Warren Phillips recruited Agee about the same time Peter Kann met Karen Elliott House. Shortly thereafter, the Kann-House relationship began to provoke Mary Cunningham–like sentiments from the *Journal* newsroom, though understandably none were ever reported in the paper itself.

The two women have some things in common. Both fell in love with the boss; both are beautiful, seductive women; both create controversy; both are ambitious, tough-minded professionals. However, in contrast to Mary Cunningham, Karen Elliott House was not forced to resign. Warren Phillips asked, "Why should the *Journal* lose such talent as Karen just because she got married?"[6]

Today Karen Elliott House, a corporate vice president, holds one of the highest positions in journalism, earns over $200,000 per year, has a Pulitzer on her mantle next to her husband's, appears on television frequently, is an active member of the Council of Foreign Relations, mothers two adorable adopted children, Petra, seven, and Jason, four, a South Korean, and is a journalist highly respected by her peers outside Dow Jones. ABC's Peter Jennings beams while exclaiming, "Karen Elliott House is simply one of the best journalists in the country, period."[7] House is especially appreciated by men of power. Alan Otten of the Washington bureau said, "Karen is like Maggie Thatcher. She loves men, loves to be around them, is defined by them, really."[8]

Immediately after Gerald Ford pardoned Richard Nixon, Watergate prosecutor Leon Jaworski retired to Texas and virtually dropped out of the public's view. Several years later, Jaworski returned to Washington for twenty-four hours to testify at a secret congressional hearing. Tipped off that he was staying at the Jefferson Hotel, House, then a *Journal* reporter in Washington, went to the hotel and, in a personal note, asked Jaworski if she could accompany him on his private plane to Texas, where she would spend a few days interviewing him on his ranch.

"I figured I had nothing to lose, and I might as well ask for the moon," House explained. To her and the Washington bureau's amazement, Jaworski agreed. "He remembered me from the *Dallas Morning News*, and it helped I was from Texas," House added. Later, Jaworski volunteered, "Karen Elliott House is the best reporter I've ever known."[9]

Why was Leon Jaworski so admiring?

"There are many advantages to being a woman," House admits. "Men are usually the subjects of interview, and women don't compete with them. Women are better listeners. Male reporters love the sound of their own voice." Tall and lithe, Karen Elliott House looks younger than forty-seven, wears her hair à la Veronica Lake, with one side of her face partially obscured by a sweeping, shining wave of blond hair. She has pretty gray-green feline eyes which regard a visitor confidently. Her Texas twang reveals an almost manly directness and candor. Yet she smiles and tears easily.

But there is nothing soft or vulnerable about her. She can be insensitive and cutting and maniacally demanding. That is why many staffers who hate her question whether it was House's brains or beauty that enabled her to win the Pulitzer Prize for international reporting, the same Pulitzer category her husband had won twelve years before. Said Alan Otten, "Karen bewitched two men to win the Pulitzer: Jordan's King Hussein and Peter."[10]

But Ellen Graham, a *Journal* reporter and wife of former *Journal* editor Don Moffett, said: "If Karen were a man, no one would begrudge her Pulitzer. It's the price she pays for having the temerity to be a brilliant journalist and a woman at the same time."[11]

In February 1983, King Hussein invited Karen Elliott House to accompany him during a month long attempt to persuade the elusive Yasir Arafat to authorize Hussein to negotiate for the Palestinians in the upcoming West Bank talks with Israel. The purpose of these talks was to create Palestinian self-government on the West Bank and in Gaza. Failure to provide the Palestinians with a homeland, Hussein knew, would cause them to emigrate into neighboring Jordan, thereby straining an already marginal economy.

Beginning in September 1982, Hussein gradually drew the conclusion that Arafat would never relinquish negotiating power even if it meant continued hardship for the Palestinians. Consequently, Hussein needed a means to tell the world that Arafat, not he, had obstructed the talks to create Palestinian self-government on the West Bank and in Gaza. Enter Karen Elliott House, diplomatic reporter for the *Wall Street Journal*, whom Hussein had known and admired for five years.

After studying secret briefing documents for a week, House traveled to Amman and, from March 3 to April 8, 1983, stayed by the king's side as he attempted but failed to gain Yasir Arafat's cooperation in President Reagan's peace plan.

House's appeal, either as a woman or as a journalist or both, became manifest when King Hussein invited her to accompany him as his only guest to attend a conference of nonaligned nations in New Delhi. On March 5, Hussein piloted his own Boeing 727 to India with Karen Elliott House sitting in the cockpit's third seat. For the next five days and nights, from March 5 to March 10, House was the only journalist permitted to stay at Hussein's hotel, the Delhi Intercontinental. Hussein spent much of the five days conferring with Egypt's Hosni Mubarak, Prince Saud of Saudi Arabia, and Chairman Arafat.

However, the king took most of his lunches and dinners with House in his suite, affording her rare glimpses of himself. Later, for example, House was able to report, "Suddenly the king is in a good mood. He bounds into the living room of his suite, smiling broadly and carrying a Sony shortwave radio the size of an overnight bag. He wolfs down his dinner."

House continued in this fashion to observe Hussein until the second week in April, when she retired to her Amman hotel and wrote a three-part leader. She then filed her series with Glynn Mapes, who had been the page-one editor since 1976, a particularly long tenure for the second most powerful job at the *Journal*. For years, *Journal* reporters were rewarded for their page-one bylines, not for how well they worked their beats.

On April 13, House called Mapes in a rage. She had just learned that he intended to reject her stories. The page-one editor remembered taking the call at 5:30 P.M., New York time, 1:30 A.M., Amman time. "Karen was very upset," Mapes said. "So upset it was hard for me to have a conversation with her."[12]

"I panicked," House admitted. "I screamed at Glynn, 'What are you doing to me? Why are you doing this to me?'"[13]

Mapes remembered replying, "Your stuff reads like a book jacket, Karen. It promises everything, but doesn't deliver."

"You can't do that to me," House screamed. "I've worked six weeks on this." She became hysterical.

"It was an open area," Mapes recalled. "People were all around me. They knew I had Karen on the line, and they knew she was upset." Fred Zimmerman, one of Karen's former mentors from the Washington bureau, who sat beside Mapes, happened to overhear the conversation. "Although Glynn was trying to muffle his words, it was obvious he and Karen were having an argument," Zimmerman said. "I grinned because I knew how tough she could get. All of a sudden, Glynn's face went white as if something terrible had just happened. Then he said nervously, 'Oh...hello, Peter.'"[14]

House later explained, "I was getting nowhere with Glynn, so I said, 'Here, talk to Peter.'"

Glynn later said, "I was amazed. One moment I'm arguing with Karen and the next moment I'm talking to Peter Kann, the associate publisher. It took me a moment to realize he wasn't in his office two floors above me, but that he was in Karen's Amman hotel room at one-thirty in the morning trying to persuade me to run her stuff. I didn't even know they were dating then."

Ignoring the question why he was visiting House's hotel room at that hour of the night, Kann did admit, "Yes, I got on the phone and said to Glynn, 'I've read these pieces and I think they're terrific stuff.'"[15]

When asked if he thought his intercession was inappropriate, Kann said, "I find it odd I have to apologize for that. I've done it with other people's stuff. My judgment was not bad. I'd do it again today. Her stuff was terrific."

After Mapes got over the shock of the argument, he claims today, he was pleased Kann had calmed things down. "I was grateful Peter became the mediator. I recovered my composure and told Peter that. I also told him I'd run her stuff, but it would be a two-parter not a three-[parter]."

Mapes then gave House's copy to Dan Kelly, a page-one rewrite man, who stayed up all night rewriting the story. The two pieces ran on the *Journal*'s front page on April 14 and 15, 1983. Fred Zimmerman said, "Dan Kelly was a genius. Karen is not a good writer, and he rewrote it with very little time. Yet, later, when the Pulitzer came out, there never was a mention of Kelly's role. Karen never even thanked him."[16]

House's ill-fated third piece in the series was resurrected by Bob Bartley, who ran it as a favor to Kann on the editorial page several weeks later.

On January 31, 1984, Norman Pearlstine nominated the House's two-parter for a Pulitzer. Pearlstine, in his three-page memo to the Pulitzer Prize board, said, "Mrs. House thus had a unique, inside view of diplomacy in the making, but she never lost sight of her own role as an on-the-record reporter covering the story for her readers."

On April 16, Peter Kann, not Norman Pearlstine, which would have been appropriate, circulated an interoffice memo he had written: "The Pulitzer Prizes have just been announced and there's doubly grand news for the *Journal*. Karen Elliott House, our foreign editor, won the Pulitzer Prize for distinguished reporting on international affairs, and Vermont Royster, our columnist and former editor, won the Pulitzer Prize for distinguished commentary."

House won out over two other finalists: David Shipler of the *New York Times*, for his reporting on Israel in which he "analyzed the mind of the nation"; and Morris Thompson of *Newsday* (Long Island), for "his thorough coverage of the island of Grenada before, during, and after the U.S. invasion."

But the award did little to boost her standing with her *Journal* colleagues. For example, Alan Otten, of the Washington bureau, said, "The Hussein stories were unremarkable."[17]

Despite Kelly's heroic rewrite, House's series is rambling and difficult to follow. And despite the Pulitzer Prize board's encomium, the series' value was not in forecasting the eventual demise of Reagan's Middle East peace plan. It was, at best, a piece about naive diplomacy. President Reagan failed to see the obvious. Any peace talks that did not provide for direct Palestinian representation would never be sanctioned by Arafat.

But Karen Elliott House did deserve the Pulitzer for uncommon access to a royal source. King Hussein even groused to House about Henry Kissinger's meddlesome ways, Reagan's naïveté, the Russians' arbitrary behavior, and the precarious position all of this put Hussein himself in as a peacemaker while maintaining good relations with his Arab neighbors, such as Saudi Arabia, Egypt, and Syria. It was an extraordinary demonstration of a journalist's greatest wish—access, the ability not only to talk openly with a source but to watch him perform historic actions.

Because House used what should have remained her private relationship with Peter Kann to defeat Mapes so publicly, she became an object of scorn, if not calumny. Had House asked her immediate boss, Washington bureau chief Mike Miller, to argue her case, she would have been well within her rights. But to enlist the intercession of the *Journal's* associate publisher, who stood three very distant rungs above her on the management ladder but right next to her in an Amman hotel bedroom, went well beyond acceptable behavior. And for Kann to get involved, especially under those compromising circumstances, exhibited a disregard for propriety and lack of judgment. Feeling as strongly as he did about House's copy, Kann could have achieved the same end by quietly calling Pearlstine and asking him to look judiciously and promptly into the problem.

Since Mapes and his many allies could not openly express their disapproval for fear of reprisal, some resorted to one of the oldest means to retaliate against women who enjoy special advantages because of their relationship with male superiors. They smeared her. *Asian Journal* reporter Joseph Manguno said on the record what many *Journal* staffers said off the record: "I know for certain Karen bedded Hussein to get those interviews,"[18] Manguno alleged.

When asked if Manguno's allegation were true, House said, "Of course, envious people are going to say or infer that. It's what I call the 'titillation factor.' It's not relevant. There's nothing I can do about it. I maintain a Caesar's wife reputation. I've stopped worrying about it long ago. But I'll say this, no one, no one, has ever patted me on the rear."[19]

Kann remained untouched by the newsroom's disapproval. It was easier for *Journal* reporters, editors, and bureau chiefs to criticize House, the foreign editor, rather than Kann, the associate publisher. It also proves there is indeed a double standard at the *Journal*, as there is in most of corporate America. Kann is every bit as seductive as House is. But in his case the label is different. It's called charm or persuasiveness.

Marriage to Kann did little to soften House's professional demeanor. In September 1984, for example, newly appointed the *Journal's* foreign editor, House distributed a menacing memo that stunned the news department worldwide. Working for the *Journal* then was like working for the post office. Time-in-grade did not make reporters and editors rich, but it bestowed upon them a sublime safety. Though grist for a plethora of complaints, even Pearlstine's tidal wave of high-paid outsiders was not life threatening. The news department had simply expanded. No one was fired.

Consequently, House's concluding sentence was frightening: "Thus, reporters will either start making significant contributions to the paper today or start looking for other jobs today." This threat was unwarranted. Reporters were not taking four-hour lunches or allowing *Business Week* to beat them on major stories. Moreover, its tone was distressing because, one, it contradicted the *Journal's* non-confrontational culture; two, this edict was presumably supported by her husband, the associate publisher; and, three, there was no room for discussion. "What a way to begin a job [foreign editor] which she should never have gotten in the first place,"[20] said Alan Otten.

Once again, following a lifelong pattern, Karen Elliott House became involved in controversy. And once again, the seminal influence of her life, Ted Elliott, a west Texas plainsman, would have been proud. "My father always told me, 'Karen Jo, it's better to be respected than to be liked,'"[21] House said recently.

House's detractors have always attributed her success to her beauty and beguiling Texas demeanor. Admirers believe House possesses energy, determination, decisiveness, and unusual persistence. "The thing that makes Karen such an unbelievable reporter is her persistence. She just keeps coming at you, five, six times, until she gets it right. She never takes no." said Norman C. "Mike" Miller, former Washington bureau chief who hired House in 1976.

Karen Elliott House was born Karen Jo Elliott on December 7, 1947, in Matador, Texas, a tiny farming and ranching community ninety miles west of Wichita Falls. Life in the west Texas plains accommodates few shades of gray. It's either white or black; either you survive or you do not. This hard-edged perspective is reflected in Matador's architecture—sturdy brick buildings with square tops built low to the ground to withstand the winds and the dust, a marble soda fountain in the drugstore to withstand time.

Next to Friday night football, men dominate the west Texas plains. At least that's how it was for Karen Jo Elliott growing up with her father, Ted Elliott. A welder of large pieces of agricultural equipment, Ted Elliott was known throughout Motley County for his strong beliefs: in himself, in the tenets of the First Baptist Church of Christ, and in the futures of his three children. Larry Elliott, Karen's older brother, is now the news director for the Lubbock television station. Karen's sister, Lynda, is the county extension agent in Silverton, Texas.

Ted Elliott's youngest child, Karen, strove to be the best, always. House said, "My father is the cause of my great eagerness to do what is right. You had to be perfect to get his attention."[22]

Ted Elliott's own father had died in the midst of the Depression when Ted was a teenager. Being the oldest of eight, he quit school to provide for his mother and siblings. For someone who worked with his hands and who lacked education, Ted Elliott was amazingly inquisitive. "My father learned German on his own by reading Goethe," House boasted. As a young girl, at her father's insistence, Karen Jo Elliott collected stamps and had pen pals all over the world. "He was always stressing places like New York, Europe, and the Far East."

Karen's mother, Bailey Elliott, was a typical housewife of the plains. "My mother is the sweetest thing in the world, the gentlest soul. Anything we did was fine with her."

Above all else, Ted Elliott was a man of God, a God of duty and purpose, a God who recoiled from the sins of the flesh. "We were not allowed to watch television, to date, to take a drive on Sundays," House said. "My father used to say, 'You're no better than anyone else unless you're morally better.'"

Charley Johnson, the principal of Matador High School, said: "The Elliotts were an archetype, people who suffered from the Depression but who refused to surrender, to give up. Ted Elliott never lost his dignity. In fact, he was bigger than life. Eventually, so were his children."

In June 1966, Karen Jo Elliott graduated from Matador High School with the highest grades ever achieved in the eighty-eight-year history of the school. "My father was mildly pleased," House said.

During her last year in high school, House worked part-time for the *Matador Tribune*, owned and operated by Douglas Meador, who became another important male influence in her life. "Mr. Meador was very patient with me. Once, at deadline, I dropped two pages of type and I was beside myself. I had to be so perfect, you see. Mr. Meador just said, 'Dear sweet child, don't give it another thought.'"

House entered the University of Texas at Austin in September 1966. Like the other women in her class, House's aims were to do well in class and be named a Bluebonnet Belle, "an honor bestowed on five girls selected for their poise, personality, beauty, activities, and campus awareness." House was one of thirty-eight semifinalists. One of the five who won the Bluebonnet Belle that year was Karen Kaye Ross, who had also won Cowboy Sweetheart of 1968 and was voted one of Texas's Ten Most Beautiful Women.

Throughout her four years at the University of Texas, Karen and the other women in her class looked like proper children of the fifties—pageboy hairstyles, pearls, and discreet dresses. Protest, drugs, and Vietnam did not exist. Besides engaging in a raft of extracurricular activities to please her father, House avidly pursued her first interest, journalism. The *Daily Texan*, the student newspaper, whose past editors included Willie Morris of later fame with *Harper's* magazine, employed House for the four years she was on campus. Eventually, she rose to the number-two slot, managing editor. Also, while working for the *Houston Chronicle* in the summer between her junior and senior years, House won a *Wall Street Journal* scholarship worth $500.

In August 1970, House joined the *Dallas Morning News*, where she was assigned a typical rookie beat—the school-board reporter. She quickly distinguished herself. "Karen was tough and tireless," said a former colleague. "She was also terribly ambitious. Within months she jumped to our Washington bureau, which, for most of us, was like becoming an astronaut."

House spent three years with the *Dallas Morning News* in Washington, covering a variety of assignments. One day she met Fred Zimmerman, then the Washington bureau's diminutive and restless page-one staff member, in the House of Representative's press gallery.

Zimmerman recalled, "There she was, pretty but frazzled, her hair swept over to one side, hunched over, taking furious notes, trying, it seems, to record the proceedings verbatim. I sidled up to her and said something smart, like 'We don't do it that way, kid.' She didn't look up until I repeated the remark but added, 'The *Wall Street Journal*.'"[23]

Zimmerman claims he hired House. But it's more likely Washington bureau chief Mike Miller did. Since the thirties, the Washington bureau had boasted any number of exceptional journalists, including Barney Kilgore, Jerry Landauer [who caused Spiro Agnew to resign in 1973], Alan Otten, Jim Gannon, and Mike Miller himself, who had won a Pulitzer in 1964 for his salad-oil-scandal exposé. When House arrived, the bureau was trying to regain some of the prestige it had lost by missing the Watergate story entirely. There was little time, therefore, for Miller to train House. For the first several years, she took great pains to compensate for her self-perceived inadequacies.

"I'm not a good writer, and I'm pretty slow," House said. "I used to go in Saturdays and Sundays to write. That's when I started to get a reputation for being a workaholic."

But House's west Texas persistence finally began to pay off when Fred Zimmerman gave her a page-one leader idea. "I suggested she spend the day in the Agricultural Department wandering from one office to another, asking anyone she sees the simple question 'What do you do?'"

House gathered eight hours' worth of responses and prepared a draft. "I then spent several days rewriting the piece," Zimmerman said, "but when it was published, it hit Washington like a bombshell." House's page-one article revealed what *Journal* readers had long suspected: The federal government was a soulless bureaucracy replete with sloth and waste, a haven for incompetents.

In 1974, Karen met Arthur House, the quintessential Connecticut Yankee, in Washington. More prominent than the Bushes or the Weickers, the House family settled in Manchester outside of Hartford in the early eighteenth century. According to *Journal* reporter Bill Mathewson, "Arthur House's grandfather, Colonel [William] House was a confidant of Woodrow Wilson's."[24] Arthur House was an insurance executive who was considering running for Congress as a Democrat when Karen Jo Elliott became Karen Elliott House on April 5, 1975.

House's next career break came when she covered the energy crisis in the mid-seventies. "This was a competitive story,"[25] Miller said. "The *Times* and the *Los Angeles Times* were all over it. Yet Karen was terrific. She was out in front, analyzing a lot of complex material quickly and writing it up pretty well, too."

In 1978, Bob Keatley, who had been the diplomatic correspondent, the bureau's most prestigious assignment, moved to New York to assume the foreign editorship. Karen Elliott House took Keatley's place. "It was a very controversial promotion," Mike Miller said. "And I was the one who gave it to her. Any number of far more senior people were angry about this, but I genuinely thought she could do it."[26]

For the next two years, House spent 134 days out of the country, mostly in the Middle East, reporting on the Carter administration's peace attempts. She won her first award for diplomatic reporting in 1980, from Georgetown University.

Once her great admirer, Mike Miller, the bureau chief, grew to dislike House because she became so ambitious.[27] Although he never openly said anything, Miller's distant manner around Kann and House conveyed his condemnation. It made House uncomfortable. Staffers either had to openly support the relationship, as Hunt and others did, or hide their disapproval. Several years later, against his wishes, Mike Miller relinquished his post to Al Hunt. Miller said, "I was called to New York by Warren Phillips in May 1983 to discuss with Peter what assignment I wanted next: Hong Kong, as editor of the *Asian Wall Street Journal*; New York, as a corporate editor type; or Washington as a senior columnist. I told them I didn't want any of them."[28]

Miller was cut from the Kilgore tradition: quiet, unassuming, shy, traits which did not hinder him from winning a Pulitzer. Al Hunt, on the other hand, is like the politicians he covers: blustery, hail-fellow-well-met, and shrewd.

Mike Miller left the *Journal* to become the national news editor of the *Los Angeles Times* in early 1984. He was a victim of the Kann-House relationship. He could not countenance nepotism, and Al Hunt could.

21

Wooing the Wrong Foreign Relations

In March 1989, when House was appointed Dow Jones vice president, international, the Kann-House marriage achieved the highest level of nepotism in corporate America. As a team, they acted out the aphorism "Power tends to corrupt and absolute power corrupts absolutely."[1]

In many ways, House's promotion was a formality since she had been comporting herself like a corporate vice president for years. Her presumption—inferring authority from marriage and not from the board of directors—caused many *Journal* superiors, peers, and subordinates to hate her.

Together, Kann and House ruled the *Journal* through a confusing and ambivalent autocracy. More specifically, Kann permitted his wife to rule through fiat while he remained in the background, everyone's seeming friend. For example, House would enter a bureau and shatter people with a flurry of nonnegotiable edicts. Later, Kann might visit the same bureau, sowing what the wounded considered were seeds of reconciliation. Only long afterward would people realize that Kann's efforts meant nothing because he never counter-manded his wife. And given the docility of CEO Warren Phillips, the Dow Jones board, and the Bancroft family, there were no appeal routes to resolve the many grievances House's conduct and decisions provoked. No one crossed her; and those who tried were fired, sometimes brutally. Her suppressive management style might have been barely tolerable for a razor-blade manufacturer. But to stifle journalists in this manner countered the *Journal*'s culture as well as its privilege of freedom of the press.

Indeed, staffers were so riled by September 1989 that Pearlstine asked reporter Alan Otten, who was about to retire after forty-five years with the *Journal*, to conduct a confidential survey to determine the morale of the news department. After visiting many bureaus and offices throughout the world, Otten came back and reported, "The one thing on everyone's mind is Karen Elliott House. Many people hate her. Behind her back, she's known as the Dragon Lady."[2] Otten also reported that Asia, an extremely important area for the *Journal*, suffered the most under House. Dow Jones's holdings in Asia include the *Asian Wall Street Journal*, the *Far Eastern Economic Review*, and the domestic *Journal*'s news bureaus in Tokyo, Hong Kong, Seoul, Singapore, Beijing, New Delhi, Jakarta, Bangkok, and Manila.

Shortly after becoming a vice president, in October 1989, House toured the Far East, evaluating the personnel. Within months of her return to New York, twelve correspondents and editors were fired. One of those terminated, John Berthlesen, fifty-three, a Singapore correspondent, said, "Karen came through Asia like the Texas chain-saw murderer. Many of us had been correspondents in countries hostile to western journalists, like Singapore. We worked under extreme stress, hardship. Karen had a view of the politics of a country, and if you didn't conform to her view, you were gone. There was no loyalty shown to us, no recognition of our loyalty either. One guy, Joe Manguno, who covered Seoul, really got shafted. It was real vindictiveness."[3]

The experience of Joseph Manguno, the *Asian Journal*'s former Seoul correspondent and twelve-year veteran covering the Far East for the domestic and *Asian Journal*, shows one picture of what it was like to work for Karen Elliott House.[4]

On her 1989 Asian tour, House stopped off in Seoul to attend an advertising conference. House was accompanied by her new boss, James Ottaway, Jr., Dow Jones senior vice president, and her friend Al Hunt, Washington bureau chief. When House was promoted, Ottaway had been appointed House's superior to create distance between her and Kann, who was Ottaway's boss. An amiable, academically oriented man, Ottaway, fifty-four, has spent his entire life in Campbell Hall, New York (population 56,000), observing his father, James Ottaway, Sr., operate a chain of fifteen small-town newspapers, mostly weeklies, whose average circulation is 22,000.

As part of her Seoul trip, House called a meeting of various *Journal* and Dow Jones Asian correspondents to meet Ottaway and to brief him on South Korea's always turbulent political situation. The meeting, which took place in the coffee shop of the Lotte Hotel, involved House, Ottaway, Hunt, and B. J. Lee of AP–Dow Jones, Damon Darlin, Seoul correspondent for the *Wall Street Journal*, Mark Clifford and Shim Jae Hoon of the *Far Eastern Economic Review*, and Manguno, Seoul correspondent for the *Asian Wall Street Journal.*⁵

Manguno, in particular, dreaded seeing House in Seoul again because, in his opinion, she maintained a close personal relationship with South Korea's president, Roh Tae Woo, which violated Manguno's journalistic ethics. He also resented House's belief, gained from Roh Tae Woo and members of the U.S. State Department and the Council on Foreign Relations with whom she socialized, that any form of government in South Korea, including a bloody military dictatorship, was preferable to communism.

A resident of Seoul since 1986, Manguno told the same stories as his counterparts at the *New York Times*, the *Washington Post*, and *Time* magazine, namely, that since 1963 South Korea had borne the repressive stamp of three harsh military dictators, the latest of whom was Roh Tae Woo. Moreover, daily life was marred by political assassinations, kidnappings, torture, police mass killings of student protesters, rigged elections, student self-immolation, and an economy which, even at its most prosperous level, failed to improve the lives of the lower and middle classes.

The first military dictator, Gen. Park Chung Hee, ruled South Korea from 1963 to 1979, when he was assassinated by his own security chief. Park's wife had been murdered seven years earlier. Though Park crushed individual freedom, he built up South Korea's economy through government sponsorship of corporations like Hyundai (computers and automobiles), Daewoo (electronics), and Samsung (electronics).

In May 1980, Gen. Chun Doo Hwan, Park's protégé, was elected president. The entire Korean army, some 600,000 strong, was ushered into voting booths by their superior officers and instructed how to vote. Protesting this sham, two hundred students were killed by Chun's special security police. After assuming the presidency, Chun sentenced his election opponent, Kim Dae Jung, to death for alleging election fraud. Chun required journalists to refer to student protesters as "Communists" and "subversives." Under Chun's rule, these "subversives" were regularly arrested, tortured, and murdered. On January 12, 1987, for example, Chun's police arrested Park Chong Chul, a twenty-one-year-old Seoul National University student. The police used electric shock to extract information from Park as to the whereabouts of other student protest leaders. Unsuccessful, the two police agents then drowned him in a bathtub.

Later that year, in June 1987, as a result of further student uprisings protesting Park's murder, Chun was driven from office, but not before designating his protégé, Gen. Roh Tae Woo, to stand election to succeed him. Two hundred thousand students, parents, laborers, and businesspeople took to the streets to protest the foregone conclusion that Roh would win through rigged elections. As a precursor to Tiananmen Square, worldwide television broadcast the grisly picture of South Korean students setting themselves aflame. Despite the bloodshed and dissent, Roh Tae Woo succeeded General Chun in February 1988. Uninvestigated accusations alleged Roh's victory was rigged via computer fraud. Riots continued through the first half of 1988, only to stop to stage the Olympics. But the following year, South Korea reverted back to form. In June 1989, three months before House and Ottaway's visit, 300,000 students and laborers protested Roh's regime, claiming South Korea was still a police state. Twelve riot policemen clubbed one student, Kang Kyung Dae, to death. To protest this killing, five students attempted suicide by fire. Four succeeded.

Early on October 12, 1989, the morning of the Ottaway coffee-shop briefing, Karen Elliott House met privately with Roh Tae Woo at the Blue House, the presidential palace. Later that morning, House began her Ottaway briefing session by stating what "a handsome, virile man he is." House then articulated the many improvements Roh Tae Woo had made "to make South Korea the democracy it is today." When she finished, House looked to the journalists for confirmation. "Isn't that right?" she asked.

An awkward silence followed. Finally, Manguno, said, "No, Karen. That's not right."

House reddened. "Are you trying to tell me that it's no better?" she snapped.

"No. Korea is moving in the right direction slowly. But lately, it's taken several steps backward," Manguno said.

"So it's not a democracy today?" House asked.

"Is Hungary any better off?" Manguno replied.

"What's Hungary got to do with it?" House said.

"It's the same thing," Manguno responded. "Some steps have been taken. But it's still not a democracy. In fact, it's less of a democracy than Hungary."

House turned to the rest of the group and asked, "Anyone else agree?"

Shim Jae Hoon, the *Far Eastern Economic Review*'s correspondent, who had been jailed for writing unflattering reports about Roh Tae Woo three years before, said, "Joe's right."

House ended the meeting abruptly and stormed out of the hotel.

A year later, Joseph Manguno, thirty-eight, was fired from the *Journal* without severance pay. A twelve-year veteran with the newspaper, Manguno had risked his life for the *Journal* covering the Seoul riots, as he had several times before in Indonesia.

Though his immediate superiors, *Asian Journal* Barry Wain and David Rosenberg, had issued some performance warnings, Peter Kann had always been highly complimentary toward Manguno. The year before, while on home leave, Manguno had dropped in on Kann in New York. Kann appeared to be very cordial. Moreover, Kann had recently sent Manguno several handwritten notes praising his work. "Peter always led me to believe I was doing great," Manguno said. According to Wain and Rosenberg, both confided separately to Manguno that his "termination resulted directly from House's vindictiveness."

Manguno sued Dow Jones for wrongful dismissal. Several months later, when Manguno and his wife and two young children returned to the United States and went to claim their belongings from a Baltimore shipping depot, Dow Jones refused to release them "unless Manguno dropped the suit."[6]

Though Manguno still rejects the suggestion that Peter Kann had anything to do with his and his family's plight, Manguno's wife said, "Peter is Pontius Pilate."

When asked for her version of the Manguno incident, House said, "Manguno and I disagree on Korea. I admire Roh Tae Woo. Admittedly, South Korea is not an American-style democracy, but it's light-years ahead of the Park or Chun regimes. I don't remember the hotel incident, nor can I shed any light on Joe's move back to the States. Barry Wain [*Asian Journal* editor] terminated Joe for performance-related reasons."[7]

Manguno and House met in 1986 on her first trip to Seoul.

According to Manguno, the two got along well as Manguno escorted her on a round of top-level interviews with leaders of industry and the political opposition. House returned to Seoul five months later to interview General Chun.

House's third trip to Korea occurred in late May 1987 when, as a board member of the Council on Foreign Relations, she accompanied a council delegation to Seoul at the invitation of General Chun to hear his explanations of the bloody uprisings. Preoccupied by the entertainment and briefings at the presidential palace, House waited ten days before she contacted Manguno. At that meeting, she criticized him for filing stories that were biased against the South Korean government.

Manguno explained, "My pieces were no different than any other correspondent's. Students were still protesting the torture and murder of Park Chong Chul [the Seoul National University student]."

When House returned to New York, she filed a news item dated June 11, 1987, which was startling. It read as if a Blue House public relations flack had written it. No editor had the courage to point out to House that her piece contradicted what Manguno and every other major newspaper in the country had been reporting for the past six months. House's article portrayed the student protesters as criminals, the police as long-suffering heroes, and Roh Tae Woo as unpretentious, candid, and an avid swimmer and tennis player. It read as a leading-man profile in a women's magazine.

On June 25, 29, and July 2, Manguno filed stories that contradicted House's article. Manguno reported that the middle class had recently joined the students to protest the Chun regime, an act that made Chun finally step down and seek shelter in a Buddhist monastery. Three weeks before, House had predicted the middle class would never join the anti-Chun protests. A month later, Kann sent a note praising Manguno for the series.

But one of Bartley's editorials, published shortly thereafter, best conveyed how the newspaper felt about Roh Tae Woo and South Korea's situation.

For the most part, there has been remarkable restraint on the part of [Roh Tae Woo and] the government in dealing with the often-violent protests of South Korea's radical fringe. What's been surprising about the demonstrations in recent years is that in all the haze of tear gas and bottle-bombs, there have been relatively few deaths.

Bartley's editorial failed to disclose the true nature of the relationship between Roh Tae Woo and Peter Kann, Karen Elliott House, and Washington bureau chief Al Hunt. In 1989, Kann and House adopted a South Korean baby boy. In the same year, Al Hunt and his wife, public TV's news commentator Judy Woodruff, adopted a South Korean baby girl. According to Damon Darlin, the *Journal's* Seoul correspondent, the head of the Korean adoption agency, a priest, revealed that Roh Tae Woo placed the Kanns' and the Hunts' names at the top of the list. Gen. Roh Tae Woo also waived the mandatory one-year waiting period for the two couples and allowed the Kanns and the Hunts to choose their babies.[8]

Besides being an exceedingly controversial manager of men, House does little to help other women at the *Journal* or Dow Jones rise through the ranks. Until recently, Mary Williams Walsh was one of the *Journal's* stars. She was young, attractive—"of the pre-Raphaelite curls?" her husband once said—and smart. Walsh graduated from the Columbia School of Journalism in 1982 where she was a Bagehot scholar, that school's version of a Baker scholar.

After Columbia, Walsh worked for the *Progressive* before joining the *Journal's* Philadelphia bureau in 1983, working for Frank Allen, "a terrific boss. Frank Allen was a great editor and no story was too big for me. He was very supportive,"[9] Walsh said.

In 1985, Walsh was promoted to Mexico City as a correspondent, working for House, then foreign editor. Walsh recalled once, "Karen came down and, together, we interviewed the minister of finance. She had the advantage of being a blond woman in Mexico. He loved her. But she was very cool, very professional."

Two years later, Walsh was transferred to Hong Kong, still working for House. "I thought she was an ideal boss and a nice person. She was very, very direct, but I didn't mind that. You knew where you stood."

Once, when Williams was on home leave from Mexico City, Karen invited her to spend the night in Princeton. "I was so excited," Walsh said. "I got to ride in the limousine with Peter and Karen and to see their perfect $2.6 million white clapboard house in Princeton, which even had a golden retriever. They were such a family. They had a Jamaican lady taking care of Petra [their young adopted daughter], and Peter helped Hilary with her homework. Then the kids had chicken wings for dinner, and at the kitchen table. Later, Peter cooked a fancy roast for the three of us. It was really nice."[10]

Both House and Williams remained in touch for the next several years, even after House's elevation to vice president.

In May 1989, Williams proposed a page-one profile to Lee Lescaze, the foreign editor who replaced House. Williams proposed to reveal how the U.S. television news media, especially CBS, had been manipulated into presenting the wrong story on Afghanistan. Given permission to do the story, Williams then spent the next six months, and nearly $100,000 in expenses, researching and writing. When she handed the article in May 1989, it was rejected—with no explanation.

Williams flew to New York and in a series of meetings with every editor except Norman Pearlstine, managing editor, tried to salvage her work. The editors kept repeating the same thing: Her piece was unfocused, and it was more the profile of one individual than the broader and more interesting story line which they had approved. The *New York Post* ran Walsh's story instead, plus an account of her problems with the *Journal*. The publicity caused the episode to become the latest Pearlstine cause célèbre.

Pearlstine retaliated by telling his version of what happened to Bill Carter of the *New York Times*. In an article that appeared in the *Times* the next day, Pearlstine was quoted as saying "Williams's piece was not up to the *Journal*'s standards," an admission that humiliated Williams and did not speak well for how Pearlstine supports his own people.

A day later, in a letter to Williams, Pearlstine wrote: "I consider you one of the most talented reporters on the paper.... I was blindsided by Carter... since I thought I was off the record... but I should know better by now, and I apologize for any embarrassment my comments might have caused you."

But Williams was unassuaged. She resigned.

"The sad part about the whole affair," said Frank Allen, Walsh's first *Journal* boss, "is it could have been avoided. Did Walsh get wrapped up in a story that probably drifted too much? Yes. But both the story and her career were salvageable. Karen should have rescued or sistered Walsh."

At the emotional height of her battles with the New York editors, Walsh wrote House a letter detailing her problem. Karen Elliott House never responded.

Years later, House admitted, "I liked Mary enormously. But she got away from me. I was not paying attention."[11]

House's failure to mentor Walsh and other women at Dow Jones becomes apparent when surveying the company's executive ranks. Very few women hold critical positions, and none, other than House herself, is a candidate for Dow Jones's top five slots—CEO, president, and three senior vice presidents.

Carol Hymnowitz, the *Journal's* Pittsburgh bureau chief, and Dorothy Coccoli Palsho, vice president, circulation, are the two highest-ranking women next to House at Dow Jones.

Hymnowitz is a highly respected manager and developer of talent. But she will probably not progress any further than another female former bureau chief, Kathleen Christiansen, who quit several years back, disillusioned with the ambiguity of her position as one of three equal spot-news editors. "We did not do a good job of giving Kathy a clear area of authority. And since she was the newest spot-news editor, she was often odd person out,"[12] Pearlstine said recently. Christiansen is now managing editor of the *Baltimore Sun*.

Palsho is a pleasant but untalented manager who was promoted to her present position nearly ten years ago because Ken Burenga wanted to look good with Phillips and Kann.[13] Back then, they were encouraging the advancement of women at Dow Jones to avoid unfavorable publicity.

Regardless of gender, the staff of Dow Jones's *Far Eastern Economic Review* (*FEER*) did not escape House's purges, either. Founded in 1946, the *Review*—Asia's business version of *Time* magazine back when Henry Luce was alive—struggled for years until post-Vietnam, when business became Asia's biggest story. The magazine then turned into a success, not only because of the reader interest in its subject, but because of the independence of its news reporting, something of a rarity in the Far East back then.

FEER's success, of course, was predicated on its news staff, which displays the unmistakable swagger of English public-school graduates, an attitude that, for the past twenty years, has enraged country dictators and Dow Jones corporate officials alike.

FEER's most famous editor, Derek Davies, Cambridge-educated and partial to the port wine and Stilton cheese served only at London's Traveller's Club, shaped the *Review* in the seventies much as Harold Ross had molded the *New Yorker* during the forties. For twenty-three years, Derek Davies was the *Far Eastern Economic Review*, refusing to bow to the Singapore government or Dow Jones's

Peter Kann or fellow Oxbridge types whose scams were not limited to London. As a result of Davies's intransigence or independence, Singapore banned *FEER*, Kann disliked Davies, and British financiers Jim Slater and Sir James Goldsmith snubbed him on Pall Mall.

Davies and Kann first clashed in Hong Kong in 1969. Davies frowned on the *Journal's* approach to journalism and told Kann so. "It was my experience," Davies said, "that *Journal*-trained reporters at *FEER* would write the story and then say, 'Now it's time to go out and fill in the quotes.'"[14]

Throughout the seventies and mid-eighties, Davies became all-powerful because of *FEER's* success. Only the *Financial Times* wielded greater influence in the English-speaking business community in Asia. In 1973, at Kann's suggestion despite his dislike of Davies, Dow Jones purchased a 40 percent share of the magazine for $500,000. A year later, it purchased an additional 10 percent from the Jardine Matheson Group and the Hong Kong and Shanghai Banking Group. But several years later, after Dow Jones owned *FEER* completely, Davies became vulnerable.

Eventually, House forced Davies to retire in 1988 after his many conflicts with Dow Jones veteran Charles Stabler, who was brought to *FEER* by Macdonald and House as publisher to sell advertising. A man who looked and acted as if he were raised on the rough streets of Brooklyn, Stabler's behavior offended the British sensibilities.

The act which most provoked the staff was when Stabler fired the incumbent advertising director, Elaine Goodwin, who had held that post for ten years. "Elaine's departure caused a major hemorrhage in our advertising revenue,"[15] said Philip Bowring, *FEER's* managing editor at the time. "It probably did the *Review* as much commercial damage as being banned from Singapore."

A year after Goodwin was fired, the *Review's* advertising revenues were $11 million, a drop of $2 million from 1987. Up until the time Goodwin left, advertising had been growing at a 12 percent annual rate. Stabler's reign, in fact, caused such turmoil at *FEER* that it became the subject of an article written by Robert Sam Anson for *Manhattan Inc.* that embarrassed Dow Jones greatly. Eventually, Stabler was replaced with another Macdonald protégé from New York, Tom Eglinton, who continued House's and Stabler's pattern of dispiriting the *FEER* staff.

"Nobody trusted Eglinton,"[16] Bowring said, "because he would pose as a journalist to gain entry to potential advertisers. Executives would see him expecting an interview, only to receive a sales pitch."

Since House had no business experience, she could not evaluate either Stabler's or Eglinton's competence to do the job. And like her husband, she trusted the retired but still active Don Macdonald, who had actually made these two appointments. "Don Macdonald is a very brilliant guy,"[17] House said. "I don't know everything, and of course I relied on him to help me in these areas."

But House did know editorial, and she replaced Derek Davies with Philip Bowring, also Cambridge educated, who had been with the *Review* for twenty years save for a three-year respite caused by a spat with Davies. Bowring ran *FEER* guided by one overriding principle: "A successful journalist accepts that controversy is inseparable from reporting the facts and views honestly."

Like his predecessor, Bowring was fiercely independent, to the point of arrogance. This demeanor, coupled with his journalistic integrity, made his relationship with House unbearable. According to Bowring, she believed that *FEER* and Bowring were anti-American; he felt that "House was always trying to force her uninformed views of Asia and the magazine down our throats."

Under Bowring, *FEER's* success continued, both in terms of journalistic influence and of circulation gains. From an initial level of 17,000 in 1972, *FEER's* circulation in 1992 grew to 74,200. Had the magazine not been censored and banned in Singapore, *FEER's* circulation would now be over 90,000.

By comparison, the *Asian Wall Street Journal's* circulation began at 12,000 in 1976 and is now at 42,000, bolstered by the questionable circulation practice of bulk deliveries of 15,000 copies. Also, the *Asian Journal* has never made a profit. Like its European counterpart, the *Asian Journal* loses on average $2 million per year. In 1991, *FEER* made an operating profit of $1,845,000.

Because of *FEER's* success, Bowring and his staff believed they were invulnerable. In November 1991, for example, Bowring was called back to New York for a budget review. In the course of discussing a decision Bowring had made unilaterally, House asked, "Why didn't you consult me? At Dow Jones, we always consult our superiors."

Bowring replied, "At the *Far Eastern Economic Review*, I am the superior."

These difficulties never were resolved. Called to New York again in March 1992, Bowring appeared before House and Ottaway, who sat side by side like judges. House coolly said, "Philip, we think it's time for a change. We're bringing someone in to replace you."

Stunned, Bowring asked, "How can you fire me when the *Review* is steadily improving and the *Asian Journal* is steadily declining?"

According to Bowring, House replied: "We don't disagree with that. But still, things here are not quite right, not quite firing on all cylinders."

The unpleasant conversation continued for several minutes. Bowring then excused himself. As he was leaving the meeting, Ottaway asked: "Are you free for dinner?"

A week later, House and Ottaway flew to Hong Kong to introduce Bowring's replacement, Gordon Crovitz, to the *FEER* staff. House referred to Crovitz as "possibly the most brilliant person at the *Journal*." Gordon Crovitz, thirty-three, had been the legal columnist for the *Journal*'s editorial page. He had never been to Asia before; he had never been a correspondent; he had never been a reporter.

Despite House's praise, forty-two *FEER* staffers were so upset by these events that they wrote a letter to Kann and Ottaway in New York, challenging Crovitz's appointment.

> We wish to place on the record our concerns arising from Philip Bowring's dismissal as Editor of the *Far Eastern Economic Review*. Philip's removal was portrayed by Dow Jones as a "rotational" exercise, but the change at the helm is anything but routine.
>
> It amounts to a drastic alteration of our pluralistic editorial culture. We have always considered that the best person to run the magazine was somebody who knows Asia inside out. Philip has been replaced by someone who does not.

The very next day, April 3, 1992, Kann and Ottaway wrote a reply to "Dow Jones colleagues who signed the April 2 letter to us."

> We do not believe Gordon's lack of specific Asian experience is a significant issue.... Gordon was selected as editor not to provide detailed Asian expertise but to provide distinguished news and editorial leadership.
>
> In all honesty, however, we find your suggestion that Gordon must somehow prove to you that Dow Jones has the *Review*'s "best interests at heart" to be at least mildly insulting.

House refused to publish Philip Bowring's farewell editorial, which was largely a letter of tribute to his *FEER* colleagues of twenty years. Instead, House ran Gordon Crovitz's first *FEER* editorial. It defended the Los Angeles Police Department's actions in the Rodney Stone beating.

Later, Bowring speculated that House was attempting to create another Kann by sending a young, inexperienced wunderkind, Crovitz, to Hong Kong so he might triumph as Kann had twenty years earlier.

As Pearlstine curried favor in New York for his own gain, so, too, did Karen Elliott House curry favor in Asia for hers. And as they did with Pearlstine, Kann and Phillips stood by nodding in tacit approval.

22

Why the *Journal* Missed the Savings and Loan Scandal

As Phillips and Kann stood by throughout the eighties, the *Journal* failed the nation in its most important duty—to keep the world of business and finance honest through unsparing and courageous investigative reporting. Instead, books, the slowest news medium of all, scooped the *Journal* on major scandals, most notably those perpetrated by the savings-and-loan industry and by Michael Milken.

Before 1980, of course, the *Journal* had made several spectacular disclosures: Ed Cony's revelation of Georgia Pacific's tax-fraud scheme, Mike Miller's expose of the salad oil swindle, Jerry Landauer's unseating of Vice President Spiro Agnew, Bill Blundell's story on Equity Funding Corporation, to name but a few.

But these stories dealt more with isolated instances than with underlying societal or Wall Street ills. As A. Kent MacDougall, professor at the UC-Berkeley Graduate School of Journalism, said: "The *Journal* exposes the rotten apples, but overlooks their barrels. They missed Watergate, the Pentagon Papers, and most importantly, Milken and the savings and loan scandals."[1]

At first glance, this accusation is astonishing. But an examination of the facts reveals MacDougall is correct.

Most people, for example, believe that the *Journal* and Jim Stewart won the 1988 Pulitzer Prize for exposing Michael Milken. But Connie Bruck's book *The Predators' Ball* and a 1988 *Forbes* magazine cover story did much more to reveal Milken's felonies than Stewart and the *Journal* did.

Stewart won the Pulitzer for two articles:[2] a retrospective examination of insider-trading felon Martin Siegel, written five months after Siegel surrendered to the authorities on his own; and "Terrible Tuesday," another retrospective piece explaining what went wrong on Black Tuesday and written one month after the debacle occurred. Like Stewart's 1991 book *Den of Thieves*, both these articles shed light on the issues, but they revisited events that had already done harm. Because they were after the fact, Stewart won the prize for explanatory, not investigative, journalism.

Many other press professionals believe the *Journal* should have done a better job alerting the country to the excesses of the eighties. Everette Dennis, head of the Freedom Forum Media Studies Center at Columbia's Graduate School of Journalism, said, "The movie *Wall Street* did far more to alert the public to the scandals of the eighties than the *Journal* did."[3]

Even Peter Jennings was disappointed with how the *Journal* covered the eighties. "The *Journal's* a great newspaper, of course, perhaps the greatest," Jennings declared. "But much of the crimes of the eighties, Milken, etc., caught them off balance a bit."[4]

Bill Kovach, curator of the Nieman Foundation at Harvard University and former editor of the *Atlanta Constitution* and, before that, Washington bureau chief of the *New York Times*, said: "None of us did a good job monitoring the eighties. Newspapers in this country tended to react to news and events long after that was sufficient. Beginning probably as far back as the fifties, with the onset of consultants who specialized in managing the public's impressions of things, there was a far greater effort made to control the news. Consequently, journalists were reporting manufactured reality. This became more true in the Reagan years with Michael Deaver, James Baker, Edward Meese, and David Gergen, new editor at large at *U.S. News and World Report*. These men, for example, knew more about us than we knew about them. They were quite adept at presenting information in a manner that controlled the way we reported it. We journalists did not catch on; we did not realize that the White House was a propagandist.

"So, with this as a backdrop, let me answer your question about the *Journal*. Because most of us focused on general news, we essentially looked to the *Wall Street Journal* to help us spot trends in the world of finance and business. There was, for example, an enormous shift of money to the S&Ls and, subsequently, to real estate when the S&Ls were deregulated. It is certain the Reagan Administration knew exactly what was happening and the *Journal* should have helped us flag this shift a lot earlier. These trends were not in the paper and we found out about them through books like *Inside Job*. Even Jim Stewart's *Den of Thieves* was after the fact. Once the system and Milken collapsed then he and the *Journal* came in. We needed to understand junk-bond financing in the early eighties when a new atmosphere was at work in Washington. They [the *Journal*] didn't do this."[5]

Jonathan Kwitny, the *Journal*'s leading investigative reporter in the seventies, agreed that the paper could have done a better job.[6] Kwitny claims that he could never get started on the story because neither Greg Hill, San Francisco bureau chief, nor Al Hunt, Washington bureau chief, would let him.[7]

Kwitny was pulled off the S&L story to write an occasional column on personal finances in early 1988. Within the year, he quit the *Journal* to pursue a career in public television to avoid further humiliation. In his single-minded and often egocentric pursuit of miscreants, Kwitny had finally stepped on too many powerful people.[8]

Investigative journalism at the *Wall Street Journal* had been on the wane since 1970, the year Ed Cony was promoted from managing editor to executive editor. Kerby and Phillips removed Cony from harm's way because they wanted more business-success, not business-excess, stories, which had been Cony's stock-in-trade.

Walt Bogdanich, a *Journal* reporter and an officer of the Investigative Reporters and Editors Association, often complained to colleagues that his efforts were not appreciated. Kwitny said, "Walt had to kick and scream to get his piece into the paper. But when it won a Pulitzer, of course, then everyone took credit for it." Bogdanich won a 1988 Pulitzer Prize in the Specialized Reporting category for a five-part series on the faulty testing practices of American medical laboratories.

Within two years of joining the *Journal*, in 1973, Kwitny wrote a series of articles that exposed the depth and breadth of white-collar crime in the United States. Many law officials considered these articles, and the resulting book, *The Fountain Pen Conspiracy*, the finest explanations of white-collar crime extant at the time.

A supremely confident and indignant man, for the next fifteen years Kwitny exposed errant businessmen, Las Vegas gangsters, and shady politicians in everything from the latest· Mafia gambit to Irangate. In the highest form of compliment, the newsroom dubbed an investigative piece a "Kwitny."

But Kwitny also had his detractors. Former *Journal* reporter Bill Paul said, "Kwitny, of course, was a great reporter. But for every story he nailed, he had twenty conspiracies that never panned out."[9]

And to several bureau chiefs and editors, Kwitny's self-righteousness and egocentricity were barely tolerable. "Jonathan could drive you wild,"[10] admitted Mike Miller, former Washington bureau chief. "Many of his investigations took him to Washington, where inevitably one of my people would already be on it. Convincing Jonathan that we could struggle through without him, or better yet, that we might be able to contribute to his investigation, was not an easy task."

Don Moffitt, an editor who at one time supervised many of the *Journal's* investigative reporters, said: "Kwitny was the best. But deadlines and tidy copy were for less talented people to worry about."[11]

Like an Arthurian knight, Kwitny feels compelled to right the world's wrongs. Therefore, he perceives conspiracies where others see only innocence, an attitude that made him increasingly unpopular in the *Journal* newsroom in the mid-eighties.[12]

According to Kwitny, Stephen Pizzo is the person most responsible for exposing what many consider the worst financial scandal since the days of the robber barons in his book *Inside Job: The Looting of America's Savings and Loans*, coauthored by Mary Fricker and Paul Muolo. Pizzo wrote this book only after Greg Hill, the *Wall Street Journal's* S&L expert and San Francisco bureau chief, rejected Pizzo's account of Centennial Savings and Loan in Guerneville, California.

In the early eighties, Pizzo sold his real estate business and bought a weekly newspaper, the *Russian River News* in Guerneville, population 1,700, which is located on the Russian River sixty miles north of San Francisco. "I wanted to be the town's Mark Twain," Pizzo said. "My only prior experience in journalism consisted of a subscription to the *San Francisco Examiner*."[13]

Stephen Pizzo soon faced the challenge of the small-town newspaper publisher: offering a legitimate news product without unduly offending advertisers. He failed this test in his first interview with Erwin Hansen, president of Guerneville's Centennial Savings and Loan.

Founded in 1977 to provide the town with a source of home

mortgages, Centennial had gone through three lackluster presidents until Erwin Hansen took over in 1980. The former chief accountant of the Federal Home Loan Board, Erv Hansen, then forty-eight, had been recruited to lead Centennial into the age of deregulation. Partial to the informality of western attire and a place called the Appaloosa Bar, Hansen frequently boasted of the deals he would make once his friends in Washington had deregulated the industry.

From 1980 to 1983, inspired by supply-side economics, Reagan, the Congress, and Richard Pratt, head of the Federal Home Loan Bank Board, deregulated the savings-and-loan industry. As a result, a simple, dull business—paying 6 percent interest on passbook savings accounts and mortgaging local homes at 9 percent interest—became a get-rich-quick outlet for real estate developers, politicians, and mobsters. Overnight, state and federal S&Ls turned their backs on community wage earners and sought out shrimp farms in the Caribbean and $100,000 CDs from commissioned money brokers on Wall Street. Before Reagan, the S&Ls had a regulation for every-thing. After 1983, the S&Ls had no regulations, period.

With deregulation, Reagan also reduced the manpower of the Federal Savings and Loan Insurance Corporation (FSLIC), the industry's regulatory body. In 1979, there were 712 examiners and in 1983, there were 634 to oversee 4,100 S&Ls throughout the country. Used to dealing with thirty-year fixed-rate mortgages, these exam-iners, many of whom were earning $14,000 per year, now had to evaluate $20 million shopping-mall deals that puzzled even the most sophisticated commercial bankers.

In January 1983, Pizzo wrote a story in the *Russian River News* exposing Centennial's acquisition of a local concern, Piombo Con-struction Company, for $14 million. Several months before, Piombo's owners had valued their company at $2.8 million. When asked how Centennial could afford the deal since it was worth only $1.87 million, Hansen said he relied on "brokered deposits to obtain the $14 million purchase price."

From 1980 onward, with the ceiling on interest rates removed, S&Ls could accept brokered funds or "hot money," which usually took the form of jumbo certificates of deposit worth $100,000 or more. Brokered funds, Pizzo explained to his readers, were deposits brought to a savings and loan by commissioned brokers who look for only one thing: the highest possible short-term interest rates for their clients, for example, pension funds, insurance companies, credit unions, government trust finds. Because deregulation also eliminated early withdrawal penalties, commission brokers would move billions of dollars each day, depending solely on where they could find the highest interest rates.

To pay the higher interest to their "hot money accounts," S&Ls had to seek increasingly risky investments, which explains why Milken's junk bonds became so popular with S&Ls. By the late eighties, S&Ls owned $18 billion in junk bonds.

Like most entrepreneurs at the time, Hansen was loath to be cautious. "You've got to use money to make money," Hansen told Pizzo in explaining Centennial's reliance on brokered accounts.

Over the next several years, Pizzo continued to chronicle Centennial's activities, which included buying and refurbishing a San Francisco penthouse for $900,000 for entertainment purposes; acquiring a Cessna twin-engined airplane and a Mercedes-Benz stretch limousine; staging a $125,000-party for Centennial shareholders; buying and renovating a building for $2.2 million, using it as Centennial's headquarters for four months, and then abandoning it; loaning the local U.S. congressman $124,000; engaging in money-laundering schemes with a Las Vegas mobster; loaning $1 million to an alleged Mafia associate; paying two-third's of Centennial's yearly profits to officers as bonuses; buying a home worth $40,000 at two P.M. and selling it back and forth between Centennial officers so that by five o'clock that same afternoon it was worth $80,000; and hiring former FSLIC examiners and public accounting auditors who helped conceal illegal transactions.

According to Pizzo, the end came when Hansen sold Piombo Construction Company for $25 million to friends. Terms of the sale meant disaster: no down payment, 10 percent in promissory notes, and 90 percent in a thirty-year mortgage, which Centennial would hold. In return, Hansen's friends took possession of Piombo's assets, which included $800,000 in cash.

Even the lax and woebegone FSLIC examiners had had enough. They declared Centennial insolvent on August 20, 1985. Centennial had assets worth $404 million, nearly ten times what they had been two years before; deposits worth $37 million, 80 percent of which was hot money; twenty-five company-owned autos; a $48,000-per-year chef. The S&L owed $187 million.

After being investigated for two years by the FBI, Erwin Hansen, Centennial's president, died in his sleep; Siddhartha Shah, Centennial's executive vice president, was convicted for drug smuggling and sentenced to seven years in prison; and another Centennial officer, Beverly Haines, was convicted of embezzling $1.6 million from Centennial.

Believing that what happened at Centennial was happening throughout the country, Pizzo approached the *Wall Street Journal*. "It had become too big a story for us,"[14]

Up until then, in mid-1985, newspapers across the country, with the notable exception of the *Journal*, had chronicled similar tales of rogue S&Ls. But there was no national, coordinated news effort to tell the story, nothing to tie Washington in with the many "zombie S&Ls" throughout the country. That's why Pizzo contacted G. Christian Hill, the *Wall Street Journal*'s San Francisco's bureau chief and the newspaper's leading S&L specialist expert, shortly before the FSLIC seized Centennial Savings.

Pizzo told Hill: "I'm sitting on a huge story, an S&L scandal. These guys are circling around me, and one lawsuit and I am out of here. You guys have to do it."[15]

Within a day, Hill had come to Guerneville, California, to take a firsthand look at Pizzo's evidence.

Pizzo, along with his business partner, Scott Kersner, took Hill to lunch at the Appaloosa Bar & Grill, to get "a flavor for things." There they ran into Erv Hansen. Seeing the three journalists together, Hansen sauntered over to them and, according to Pizzo, said: "Well, well, are you guys going to get me?"

After lunch, Pizzo and Kersner took Hill to the office of the *Russian River News*, where they examined three years' worth of evidence, notes, and clips. At the end, according to Pizzo, Hill said: "'This is a fucking race horse of a story.'

"Hill led us to believe the *Journal* was going to take over the story," Pizzo recalled. "But he never contacted us again. In fact, he would never take my calls when I tried to follow up. Finally, I gave up and concluded the *Journal* just wouldn't do it."

It was at this juncture that Pizzo, together with two associates, Mary Fricker, a housewife turned reporter for the *Russian River News*, and Paul Muolo, associate editor of the *National Mortgage News* in Washington, D.C., decided to write the story of the savings-and-loan scandal themselves in book form. The trio soon discovered, as they had suspected, that Centennial's crimes were being replicated throughout the country by much larger S&Ls with much larger consequences.

On one of their research trips, Pizzo and Fricker went to Shreveport, Louisiana, to investigate Herman Beebe, an associate of former Texas governor John Connally. With Greg Hill in Dallas, less than one hundred miles away, Herman Beebe built what was reputed to be the most extensive illegal banking and S&L network in the world, 109 banking and savings-and-loan institutions throughout Louisiana and Texas.

Joseph Cage, the U.S. attorney prosecuting Beebe, urged Pizzo to read Jonathan Kwitny's *Fountain Pen Conspiracy.* Apparently, some of the mobsters Kwitny cited in his book—Sam Calabrese, Lionel Reifler, Tony "Little Pussy" Russo, and Mort Zimmerman—were also involved in the S&L scandals. Cage also urged Pizzo to seek Kwitny's help at the *Journal.* "So with some trepidation based on our prior experience with the *Journal,* we called Kwitny," Pizzo said. "We were delighted to find he was a soul mate. He encouraged us greatly. He said he would do some stories in the *Journal* to help us. But Kwitny ran across the same thing we did. He and Hill butted heads, I know. It was a territorial thing. But Hill never did anything."

Pizzo's coauthor, Mary Fricker, said, "I was enormously disappointed by the *Journal's* reaction. Sometimes they do some great stuff, but other times you just wonder where they are."[16]

Pizzo was even more critical. "The *Journal* went through an ethical melt-down," Pizzo said. "Boesky, Milken, the S&Ls, the Big Eight accounting firms selling everyone down the river, yet the *Journal* never did anything."[17]

Pizzo, Fricker, and Muolo went on to publish their book to substantial acclaim. Writing in the *San Francisco Examiner*, Warren Hinckle said: "When it comes to understanding the eighties, *Inside Job* plays the same role that Upton Sinclair's *The Jungle'* or Lincoln Steffens's *The Shame of the Cities* did at the turn of the century."[18]

Also writing in the *Examiner*, Susan Burkhart said, "Three little guys, including an ex-housewife, uncovered one of the great scandals of the century. They scooped the establishment press who were too big and too corporate ever to notice, much less expose, what's been happening across America in the last eight years."[19]

When asked to comment on what Pizzo, Fricker, and Kwitny had alleged about him, the *Journal's* Greg Hill said: "Yes, I went up there.

But the Centennial story was too small for us, too local, small potatoes. It was a $20 million scandal. We needed twenty Centennials before the *Journal* could do a story."

But then, almost in the same breath, Hill admitted, "I had a hunch it [the Centennial situation] was going on everywhere."[20]

Conceding that the *Journal* missed the S&L scandal, Hill added, "No national publication did a good job uncovering the savings and loan scandal. With us, it was a question of territorial imperatives. The Balkanized structure of the bureaus didn't allow for national cooperation and coordination."[21]

Hill was the *Journal*'s national savings and loan beat reporter working out of Los Angeles in the early eighties. An examination of articles reveals his coverage centered on the economic hardships most S&Ls experienced from paying 10 percent interest to depositors and earning only 9.5 percent interest from home mortgages. Hill's stories, usually buried deep within the paper, were written as if he were an economist concerned with theory instead of the reality of the situation. For instance, 439 S&Ls failed in Reagan's first three years in office, yet Hill never ran a page-one piece chronicling these failures. Before 1980, the largest number of S&L failures in a year was 13, and that occurred in 1941.

After several years in Los Angeles, Hill accepted a promotion to Dallas as a general reporter "who also would do a little editing. I wanted to continue the S&L beat in Texas, but Pearlstine kept it in LA with Hilder [David Hilder, former *Journal* reporter]. I was concerned that Hilder was taking over because he was weak. But Pearlstine didn't think it was that important, and there was nothing I could do. I would occasionally write suggestions to the LA and Washington bureau chiefs but they didn't seem to need my help."[22]

From 1983 to 1986, with the industry completely deregulated, S&Ls were either succeeding or failing with manic intensity. The vortex of this business activity swirled around Hill's front yard, Texas and California.

As early as March 1984, Empire Savings and Loan turned a Dallas suburb into a ghost town of unwanted condominiums. Beginning in 1983, Empire officers, aided by Arthur Young (now Ernst & Young), the public accounting firm, flipped these condos among themselves, elevating their value by tens of millions. A sudden surge in unemployment in Dallas caused the home market to collapse and Empire's scheme to unravel. By 1985, Empire had been declared insolvent, costing taxpayers $300 million. The *Dallas Morning News* scooped the story. The *Journal* never mentioned it.

Meanwhile, back in Los Angeles, right under Greg Hill's nose, perhaps the worst of the S&L offenders, Charles Keating, Jr., acquired Lincoln Savings of Irvine, California, with the help of $50 million in junk bonds from Michael Milken. He perpetrated schemes that eventually caused a photo of him in manacles and chains to appear on the front page of the *New York Times*. Somehow the *Journal's* Los Angeles bureau, headed by Barney Calame at the time, missed the story.

There were many things Lincoln did that should have roused the suspicions of the *Journal*. From 1984 to 1986, for example, Lincoln made fifty-two real estate loans to borrowers who were not required to submit credit reports with their loan applications. Another instance occurred when FSLIC examiners found that Lincoln had made a $12 million paper profit by selling a loan to another bank which was rescinded within hours: Lincoln never took the $12 million from its books. Also, Lincoln's auditors, the public accounting firm of Arthur Young, stuffed loan files with postdated documents so they might pass the scrutiny of FHLB-SF examiners.

Yet neither Hill nor the *Journal* wrote a page-one leader on Keating, or David Paul of CenTrust, or M. Danny Wall of the Federal Home Loan Bank Board, or Cong. Fernand St. Germain, or Sen. Jake Garn, the Washington politicians most responsible for deregulating the industry, or Leonard Taggart, California's savings-and-lan commissioner who approved the start-ups of two hundred thrifts, all of which failed within two years.

Had Hill cooperated with Pizzo in 1985, or Pearlstine allowed Kwitny to cooperate with Pizzo in 1987, perhaps the meeting of five senators to intercede with three Federal Home Loan Bank–San Francisco officials on behalf of their patron, Charles Keating, Jr., would have been revealed in time to do some good.

The senators attending that meeting on April 9, 1987, were Alan Cranston, John Glenn, Dennis DeConcini, John McCain, and Don Riegle. Minutes of the meeting, published in *Inside Job*, reveal that the examiners told the senators that Keating's Lincoln Savings was guilty of criminal activities.

Responding to questions asked by Senator Reigle, Michael Patriarca, director of Agency Functions of the Federal Home Loan Board–San Francisco, said: "We're sending a criminal referral on

Lincoln to the Justice Department. Not maybe. We're sending one. This is an extraordinarily serious matter."[23] Patriarca was referring to Lincoln's claim that it made $49 million in profits for 1986, when in fact the firm had posted a loss.

When pressed about the *Journal's* lack of coverage of Charles Keating, Hill conceded, "Yeah, we should've done profiles on Keating and on David Paul of CenTrust and on Spiegel of Columbia Savings."[24]

When asked why the *Journal* failed to profile Keating and the others, Hill replied: "Because Danny Wall [head of the Federal Home Loan Bank Board] would never let us in."

It is difficult to imagine Al Hunt, the *Journal's* Washington bureau chief, being stymied by Danny Wall, a third-tier Washington official.

It is also difficult to understand why Hunt did not use his power to ferret out other politicians corrupted by the savings-and-loan scandal, men like House Speaker Jim Wright or California congressmen Tony Coelho. Both men resigned—Wright from his speakership and Coelho from Congress—because of their S&L sins. Another friend, Alan Greenspan, who wrote the famous letter vouching for Charles Keating, Jr.'s competence as a savings-and-loan executive, spends every Christmas at Hunt's home. If George and Barbara Bush can attend a black-tie dinner in Hunt's home, one would suppose that Hunt could get access to whomever the *Journal* needed to interview to obtain a story.

Neil Bush, the president's youngest son, was a director of Silverado Savings and Loan of Denver, Colorado. Bush had fiduciary relationships with two of Silverado's biggest borrowers, William Walters and Kenneth Good, which Bush concealed from the rest of the Silverado board. Whenever a loan for either Walters or Good came to the board for approval, Bush would endorse it. Eventually, Good and Walters defaulted $100 million in loans to Silverado, whose total losses were nearly $1 billion. On November 8, 1988, exactly twenty-four hours after his father won the presidency, Neil Bush's Silverado was declared insolvent.

Though thousands of middle-class Americans lost their life savings through the misdeeds of men like Charles Keating, Jr., some billionaires did quite well by them. In an article entitled "The Screwiest S&L Bailout Ever," *Fortune* magazine chronicled how Ron Perelman, friend of Norman Pearlstine's and employer of Nancy Friday's, bought a package of distressed thrifts, headed by First

Gibraltar of Houston, for $315 million. In return, Perelman took title to $7.1 billion in assets, including $5.1 billion in cash and a $900 million tax break for Perelman's MacAndrews and Forbes Holding Inc.

Eli Jacobs, another Pearlstine friend and subject of a negative profile by *Journal* reporter Laurie Cohen that was never published, acquired the Memorex Corporation in 1986 for $550 million. Jacobs put up $1.2 million of his own cash and supplied the balance, $547.5 million, in junk bonds provided by Michael Milken. Jacobs and Milken then sold $66 million of Memorex's junk bonds to Charles Keating, Jr., of Lincoln and David Paul of Centrust. Over the next eight days, Keating and Paul sold these junk bonds back and forth to each other, inflating their worth to $145 million.

In January 1989, after President Reagan exited Washington, the Brady Commission, formed to investigate the collapse of the savings-and-loan industry, announced that $96 billion would be required to restore it to health. At the time, few people realized the final bailout estimate would increase to $500 billion.

The savings-and-loan debacle was one of the twentieth century's most devastating but well-kept secrets. In November 1990, the *Journal* finally published a two-part series on the scandal, reiterating many of the problems that Stephen Pizzo had exposed seven years before in the *Russian River News*. It was a thorough, lucid, and retrospective explanation of an event that had begun in 1982. But as Jonathan Kwitny said, had the two-parter been published when it could have done some good, say, in 1985 or 1986, the country would have been spared much money and misery.

Many reporters from other newspapers did a better job than the *Journal*. They include Pete Brewton of the *Houston Post*, Kathleen Day of the *Washington Post*, Jeff Gerth of the *New York Times*, Jerry Knight of the *Washington Post*, and Tom Furlong of the *Los Angeles Times*.

In June 1990, as part of his duties as the keynote speaker at the annual convention of the Investigative Reporters and Editors convention, Norman Pearlstine presented the IRE yearly awards for outstanding achievement in investigative journalism. The Investigative Reporters & Editor's Best Book Award went to *Inside Job: The Looting of America's Savings and Loans*, by Stephen Pizzo, Mary Fricker, and Paul Muolo.

Michael Milken: The Exposé That Never Happened

Besides missing the savings-and-loan scandals, the *Journal* also failed to investigate and expose the corrupt world personified by Michael Milken. Former *Journal* editor Jim Stewart denied this assertion when he recently told *New York Newsday*, "I spent five years of my life on the Milken case. And as far as I know, the *Journal* was the first to raise the issue of potential wrongdoing by Milken."[1]

But in truth neither Stewart nor the *Wall Street Journal* alerted the nation to Milken's crimes and the era of greed he epitomized. Instead, Milken was exposed by Connie Bruck in her book *The Predators' Ball*, which Jason McManus, Time Inc.'s editor in chief, regarded as "the finest piece of business investigative journalism since the turn-of-the-century muckrakers, Lincoln Steffens and Upton Sinclair."

Unfortunately, throughout the eighties, Pearlstine's fraternization with Wall Street tycoons, tacitly endorsed by Phillips and Kann sapped the *Journal's* will to investigate and expose business conduct contrary to the public interest. A search of the *Journal's* ten-year coverage of Ron Perelman, Norman Pearlstine's friend and Nancy Friday's employer, reveals that not once did the paper report how Michael Milken helped make Perelman a multibillionaire.[2] Nor did the *Journal's* Daniel Hertzberg, in reporting Perelman's 1985 acquisition of Revlon, referred to as "the deal of the century," mention

Michael Milken by name. Yet Milken and Perelman spoke as often as ten times per day arranging the $1.3 billion in junk-bond financing that enabled Perelman to complete what to Wall Street appeared to be a preposterous deal. Hertzberg and the *Journal* did make reference to Drexel Burnham Lambert, Milken's firm. But they did not reveal that Milken was Drexel's junk-bond department and that he operated like a separate nation far from Drexel's New York headquarters.

The *Journal's* news department appeared to abandon its objectivity and adopt the bias of its editorial page. What many people saw as the decade of greed, Pearlstine saw as "the decade of prosperity."[3] Infected by the power and money of Wall Street, Pearlstine and the *Journal's* rank-and-file reporters resorted to go-go journalism.

Even when it became apparent Milken was a suspected felon, the *Wall Street Journal* continued to champion him.

In June 1986, a full month after Drexel banker Dennis Levine, who later went to jail, had implicated Milken and Ivan Boesky in his insider trading conspiracy, the *Wall Street Journal* wrote a page-one leader entitled "Street Fighter: Fast Growing Drexel Irritates Many Rivals With Its Tough Tactics." As the headline indicates, the *Journal* treated Drexel and Milken as if they were pranksters, not the subjects of federal indictments. *Journal* reporters Daniel Hertzberg, Steve Swartz, and George Anders described Michael Milken's accomplishments and work habits admiringly. Moreover, they sacrified something to accuracy. Milken's 1985 income, the piece said, was $20 million. In actual fact, Milken made $550 million that year.

On February 5, 1987, Stewart finally reported "Drexel's Michael Milken Called a Focus of Probe of Suspected Boesky Scheme" on the *Journal's* page three. However, Robert Coles of the *New York Times* had reported the same story in November 1986.

From the fifties onward, the *Journal* was so superior to *Fortune*, *Forbes*, *Business Week*, and the business department of major newspapers that the rest of the press always delayed taking up a story until the *Journal* decided it was newsworthy. *Times* reporter Robert Cole and his editor, Fred Andrews, were the first financial journalists to realize the *Journal* was slow to report on the Milken-Boesky scandal. Despite Pearlstine's swarms of new recruits, the *Journal* came in last on a story that should have been its Watergate.

Fortune magazine was the first news medium to suspect Milken. In its August 6, 1984 issue, *Fortune* hinted at the illegality of the

Milken-Boesky connection. Five months later, in the December 1984 issue of the *Atlantic*, Connie Bruck expanded on the Milken-Boesky relationship and then later, in her book *The Predators' Ball*, cracked the scandal wide open. To add to her achievement, Bruck withstood Milken's attempt to bribe her not to publish the book to the tune of $250,000. Rebuffed, Milken then hired Pearlstine's former girlfriend, Linda Gosden Robinson, who launched a vigorous campaign to discredit *The Predators' Ball*.[4] It was Linda Robinson who recommended that Milken take 1,700 underprivileged youngsters to a New York Mets baseball game as a publicity gimmick to show he was kindhearted. The nation's newspapers excoriated Milken for such a transparent ruse.

Though Stewart and the *Journal* never exposed Milken's crimes, they did a creditable job of reporting the junk-bond king's four-year-long legal machinations to avoid jail. The drawn-out process worked to the *Journal's* advantage. Toward the end, right before Milken received his sentence, it was difficult to remember what the scandal was about, much less which newspaper had reported it first. Because people had been dulled by the avalanche of Milken's illegal insider-trading activities after 1988, they incorrectly assumed that Stewart and the *Journal* had covered Milken just as conscientiously before 1985.

The *Journal's* role was further inflated—misleadingly so—when Pearlstine excerpted Stewart's bestseller *Den of Thieves* on the front page of the second section in October 1991. *Den of Thieves* revisits the crimes and conspiracies of Milken, Boesky, Levine, and Siegel through layer upon layer of fascinating detail. The problem with the excerpt, however, is that its author should have reported its revelations in 1985, in the *Wall Street Journal* when they could have done some good. Yet readers quite naturally assumed the *Journal* was on top of the story back then, as Stewart is with it today.

One glaring example of Milken's misdeeds, which occurred right under the nose of the *Journal's* Los Angeles bureau, passed unnoticed. Six years later, Stewart wrote about it in *Den of Thieves*, as if he had uncovered the miscreants in the *Journal* in 1985.

One of Michael Milken's closest friends was Thomas Spiegel, CEO of Columbia Savings and Loan of Los Angeles. The two men shared ownership of an airplane, and Columbia maintained a branch office one floor above Milken's Beverly Hills headquarters. Whenever Milken needed to find a buyer for his risky junk bonds, he would "sell" the bonds to Columbia, frequently without consulting Spiegel or anyone else there. By 1985, Columbia had bought $4 billion worth of Milken's junk bonds, four times more than Charles Keating, Jr., had purchased.

In 1987, the Federal Home Loan Bank Board seized Columbia and ousted Spiegel after a number of Milken's bonds defaulted. The *Journal's* national savings-and-loan reporter was located twenty minutes away.

What went wrong here? Stewart is a first-rate reporter. Why didn't he, instead of Connie Bruck, write *Predators' Ball?* And why didn't a book like this by a *Journal* reporter get excerpted in its pages?

The answer lies with Norman Pearlstine, Peter Kann, and Warren Phillips. The power and money of Michael Milken and his clients, most notably billionaire raider and greenmailer Ronnie Perelman, seduced Norman Pearlstine. Through his wife, Nancy Friday, and his position as the *Journal's* managing editor, Pearlstine became Perelman's token journalist-friend. Perelman and his glamour intoxicated Pearlstine, who in turn intoxicated the *Journal* news department, while Peter Kann and Warren Phillips stood by. And in their state of Perelman-induced inebriation, Pearlstine and his subordinates lost perspective.

"Yes," admitted Pearlstine, "I'm a friend of Ronnie's, and Nancy's on his payroll. Peter and Warren know all that. . . .

"Yes, I've been to Seder at Ronnie's, and so have a lot of other people like Joe Flom, Eli [Jacobs], and others. . . .

"Ronnie and I come from the same suburban Philadelphia background. . . .

"Besides, I like to know the people we write about. . . .

"But I never get involved when we write about him."[5]

Pearlstine may think he has a lot in common with Perelman, but the numbers say otherwise. In 1990, for instance, Norman Pearlstine earned $329,000 and Nancy Friday earned $678,819. Between them they had a net worth of $2.3 million. That same year, Ronnie Perelman earned $192 million and had a net worth of $3.2 billion.

Since 1980, Perelman had relied on Michael Milken and his junk bonds to finance three increasingly larger and vitriolic raids. The last, Pantry Pride, a supermarket chain, had a $300 million tax carry-over which Perelman used, together with $1.3 billion worth of Milken's junk bonds, to acquire Revlon in a hostile takeover that raged throughout most of the fall of 1985.

The battle for this premier cosmetics company pitted Perelman, short, insecure, a saliva-laden cigar always in hand, against Revlon's chief executive officer, Michel Bergerac, sleek, imperious, French. The acquiring company, Perelman's Pantry Pride, was one-eighth the size of Revlon. Felix Rohaytn dismissed the idea as "preposterous." No one on Wall Street thought it could be done.

Though an M.B.A. from Wharton, Perelman preferred to approach business viscerally and collegially. Like twelve-year-old boys hanging outside a candy store, Perelman and three aides, who earned $10 million apiece, spent all day together, kvetching. Bergerac, on the other hand, was the quintessential executive, fully conversant with five-year plans and matrix analyses.

Once the battle was joined, Michael Milken and Dennis Levine, the Drexel banker who six months later would be arrested for insider trading, provided Perelman with the junk-bond financing that defeated Bergerac and his ally, Forstmann-Little.

Throughout the struggle, Norman Pearlstine and Nancy Friday offered their friend encouragement and advice, an attitude that troubled some *Journal* newspeople. "Do you think when Ronnie and Norman were having Seder together that Ronnie was telling Norman to watch out for Milken?"[6] asked Bill Paul, a former *Journal* reporter.

The *Journal's* penchant for omitting embarrassing facts about Perelman continued into the nineties. In a *Journal* page-one leader on Perelman, dated March 27, 1990, Randall Smith and David Wessel again failed to mention how Milken aided Perelman in acquiring Revlon. Smith and Wessel did note that Perelman had hired Linda Robinson as a public relations consultant, but they failed to report Linda Robinson's special relationship with Norman Pearlstine.

Nor did the profile mention that weeks before the Revlon acquisition had closed, Dennis Levine illegally leaked insider information about the pending deal to Ivan Boesky. The average sales volume of Revlon stock before Perelman approached the company was 200,000 shares per day. One week prior to the closing of the Revlon deal, the average had shot up to 1,200,000 shares per day.

The *Journal* page-one leader also neglected to report a lawsuit that resulted from Perelman's acquisition of Technicolor in September 1982. Of this lawsuit Connie Bruck says: "Taken as a whole, the complaint paints a picture of Perelman allegedly using deceit and secret deals—money here, position there, whatever it took—to buy off the necessary people and get the company."[7]

The *Journal's* reluctance to report potentially embarrassing facts about Perelman also extended to Stewart's book *Den of Thieves*. In his bestseller, Stewart allocates nearly five hundred pages to Milken and the three other criminals. He even rakes up Foster Winans's "homosexual lover" relationships and how former SEC compliance chief John Fedders beat his wife. Yet, like his *Journal* colleagues, he fails to articulate Milken and Levine's intimate relationship with Perelman, Norman Pearlstine's friend.

Norman Pearlstine helped Jim Stewart earn an estimated million dollars plus from *Den of Thieves* by excerpting it on the front page of the *Journal's* second section; printing a photograph of the book's cover on the *Journal's* front page; allowing *Journal* reporters to work it; permitting *Journal* property—*Journal* interview information—to be used in the book; and by hosting a publication party.[8]

Ethical laxity continued to infect the *Journal's* news department in June 1991, when the *New York Post* printed the allegation that a *Journal* reporter had extorted fight tickets from Donald Trump in return for favorable press treatment in the *Journal*.

The incident began when Trump gave *Journal* reporter Neil Barsky one ticket, worth $1,000, for the April 1991 Holyfield-Foreman fight in Atlantic City. Violating Dow Jones policy, Barsky accepted this first ticket but failed to pay for it. "It got Neil into an area where his best sources were sitting,"[9] wrote managing editor Norman Pearlstine and his assistant, Paul Steiger, to their worldwide *Journal* news colleagues in an interoffice memo explaining the incident.

Four years before, Pearlstine used a variation of this reasoning to explain why he, too, accepted Trump's invitation to attend the 1987 Tyson-Foreman championship bout in Atlantic City. "I like to know the people we write about,"[10] Pearlstine said.

Several days after receiving the first fight ticket, Neil Barsky compounded his violation of Dow Jones policy and journalistic ethics by asking for two additional tickets. "Neil told us they were for his father and brother,"[11] said Robert Trump, Donald's brother and executive vice president of the Trump Organization. "We felt pressured. But considering he represented the *Wall Street Journal*, we thought it best not to refuse him."

Four years before, Norman Pearlstine had asked Trump if he could bring Nancy Friday to the Tyson-Foreman fight, as well.

Barsky had told his immediate boss, Fred Bleakley, about the first ticket, but failed to mention the two tickets for his father and brother.

Pearlstine and Steiger frowned on this omission. "Neil agrees with us that no case can be made for taking the second and third tickets," wrote Pearlstine and Steiger to their *Journal* news colleagues. Their use of the verb "take" is curious. Again, in the same memo to their colleagues, the two editors maintained: "Donald Trump has publicly asserted that Neil demanded the tickets from the Trump Organization and that the organization felt pressured to provide them. Neil says the opposite is the case— that the Trump people pressed him to take the additional tickets. We believe Neil. We don't believe Donald Trump."[12]

Donald and Robert Trump believed Barsky, his father, and brother "enjoyed themselves immensely" at the twelve-round fight, which Holyfield won by decision. So much so that Donald Trump felt betrayed when, a month later, Barsky reported in the *Journal* that "Trump was so strapped for cash he was considering borrowing money from his eighty-five-year-old father, Fred."

Enraged, Donald Trump retaliated by telling the *New York Post*, "Barsky's piece was evil, vicious, false, and misleading, and... the *Journal* should take appropriate action against Barsky over the fight tickets."

According to Robert Trump, Donald Trump had been a friend of Pearlstine's for years and could not believe the *Journal* would write something so personal and so demeaning about the Trump family. "He went to his wedding, for God's sake,"[13] Trump said. "But the fight tickets were nothing. You have no idea what the *Journal* has asked us for over the years."

Pearlstine and Steiger admitted that "Neil is the first to acknowledge that it was a mistake in judgment and a clear violation of the Dow Jones Conflicts of Interest Policy which holds that 'employees should not accept, directly or indirectly, any gift, entertainment, or reimbursement of expenses of more than nominal value or that exceeds customary courtesies....' We have sent the Trump Organization a check for $3,000 and at Neil's behest, we have accepted his check for $2,000 to cover the second and third tickets."

Neither Dow Jones nor Norman Pearlstine reimbursed the Trump Organization for the expenses he and Nancy Friday incurred during their 1987 junket to the Tyson-Foreman fight.

Pearlstine and Steiger conceded that the incident was "both unpleasant and a source of embarrassment to the *Journal* and Dow Jones." While still defending Barsky's reporting staunchly, Pearlstine and Steiger reassigned him to another beat.

Frank Allen, the *Journal's* environmental reporter, said, "Someone at a Dow Jones board meeting asked why Barsky wasn't fired. The unspoken answer, of course, was if Barsky were fired, then Pearlstine should be fired, too." [14]

When asked if this were true, Bill Cox, member of the Dow Jones board of directors, said: "It was discussed. But Warren [Phillips] felt it best to handle the matter in a different way."[15]

In June 1991, shortly after the Trump incident, Norman Pearlstine was appointed executive editor of the *Wall Street Journal*, and Paul Steiger succeeded him as managing editor. Besides overseeing the *Journal* and exploring new opportunities, the announcement said, Pearlstine would continue to oversee the test of a new magazine called *SmartMoney*, a joint venture with Hearst magazines. The announcement was made with the usual flourish, encouraging Pearlstine's many supporters to believe it was a promotion, the next step in his natural progression to the top.

But in truth, Norman Pearlstine had just been fired, *Journal* style. The Trump incident was the last straw. All the fanfare of his promotion to the contrary, Pearlstine, like Cony, Taylor, and O'Donnell before him, had little to do in his new post.

Similar to the 1980 magazine project that occupied Taylor for a brief time when he was made executive editor, *SmartMoney* was a small-potatoes project that was relegated to a junior editor almost immediately. Pearlstine occasionally lunched with the Hearst folks, but John Mack Carter, Hearst's interface with Dow Jones on *SmartMoney*, admitted, "I really don't know anything about this guy."[16]

Eleven months later, Norman Pearlstine resigned from Dow Jones "to explore my interests and new horizons...with people with whom I couldn't negotiate so long as I was responsible for the *Journal's* news coverage."[17]

On May 28, 1992, at a Long Island, New York, conference center, on the occasion of the *Journal's* annual editors/bureau chiefs meeting, Peter Kann, Warren Phillips, Al Hunt, Ken Burenga, and others gave Pearlstine a farewell roast. In a videotaped skit entitled "Why Pearlstine Quit," the *Journal's* Consuela Mack, playing a fictional television anchorperson, revealed that Pearlstine quit to coauthor with his wife, Nancy Friday, a book to be entitled *Money and Sex*. *Journal* environmental reporter Frank Allen was surprised "by the bluntness of all the sexual allusions to Norman and Nancy. They rang true, however."[18] But Pearlstine took the teasing well, Allen added, even the question asked of Peter Kann throughout the night, "Why did you keep promoting this man?"[19]

Warren Phillips struck the evening's only serious note when he presented Pearlstine with a videocamera and said how over the years "Norman always exceeded his goals." The remark prompted an anonymous heckler to add, "especially in hiring."

Everyone participated in the roast with one notable exception, Karen Elliott House. Though few know this, Pearlstine's demise began in 1984 when he expressed, sotto voce, his disapproval of House's promotion to foreign editor. By so doing, he made an enemy of his boss's wife, a misstep that was to come back to haunt him over the ensuing years.

By 1986, House had begun to express her negative views of Pearlstine more freely. Derek Davies, retired editor of Dow Jones's *Far Eastern Economic Review*, remembered a 1986 dinner with House and Peter Kann at the couple's favorite Greenwich Village Italian restaurant. He recalled, "Karen was merciless with her criticism of Norman to Peter. Apparently, Norman had just hired twelve more reporters and Karen was saying the entire news department was livid. She kept saying, 'Peter, you've got to do something. You just can't sit back and let him get away with this.'"[20]

By 1987, Kann had manipulated Pearlstine into delegating virtually all day-to-day responsibilities, even emergencies and landmark stories, to Paul Steiger. Presumably that's why Pearlstine, with Kann's approval, traveled so extensively. Even Bob Sack, the *Journal*'s outside libel counsel, said, "From 1986 on, I dealt exclusively with Paul."[21]

Though the world of New York and western Connecticut society, as well as much of the *Journal* news department, believed Pearlstine was doing well throughout this period, the story of Pearlstine's decline was told through his titles. Pearlstine never rose above the rank of *Wall Street Journal* vice president and member of the management committee, two impressive-sounding but hollow honorariums. The real power came from being named a Dow Jones corporate vice president and becoming a member of Kann's inner circle, two talismans Pearlstine never received.

In fact, if it hadn't been for Warren Phillips's protection of Pearlstine, Kann would probably have listened to his wife and banished his onetime close friend several years previously. But Phillips remained loyal to the end, crediting Pearlstine with developing the paper's third section and expanding its coverage into law, marketing, small business, and other areas of commerce and finance.

Pearlstine also lifted the *Journal's* ban on staff-written books. After the war, Kilgore had outlawed the practice. In explaining the ban to Dow Jones vice chairman Don Macdonald, Kilgore said, "The *Journal* competes with books. If a news item is good enough for a book, it's good enough for the *Journal* first. If it's in the *Journal* first, there's no need for the book. If a reporter holds back on a *Journal* news item to make his book better, he shouldn't be a *Journal* reporter."[22]

In a discussion of the appropriateness of allowing *Journal* reporters to write books, Warren Phillips said: "Though the *New York Times* discourages its staff from writing books—too many conflict-of-interest issues raised, they say—we feel it is an appropriate policy for the *Journal* today. We have no fear that our reporters will become too big. We know Jim Stewart, for example. He's not an opportunist."[23]

Within six months of Warren Phillips retiring from Dow Jones, in January 1992, Norman Pearlstine, Bryan Burrough, and Jim Stewart all resigned.

24

A Pulitzer Prize:
Just One More Time

In February 1992, another reporter-turned-author, Susan Faludi, thirty-two, resigned from the *Wall Street Journal* "to handle the flood of speaking requests her book has generated," according to a cover story on Faludi and Gloria Steinem that appeared in *Time* magazine.[1] *Time's* coverage was prompted by Faludi's book *Backlash: The Undeclared War Against American Women*, which had become the number-two bestseller, right behind Gloria Steinem's *Revolution From Within*.

Both authors could not have chosen a better moment for their feminist books to be published, as America confronted sexual harassment, date rape, and other women's issues raised by the Clarence Thomas hearings, William Kennedy Smith's rape trial, and the increasingly strident abortion–pro-life clashes.

In *Backlash*, Faludi "describes how flawed statistics, media manipulation, hypocrisy, misogyny, and female masochism combine to undermine women at home and in the workplace,"[2] said the *Wall Street Journal's* Manuela Hoelterhoff, who reviewed her fellow worker favorably in the *Journal*. Besides the book's timeliness and controversial thesis, *Backlash* was further enhanced by Faludi's professional credentials: She was a reporter for the *Wall Street Journal* who had won a Pulitzer Prize just six months before.

Soft-spoken to a whispering degree, Susan Faludi hardly seems capable of debunking anything, much less antifeminism. But as a *Journal* reporter (a paradoxical job considering *Backlash* was so antimedia), Faludi's self-effacing demeanor and teenage looks prompted sources to relax and open up.

According to Accuracy in Media Reports, before joining the *Journal* Faludi had published only three articles in a national publication, and all three appeared in *Mother Jones*. Two dealt with feminist issues, and the other profiled a peace group called "Beyond War."[3] In the two years Faludi worked for the *Journal*, she published two stories, one on Nordstrom's, the Seattle-based department store, and the other, which earned her the Pulitzer Prize, on Safeway Stores.

Faludi's first story for the *Journal* appeared on February 20, 1990. It was about Nordstrom's, the Seattle-based department store renowned for its quality service. Faludi claimed that Nordstrom may look responsive on the outside, but that its 30,000 employees are often underpaid, especially with respect to overtime.

Predictably, Nordstrom's was not happy. In a letter to Warren Phillips, which the *Journal* did not publish, James Nordstrom asserted Faludi's piece was biased and inaccurate. He further charged that Faludi had based her conclusions on evidence provided by members of the local retail clerk's union, evidence which, Nordstrom claimed, the *Journal* published without substantiation. Nordstrom also said that Faludi failed to interview any of the store's top executives.

Several months later, in April 1990, Greg Hill, Faludi's San Francisco boss, received a telephone call from Pearlstine. "Norman had this great idea,"[4] Hill said. "He wanted Faludi and Hilder [David] to do a piece on Safeway's LBO [a leveraged buyout that occurred in 1986]. Norman said, 'KKR [Kravis, Kohlberg, and Roberts] made a lot of money off that deal. Was that good for the country?'"

In 1986, Safeway Stores was a $20 billion company that maintained 2,300 supermarkets worldwide and employed 175,000 people. In May of that year, to foil the corporate raiders Herbert and Robert Haft from taking over Safeway Stores, Peter Magowan, Safeway's CEO, bought back all of Safeway's stock from the public, effectively removing Safeway from the Hafts' outstretched grasp. The financial maneuver, known as a leveraged buyout or LBO, was much in vogue in the mid-eighties when hostile raiders were stalking corporate

America in full force. KKR were specialists in LBOs, a term derived from the fact that a small down payment was usually leveraged to the hilt with debt financing to complete the buyback.

Even though LBOs were long since outdated, the assignment was a coup for Faludi because it came from Norman Pearlstine, the person who still determined which *Journal* reporters would be nominated for Pulitzer Prizes.

Faludi had spent much of her life in journalism, but never in one place for long. After graduating from Harvard College in 1981, she held six jobs in eight years, an exhaustive accomplishment. Faludi was the editor of her high school newspaper in the affluent suburb of Yorktown Heights, New York, a post she also achieved at the *Crimson*. After Harvard, she became a *New York Times* "copy kid, collecting people's dry cleaning."[5] From there she went to the *Miami Herald*, where she worked in a suburban bureau rewriting church press releases. After eight months in Miami, Faludi became a general assignment reporter for the *Atlanta Constitution*. In 1985, she joined *West* magazine as a staff writer, then quit in 1987 to write *Backlash*. In January 1990, Faludi joined the *Journal* in San Francisco, working for bureau chief and savings-and-loan expert Greg Hill.

On May 2, 1990, Faludi and Hilder set out to Safeway headquarters in Oakland, California, where they learned in a three-hour interview with CEO Peter Magowan his version of the whys and hows of Safeway's LBO. Almost four years to the day, May 15, 1986, the feared corporate raiders Herbert and Robert Haft, a father-and-son team, had bought 3 million shares of Safeway Stores, Inc. for $121 million. Their purchase "put Safeway in play," which meant a raid was about to be launched and any other raider or defender could join in. Assuming Magowan would hate the notion of being acquired, George Roberts of KKR called and suggested an LBO.

With KKR's financing and counsel, Roberts assured Magowan he could, one, buy Safeway's stock back from the public with almost 100 percent financing; two, sell off several Safeway divisions to pay down the KKR-provided debt; three, operate the down-sized Safeway at a profit for a few years; and then four, sell the "improved Safeway" stock back to the public; five, make anywhere from ten to twenty times his original investment; six, not have to work for the Hafts.

Roberts clinched the deal when he cited the recent example of how KKR, with $2.5 billion in Milken's junk bonds, bought Beatrice Foods for $6.2 billion and then, within months, sold off Beatrice's businesses, such as Avis, Hunt-Wesson Foods, and International Playtex, for $10 billion. On July 28, 1986, KKR and Magowan together defeated the Hafts and bought Safeway for $5.65 billion.[6]

Immediately, Safeway proceeded to "restructure," another gut-wrenching phrase of the eighties, a euphemism for the process of selling off various assets and firing employees to pay down debt—in this case the loaned money KKR raised to buy the company. By the following spring, Safeway had sold several divisions, thereby reducing its employee rolls by 63,000. Most of these people did not lose their jobs, however. The acquiring companies continued their employment.

But a few unprofitable divisions could not be sold: Safeway then closed these divisions to avoid further losses. One such division was in Dallas. The focus of Faludi and Hilder's investigation, this division consisted of 141 stores in Oklahoma, Arkansas, Louisiana, and Texas and employed 8,814 people. Most of the stores and employees, however, were clustered in the Dallas–Fort Worth area.

For some inexplicable reason, Hilder was taken off the story and Faludi, on her own, conducted more than a hundred interviews with a wide range of people, from grocery baggers to investment bankers. Three weeks later, on May 16, 1990, "The Reckoning: Safeway LBO Yields Vast Profits But Exacts a Heavy Human Toll" appeared on page one, bylined by Susan Faludi and tag-lined by David Hilder. It compared the fate of Safeway's unemployed workers, depression, heart attacks, and suicide, to the fate of Magowan and KKR, wealth, security, and power. Faludi spent many of her 8,500 words making Magowan look ridiculous.

Sitting in his CEO office in Oakland, his stock now worth $800 million, Magowan presented one view of the Safeway world; the employees presented another. Magowan looked like an egocentric, out-of-touch executive who had made a Faustian bargain with KKR and was now rationalizing the harm that resulted. Again, not surprisingly, neither Magowan nor his mother was happy with Faludi's reporting. In a letter to Phillips, Magowan alleged that his mother had been ambushed at home by Faludi, but that Mrs. Magowan had still refused to talk with her. Nevertheless, Faludi included a critical quote in her article that she attributed to Mrs. Magowan. Most journalists, of course, frequently contend with charges from sources that allege misquotation or quotation despite stipulations that remarks are strictly off the record.

In January 1991, Pearlstine nominated Faludi's piece for a Pulitzer Prize. In April 1991, Faludi won the prize for explanatory journalism, the fourteenth to go to the *Journal*. According to the Pulitzer board, explanatory journalism is "any distinguished piece of journalism which illuminates a significant and complex issue."

Within a week, however, apparently provoked by the Pulitzer publicity, a disturbing fact surfaced. It seemed that the *Texas Observer*, a small but respected publication once edited by Willie Morris, had published an article on December 23, 1988, entitled "Leveraged Lives." The article, written by Austin free-lance writer Bill Adler, dealt with the human cost of the Safeway LBO on the Dallas division.

Comparing Faludi's Pulitzer Prize–winning piece to Adler's piece revealed the following.

Theme: the same; namely, the human cost of the Safeway LBO.

Focus of story: the same; namely, Dallas division of the Safeway. There were other LBOs as well as Safeway divisions whose employees lost their jobs and suffered.

Sources: See below.

Adler/*Texas Observer*
December 23, 1988

William L. Mayfield, Jr., reported to his maintenance job at Safeway's milk plant in Garland, a suburb northeast of Dallas.

Once, Mayfield said, he stuck a .45 automatic pistol in his side and pulled the trigger. The gun didn't fire, so he promptly picked up his .22 caliber rifle and tried again. This time the gun went off, but the bullet, narrowly missing his liver and kidneys, lodged in his hipbone. He stayed a week in the hospital.

The last time Bill Mayfield tried to commit suicide, he almost succeeded. After filling his bathtub with hot water, he said, he lay back in the tub and "cut my wrists to the bone" with a Gillette double-edged razor.

Faludi/*Wall Street Journal*
May 16, 1990

One was Bill Mayfield, Jr., a mechanic in the Safeway dairy since it opened in 1973, who slashed his wrists, then shot himself in the stomach; the bullet just missed his vital organs and he survived.

Adler/*Texas Observer*
December 23, 1988

Kay Seabolt, who worked in the company's human resources department, said she stopped by the club every Friday evening after work for "six or seven years running." She met her husband, a fellow Safeway employee, there, but they married in a church.

Faludi/*Wall Street Journal*
May 16, 1990

The Seabolts lost three: Husband, wife and daughter all get their pink slips on the same day. Ron Seabolt, who worked in the company's distribution center for 17 years, searched for months before taking a job as a janitor. Now he works at the post office. Kay Seabolt, a human resources supervisor at Safeway and a 17-year company veteran, counseled ex-employees for a year under a state job-placement retraining program.

Adler/*Texas Observer*
December 23, 1988

Tomorrow, as they filled out forms for unemployment benefits, they would begin to pick up the pieces. It would be the first time the local office of the Texas Employment Commission opened on a Saturday.

Faludi/*Wall Street Journal*
May 16, 1990

When the Dallas division shut down, the state unemployment office had to open on the weekend—for the first time ever—just to accommodate the Safeway crowds.

Adler/*Texas Observer*
December 23, 1988

James White had spent half of his 58 years working for Safeway.

James T. White nodded, smiling softly toward the newly arrived people he recognized, other truck drivers mostly.

James White was not there either. A few minutes before 11 that warm, clear morning, he had walked into the bathroom of his tidy home. As he did so, he told his wife, as he often did, that he loved her. "I know, and I love you too," Helen White replied from the living room, where she was folding laundry. Then he closed the door. A few moments later, Mrs. White heard a thump; she thought perhaps James's mother had fallen in her bedroom. She hadn't. The faint noise came from the bathroom. James White had ended his life as quietly as he lived it; he had shot himself in the head.

There were tears in White's eyes as he told his wife, "Oh my God, there go my 30 years with Safeway." That night, recalled Helen, "He and I cried over it. It was like our world collapsed."

On Saturday, April 23, 1988, a year to the day after James White worked his final day for Safeway. . . .

Faludi/*Wall Street Journal*
May 16, 1990

James White, a Safeway trucker for nearly 30 years in Dallas, was among the 60%.

In 1988, he marked the one-year anniversary of his last shift at Safeway this way: First he told his wife he loved her, then he locked the bathroom door, loaded his .22-caliber hunting rifle and blew his brains out.

"Safeway was James's whole life," says his widow, Helen. "He'd near stand up and salute whenever one of those trucks went by." When Safeway dismissed him, she says, "It was like he turned into a piece of stone."

Adler/*Texas Observer*
December 23, 1988

It also organized volunteers for local charities, such as the North Texas Food Bank. The association was instrumental in forming the food bank in 1982 and Safeway remained the single largest donor—averaging 45,300 pounds of food per month—until the closing. "We're not only losing a source of food, we're losing a friend," said food bank director Lori Palmer at the time the closing was announced.

Faludi/*Wall Street Journal*
May 16, 1990

The North Texas Food Bank suffered, too. It lost a founding member and its leading contributor; Safeway used to donate 600,000 pounds of food a year. "The bottom line," food-bank director Lori Palmer says, "is fewer people ate."

Adler/*Texas Observer*
December 23, 1988

The credit union has repossessed so many vehicles from laid-off Safeway employees that it has had to expand its parking lot—twice.

Faludi/*Wall Street Journal*
May 16, 1990

"I would say [the layoff] devastated about 80% of the people in the division," says Gary Jones, president of Safeway's credit union in Dallas, which eventually had to write off $4 million in loans. "Overnight we turned from a lending institution into a collection agency." At one point, more than 250 repossessed cars were sitting in his parking lot.

When asked specifically, "What do you feel about Susan Faludi's Safeway article?" Bill Adler, writer of the first piece, said: "Well...there are similarities...yes...suicide attempts, union people, local Safeway stores closed...but I don't think there's any plagiarism."[7]

When Susan Faludi was asked if she were aware of Bill Adler's article "Leveraged Lives," Faludi said, "Yes, I had Adler's article before I wrote my own. In fact, when I was in Dallas, I interviewed him."[8]

When asked if she felt there were similarities between her article and Adler's, Ms. Faludi said, "Many papers, including *Mother Jones*, did pieces on the human effects of the Safeway LBO. Take Michael Milken, for example. Everybody was rereporting him, and no one was attributing the rereported facts back to the original reporter. It was the same way with Safeway."[9]

When asked if she should have included a line of attribution to Bill Adler in her *Journal* article, Faludi replied, "No. There was no need for me to attribute anything to anyone."[10]

When asked for his thoughts on the Faludi-Adler matter, *Journal* San Francisco bureau chief Greg Hill, Faludi's immediate boss who worked "every step of the way" on the article, said, "I was not aware of Bill Adler or his article or the *Texas Observer*, for that matter, while I was helping Susan with the piece. I've seen it since, of course, and all I can say is that Susan never borrowed from anyone's work. She merely took Adler's sources and interviewed them herself, rereported them. The *Trib* [*Oakland Tribune*] and the *Examiner* [San Francisco] did similar pieces, too."[11]

In an unrelated case involving a former *Journal* reporter, the noted libel attorney Martin Garbus used this term—*rereporting*—to defend his client, Jonathan Kandell, who was suing Dow Jones because "the *Journal* wrongfully accused him [Kandell] of being a plagiarist...."[12]

Mr. Garbus wrote:

Even Pulitzer Prize-winning articles can be partially based on subjects previously reported by other publications. For example, a few weeks ago, the *Journal* won a Pulitzer Prize for a May 16, 1990, front-page article on the leveraged buy out of Safeway, the world's largest supermarket chain. But a significant portion of the article—on the troubles of employees in Safeway's Dallas division—went over ground already covered by the *Texas Observer* in its December 23, 1988, issue. I have been advised that the *Journal* reporter, Susan C. Faludi, requested and obtained a copy of the *Texas Observer* article prior to the publication of her Pulitzer Prize-winning article. Not coincidentally, the *Journal* story mentions persons, incidents, facts, and ideas contained in the *Texas Observer* without acknowledging that publication as a source.[13]

For the *Journal* story to mention "persons, incidents, facts, and ideas contained in the *Texas Observer* without acknowledging that publication as a source," as Martin Garbus writes, hardly constitutes what Pearlstine once described as Faludi's "brilliant reporting and penetrating analysis."

Moreover, for Faludi to have taken, as *Journal* bureau chief Greg Hill said, "Adler's sources and interviewed them herself, rereported them,"[14] hardly constitutes brilliant reporting, either.

Though the word itself is cumbersome, *rereporting* is both an acceptable and necessary element in journalism—provided it is restricted to certain immutable facts relating to hard-news stories. Michael Milken's guilt and ten-year prison sentence, for example, are immutable facts that can be freely reiterated without attribution to the journalist who first reported them.

But the human toll of Safeway's LBO is a soft-news or feature idea created by Paul Farhi of the *San Francisco Examiner*, who wrote a five-part series on the subject in February 1987. It did not spring from the news event itself. Therefore, the human toll of Safeway is not an immutable fact and not subject to being "rereported" without attribution.

Although conceding there are overlaps between Adler's and Faludi's stories, supporters believe Faludi's article is a better piece of journalism. Greg Hill, Faludi's boss, said, "Susan did an infinitely better job of reporting this story. She interviewed far more people than Adler did, for example. She also went to other Safeway divisions, and she went to Kroger and compared how it handled its LBO far better than Safeway."[15] Adler's *Texas Observer* Safeway piece was 2,000 words in length, while Faludi's was 8,000 words. Paul Farhi's five-part series in the *San Francisco Examiner* on the Safeway LBO, entitled "Anatomy of a Takeover," was 12,000 words.

No doubt, Faludi's piece shed additional light on a subject the public needed to know about. But like most *Journal* stories that dealt with the greed and excess of the eighties, it was published several years too late. Also, had Pearlstine assigned Faludi to report on Ron Perelman's takeover of Revlon and its effect on employees, or Eli Jacobs's takeover of Memorex, her effort might have been more original.

However, the important question remains, was Faludi's story worthy of a Pulitzer Prize, journalism's highest recognition of excellence?

When J. Douglas Bates, author of *The Pulitzer Prize: The Inside Story of America's Most Prestigious Award*, was asked why Faludi and the *Journal* won a Pulitzer for an article about a soft-news or feature story which included reporting, Bates said: "It's not surprising. In fact, I knew the *Wall Street Journal* would win a 1991 Pulitzer as far back as April 1990. I was there at Columbia trying to interview the Prize Board as they deliberated on the 1990 awards. That year, Kann came away without a prize. I knew in my bones they'd make up for it next year. All that phony jockeying. I knew the *Journal* would get theirs in 1991."[16]

Ironically, Robert Maynard, editor and publisher of the *Oakland Tribune*, and Burl Osborne, editor and president of the *Dallas Morning News*, sat on the 1991 Pulitzer Prize board and gave the award to Faludi, bypassing their own reporter who had done a better and more timely job.

David Hilder, it seems, was not the only contributor to Faludi's Pulitzer Prize–winning article who went unheralded.

Bill Adler of the *Texas Observer*, Robert Tomsho of the *Dallas Morning News*, the *Oakland Tribune*, Paul Farhi of the *San Francisco Examiner*, the *San Francisco Chronicle*, *Mother Jones*, and *Grocery Marketing News* were ignored, too. All these writers and publications had taken note of this soft-news subject—the human toll of Safeway's LBO—anywhere from two to four years before the Faludi article appeared in the *Journal*.

Telerate and FNN:
Too Little and Too Late

In its desire to report on the human toll of acquisitions and leveraged buyouts, the *Journal* could have written about two of its own recent experiences: Phillips's four-year-installment purchase of Telerate, Inc., an electronic publisher of financial data; and Peter Kann's defeat by Robert Wright, president of NBC, in a head-to-head competition to acquire *Financial News Network*, a 35-million-household cable television network.

In the fight to acquire FNN, only $20 million separated Dow Jones's losing bid from NBC's winning one ($145 million versus $125 million), a trifling sum when compared to the enormous technological advantages FNN would have bestowed on Dow Jones. For instance, Dow Jones owns an extensive library of facts and figures which today is used by a tiny sliver of the business market. A vastly greater, and more profitable, potential for the library exists with consumers. But just as Dow Jones needs newsstands to distribute the *Journal*, the company also should have a means to distribute its data bases into homes. Since home ownership of computers is still quite low, a practical alternative would have been to use television broadcast microwaves and a television monitor. FNN, with its 35 million households, would have fulfilled this need nicely. Simply by turning on the television set, zapping on the FNN channel, and calling up the Dow Jones library menu, a consumer could have shopped for a dining-room table, made an airline reservation to Chicago, or looked up the *Journal* article that conveyed the particulars of last week's stock market. And, unfortunately for Dow Jones, the chance to acquire a 35-million-household cable network is rare indeed.

In the case of Telerate, the errors were twofold. First, Phillips could have bought Telerate in 1974 for $1 million; in 1981 for $80 million; and in 1986 for $800 million. Instead, he elected to buy the company piecemeal over four years, from 1986 to 1990, for $1.6 billion. Second, once the deal was finally consummated, Phillips and Kann "Dow Jonesized" Telerate, that is, they turned the electronic publisher from a highly successful entrepreneurship, where decisions were conceived by experienced individuals instantly, into a faltering bureaucracy where decisions were conceived by inexperienced committees long after they were relevant.

As a result, the competition proliferated, and Telerate's once large share of the financial electronic publishing market shrank substantially. If they were so bent on converting Telerate into the image and likeness of Dow Jones, Phillips and Kann could have created a Dow Jones electronic publishing venture at a fraction of Telerate's $1.6 billion purchase price.

At one time, on paper at least, Telerate looked like the perfect acquisition to lead Dow Jones into the twenty-first century. High hopes were pinned on Telerate's ability to convey instant financial information to its subscribers in contrast to the *Journal*, which requires fourteen hours to do essentially the same thing. Telerate's information includes reports on U.S. government securities, world money markets, foreign exchanges, precious metals, energy markets, and futures. Some two thousand brokers and dealers directly contribute live data and market commentary to Telerate's electronic network, which in turn instantly transmits this information to Telerate's 100,000 computer terminals in banks, securities traders, brokerage firms, corporations, and individual investor offices located in sixty countries throughout the world.

Founded in 1969 by Neil S. Hirsch, a twenty-one-year-old University of Bridgeport dropout, Telerate provided quotes for commercial paper, a type of short-term investment favored by corporate treasurers, in its first several years of operation. But in 1972, Telerate's sales started to boom when Hirsch convinced Cantor Fitzgerald Securities Corp., a bond brokerage firm, to acquire a 70 percent stake in Telerate. In turn, Cantor Fitzgerald gave Telerate exclusive rights to publish electronically U.S. Treasury quotes.

In 1974, Hirsch approached Ray Shaw, then general manager, who was setting up Dow Jones's Information Services Group. Hirsch proposed that Dow Jones buy the company, including Cantor's stake, for $1 million. Reflecting Phillips's timidity, Shaw offered a counter-proposal instead: a joint venture making Dow Jones and the Associated Press sales agents for Telerate in Europe. Three years later, Hirsch accepted Shaw's offer and by 1981, Telerate's yearly revenues were $27.6 million, and its after-tax profits were $6.6 million, a staggering 24 percent margin.

That same year, 1981, Hirsch approached Shaw and Bill Dunn, who had taken over for Shaw as head of the Information Service Group several years before. "I wanted Dow Jones to buy Telerate, lock, stock and barrel, for $80 million this time," Hirsch said. "It was a bargain, only twelve times earnings, when other companies were going for twice that multiple."

But Phillips, as chief executive officer, turned Hirsch down again, preferring to buy 25 percent of a cable network, Continental Cablevision Inc., for $79 million. In 1981, before the Continental purchase, Dow Jones carried only $8 million in long-term debt, which meant Phillips could have easily financed both purchases. No doubt Phillips was suffering at this time from the many management problems associated with the *Book Digest* acquisition. Continental Cablevision represented a passive investment. Telerate, like *Book Digest*, would have required heavy Dow Jones management involvement, which Phillips was reluctant to promise.

In January 1983, Telerate went public and raised $900 million in capital. Hirsch's 7.6 percent stake in the company was worth $70 million. Later, Dow Jones sold its interest in Continental Cablevision, before the cable-television boom swept the country, earning an after-tax profit of $249 million. A similar investment in Telerate would have earned Dow Jones six times this amount.

By 1985, Telerate's sales were growing 35 percent annually and its profits by even more. It was then that Bill Dunn, executive vice president, who had watched Telerate's growth for eleven years, stormed Phillips's office. "Enough is enough,"[1] Dunn said to Phillips. "We've just got to do this deal. It's our future, for chrissake. Print's dying. Electronics are the future."

Dunn wanted to purchase Telerate outright, but Ken Burenga

persuaded Phillips to buy 28 million shares of Telerate stock for $285 million. The former circulation director, Burenga, had been named Dow Jones chief financial officer the year before.

By 1987, Telerate's revenues were $336 million, up from $148 in 1985; its income was $75.2 million, up from $33.9 in 1985. Again, Dunn pressed to acquire the entire company. He was anxious to expand his Information Services Group, which, after some thirteen years of well-publicized promises, would post its first profit in 1987, an insignificant $17 million. By acquiring all of Telerate and folding it into Information Services Group, Dunn would rival Kann in fiscal responsibility. In 1987, as the associate publisher of the *Journal*, Kann was responsible for more than $800 million in revenue.

But Burenga prevailed again, and Phillips authorized three more purchasing waves of Telerate's stock for an additional $416 million, bringing Dow Jones's total investment in the company to 56 percent. "It baffled me why Phillips kept doling out the money this way," Dunn said. "It was a fuckin' expensive way to do business."

Assuming the same number of outstanding shares in Telerate throughout this period, what would have cost Dow Jones 1¢ per share in 1974, $1 per share in 1981, or $10 per share in 1985 was now costing Dow Jones $18 per share in 1987.

In an attempt to explain Phillips's installment purchases of Telerate, Ken Burenga, said: "It was the Dow Jones way not to incur debt."[2]

But Al Neuharth, founder of *USA Today* and CEO of Gannett Newspapers, Inc., offered another explanation. "Warren [Phillips] does not have the guts to do a deal, to hang in there. He always has to have a[3] partner, a back door, some avenue of escape, someone to share the blame with if the deal goes wrong."[3] Eight years before, as part of an acquisition wave for Gannett Newspapers, Neuharth had outbid Warren Phillips and others to buy the *Des Moines Register*.

Irrespective of Dow Jones's partial ownership of Telerate, Shaw and Dunn, who were now on Telerate's board of directors, were pleased with Hirsch and his company's increasing profits. In fact, to the amusement of Kann and Pearlstine, Hirsch, now worth $112 million, started to squire Bianca Jagger and other beautiful women around New York as one indication of his growing prosperity.

In 1987, Dow Jones's pro rata share of Telerate's earnings, some $35 million, all but erased the *Journal's* advertising and circulation decreases, which had grown alarmingly after Black Monday. Dunn, in his rivalry with Kann to succeed Phillips as Dow Jones CEO, was feeling very cocky. "It took the Information Services Group to bail the *Journal* out," said Dunn.

Meanwhile, Hirsch regarded both Shaw and Dunn warmly because "they left us alone. We were bringing in the numbers."

In March 1988, Ray Shaw surprised everyone at Dow Jones by announcing his retirement as president, effective a year hence. Dow Jones, especially Warren Phillips, had taken Shaw for granted for twenty-eight years, ever since he had joined the company in 1960. Throughout all those years, Shaw had worked only for Phillips, struggling between being his own man and being Phillips's man. Phillips always won. To have risen to president of Dow Jones should have been enough. But Shaw could be satisfied by only one thing— Warren Phillips's approval.

Phillips, however, was incapable of conveying approval to anyone. And so, for thirty years, Phillips and Shaw remained locked in an unsatisfying relationship. Together, the pair was singularly uninspiring.

If there was ever a doubt as to how Phillips regarded Shaw, it was dispelled in Phillips's 1989 letter to Dow Jones shareholders. Buried at the end of a long recitation of accomplishments for the previous year, Phillips wrote: "Ray Shaw retired as president and director April 1, as last year's annual report said he planned to do."

Neither Phillips nor Shaw ever admitted the other was less than perfect. No less was required to keep up appearances for shareholders, the Dow Jones board of directors, and the Bancrofts. The closest Shaw ever came to acknowledging anything was even remotely awry in his relationship with Phillips occurred when he said: "Nothing irks me more then when people speculate I resigned because I was passed over, because I was not going to succeed Warren. I was clearly in line to be CEO, but I didn't want it. Business was not fun for me anymore and, besides, I had a bypass in '84 and there were other health problems, plus personal family reasons."[4]

Within sixty days of leaving Dow Jones, Shaw must have experienced a miraculous recovery because he became the CEO of a $100-million communications company.

In retrospect, Shaw was Dow Jones's Harry Truman. Others always managed to preempt the credit for successes that were due to Shaw. Shaw founded the AP–Dow Jones joint venture, which led to the creation of the *Asian* and *European Wall Street Journals*. In 1977, he also rescued the *Journal*'s ailing circulation department by replacing its head, then senior vice president Don Macdonald, with Joe Perrone.

And it was Shaw who, in 1974, established Dow Jones's Information Service Group, which eventually eclipsed the *Journal* in size and possibly in importance. Shaw's greatest accomplishment, however, one he shared with Executive Vice President Bill Dunn, was to have promoted Telerate. When he left, it fell to Bill Dunn to keep Neil Hirsch and his Telerate colleagues happy.

But from Peter Kann's point of view, Shaw's resignation was a relief. It meant now only one person, Bill Dunn, the explosive head of Dow Jones Information Services Group, remained a so-called rival to succeed Warren. Mercifully, Kann had to keep up that pretense for only another year.

In July 1989, a week after President Bush attended the *Journal*'s black-tie one hundredth anniversary celebration, Warren Phillips summoned Bill Dunn to New York.

"It was Monday, July 17, 1989, at five o'clock," Dunn said in a typical stream-of-consciousness response to a question. "Warren had called me up from South Brunswick for a chat. I knew Phillips was going to announce who would succeed him, Kann or me. For the previous five years, I had repeated a phrase almost as if it were a mantra to prepare myself for how I would react to his decision. It was not a practice set and I wanted to be ready. I did not want to be swayed by the emotion of the moment. When it happened, I had to be ready to act. The saying was: 'If Kann gets it, I quit. If I'm offered it, I'll consider it.'

"So there we were, Phillips and I, staring at each other in his big, spare office. Finally, Warren leans over, winces and says, 'I've decided to name Peter Kann....'

" 'I quit,' I said. Warren never finished the sentence."

"That was the end of the conversation. I was enraged and he looked upset and baffled. Both of us kept our composure by remaining mute.

"I broke the silence by saying, 'I resign, effective January 1, 1991.'

"When I heard myself say those words, I thought, Oh, fuck! I've really gone ahead and done the thing I threatened to do for five years. How old am I? How old will I be when I resign? I was fifty-three then.

"Acting as if we were two semiliterates, the two of us tried to figure out when that date was. We couldn't for the fucking life of us determine if it were the following January or the January after that. My voice kept quaking and Phillips was equally rattled. His hands trembled as he looked the date up in his diary.

"The two of us gained enough composure for Phillips to then ask, perfunctorily, if I would reconsider. But I had ironcladded the thing. I refused.

"Then Peter came into the room, and tried to be conciliatory. But I cut him off and said, 'The bird is out of the cage. It's free.'

"It was evident to me then that Phillips had known for a long time he was going to choose Kann. He had lied about it because Warren kept saying to everyone he had not chosen a successor. He even wrote memos about it.

"Why was I surprised? I don't know. I guess I always dreamed I could do it, that I should do it. People told me I was naive to have wanted it so bad. They cited the company tradition, beginning with Kilgore, that the CEO of Dow Jones had to be a news guy. Kilgore was great because he was a great news guy, so the company thinking goes. Not true. Kilgore was great because he was great. He just happened to be a newsman. But it doesn't follow. Newsman and business executive often have nothing to do with one another. Two different sets of skills. And if Kilgore were alive today, he would be the first to agree with me....

"I did not want to stay on as Number Two because I watched others stay too long. I saw Don Macdonald [Dow Jones vice chairman] wander the halls, doing and saying things that no one ever paid any attention to. Then he played golf with the Japs long after he should have. I saw George Flynn [Dunn's mentor at Dow Jones] drink too much. It caused his death. The two of them copped a plea. When you sit alone in the morning, taking a shit, you know whether you copped a plea. Kann was not going to take my life and trash it just because I went to the wrong meetings, hung out with the wrong people, and said 'fuck' and drank too much....

"Peter said to me on two separate occasions that he would have served under me. Easy for him to say then. But I told him I would never have worked for him. Why? It's personal. If he were an asshole buddy, we could have worked it out. But he wasn't, and we didn't. I've got enough money today, and I didn't want ten more years of agony....

"The day I quit, people in South Brunswick wore black armbands.

Young Bill Cox [son of William Cox, Jr.] was real upset about it. He said: 'You out-Kilgored Kilgore.'"

Young Cox paid Dunn the highest Dow Jones compliment. Dunn, in young Cox's opinion, was even more innovative and inventive than Kilgore.

"With newspapers and magazines, the cost of doing business—transportation, labor, energy, cost of manufacture, paper expenses—have all gone up. But the value of the products have not increased. The *Wall Street Journal* or *Time* magazine is still the same. They aren't any better today than they were ten years ago when they cost less. But in electronic transmission, the costs have gone down.

"As one reporter put it, Phillips chose the past instead of the future. But Warren does not know what the future holds. Look at my noncompete list: Reuters, Quotron, Apple. [Companies that Dunn, by contractual agreement, may not work for until 1996.] These names are evidence of their ignorance. The new technology is not going to come from companies like these because they are just like Dow Jones....

"There has been a fundamental change in the marketplace. The news model has changed, shifted. When Don Macdonald said it, it was noteworthy. People at Dow Jones are now waiting for the economy to improve because they think the *Journal* will improve automatically, too. But the news model has changed, and the printed version of the *Journal* will never come back to its former heights."[5]

Warren Phillips essentially confirmed Bill Dunn's account of their uncomfortable confrontation, with one variation. "Dunn didn't say, 'I quit.' He said, 'I'm outta here.'"[6]

But Phillips cited an entirely different reason why Dunn did not succeed him. "Bill Dunn was smart, brilliant, a visionary. But in the last year or so his behavior was off the charts. There was an instability about him, as if he were reacting to some inner tension, which made me fear he could not do the job."[7]

When asked for an example of Dunn's unstable behavior, Phillips hesitated for a moment and then replied: "Well... there was the *Journal*'s Centennial dinner where the President of the United States helped us celebrate the *Journal*'s hundredth anniversary. It was in July 1989, and as early as the previous December, I notified all the directors and top people to reserve that date. Come the big night, who's the only director and executive who's not at the dinner? Bill Dunn. He had a hiking date in the Grand Canyon."

When asked to respond to Phillips's comment, Dunn said: "My priority was correct. Rather than attend that sideshow in New York, that Bonfire of the Vanities with Karen Elliott House running around with hot pants and a tuxedo jacket, I was in the bottom of the Grand Canyon. My priorities were correct on that one. It took me six months to get reservations at the Phantom Ranch, and I wanted to go."[8]

Dunn exhibits the frustration and anger of a person seldom understood. Like Macdonald, he was Dow Jones's idiot savant who talked in riddles but who foresaw the future accurately. But no one listened to him. Phillips suggested some of Dunn's former associates would support his own opinion that Bill Dunn acted peculiarly toward the end of his career with Dow Jones.

Immediately after quitting, Dunn tracked down his closest Dow Jones friend, Carl Valenti, who was asleep in Seoul, Korea. "Bill talked to me for three hours that night," Valenti said. "But I didn't try to dissuade him [from quitting]. Bill was not an operator. He was no longer needed at Dow Jones."[9] Two weeks after Dunn resigned, Carl Valenti replaced him as head of the Information Services Group.

Perhaps Dunn was not an operator, as Valenti suggests. But those who worked for him, including Valenti at one time, worshiped Bill Dunn. And they produced for him. Dunn and his people created the Dow Jones News Retrieval, which sprang from a joint venture with Bunker Ramo. Today it is one of the country's largest suppliers of data bases to financial professionals. Some other innovations include increasing the number of printing plants from ten in 1975 to eighteen in 1989; and creating the Dow Jones alternative delivery service, which delivers nearly a million copies of the *Journal* and *Barron's* privately, allowing close to 60 percent of the *Journal's* and *Barron's* combined circulation to bypass the slow and costly U.S. Postal Service.

In 1975, when Dunn succeeded Shaw, the Information Services Group revenues were $29 million. In 1989, when Dunn quit, the ISG had revenues of $696 million and profits of $214 million, which accounted for two-thirds of Dow Jones's total operating income.

In contrast, the *Journal's* operating income in 1977 was $65 million. In 1989, it was $69 million, which, factoring out inflation and rate increases, meant that the *Journal* declined at an annual average of 7.6 percent during this period.

Beginning in the summer of 1989, the absence of Ray Shaw and Bill

Dunn was felt most by Neil Hirsch and Telerate. Telerate had gotten smug. Salespeople were more interested in selling than servicing, and Telerate's terminals had become outdated. Two additional rivals, the brand-new Bloomberg Financial Markets and Knight Ridder, for instance, had introduced a service through which subscribers could receive data on their personal computers and then analyze them further with a software package tailored to their informational needs. Telerate countered with "analytics," a system called Matrix that proved disappointing almost immediately.

And then, in the fall of 1989, Phillips decided Telerate should seek superiority over its competitors with a $700-billion-a-day foreign-exchange market, just as it had once enjoyed superiority in the government bond market. Phillips authorized Telerate to buy out its partner, AT&T, in the Trading System, an electronic service traders use to negotiate and execute currency deals. By December 31, 1989, the Trading Service had lost $51 million.

Phillips was not pleased. And Dow Jones history began to repeat itself. Although the numbers were a hundred times greater and the impact on Dow Jones greater still, Phillips, Macdonald, Kann, and others—in Shaw's and Dunn's absence—were beginning to express their disappointment in Telerate in the same manner they had once expressed their disappointment in *Book Digest*.

"We kept buying bigger stakes in Telerate," said Don Macdonald, "and with each stake, more shocks would be revealed. It was as if Telerate waited until the sale was completed before they exposed the problems."[10]

"That's nonsense," Neil Hirsch retorted. "We sold them a clean company, a good company. Ray Shaw and Bill Dunn were on our board. They knew me for fifteen years. We concealed nothing."[11] Warren Phillips, Peter Kann, Ken Burenga, Dow Jones chief financial officer Kevin Roche, and Dow Jones general counsel Peter Skinner also served on the Telerate board.

By the summer of 1989, Hirsch had begun to tire of Dow Jones. An associate, Telerate's John Jessop, related, "Neil hated those interminable Dow Jones meetings where nothing ever gets decided. Toward the end, he would either walk out or start to play Nintendo." Jessop was referring to the Dow Jones management committee, a group of twenty-eight department whose heads convene monthly to share with each other the developments, successes, and problems of their respective areas.

"It was a conflict of two cultures," Hirsch said. "Telerate was entrepreneurial. We had ideas and carried them out with a minimum of fuss, a minimum of approvals. Dow Jones did not run that way. Lots of committees but no decisions. People sat around, talking all day."[12]

Phillips was not pleased with Hirsch, either. Phillips believed Hirsch's extracurricular activities were affecting Telerate. "After suffering several heart attacks, though he was only thirty-eight, Neil became preoccupied with a night club he owned called Caroline's,"[13] Jessop recalled.

After an initial contribution of robust revenues and profits to Dow Jones and after Shaw and Dunn had left, Telerate started to lose market share to Reuter's overseas and to Knight-Ridder and Bloomberg domestically. Also, Telerate suffered from the collapse of the savings-and-loan industry, which at one time represented 25 percent of the company's domestic sales.

"The economic downturn in '89-'90 was severe," Phillips said. "We were laying off people right and left. It was a tough time. And in this environment, some of Telerate's costs and other problems started to surface. Telerate's customer service, for example, was less than perfect. That's why we offered the price we did for the last of the Telerate shares [$18 per share]."[14]

The economic downturn did not deter Dow Jones's board from authorizing a special $1 million bonus for Warren Phillips in 1989. The special bonus was in addition to his $1.5 million in regular salary and incentive compensation for the year. Rand Aroskog, CEO of ITT and Dow Jones board member, suggested Phillips's reward. In 1990, according to Graef Crystal, the executive compensation specialist, Aroskag made $11.2 million in annual salary, bonus, and incentive compensation. Crystal criticized Aroskog for ITT's poor record over the last twenty years.[15]

In August 1989, Phillips and Kann met with Hirsch to discuss the future. Hirsch admitted he was bored with the day-to-day routines of Telerate and readily agreed to focus more of his attention on developing new services. To fill the void this shift created, Hirsch also agreed to appoint John Jessop, a Telerate veteran, the company's chief operating officer in January 1990, when Dow Jones would own Telerate completely. For Hirsch it was an amicable meeting.

Between August and January, the conflict over the proper share price for Telerate became heated. Genuinely annoyed, and also determined to get the fairest price for the shareholders, Hirsch rejected Dow Jones's $18-per-share offer.

"What annoyed me the most," Hirsch said, "is that Phillips could have bought the company in 1986 for $880 million, half what he eventually paid for it. But now that it was a foregone conclusion the acquisition would go through, he was trying to low-ball us."[16]

Phillips disagreed. "That's hindsight bullshit. We bought it over several years to limit our debt. We also wanted to let Hirsch, an entrepreneur, grow the company as quickly as possible."[17]

From September through December 1989, the struggle over the price for Telerate's shares grew heated. Finally, in a move that startled even Wall Street, Hirsch commissioned a full-page newspaper ad to be created that advised Telerate's shareholders to reject Dow Jones's insultingly low tender offer. Its headline blared the rhetorical question: "What Now Dow Jones?" Hirsch then tried to run the ad in the *Journal*. "I wanted to see if the *Journal* extended free speech to others as much as it protected it for itself."[18]

It didn't. Phillips, perhaps playing right into Hirsch's hands, rejected the ad. Before the day was out, every major newspaper in America told the story of how Dow Jones refused Hirsch's ad. Before the week was over, Phillips agreed to Hirsch's price of $21 per share for Telerate's remaining stock.

But Phillips had the last word. In January 1990, Hirsch met with Phillips and Kann again. Phillips reviewed their August conversation in which Hirsch agreed to devote most of his energies to new products and John Jessop would be appointed Telerate's day-to-day boss. And then Phillips made what, according to Hirsch, was an extraordinary announcement. "We're also bringing in one of our people, Carl Valenti, as the president of Telerate. You'll still be CEO, but Carl will report to Peter, as you will. Jessop, of course, will report to Carl."

At the same meeting, Phillips informed Hirsch that Dow Jones was not renewing "your million-dollar-per-year contract and car and driver. From now on your salary will be $250,000, period."[19]

Neil Hirsch had been fired, *Journal* style. Hirsch mildly protested, his objections tempered by the $90 million Phillips had just paid him for the remainder of his Telerate stock.

Hirsch said, "We all knew Valenti was a lightweight, Bill Dunn's bag carrier. I said so, but I didn't beat on the desk. I figured Jessop would never take the job."[20]

But Jessop did take the job. In February 1990, Jessop accepted Kann's offer to be Telerate's executive vice president at an annual salary of $400,000. It represented a $100,000 raise for Jessop.

John Jessop was a working-class Britisher from south London who had established Telerate in Europe before coming to the United States in 1987. He once described himself as "a good bloke, really, who's been married three times and loves antiques, oriental rugs, wine, and anything else that is frowned upon."[21]

On the surface, Carl Valenti has much in common with John Jessop. A high school dropout, he was one of Bill Dunn's wildest and most willing drinking companions. A millionaire from his $500,000-per-year salary and Dow Jones's stock options, Valenti rose through the Information Services Group's ranks principally because everyone—Ray Shaw, and then Bill Dunn, most of all—liked him so much. Still speaking with the accent of Manhattan's Lower East Side, where he spent much of his boyhood, Valenti conceded, "I never asked for a raise, I loved working for those guys so much."

Valenti moved to Rocky Hill, New Jersey, when he was fifteen and attended Princeton High School, Kann's alma mater. "But I quit before graduating and joined the navy. Princeton High wasn't for me, not after where I came from," Valenti said, smiling.

Jessop and Valenti worked together for only three months, from February 1 to May 10, 1990. "Right from the first day, I argued with Carl endlessly," Jessop said. "I didn't like his approach to business. He avoided decisions and trouble. He was a corporate creature who knew how to play corporate politics well. He came from a different culture than what I came from. He was always nitpicking, and he was far too concerned about Dow Jones than representing Telerate to Dow Jones. He did not speak his mind.

"After two months working for him, I couldn't take it anymore. I had just come back from a long, liquid lunch and I called him. I was very pissed off. I said, 'Carl, Telerate is in turmoil because of some of the things you've been saying. You're alarming and confusing us.'"

Valenti responded, according to Jessop, by saying, "That's my style."

To which Jessop said, "Style is not what I would apply to that approach. Maybe we should have a meeting to clear the air. Maybe Peter [Kann] should be involved."

A few minutes later, Valenti called back and said, "How about eleven o'clock tomorrow. You, me, and Peter."

Jessop continued, "The next day, at the appointed time, I met Carl in his office, which is right across the hall from Peter's. We exchanged pleasantries after I apologized for being rude the day before on the phone. We were then ushered into Peter's plush corner office, mahogany paneling, nice carpeting, display case of Oriental weapons. Peter was affable as he sat there smoking one of his little cigars. Then he turned to me and said, 'Your nickel.'"

Jessop added, "I made a two-minute statement which expressed my concerns over merging the two corporate cultures and the need to define my role better and what Dow Jones wanted. After I said my piece, Peter didn't appear happy.

"Peter said, 'That's typical of Telerate, not being loyal to Dow Jones. But people better get used to taking orders.'

"I got pissed off. I took umbrage at what he said. I said back, 'I am not being disloyal. Nor am I refusing to comply to Dow Jones. But I do need to understand Valenti better. I do not want to stand around and take orders blindly.' My anger focused on Peter.

"Finally, Peter leaned over and said, 'You present your resignation, and I'll accept it.'

"And I did. I was stunned. Peter disappointed me. He should have cut me off so it never got to that point. Peter was not rational. I acted in character. He did not.

"Later, Peter admitted to Neil [Hirsch] he may have been too direct with me, but it was too late then. I was gone, and Valenti now had a free hand to operate Telerate without any interference.

"I think he wanted me out. All of us at Telerate had reputations for being wild, chasing women. But it still was a funny way to treat someone who, six weeks before, he gave a $100,000 raise to.

"Peter Kann is a great writer, but he needs to surround himself with more capable people. He's not a good businessman. Doesn't have the background. Things today at Telerate under Carl Valenti are in turmoil."[22]

Valenti, of course, has a different version of what happened, though he refused to articulate it precisely. On September 4, 1991, Valenti did say: "I'm feeling real good right now. I took over as president of Telerate in May 1990, and we're probably going to do 20 percent better this year than last."

What Valenti failed to mention was that 1990 was a disaster for Telerate, because the company's revenues were down 39.7 percent from 1989. Thus, what Valenti tried to pass off as a triumph is actually a company that is still running 20 percent behind in sales from where it was two years before—when Shaw and Dunn were still at Dow Jones.

Moreover, on November 6, 1991, Dow Jones announced it would write down or reduce its 1991 after-tax profits by $31.8 million to reflect the company's decision to shut down Telerate's Trading Service, a foreign-exchange-currency automated trading service introduced just eighteen months before which had then been heralded as the bulwark for Telerate's and Dow Jones's future.

When asked what this meant, Neil Hirsch said, "It's incredibly sad. It means Valenti failed to make a go of what was going to be the saving grace for Telerate."[23]

When asked the same question, Bill Dunn said, "I was at Dow Jones today. I asked the chief financial officer [Kevin Roche], 'How come there's a $32-million write-down for Telerate?' He said, 'It was the Telerate board who decided to do that.' I wanted to puke. There is no Telerate board. It went out of existence when we bought them out last year. There's no one who will claim responsibility for anything. There's no leadership."[24]

In a memo to the staff announcing the $32 million write-down of Telerate's Trading Service, Peter Kann said, "The announcement last week of a write-off of development costs and goodwill for the Telerate Trading Service obviously will reduce the company's fourth-quarter and full-year net income substantially. But, as we said earlier, this affects reported net income, not operating results or cash flow. In fact, the write-off should help the company results next year."[25]

Dow Jones's earnings per share in 1991 was $0.71 per share, the lowest it has been since 1943, which was before Kilgore's reinvention of the *Journal* started to take hold. In 1990, Dow Jones's earnings per share came to $1.09, the lowest it has been since 1956. In 1989, Dow Jones's was earning $3.15 per share. But stripping away nonrecurring profits, which do not come from operations, Dow Jones earnings per share was $1.52, the lowest it has been since 1969.

Two weeks after becoming Dow Jones's CEO in January 1991, Kann faced his first real test. One of Bill Dunn's most valuable legacies was the realization that if the *Journal* were to be the business newspaper of the twenty-first century, it had to acquire a means to communicate electronically with tens of millions of people. Television could be that means, Dunn told his colleagues before he quit. Thus, Kann and his lieutenant, Peter G. Skinner, a Dow Jones senior vice president, had been searching for a suitable television vehicle for several years, a daunting mission considering television properties seldom become available.

But in November 1990, Kann and Skinner came across a remarkable opportunity. The Financial News Network, a cable network
specializing in business news, was put up for sale. FNN's greatest
asset was its subscriber base of 35 million households, most of which
were located in affluent markets.

When Kann and Skinner learned of FNN's availability, they
resorted to a time-honored Dow Jones acquisition practice. They
sought a partner to acquire FNN together. "We didn't have experience in television,"[26] Skinner said.

It was the same lack of confidence that had caused Phillips to seek
safety in numbers with *Digest*, Telerate, and Continental Cablevision, all marriages that had ended in disaster.

In their attempt to bolster their self-doubt, Kann and Skinner
failed to see the obvious: FNN did not require an operating partner.
Its current $78 million deficit was not caused by incompetence, but
by its chairman's overly aggressive accounting methods, which
Touche Ross, the auditing firm, eventually reversed. In fact, in the
rough-and-tumble cable world, FNN was performing well. In all
probability, no outside cable television operating partner, no matter
how skilled, could have done a better job operating FNN than FNN's
incumbent management.

Nevertheless, Kann and Skinner sought out and obtained Paramount's agreement to join forces with Dow Jones to acquire FNN.
For the next three months, Kann and Skinner worked out an
agreement by which Dow Jones and Paramount, as equal partners,
would submit an offer to buy FNN for $90 million, an extremely low
bid considering FNN had liabilities that alone amounted to $140
million. There was also a difference in how the two companies
viewed the potential of FNN. The cable network did not offer
Paramount the same degree of salvation it offered Dow Jones.
Nevertheless, when determining the bid, Kann and Skinner deferred
to their more experienced television partner.

On Thursday, February 6, 1991, the day before the bid was to be
submitted, Paramount called Kann and unexpectedly backed out of
the deal. Skinner said, "Paramount told us that because it owned a
part of USA Network [a competing cable network], they would have
to withdraw." Skinner could not answer why this preexisting condition become a deal-breaking obstacle at the last possible moment.

But rather than proceed alone on the FNN deal, Kann and Skinner
still preferred to spread the risk. "We called Westinghouse that

afternoon and asked them if they'd be interested in coming in with us," Skinner recalled.

The following Monday morning, Donald Mitzner, Westinghouse Broadcasting's president, agreed to the last-minute venture. The next three days were spent convincing Westinghouse that $90 million was the proper opening bid.

In explaining how they arrived at that price, Skinner said, "Our people analyzed FNN's advertising and estimated how much growth we could expect in the next five years." Basing the bid on an estimate prepared by Dow Jones accountants who were totally unfamiliar with cable advertising patterns seemed a curious reference for Kann and Skinner to depend on.

On Thursday, February 13, 1991, Kann and Skinner announced that Dow Jones and Westinghouse had signed a letter of agreement to acquire the assets of FNN for $90 million. The newspapers reiterated the venture's many advantages: Westinghouse had experience in cable (a country-and-western music network) and, of course, Dow Jones had experience in business news. And FNN's enviable asset was its subscriber base of 35 million households, most of which were located in major and lucrative markets throughout the country.

Even Bill Dunn conceded it was a smart acquisition. Privately, Kann and Skinner were congratulating themselves. Following the Phillips tradition of always bidding low, Dow Jones had managed to buy its way into the cable business for only $90 million. FNN's investment bankers had hoped the company would fetch $150 million.

Several weeks later, FNN filed for Chapter 11 bankruptcy. Since the pending sale did not involve FNN's liabilities, the investment bankers explained, FNN needed the temporary relief from its creditors. No one at the time realized that once FNN was under the protection of a bankruptcy court, any recent sale of assets was subject to cancellation if the presiding judge believed the assets could bring a higher price.

It was as if General Electric, once Westinghouse's archrival, had been standing in the wings, waiting for this very development to occur. Once FNN became a ward of the bankruptcy court, General Electric—the owner of NBC Television, a station that had just launched its own cable network, CNBC—stepped forward and bid, first, $105 million and then $115 million for FNN.

Kann and Skinner were stunned.

Under Jack Welch's aggressive stewardship, General Electric was not a company that would give up easily. Though GE's need for FNN could be considered more short term, it was no less urgent than Dow Jones's. GE wanted FNN for its 35 million subscribing households, which it planned to add to CNBC's 18 million. Like the other two networks, NBC had been losing too many viewers to CNN and other cable systems recently.

Had they been more experienced, and perhaps less afraid to fail, Kann and Skinner would have submitted a preemptive bid that reflected the price Dow Jones was willing to pay to enter a market, television, that was the gateway to its future survival.

"Here it was, readymade. We could not create a network of 35 million households if we had all the fuckin' money in the world," Dunn said.

But rather than go for broke, Kann, Skinner, and Westinghouse countered with a bid of $115 million. Then Dow Jones appealed to the FTC to rule whether the proposed CNBC and FNN combination would violate antitrust laws, a curious position for the *Wall Street Journal* to take, considering its lifelong history of fighting government interference in just such matters as this.

When the FTC announced that the CNBC and NBC combination would not violate antitrust laws, Kann and Skinner grumbled. Skinner told the *New York Times*, "We believe there is something fundamentally wrong with CNBC acquiring a competitor just to put it out of business." Skinner was referring to CNBC's announced plans to terminate all but fifty of FNN's two hundred eighty employees and close down its programming facilities. Skinner's remark contradicted the *Journal's* editorial page, which regularly praised hostile raiders for cutting costs by "downsizing" the payrolls of the companies they acquired.

After the FTC ruling, the matter reverted to the U.S. Bankruptcy Court, where Judge Francis G. Conrad presided over what then became an auction between General Electric and Dow Jones/Westinghouse. Several more rounds of cautious bidding took place until Kann and Skinner countered with a bid of $167.1 million, but with only $125 million in cash. The balance—$42.1 million—would be paid only if certain operating goals were achieved by FNN in the next three years.

General Electric came back with a bid of $154.3 million, all but $9 million in cash.

FNN obviously favored Dow Jones because it meant two hundred eighty employees would retain their jobs. FNN's creditors, together with the investment bankers, preferred General Electric because it would provide more cash-in-hand for creditors. However, Judge Conrad had little choice but to rule in favor of General Electric since his first obligation was to FNN's creditors, too. Kann and Skinner threatened legal action, but a week later, Westinghouse backed out of the partnership.

When asked if Dow Jones had any other television alternatives, Skinner replied, "We might grow our own."[27]

"There will never be another opportunity like FNN," said Bill Dunn. "Cable has now matured to where that many subscribers, 35 million, will probably never be for sale again. It was a monumental stumble."

Of all the opinions expressed about the Dow Jones-Westinghouse-FNN deal, Amy Silverberg, a young assistant producer at FNN, said what many other observers thought: "I can't believe the *Wall Street Journal* was so stupid. Why didn't they just make a winning bid and be done with it?"

The *Wall Street Journal:* Today and Tomorrow

Every two weeks or so, the *Journal's* front page inspires readers by addressing important social issues which, though they lack the urgency of breaking news, still gnaw at the nation's consciousness. One such article, written by Alex Freedman, explained how fast-food restaurants, seemingly so wholesome, add to the plight of the ghetto. Poverty and ignorance have seduced the disadvantaged into becoming too dependent on a fat-laden diet of hamburgers, french fries, and milk shakes. The results, Freedman wrote, are raised cholesterol levels and a disproportionate risk of heart disease in the inner cities. Besides illuminating an important concern, Freedman's piece read as if Truman Capote, at his zenith, had written it for the *New Yorker.* "Where else could I read an article like that and then turn the page and read another beautifully written article on puts and calls?" a reader asked.

Though articles dealing with social issues continue to appear in the *Journal* frequently, they are more the result of enterprising reporters like Freedman than of encouragement from Paul Steiger, the *Journal's* new managing editor. As the leader of the news department, Steiger balances his determination and steadiness with an equal measure of dullness. Steiger shares, for example, Warren Phillips's fondness for page-one stories that herald business success, the type former *Journal* managing editor Ed Cony derided as "frisky furniture" pieces.

Lack of ego made Steiger the perfect assistant to Norman Pearlstine for nearly eight years. While Pearlstine took all the kudos, Steiger did all the work, happily and competently. Normally, when someone plays the understudy role this well, it's owing more to lack of courage than to serenity. But Steiger is neither timid nor vacillating. Just beneath his bland exterior lies unshakable self-confidence and determination.

Fred Taylor, Steiger's boss in the *Journal's* San Francisco bureau in the late sixties, said, "Though Steiger looks like an accountant, he can be tough, very tough. He had to be to withstand Norman [Pearlstine] all those years."[1] Inner strength also enables Steiger to enjoy a good relationship with his boss, Peter Kann, while enduring Kann's wife, Karen Elliott House, who sits next door.

But aside from his stamina, Paul Steiger remains a corporate editor, more the efficient plant manager than a great journalist. He keeps the newsroom's assembly lines operating at peak efficiencies so that the product, the daily *Journal*, goes out the door every morning on time. Though Steiger's sense of right and wrong is more refined than Pearlstine's, he is seldom bothered by these distinctions in his work. Compare how the *Journal* and the *New York Times* recently treated a story relating to the tobacco industry.

On Saturday, February 9, 1992, the *Times* ran a front-page story with this headline: "Judge Cites Possible Fraud in Tobacco Research." The prominent, 800-word story reported how Judge H. Lee Sorokin of the federal district court ruled for the plaintiff in a wrongful-death suit against a cigarette manufacturer. In rendering his decision, Judge Sorkin said that the tobacco industry's decades-old vow to disclose its research findings was "nothing but a public-relations ploy—a fraud—to deflect the growing evidence against the industry, to encourage smokers to continue and nonsmokers to begin, and to reassure the public that adverse information would be disclosed. Despite some rising pretenders, the tobacco industry may be the king of concealment and disinformation."

On Monday, February 11, 1992, the *Journal* reported the same event quite differently. In the issue's second section, page B6, the eighteen-point-type headline "Wedtech Securities Fraud Case Is Settled" heralded the first of several items in the Law column. The first item consisted of eleven paragraphs dealing with the resolution of the Wedtech scandal. The second item in the column appeared under a 6-point headline: "Tobacco Plaintiff Wins Right to See Documents." The *Journal* text contained the tobacco industry's answer to Judge Sorokin's charges, but little as to what Sorokin actually said.

Asked to comment on the contrast between how the *Times* and the *Journal* played this story, Ellen Pollack, the *Journal* editor who wrote the story and determined its position, said, "I played it the way it should be played. It [Sorokin's ruling] occurred over the weekend and it was old news."[2] But a *Wall Street Journal* reporter who did not wish to be identified said: "I don't know for sure, but it is not unreasonable to assume we downplayed the story not to offend an advertiser."

As managing editor, Steiger has also permitted a noticeable anti-Clinton bias to rule the *Journal*'s coverage of the new president. After *Journal* reporter Jeffrey Birnbaum uncovered Clinton's questionable draft status, which was a legitimate revelation, the paper's coverage of the president became so prejudicial that today most *Journal* news articles on Clinton read like opinion pieces better suited for the editorial page. For example, on February 18, 1993, two days after Clinton unfurled his economic plan, the *Journal* fully reported the dissenting reactions of Republican political leaders but failed to mention the country's and corporate America's overall endorsement. On that same day, in a front-page feature, the *Journal* devoted 4,000 words to comparing Clinton's hands-on management to Reagan's style of delegating responsibility. Clinton, of course, was found lacking.

But aside from its antipathy toward Democrats, the *Journal* reflects Steiger's lack of passion or outrage. It's unimaginable, for example, that Steiger's *Journal* would investigate whether beer television commercials contribute to the 19,000 annual deaths caused by minors driving while drunk on beer, as many medical and alcohol-abuse officials allege.[3] The breweries, of course, articulate strong arguments to counter these allegations. A story presenting both sides of this issue would be ideal for the *Journal*. Yet there is little chance it will appear because the beer industry controls the advertising agencies, and they control the *Journal*'s advertising revenue.

For example, Anheuser-Busch Miller, Coors, and Strohs, spend $750 million annually with ad agencies for television advertising.[4] Afraid of losing this revenue through a ban on beer advertising, agencies frown on those media that shed too bright a light on alcohol-related problems. And since the *Journal* depends on these same ad agencies for beer advertising, and other types as well, Steiger and his staff, as Arthur Hayes said, are careful not to offend the advertising industries.

As a further example of how the *Journal* reacts to advertisers, Pamela Sebastian, a *Journal* reporter, wrote an article on Fidelity Mutual, a huge *Journal* advertiser, several years ago. Fidelity objected to the story so strenuously that both Warren Phillips and Peter Kann flew to Boston to placate Fidelity's management.

Don Moffitt, a *Journal* editor at the time, reported, "After Warren and Peter visited Fidelity, Pamela no longer covered the company. Can you imagine Barney [Kilgore] ever doing that? Can you imagine him flying to Boston to see an advertiser?"[5]

Now that Pearlstine has left the company, Paul Steiger joins Kann and Dow Jones president Ken Burenga, Telerate president Carl Valenti, Dow Jones senior vice president Peter Skinner, and Dow Jones chief financial officer Kevin Roche to form the inner circle responsible for leading Dow Jones and the *Journal* into the nineties. With the exception of Steiger, who occupies Pearlstine's old office on the ninth floor, and Roche, who prefers Dow Jones's South Brunswick office complex, these men maintain offices on the seventeenth floor of the Dow Jones Building, a floor that resembles the throne room of the Ming dynasty, with its expensive Oriental weapons, screens, furniture, and vases. And yet, disappointingly, none of Kann's subordinates appears comfortable in these surroundings, any more than they can rival Kann for wit, charm, or intelligence.

In December 1990, Kann and his inner circle appeared at a Paine Webber forum held for analysts to discuss the future of Dow Jones. Kann and his group were singularly disappointing. So frequently did they cite the 1987 stock market crash and the subsequent Gulf War to explain the *Journal's* operating declines—circulation down from 2 million in 1984 to 1.8 million in 1992, advertising lineage down 28 percent in the last six years—that had these two catastrophes not occurred, Kann and his people would surely have had to invent them. Words and phrases like "strategizing," "without getting into the specifics," "running a tighter ship," "metadata," and "fully integrated" rang through the air as the two hundred analysts grew more and more glassy eyed. Finally, the presentation ended without the analysts' learning that in the following year, 1991, Dow Jones's earnings would hit a fifty-year low of 71¢ per share, down from $3.12 per share in 1988.

When later asked how he was going to solve this problem, Kann said, "We don't have a problem. The economy is the problem. When it bounces back, we'll bounce back."[6]

But Don Macdonald, Dow Jones vice chairman disagrees. Recently Macdonald said, "Everyone around here is asking the question, Is this publishing company going to come back once the economy recovers? Too many people think that it is, and that's the danger. They are just sitting back, doing nothing, waiting for the economy to solve their problems. Well I believe that even when the economy improves, publishing in general and the *Journal* in particular are never coming back. We need to reinvent the *Journal* as radically as Kilgore did in 1941 or face extinction."[7]

Since Kann made that promise in October 1991, the Dow Jones Industrials have soared to 3,300 and Wall Street bonuses are bigger than ever, reflecting the $800 billion in mergers and acquisitions completed in 1992. Yet the *Journal* continues in its eight-year advertising and circulation slide, and Dow Jones's 1992 earnings were $1.06 per share, the second worst performance in fifty years. These financial disappointments are the symptoms of an unhealthy condition pleading for a remedy.

Fifty years have lapsed since Kilgore reinvented the *Journal*, an unusually long life for any national publication. Today, the *Journal* is at the end of another life, its third since 1889. For the *Journal* to continue into the twenty-first century, it needs to be transformed again. Yet, like Cassandra's prophecy, the prognosis goes unheeded. Not many people, Kann least of all, believe another *Journal* resurrection is necessary. Citing the false but comforting god of reader loyalty, Kann forgets that readers are often the last to know when a publication, and its parent company, are troubled, as the former subscribers of the *American Mercury, Colliers*, the *Saturday Evening Post*, the *New York Herald Tribune*, and the *National Observer* will attest.

It's difficult, almost blasphemous, to accept that Dow Jones is in trouble. It is also difficult, almost blasphemous, to accept that General Motors, IBM, American Express, or Sears were in trouble. It's easier to forget what Kann and his mentor, Warren Phillips, were responsible for: acquiring *Book Digest* and Telerate; rejecting the chance to buy Apple Computer; mismanaging Telerate; flubbing the

FNN opportunity; permitting Norman Pearlstine to use the *Journal* for his social aggrandizement; allowing Karen Elliott House to menace her staff; refusing to accept blame for the Foster Winans scandal; tolerating a disorganized and unresponsive news department that has missed Watergate, Milken, and the savings-and-loan scandals; tearing down the division between the *Journal's* editorial department and the news department; allowing the news and editorial departments to become distracted with book contracts and book excerpt agreements; keeping an inept board of directors and the hapless owners, the Bancroft family, continually in the dark.

Over its one-hundred-plus years of existence, Dow Jones has spawned many hero-journalists. But history will remember only three: Clarence Barron, for rescuing the company in the twenties; Barney Kilgore, for rescuing the *Journal* in the forties; and Peter Kann, for his rescuing or failing to rescue Dow Jones in the nineties.

A NOTE ON THE RESEARCH

The Power and the Money is drawn from three sources: personal interviews, my observations gained as a Dow Jones employee, and secondary references.

Over a period of eighteen months, I interviewed 313 people, 153 of whom are either present or former *Journal* news staffers. The bulk of these interviews took place in New York City and South Brunswick, New Jersey. Others occurred in Paris, London, Rome, Washington, D.C., Chicago, Los Angeles, San Francisco, and Coos Bay, Oregon. All but 27 were in person; all but 31 were tape-recorded. This phase of the research took me to the highest reaches of Dow Jones—three members of the Bancroft family, six members of the board of directors, and virtually every key Dow Jones executive. Many times it was necessary to interview people more than once. Warren Phillips, for example, allowed me to interview him on four different occasions.

I joined Dow Jones in July 1977 as an advertising salesperson for the *Wall Street Journal*. Ten months later, I was appointed sales development manager. In October 1979, I was named general manager of Dow Jones's *Book Digest* magazine. Twelve months later, I was named a vice president. In July 1982, when *Book Digest* ceased publishing, Dow Jones invited me back to the *Journal*. Instead, I joined the New York Times Company as publisher of *Tennis* magazine. Dow Jones generously gave me a year's salary in severance pay.

Two professional researchers and I separately plumbed the depths of various public and private libraries, archives, and data bases located in such places as Matador, Texas; South Brunswick, New Jersey; Queens, New York; and Cambridge, Massachusetts. All newspapers, magazines, and books are cited in the text or the endnotes or bibliography.

In the spring of 1991, Carol Publishing Group became the distributor of *Final Exit*, a book just published by the Hemlock Society. In the course of promoting the book, Steven Schragis, publisher of Carol, dined with Meg Cox, a *Journal* reporter. Later, Schragis followed up with a letter to Cox, the gist of which he also sent to Norman Pearlstine, the *Journal's* executive editor. In his letters, Schragis urged the *Journal* to write a story on *Final Exit*, a book which dealt with assisted suicide for the dying. On July 12, 1991, a story on *Final Exit* appeared on the front page of the *Journal's* second section. From April to June 1991, *Final Exit's* sales were fewer than five hundred copies. After the *Journal* article appeared, however, sales skyrocketed.

Notes

Chapter 1

1. Al Neuharth interview, April 9, 1991.
2. The basis for the remark that Kann permits his wife to terrorize the *Journal* was drawn from interviews with 153 present and former *Journal* news staffers. Of this group, 107 reported that House mistreats people, sometimes quite cruelly. Most alarming, according to these same staffers, was the belief that House's alleged victims have no chance for appeal because Peter Kann, Dow Jones CEO, will not countermand her.
3. A search through the *Journal*'s news index and Dow Jones News Retrieval reveals that between 1975 and 1985 the *Journal* mentioned Milken's name twice, both times in passing, even though Milken created the junk bond during this period. Milken's name first appeared in the *Journal* on March 27, 1975; the second appearance was December 13, 1985.

On December 6, 1984, at the peak of the junk-bond financing mania, the *Journal* ran an article entitled "How Junk Financing Aids Corporate Raiders in Hostile Acquisitions." The article focused on Drexel Burnham and never mentioned Michael Milken by name, an omission comparable to reporting on a typical day at the White House without mentioning the president.

4. A search of major newspapers and magazines from 1945 to 1992 revealed only one article, a cover profile in *Forbes*, February 3, 1992, that criticized the *Journal*. The *Forbes* pieces discussed Dow Jones's recent problems, especially the company's 1990 acquisition of Telerate. Unaccustomed to such scrutiny, the *Journal* bristled. In an interoffice memo denouncing the story, Dow Jones CEO Peter Kann denied he had told *Forbes*, "We're [Dow Jones] afraid to fail." The *Forbes* coreporter, Subrata N. Chakravarty, a fifteen-year veteran, claimed Kann made this observation "not once but twice, both times on tape."
5. Dow Jones Archives, South Brunswick, N.J.
6. Ibid.
7. Ibid.

Chapter 2

Much of the information in this chapter pertaining to Clarence Barron and Hugh Bancroft came from interviews with Bill Cox, Jr., step-great-grandson and grandson of the two, and with two other Barron descendants who wish to remain anonymous.

1. Barron to Christopher Lambeth, Dow Jones Archives, South Brunswick, N.J.
2. Arthur Pound and Samuel Taylor Moore, *Told to Barron* (New York: Harper & Brothers, 1930), p. 32.
3. *Boston Transcript*, March 11, 1876, p. 1.
4. *Boston Transcript*, September 29, 1873, p. 1.
5. Boston News Bureau, October 22, 1882, p. 1.
6. Boston News Bureau, July 24, 1894. p. 1.
7. C.W. Barron to Martha Waldron, August 3, 1900.
8. W.S.J. Moise, ed., Barron Manuscripts, Dow Jones Archives, South Brunswick, N.J.
9. William Cox, Jr., interview, October 15, 1991.
10. Ibid.
11. C.W. Barron to Maurice Leventhall, June 22, 1900.
12. Edward Stein memo, September 23, 1912.
13. Barron Manuscripts.
14. Ibid.
15. William Cox, Jr., interview, October 15, 1991.
16. Ibid.
17. Ibid.

Chapter 3

Interviews with James Kilgore provided much of the information on the early life of his father, Bernard Kilgore.
1. Dow Jones Archives, South Brunswick, N.J.
2. Ibid.
3. Dow Jones Archives, South Brunswick, N.J.
4. Fred Taylor interview, February 22, 1991.
5. Ibid.
6. Dow Jones Archives, South Brunswick, N.J.
7. Eleanor Cammack interview, May 11, 1992.
8. Kit Melick interview, September 23, 1991.
9. William Cox, Jr., interview, October 15, 1991.
10. Dow Jones Archives, South Brunswick, N.J.
11. Ibid.

Chapter 4

1. Papers of Thomas Woodcock, Dow Jones Archives, South Brunswick, N.J.
2. Ibid.

Chapter 5

1. William F. Kerby, *A Proud Profession* (Homewood, Ill.: Dow Jones-Irwin, 1981), p. 30.
2. Dow Jones Archives, South Brunswick, N.J.
3. Kit Melick interview, September 9, 1991.

Chapter 6

From May 1969 to February 1975, I worked at Batten, Barton, Durstine & Osborne on the *Wall Street Journal* and *National Observer* advertising accouunts as an account executive. John Caples related the Feemster anecdote to me.

Chapter 7

1. Vermont Royster, *A Pride and Prejudice* (New York: Simon & Schuster, 1967), p. xi.
2. *Wall Street Journal*, editorial page, December 22, 1964.
3. *Wall Street Journal*, editorial page, February 4, 1964.
4. *Wall Street Journal*, editorial page, February 11, 1966.

Chapter 8

1. James Kilgore interview, May 12, 1992.
2. Ibid.
3. Tom Dillon interview, November 4, 1972.
4. Fred Taylor interview, February 26, 1990.
5. Dow Jones Archives, South Brunswick, N.J.

Chapter 9

1. Descriptions of Warren Phillips's carriage and bearing are based on my firsthand observations. I became acquainted with Phillips in August 1977. From October 1979 to May 1982, as a vice president of *Book Digest,* I periodically met with him in the company of others to discuss operational-management matters. Additionally, Phillips served on a Dow Jones subsidiary board of directors whose meetings I regularly attended.
2. Certain huge corporations, Dow Jones, IBM, and General Motors among them, made poor choices in selecting the men who would lead them in the seventies and eighties. These men were chosen for them ability to comply, not lead. They did what they were told; they followed orders perfectly.
3. Dow Jones Archives, South Brunswick, N.J.
4. My sources for this conversation are Warren Phillips and Fred Taylor, former managing editor, the *Wall Street Journal.*
5. Over the years, Phillips's mistakes regarding personnel and acquisition selection included: Rand Araskog and Bill Agee for the Dow Jones board of directors; Larry O'Donnell for the *Journal's* managing editor in 1977; Norman Pearlstine for the *Journal's* national news editor in 1981 and managing editor in 1983; Donald A. Macdonald to replace John Veronis at *Book Digest; Reader's Digest* as a joint venture partner for *Book Digest;* rejecting Dunn's advice on investing in Apple Computer in 1975; Karen Elliott House for, first, *Journal* foreign editor and, then, four years later, Dow Jones vice president, international; Peter Kann as Dow Jones CEO; acquisition of *Book Digest* for $10 million when it was worth $3 million; acquisition of Telerate for $1.6 billion when, on three previous occasions, Phillips could have bought the company for $1 million, $80 million, or $800 million.
6. William Cox, Jr., disclosed that Araskog was the "prime mover" behind the $1 million bonus, interview, October 15, 1991.
7. Warren Phillips interview, August 28, 1991.
8. Ibid.
9. Anthony Lewis to the author, March 23, 1991.
10. Warren Phillips interview, August 28, 1991.
11. Katherine Melick interview, August 18, 1991.
12. Henry Gemmill interview, September 28, 1991.
13. Nathan Margolin interview, September 12, 1991.
14. Warren Phillips interview, August 28, 1991.
15. Fred Taylor interview, February 21, 1991.
16. Nathan Margolin interview, September 12, 1991.
17. William Clabby interview, September 12, 1991.
18. Warren Phillips was a reporter, specifically a correspondent, for the *Wall Street Journal* for eighteen months, from January 1949 to June 1950. According to my interviews

with two former managing editors, Norman Pearlstine and Fred Taylor, and two of Phillips's contemporaries in the newsroom at the time, Alan Otten and Kit Melick, Phillips's stories required extensive rewrites before the *Journal* would publish them. Kit Melick, in fact, stated that Phillips was a "mediocre reporter and writer, at best." However, Phillips drew praise for his copyediting abilities.

19. Sterling E. Soderlind interview, October 31, 1991.
20. Paul Lancaster interview, October 21, 1991.
21. Sterling Soderlind interview, September 12, 1991.
22. Richard Leger interview, February 12, 1991.
23. Ibid.
24. Fred Taylor interview, February 28, 1991.
25. Ibid.
26. Fred Taylor, interview, February 26, 1991.
27. Roger Ricklefs interview, October 21, 1991.
28. Paul Lancaster interviews, October 22 and 23, 1991.
29. Paul Lancaster interview, October 22, 1991.

Chapter 10

1. Interviews with twenty-three present and former *Journal* staffers confirmed this observation.
2. While Macdonald headed the *National Observer* and *Book Digest*, both publications failed. They suffered from difficulties in advertising and circulation, Macdonald's areas of expertise.
3. Donald Macdonald is the source for this scene in the Downtown Athletic Club.
4. Donald Macdonald interview, August 21, 1992.
5. Ibid.
6. There are three sources for the meeting at the Chicopee Circulation Center in 1970: Donald Macdonald, William Cox, Jr., and Kevin McGarry, former *Journal* advertising executive who was Cox's immediate superior in Detroit.
7. William Cox, Jr., interview, October 15, 1991.
8. Donald A. Macdonald interview, August 21, 1992.
9. Kevin McGarry interview, July 30, 1992.
10. Dow Jones Archives, South Brunswick, N.J.
11. Kevin McGarry interview, July 30, 1991.

Chapter 11

1. Fred Taylor interview, February 21, 1991.
2. Fred Taylor interview, February 28, 1991.
3. Ibid.
4. Sources for this scene on the *Low Profile* were Donald Macdonald, Peter Kann, Martha Sorenson (Kann's former sister-in-law), and A. Meyer (Kann's former father-in-law).
5. Florence Sommers interview, August 22, 1991.
6. Roslyn Denard interview, June 12, 1992.
7. David McClintick interview, September 9, 1991.
8. David Halberstam interview, April 18, 1991.
9. Bernard T. Flanagan interview, August 21, 1991.
10. Michael Gartner interview, August 13, 1991.
11. A. Kent MacDougall worked for the *Wall Street Journal* from 1960 to 1972 and for the *Los Angeles Times* from 1972 to 1985. In 1988, writing in the *Monthly Review*, MacDougall confessed to being "an anti-Establishment reporter who always tried to introduce to readers the radical historians, radical economists, and the left- wing journalist I. F. Stone."
12. David Halberstam interview, April 18, 1992. Besides Halberstam, former *Journal* editors Fred Taylor and Michael Gartner were surprised by Kann's support of the U.S.

government's position in Vietnam. Most journalists Kann's age were against the war, and, like Halberstam, the two editors assumed Kann would be, too.

13. Peter Arnett interview, October 2, 1991.
14. Peter Arnett interview, October 2, 1991.

Chapter 12

1. On two separate occasions Phillips denied being partial to Kann. Moreover, he scoffed at the notion that Kann represented a surrogate son. "I'll leave that to the armchair psychiatrists," he said.

2. Seth Lipsky interview, February 15, 1991. Lipsky's admiration for Kann, though shaded by the fact that his wife, Amity Schlaes, still works for the *Journal*, was quite genuine. In fact, out of the 153 interviews with present and former *Journal* newspeople, virtually everyone old enough to remember Kann's pieces from 1967 to 1975 remarked that he was an extraordinary correspondent. Some veteran correspondents, like Barry Newman in London and Phil Revzin in Brussels, recited verbatim from Kann's stories twenty years after they were published.

3. Fred Taylor interview, February 26, 1991. Taylor claimed that sources, mutual to both the *Journal* and *Forbes* in Asia, told him that Pearlstine was passing out *Forbes* business cards while still employed by the *Asian Journal*. Pam Hollie, a former *Journal* reporter who knew Pearlstine well at the time he went from the *Journal* to *Forbes*, confirmed that Pearlstine circulated his *Forbes* business cards while still at the *Asian Journal*.

4. Ibid.
5. In Pearlstine's official Dow Jones biography, he fails to mention his stint at the *New York Times*.
6. Barry Newman interview, April 14, 1991.
7. Pamela Hollie interview, December 13, 1991.
8. Herbert Lawson interview, December 18, 1991.
9. Lawrence O'Donnell interview, September 24, 1991.
10. Norman Pearlstine interview, September 11, 1991.
11. Interview with I. Norman Pearlstine, executive editor, the *Wall Street Journal*. September 11, 1991.
12. *Wall Street Journal*, September 20, 1971, p. 1.
13. Fred Taylor interview, February 26, 1991.
14. Memo, Barney Kilgore to William Kerby, December 23, 1940.
15. Fred Taylor interview, February 26, 1991.
16. William Blundell interview, December 3, 1991.
17. Pamela Hollie, December 13, 1991.
18. Up until 1978, Norman Pearlstine was universally liked and respected by his peers in the *Journal* news department. He was regarded as a resourceful reporter and an engaging, nice person.
19. William Blundell interview, December 3, 1991.
20. Bill Hartley interview, April 24, 1991.
21. Norman Pearlstine interview, September 11, 1991.
22. William Cox, Jr., interview, October 15, 1991.
23. Fred Taylor inteview, February 28, 1991.
24. Fred Taylor interview, February 26, 1991.
25. Michael Gartner, August 13, 1991.
26. Mary Bralove interview, April 23, 1991.
27. Fred Taylor interview, February 26, 1991.
28. Warren Phillips interview, October 24, 1991.
29. After Fred Taylor resigned from the *Journal* at the age of fifty-four, he bought and operated a weekly newspaper in a small coastal town in Oregon. The newspaper failed in 1989, and Taylor retired.
30. Out of 153 interviews with past and present *Journal* news staffers, 94 journalists described O'Donnell in these terms.

31. Mack Solomon interview, January 8, 1992.
32. Lawrence G. O'Donnell interview, September 24, 1991.
33. David McClintick interview, January 7, 1991.
34. David McClintick interview, January 3, 1992.

Chapter 13

1. The source for this account of the acquisition of Ottaway Newspapers was James Ottaway, Jr.
2. William Dunn interview, September 10, 1991.
3. Joseph Perrone interview, February 28, 1991.
4. *Wall Street Journal,* August 11, 1978, p.6.
5. Leonard Doughtery, now Dow Jones treasurer, related to me how he reported to Fred Harris in this manner. Don Macdonald corroborated this procedure.
6. In separate interviews with Ray Shaw, former president of Dow Jones who took over the circulation department from Macdonald in 1976, and with Joe Perrone and Ken Burenga, the two people whom Shaw installed as day-to-day heads of the *Journal's* circulation department that same year, all three men confirmed that the department was in a shambles when they arrived on the scene, due mostly to Macdonald's negligence.
7. I attended this meeting.
8. I attended this meeting.
9. I was Roger Miller's boss.

Chapter 14

1. Fred Taylor interview, February 26, 1991.
2. Ibid.
3. I attended this meeting.
4. William L. Dunn interview, September 10, 1991.
5. Interviews with Carl Valenti and Bill Dunn both revealed they were divorced. In my interview with Valenti, he characterized Dunn as a prodigious drinker. In my interview with Dunn, he alluded to his drinking several times.

Chapter 15

1. Don Macdonald interview, September 12, 1991.
2. Macdonald did not elaborate on why people disliked Henry Marx. Bill Cox, Jr., told me he intensely disliked Marx. "Nobody liked" Heffner because he was not born to the *Journal* culture (he came from Time Inc.) and because he was sour and aloof.
3. I attended the sales convention and witnessed the incident. Kann made his remark to several people who were distressed by Macdonald's conduct.
4. Joseph Perrone interview, April 4, 1991.
5. Ray Shaw interview, September 12, 1991.
6. Thomas O'Mara interview, December 12, 1991.
7. Fred Zimmerman interview, April 3, 1991.
8. Fred Taylor interview, February 26, 1991.
9. Ibid.
10. Pamela Hollie interview, December 13, 1991. Six other *Journal* news staffers shared Hollie's assessment that Pearlstine purposely moved to *Forbes* to increase his worth at Dow Jones. Fred Taylor suspected Kann participated in Pearlstine's scheme.
11. Nancy Cardwell interview, February 21, 1991.
12. These early stages of the Kann-House relationship were confirmed by interviews with former *Journal* editor Fred Zimmerman, one of House's early mentors at the paper; Fred

Taylor, former managing editor; Alan Otten, a veteran reporter in the Washington bureau; Norman C. Miller, former Washington bureau chief; Glynn Mapes, former page-one editor and London bureau chief; and twenty-two other *Journal* news staffers.

13. Fred Taylor interview, February 28, 1991.
14. Alan Otten interview, May 8, 1991.

Chapter 16

1. Robert L. Bartley interview, September 27, 1991.
2. I played tennis with Peter Kann, Bob Bartley, Tom Herman, and Tom Bray every week.
3. Finding of Justice James A. Boyle in his report on the inquest into the death of Mary Jo Kopechne which appeared in the final papragraph of the article entitled "A Judge's Remarks on Chappaquiddick," *Wall Street Journal*, November 6, 1979, p. 26, col.
4. Robert L. Bartley interview, September 27, 1991.
5. Ibid.
6. Ms. Broderick passed this remark on to me on September 27, 1992, when I was about to interview Mr. Bartley.
7. Peter R. Kann interview, October 23, 1991.
8. Peter R. Kann interview, July 10, 1991.
9. Ibid.
10. Norman Pearlstine interview, September 21, 1991.
11. Robert L. Bartley, September 27, 1991.
12. I played a role in Ray Sokolov's joining *Book Digest* as editor. In my interview with Sokolov, and several times thereafter, he volunteered he was fired from the *Times*.
13. Karen Elliott House interview, September 11, 1992.

Chapter 17

Sources for this chapter include a *Journal* executive who is the neighbor of Everett Groseclose, the man who hired Winans; Laurie Cohen, *Journal* reporter who used to work for Dick Rustin, Foster Winan's boss; a former *Journal* reporter; Fred Taylor, *Journal* executive editor at the time; Larry O'Donnell, *Journal* managing editor for part of the time when Winans was at the paper; Norman Pearlstine, who succeeded O'Donnell as managing editor; Peter Kann, associate publisher at the time; Warren Phillips, Dow Jones CEO at the time; Bill Cox, Jr., Dow Jones director at the time; Donald Macdonald, vice chairman, Dow Jones, at the time; Don Moffett, *Journal* copy editor at the time; Bill Paul, *Journal* reporter at the time; Karen Elliott House, *Journal* foreign editor at the time; Bill Mathewson, *Journal* reporter; Mac Solomon, *Journal* page-one editor at the time; Jonathan Kwitny, former *Journal* reporter; Len Kessler, a public relations consultant, frequent *Journal* source, and friend of Foster Winan's.

1. Fred Taylor interview, February 28, 1991.
2. Ibid.
3. Opinion, *United States v. Winans*, Stewart, District Judge, p. 831.
4. R. Foster Winans, *Trading Secrets* (London: Macmillan, 1986), p. 167.
5. Robert Sack interview, October 2, 1992. Sack was Dow Jones general counsel and partner, Gibson, Dunn & Criutcher.
6. Laurie Cohen, *Journal* reporter, who is a close friend of Stewart's and who researched *Den of Thieves*, volunteered that Stewart was homosexual. I then corroborated her assertion with Bill Mathewson, *Journal* reporter, and Frank Allen, Philadelphia bureau chief, and a former *Journal* reporter.

Chapter 18

1. Norman Pearlstine interview, September 11, 1991.
2. Don Moffett interview, April 9, 1991.
3. Fred Taylor interview, February 28, 1991.
4. Frank Allen interview, September 20, 1991.
5. Laura Landro interview, October 9, 1991.
6. Frank Allen interview, September 20, 1991.
7. Stephen Schwarzman interview, May 13, 1991.
8. Don Moffett interview, April 9, 1991.
9. Don Moffett interview, April 9, 1991.
10. William Paul interview, January 9, 1991.
11. Laurie Cohen interview, May 1, 1991.
12. Norman Pearlstine interview, October 1, 1991.
13. Connie Bruck, "Undoing the Eighties," *New Yorker*, July 23, 1990, p. 69.
14. Norman Pearlstine interview, October 1, 1991.
15. *Esquire* magazine dates the Pearlstine-Friday relationship to December 1981, but Pearlstine told me he had met Friday the previous December.
16. Norman Pearlstine interview, September 11, 1991.
17. William Paul interview, January 17, 1991.
18. Warren Phillips interview, October 12, 1991.
19. Fred Taylor interview, February 28, 1991.
20. David Halberstam interview, April 11, 1991.
21. Norman Pearlstine interview, October 1, 1991.
22. Laurie Cohen interview, May 1, 1991.
23. Ibid.
24. Ibid.
25. Paul Steiger interview, October 18, 1991.
26. Stephen Schwarzman interview, May 10, 1991.
27. Stephen A. Schwarzman interview, May 17, 1991.
28. Sarah Bartlett, *The Money Machine: How KKR Manufactured Power and Profits* (New York: Warner Books, 1991), p. 317.
29. Interview with Davis Weinstock, of Clark and Weinstock, August 19, 1991.
30. Bob Dallos interview, August 18, 1991.
31. Laurie Cohen reporter, May 1, 1991.
32. Donald A. Macdonald interview, August 21, 1991.

Chapter 19

1. Tim Metz, *Black Monday: The Catastrophe of October 19, 1987, and Beyond* (New York: William Morrow, 1988), p. 167; and Metz interview, January 29, 1991.
2. Norman Pearlstine interview, September 11, 1991.
3. Alan Otten interview, May 9, 1991.
4. Fred Taylor interview, February 26, 1991.
5. Alan Otten interview, May 9, 1991.
6. Norman Pearlstine interview, October 1, 1991.
7. Tim Metz interview, January 29, 1991.
8. Donald A. Macdonald interview, August 21, 1991.
9. Bernard Flanagan interview, August 15, 1991.
10. Robert Coen interview, March 12, 1991.
11. Paul Atkinson interview, September 4, 1991.
12. Peter Kann interview, July 9, 1991.

Chapter 20

Much of this chapter came from my interviews with 153 present and former *Journal* news staffers. Inevitably, respondents volunteered two comments: on Karen Elliott House and the conflict of interest her marriage to Peter Kann does or does not represent; and on the improprieties of Norman Pearlstine.

I first met Norman Pearlstine on September 11, 1991, the date of my first interview with him. I had met Karen Elliott House at a party in December 1981, when she was dating Peter Kann. We had a pleasant, perfunctory conversation then. At our next meeting, in September 1991, I interviewed her for this book.

With respect to House, at least 75 percent of the staffers I interviewed harbored strong negative emotions about her.

I have worked at reasonably senior levels for Dow Jones, the *New York Times*, CBS, and Time Inc. Never have I observed a system so autocratic and unfair as the one that exists under House at Dow Jones. Everyone, of course, is victimized sooner or later by a superior. Yet if this occurs at the *Times*, CBS, or Time Inc., the alleged victim can always seek a hearing from his or her superiors. This route of appeal dissuades managers from becoming unnecessarily autocratic. Such a system of checks does not exist at Dow Jones. Joseph Manguno, for example, was dismissed from the *Journal* after twelve years of service without severance pay. Dow Jones then embargoed his family's belongings. This would have been unheard of at the *Times*, CBS, Time Inc., or, when Barney Kilgore was alive.

The Mapes-House-Hussein incident described in this chapter was corroborated by three sources: Karen House, Mapes, and Zimmerman. In my interview with House, she discussed at length her relationship with Kann and its effect on the staff. I also discussed the relationship with Kann, whose response is included here as well.

1. Fred Zimmerman interview, April 3, 1991.
2. Alan Otten interview, May 9, 1991.
3. Fred Zimmerman interview, April 3, 1991.
4. Fred Taylor interview, February 28, 1991.
5. These seven questions were raised by most of the 153 present and former *Journal* news people whom I interviewed.
6. Warren Phillips interview, August 28, 1991.
7. Peter Jennings interview, January 10, 1992.
8. Alan Otten interview, May 9, 1991.
9. Leon Jaworski interview, July 12, 1978.
10. Alan Otten interview, May 8, 1991.
11. Ellen Graham interview, April 2, 1991.
12. Glynn Mapes interview, April 15, 1991.
13. Karen Elliott House interview, September 17, 1991.
14. Fred Zimmerman interview, April 3, 1991.
15. Peter Kann interview, October 23, 1991.
16. Fred Zimmerman interview, April 3, 1991.
17. Alan Otten interview, May 8, 1991.
18. James Manguno interview, May 9, 1991. Manguno cited as his source for this unseemly remark a woman reporter for the *Financial Times*, Maggie Ford, who attended the New Delhi Conference. Five other *Journal* news staffers made the same allegation.
I quoted Manguno's allegation to House verbatim. House was neither startled nor insulted by the question. She answered it coolly by relating in some detail the trip she took to New Delhi with Hussein.
19. Karen Elliott House interview, September 17, 1991.
20. Alan Otten interview, May 8, 1991.
21. Karen Elliott House interview, September 17, 1991.
22. Ibid.
23. Fred Zimmerman interview, April 3, 1991.
24. William Mathewson interview, May 9, 1991.
25. Norman C. Miller interview, February 28, 1991.
26. Ibid.

27. Miller was a *Journal* lifer, a Pulitzer Prize winner, and a distinguished, highly respected journalist, both in and out of the *Journal*. He hired House, promoted her, and played a key role in her attending the Kennedy School of Government at Harvard University. Then, a year later, he lost his job to Al Hunt. To observe Miller telling this story, as I did, is to see that he intensely dislikes Karen Elliott House.

28. Ibid.

Chapter 21

1. The comparison stems from interviews with 153 present and former *Journal* news staffers. The composite reaction was that the nepotic relationship of Kann and House has caused the *Journal's* standard of moral soundness to deteriorate.

For example, eight staffers felt it was unsound for House to write a news item—not an editorial—that portrayed South Korea's military dictator Roh Tae Woo glowingly and did not disclose that Roh is a close personal friend who expedited the adoption of her youngest son, Jason, a South Korean orphan. What also stands out in this situation is the vivid contrast between House's news account of Roh and the *New York Times's* or the *Washington Post's*. This incident, described in detail in this chapter, represented a substantial change in *Journal* standards, according to staffers. Under the Kilgore regime, nepotism was not allowed, and House would not have covered Roh because of her personal relationship with him.

Thirteen staffers felt terminating Joseph Manguno without severance pay, also described in this chapter, exceeded the bounds of decency, especially Kilgore's boundaries of decency. They felt strongly that Manguno should have been given severance pay as determined by the Dow Jones Policy Manual.

2. Alan Otten interview, May 9, 1991.

3. John Berthlesen interview, April 2, 1991. Other *Journal* reporters who either were fired or resigned from the paper as a result of House include, in addition to Berthlesen, Rusty Todd, *Asian Journal* correspondence; Tony Spaeth, *Journal* New Delhi correspondent; Mike Miller, Washington bureau chief; David Ignatius, Middle East correspondent; S. K. Witcher, Australian correspondent; Matt Miller, *Asian Journal* reporter; and James Leung, former *Asian Journal* reporter.

4 I corroborated the Manguno incident with Philip Bowring, former editor, *FEER*, Derek Davies, former editor, *FEER*; John Berthelesen, former *Asian Journal* correspondent; Mary Williams Walsh, former *Asian Journal* correspondent; a former *Journal* China correspondent; as well as House. With the exception of House, all thought she had terminated Manguno vindictively. I interviewed Manguno for over four hours on two separate occasions in Washington, D.C. I found him to be a sober, responsible, and competent person.

5. Sources for this description of the briefing of Ottaway at the coffee shop are House, Jim Ottaway, Jr., Philip Bowring, and Joseph Manguno.

6. John Berthleson interview, April 2, 1991.

7. Karen Elliott House interview, September 17, 1991.

8. Joseph Manguno interview, May 9, 1991.

9. Mary Williams Walsh interview, April 2, 1991.

10. Mary Williams Walsh interview, April 27, 1991.

11. Karen Elliott House interview, September 17, 1991.

12. Norman Pearlstine interview, October 1, 1991.

13. The comment about Dorothy Palsho is based on my own observation and is corroborated by two *Journal* business executives who work with Palsho and by a circulation director from a competitive publication.

14. Derek Davies interview, June 1, 1992.

15. Philip Bowring interview, June 1, 1992.

16. Ibid.

17. Karen Elliott House interview, September 17, 1991.

Chapter 22

1. After searching the *Wall Street Journal* news index and Dow Jones News Retrieval Systems, I found no stories pertaining to the savings and loan scandal until late 1989 and 1990, date from 1976 to the present which were well after the fact. I then commissioned a professional researcher to double-check my efforts. He came up with the same finding.

Then, in separate face-to-face interviews conducted in September 1991, I asked Norman Pearlstine, the *Journal's* managing editor, and Paul Steiger, the *Journal's* assistant managing editor, why the *Journal* missed the S&L scandal. Both men disagreed with the assertion. Pearlstine claimed, "Greg Hill [the *Journal's* S&L beat reporter] did a superior job of covering the industry throughout the eighties." Barney Calame, a *Journal* senior editor, was assigned the task of providing me with the stories that would prove their opinions. Several weeks later, Clame messengered to me sixteen *Journal* stories relating to the savings and loan industry. Most were written by Greg Hill between 1981 and 1987. None revealed the particulars of the S&L scandal.

In November 1991 I flew to San Francisco and asked Greg Hill, then the *Journal's* San Francisco bureau chief, why the newspaper missed the scandal. Unlike Messrs. Pearlstine and Steiger, Hill did not deny the allegation. He merely replied, "No newspaper did a good job on that story." Hill went on to admit the *Journal* even failed to profile the S&L main felons, e.g., Charles Keating, Jr., because of "turf battles between the *Journal* bureaus. Hunt [*Journal* Washington bureau chief] would never let me do a story on Danny Wall [head of the FHLBB in Washington], nor would Barney [Calame, then Los Angeles bureau chief] let me in to L.A. to do a story on Keating [who operated in Irvine, California, a suburb of Los Angeles]."

2. Coauthored by *Journal* reporter Daniel Hertzberg.

3. Everette E. Dennis interview, May 16, 1991.

4. Peter Jennings interview, ABC News, January 10, 1992.

5. William Kovach interview, November 11, 1991.

6. Jonathan Kwitny interview, April 26, 1991.

7. Ibid. Norman Pearlstine, Barney Calame, a *Journal* senior editor who oversaw much of the *Journal's* savings-and-loan coverage, and Greg Hill, San Francisco bureau chief and the *Journal's* best savings-and-loan reporter, confirmed that Jonathon Kwitny was not allowed to cover the story in any part of the country.

8. Ibid.

9. Bill Paul interview, January 17, 1991.

10. Norman C. Miller interview, February 28, 1991.

11. Donald Moffett interview, April 9, 1991.

12. Jonathan Kwitny interview, April 26, 1991, and Norman Pearlstine interview, October 1, 1991.

13. Stephen Pizzo interview, April 30, 1991.

14. Stephen Pizzo interview, April 16, 1991.

15. Stephen Pizzo interview, April 13, 1991.

16. Mary Fricker interview, April 30, 1991.

17. Stephen Pizzo interview, April 26, 1991.

18. Warren Hinckle book review, July 15, 1990.

19. Susan Burkhart, *San Francisco Examiner*, Business Section, June 24, 1990, p. D1.

20. G. Christian Hill interview, November 20, 1991.

21. Ibid.

22. Ibid.

23. Stephen Pizzo, Mary Fricker, Paul Muolo, *Inside Job: The Looting of America's Savings and Loans* (New York: Harper Perennial, 1990), p. 520.

24. G. Christian Hill interview, November 20, 1991.

Chapter 23

1. "Giving Credit," *New York Newsday*, January 21, 1992, p. 6.

2. I personally reviewed the *Journal's* coverage of Ron Perleman from 1979 to 1982 by consulting the *Wall Street Journal* news index and by also running a search on the Dow

Jones News Retrieval System. The researcher I employed, Michael Sheridan, duplicated my efforts.

3. Norman Pearlstine interview, September 11, 1991.

4. Robinson's efforts to discredit *The Predators' Ball* were widely known. In fact, Robinson's public relations ineptness brought so much attention to the book, it became a bestseller.

5. Norman Pearlstine interview, September 11, 1991.

6. Bill Paul interview, January 14, 1991. My research revealed that many other people, in and out of Dow Jones, shared Bill Paul's reaction. They were offended for these reasons: (1) In the Kilgore tradition, *Journal* newspeople have a responsiblity to comport themselves, personally and professionally, in a manner that will not cast any doubt on their ability to be perceived as objective and fair. The *Journal*'s managing editor, of course, has the greatest responsibility to uphold this standard, since he sets the example for the entire news department. When *New York* magazine's Julie Baumgold captured Pearlstine fawning over Donald Trump, his conduct and judgment were called into question. In fact, many *Journal* news staffers told me they were enraged. (2) What troubled the people I interviewed even more was that Trump's party was not a press junket where Pearlstine would be in the company of other journalists. In a *New York* magazine article, the Atlantic City fights junket was a public relations scheme which Trump dreamed up to publicize his new gambling casinos. The guests included Cheryl Tiegs, Jack Nicholson, a former Miss America, and Steve Rubell. What hurt these *Journal* newspeople even more was that Baumgold's story satirized Trump mercilessly, and here was Norman Pearlstine currying favor with the object of Baumgold's scorn. Even a cursory examination of the quoted dialogue between Trump and Pearlstine reveals that Pearlstine was trying to endear himself with Trump through the accomplishments of Nancy Friday. A twenty-year *Journal* reporter said, "Pearlstine was kissing Trump's ass shamelessly. How can the *Journal* ever cover Trump again objectively?" (3) Even more troubling was that Norman Pearlstine never reimbursed Trump for any of the expenses, nor did he write a piece about the junket.

Other people who expressed a negative view of the January 1988 Pearlstine-Trump affair to me include:

A. Donald Macdonald, vice chairman, Dow Jones. When asked to comment on the Barsky-Pearlstine-Trump affair in August 27, 1991, Macdonald replied, "He [Pearlstine] sullied the *Journal*'s reputation, that great halo."

B. William Cox, Jr., scion of the Bancroft family and member of the Dow Jones board of directors. On October 15, 1991, I asked Cox in an interview: "Frank Allen, *Journal* Philadelphia bureau chief and environmental beat reporter, told me that Pearlstine was almost recently fired at a Dow Jones board meeting when a board member asked, Why don't we fire Barksy? The answer was given that if we fire Barsky, we'll have to fire Pearlstine. Is that true?"

After muttering a profane pejorative about Norman Pearlstine, Cox said: "It [firing Pearlstine] was discussed. But Warren [Phillips] felt it best to handle the matter in a different way." Cox blamed Pearlstine for the Barsky-Trunp affair in his gestures and exclamation.

The *Journal* staffers believed that had Norman Pearlstine not accepted Trump's hospitality in January 1988, it's highly unlikely Barsky would have sought Trump's hospitality in 1991. They were not excusing Barsky's behavior, but merely explaining how he rationalized a serious breech in journalistic ethics. At any other newspaper iin the country, those interviewers asserted, Barsky would have been fired instantly. Yet the *Journal* chose not to take this action because it would have meant, as Bill Cox confirmed, Pearlstine would have to be fired as well.

7. Connie Bruck, *The Predators' Ball: The Inside Story of Drexal Burnham and the Rise and Fall of Junk Bond Raiders* (New York: Penguin Books, 1980), p. 201.

8. Barney Calame, *Journal* senior editor, said that in 1991, the year Stewart's *Den of Thieves* was published, thirteen other books authored by *Journal* news staffers also were published. None of these other books received the same treatment the *Journal* accorded *Den of Thieves*.

9. Interoffice memo from Norman Pearlstine and Paul Steiger to the *Journal* news department, June 26, 1991.

10. Norman Pearlstine interview, September 11, 1991.

11. Robert Trump interview, November 12, 1991.

12. Interoffice memo, Pearlstine and Steiger to the *Journal's* news department, June 26, 1991.

13. Robert Trump interview, November 12, 1991.

14. Frank Allen interview, September 20, 1991.

15. William Cox, Jr., interview, October 15, 1991.

16. John Mack Carter's handwritten response to author's letter, dated February 9, 1991.

17. "U.S. *Journal's* Executive Editor Pearlstine to Resign and Start His Own Media Firm," *Wall Street Journal*, May 14, 1992, p. 5.

18. Frank Allen interview, June 1, 1992.

19. Ibid.

20. Derek Davies interview, May 12, 1992.

21. Robert Sack interview, October 1, 1991.

22. Donald A. Macdonald interview, August 21, 1991.

23. Warren Phillips interview, October 24, 1991.

Chapter 24

The key consideration of this chapter is: Was Faludi's story worthy of a Pulitzer, journalism's highest recognition of excellence?

There is the matter of the soft feature's subject: the human toll of Safeway's LBO. It had been done two to four years before by Bill Adler and the *Texas Observer*, Robert Tomsho of the *Dallas Morning News*, the *Oakland Tribune*, Paul Farhi of the *San Francisco Examiner*, the *San Francisco Chronicle*, *Mother Jones*, and *Grocery Marketing News*. Since this was not breaking news, the subject should not have been duplicated.

In answering whether her piece is worthy of a Pulitzer Prize, one must also consider that Faludi interviewed Adler and read his piece on Safeway-Dallas before preparing her story on the same subject. Safeway had stores throughout the United States. She could have gone to any one of them. Yet she chose Dallas.

Perhaps the best quote describing the current state of affairs of the Pulitzer Prize occurred when a veteran *Journal* reporter said, "Mike Miller won a Pulitzer [1964] back in the days before he knew he was going to win it."

1. Nancy Gibbs, "The War Against Feminism," *Time*, March 9, 1992, p. 51.

2. Manuela Hoelterhoff, "Women Kept in Their Place," *Wall Street Journal*, October 5, 1991.

3. *Accuracy in Media Report*, June 8, 1990, p. 2.

4. G. Christian Hill interview, November 20, 1991.

5. Susan Faludi interview, November 20, 1991.

6. Paul Farhi, "Anatomy of a Takeover," *San Francisco Examiner*, February 8-12, 1987.

7. William Adler interview, May 7, 1991.

8. Susan C. Faludi interview, November 20, 1991.

9. Ibid.

10. Ibid.

11. G. Christian Hill interview, November 20, 1991.

12. Affidavit of Martin Garbus in the matter of *Jonathan Kandell* v. *Dow Jones & Company, Inc.*, p. 2.

13. Ibid.

14. G. Christian Hill interview, November 20, 1991.

15. Ibid.

16. J. Douglas Bates interview, May 3, 1991.

Chapter 25

1. William Dunn interview, September 23, 1991.

2. Ken Burenga interview, September 3, 1991.

3. Alan Neuharth interview, April 22, 1991.
4. Ray Shaw interview, August 12, 1991.
5. William Dunn interview, September 10, 1991.
6. Warren Phillips interview, October 24, 1991.
7. Ibid.
8. William Dunn interview, November 8, 1991.
9. Carl Valenti interview, September 4, 1991.
10. Don Macdonald interview, August 21, 1991.
11. Neil Hirsch interview, October 3, 1991.
12. Ibid.
13. John Jessop interview, February 20, 1991.
14. Warren Phillips interview, October 16, 1991.
15. Graef S. Crystal, *In Search of Excess* (New York: W. W. Norton, 1991), p. 100.
16. Neil Hirsch interview, October 3, 1991.
17. Warren Phillips interview, October 16, 1991.
18. Neil Hirsch interview, October 3, 1991.
19. John Jessop interview, May 15, 1991.
20. Ibid.
21. John Jessop interview, February 20, 1991.
22. Ibid.
23. Neil Hirsch interview, November 8, 1991.
24. William Dunn interview, November 8, 1991.
25. Interoffice memo from Peter Kann and Ken Burenga to staff, November 14, 1991.
26. Peter G. Skinner interview, October 9, 1991.
27. Ibid.

Chapter 26

1. Fred Taylor interview, February 28, 1991.
2. Ellen Pollack interview, February 12, 1992.
3. NHTSA Data published by MADD, September 1989.
4. Television Bureau Research Department.
5. Don Moffett interview, April 9, 1991.
6. Peter Kann interview, October 23, 1991.
7. Donald A. Macdonald interview, August 21, 1991.

BIBLIOGRAPHY

ADLER, R. *Reckless Disregard*. New York: Knopf, 1986.

AULETTA, KEN. *Three Blind Mice: How the TV Networks Lost Their Way.* New York: Random House, 1991.

BAGDIKIAN, BEN H. *The Media Monopoly.* Boston: Beacon Press, 1987.

_____. *The Effete Conspiracy and Other Crimes by the Press.* New York: Harper & Row, 1972.

BARTLETT, SARAH. *The Money Machine: How KKR Manufactured Power and Profits.* New York: Warner Books, 1991.

BATES, DOUGLAS J. *The Pulitzer Prize: The Inside Story of America's Most Prestigious Award.* New York: Birch Lane Press, 1991.

BRUCK, CONNIE. *The Preditor's Ball.* New York: Simon and Schuster, 1988.

CHERNOW, RON. *The House of Morgan.* New York: Atlantic Monthly Press, 1990.

DRAPER, R. *Rolling Stone Magazine: The Uncensored History.* New York: Doubleday, 1990.

GOULDEN, J. *Fit to Print.* New York: Lyle Stuart, 1988.

CRYSTAL, GRAF S. *In Search of Excess* New York: Norton, 1991.

HALBERSTAM, D. *The Powers That Be.* New York: Knopf, 1979.

_____. *The Reckoning.* New York: William Morrow, 1986.

HORWITZ, TONY. *Baghdad Without a Map and Other Misadventures in Arabia.* New York: Dutton, 1991.

KEELER, R. *Newsday: A Candid History of the Tabloid.* New York, William Morrow, 1990.

KLUGER, RICHARD. *The Paper: The Life and Death of the New York Herald Tribune.* New York: Random House, 1987.

LEE, M., AND N. SOLOMON. *Unreliable Sources: A Guide to Detecting Bias in News Media* New York: Lyle Stuart, 1990.

LEVINE, FAYE. *Splendor & Misery: A Novel of Harvard.* New York: St. Martin's, 1983.

MALCOLM, JANET. *The Journalist and the Murderer.* New York: Vintage, 1990.

MARTON, KATI. *The Polk Conspiracy: Murder and Coverup in the Case of CBS News Correspondent George Polk.* New York: Farrar, Straus & Giroux, 1990.

McCLINTICK, DAVID. *Indecent Exposure.* New York: Wiliam Morrow, 1982.

McKERNS, J., ED. *Biographical Dictionary of American Journalism.* New York: Greenwood Press, 1989.

MERILL, JOHN C. *The Dialectic in Journalism: Toward a Responsible Use of Press Freedom.* Baton Rouge: Louisiana State University Press, 1989.

METZ, TIM. *Black Monday: The Catastrophe of October 19, 1987...And Beyond.* New York: William Morrow, 1988.

NEUHARTH, AL. *Confessions of an S.O.B.* New York: Doubleday, 1989.

PIZZO, STEPHEN, MARY FLICKER, AND PAUL MUOLO. *Inside Job: The Looting of America's Savings and Loans.* New York: McGraw-Hill, 1990.

POUND, ARTHUR, AND SAMUEL TAYLOR MOORE. *They Told Barron.* New York: Harper & Brothers, 1930.

———. *More They Told Barron.* New York: Harper and Brothers, 1931.

ROSENBERG, J. *Inside the Wall Street Journal.* New York: Macmillan, 1982.

SABATO, LARRY J. *Feeding Frenzy: How Attack Journalism Has Transformed American Politics.* New York: Free Press, 1991.

SAFER, M. *Flashbacks: On Returning to Vietnam.* New York, Random House, 1990.

SCHARF, E. *Worldly Powers.* New York: Beaufort Publishing, 1986.

STEEL, RONALD. *Walter Lippmann and the Twentieth Century.* Boston: Atlantic, 1980.

SWANBERG, W. A. *Luce and His Empire.* New York: Scribners, 1972.

TALESE, G. *The Kingdom and the Powqer.* New York: World Publishing Company, 1969.

TEEL, L. AND R. TAYLOR. *Into the Newsroom.* Chester, Conn.: Globe Pequot Press, 1983.

WENDT, L. *The Wall Street Journal.* New York: Rand McNally, 1982.

WINANS, CHRISTOPHER. *Malcolm Forbes: The Man Who Had Everything.* New York: St. Martin's, 1990.

WINANS, R. FOSTER. *Trading Secrets.* New York: St. Martin's, 1986.

Index

"Abreast of the Market" (column),
221
Ackell, Joseph J., 29–30, 41–42, 46,
56–60, 185–86
Adler, Bill, 318, 322–24
Advertising, 115–17
Agee, William, 95, 267–68
Allen, Frank, 238–39
American Express, 241–43
American Stock Exchange, 226–27
American Surgery, 224, 231
American Tobacco Company, 66
Anders, George, 221, 250–51
Andrews, Fred, 305
Apple computers, 166
Arafat, Yasir, 270
Araskog, Rand, 95
Asian Wall Street Journal, 143,·
145–47, 157–58, 183, 289
Atkinson, Paul, 193–94, 261–63
Auletta, Ken, 216
Austin, Paul J., 90

Backlash: The Undeclared War
Against American Women
(Faludi), 314–24
Baker, James, 256
Bancroft, Hugh, 21–23, 28, 30–31
Bancroft, Jane, 31
Bancroft family, 10, 110, 123, 219
Bankruptcy Court, U.S., 342–43

Barbarians at the Gate (Burrough
and Helyar), 240–42
Barron, Clarence Walker, 13, 16–31,
50, 52, 180, 349
early career of, 16–19
as publisher of Wall Street
Journal, 21–31
Barron, Jessie Waldron, 20–23
Barron's National Business and
Financial Weekly, 8, 27
Barsky, Neil, 309–11
Bartlett, Sarah, 250–51
Bartley, Robert L., 206, 254–56
Bates, J. Douglas, 323–24
Beattie, Dick, 250–51
Begelman, David, 158–62
Bell, Alexander Graham, 18
Bendix Corporation, 267–68
Bennet, James Gordon, Jr., 25
Berentsen, Ingrid, 193
Bergerac, Michel, 308
Bergstresser, Charles, 13, 15, 21,
185
Bernstein, Carl, 128–29
Black Monday: The Catastrophe of
October 19, 1987 and Beyond
(Metz), 252–53
Blackstone Group, 248–49
Bleakley, Fred, 309–10
Blundell, William, 153–54
Boesky, Ivan, 305

Bogdanich, Walt, 294
Book Digest, 166–79, 327
Boston News Bureau, 19–20
Boston Transcript, 18–19
Bowring, Philip, 288–91
Bradlee, Ben, 128
Brady Commission, 303
Brant, Peter, 224–28, 235
Bray, Tom, 206–9
Broderick, Pat, 211
Brooks, Geraldine, 4
Brooks, James, 153
Brown v. Board of Education, 70, 72, 102
Bruck, Connie, 241, 292, 304, 306
Bundesbank, 256
Burenga, Ken, 168, 195–99, 236–37, 327–28
Burrough, Bryan, 241–44, 313
Bush, Neil, 302

Calame, Barney, 247–50
Callis, Ted, 68, 82, 111–13, 120
Cantor Fitzgerald Securities Corporation, 326–27
Caples, John, 67–68
Carpenter, David, 220, 222, 224, 226, 229, 232–33, 235
Carrington, Tim, 258
Cella, Joseph, 226–27, 229, 232–33, 235
Centennial Savings and Loan, 295, 297–98
Central High School (Little Rock), 102
"Chappaquiddick and Credibility" (Bartley), 209–11
Chicopee, 186
Christiansen, Kathleen, 287
Chun Doo Hwan, 281
Clabby, Bill, 218–19
Clark, David W. C., 226
Clinton, Bill, 346
Cockburn, Alexander, 214
Cohen, Laurie P., 240, 247–48
Cohen, Peter, 241
Cole, Ron, 175–77
Coles, Robert, 305
Columbia Savings and Loan, 306–9
Conrad, Francis G., 342–43
Continental Cablevision, 327

Cony, Edward, 97, 106, 129–33, 138–39, 157–58, 247
    Pulitzer Prize of, 106–7, 127
Cook, Jane Bancroft, 40
Cooke, Jay, 18–19
Cox, Bill, Jr., 40, 112, 121
Cox, Jessie Bancroft, 40, 68, 99, 123, 126
Cox, Martha Whiting, 125
Cox, William Coburn, Jr., 20, 121–26, 332
Craig, Paul Roberts, 210
Crimson, The (magazine), 136–37
Crovitz, Gordon, 290–91
Cubism, 25–26
Cunninghan, Mary, 267–69

Dallos, Bob, 252
Davies, Derek, 287–88
Dennis, Everette, 293
Den of Thieves (Stewart), 244, 306, 309
DePauw University, 35–36
Dillon, Tom, 84
Donnelley, Betty, 99
Dorfman, Dan, 223–24
Dow, Charles, 13, 15, 21–22, 52
Dow Jones averages, 14
Dow Jones & Company
    bought by Barron, Clarence Walker, 21
    expansion of, 79–84, 89–90, 109, 155–56, 163, 165–79, 189, 219, 264, 325–34
    financial reverses of, 10–12, 23–26, 92, 236, 339, 347–49
    formation of, 13–15
    growth of, 8–10, 29
    position of women at, 285–87
Dow Jones Industrials, 254–57
Dow Jones Interactive Cable, 187
Dow Jones Management Committee, 79
Dow Jones News Retrieval, 9, 187, 333
Dow Jones News Service, 9
Dow Jones News Ticker, 218–35
Dow Jones's Afternoon News Letter, 13
Duffield, Gene, 58
Dunn, William L., 166, 180–88, 191, 327–33, 339

Eglinton, Tom, 288
El Salvador, 211
Employment Weekly, 199–200

Faludi, Susan, 314–24
*Far Eastern Economic Review
(FEER),* 287–91
Federal Savings and Loan Insurance
Corporation (FSLIC), 296–97
Feemster, Robert McCleary, 80–83,
85, 115, 119–20
advertising policy of *Wall Street
Journal* and, 62–69, 112–13
Felis, Kenneth, 226, 235
Fidelity Mutual, 347
Financial News Network (FNN),
325–26, 340–43
Flanagan, Bernard T., 194, 261–63
Flom, Joe, 242, 250
Flynn, George, 185–86
Ford, Henry, 28
Ford Motor Company, 65
Fortune (magazine), 305–6
Fountain Pen Conspiracy, The
(Kwitny), 294, 299–300
Freedman, Alex, 344
Fricker, Mary, 298–99
Friday, Nancy, 241, 244–45

Garbus, Martin, 322
Garment, Suzanne, 212–13
Gartner, Michael, 92, 139–40
Gemmill, Henry, 84, 102
General Electric, 341–43
Giles, Bill, 82, 84
Gingold, Oliver, 223
Goodwin, Elaine, 288
Graham, Katherine, 128
Great Depression, 32–34, 38,
40–41, 43, 46
Greenspan, Alan, 256
Grimes, William Henry, 33, 41–43,
45–52, 71–72, 99
Pulitzer Prize of, 49, 52–53, 74
Groseclose, Everett, 218–19, 221
Gross, Martin, 173–75, 177
Guilfoyle, Joe, 102

Haft, Herbert and Robert, 315–16
Halberstam, David, 138–41, 246
Hamilton, William, 23, 29–30, 52,
73–74

Hansen, Erwin, 295–98
Harris, Fred, 168
Hartley, Bill, 154–55
Harvard College, 136–37
Harvard Graduate School of
Business Administration, 190
"Heard on the Street" (column),
221–35
Heffner, Lee, 183–84, 192
Helyar, John, 241–44
Henninger, Dan, 212–13
Herman, Tom, 206–9
Hertzberg, Dan, 247, 260
Hilder, David, 315–17, 324
Hill, Greg, 299–300, 322–23
Hirsch, Neil S., 9, 325–26, 334–36,
339
Hogate, Kenneth Craven (Casey),
28, 30–31, 37, 43, 49–50, 54–55
Hollie, Pam, 203–4
Hong Kong, 144
Horowitz, Tony, 4
House, Karen Elliot, 11–12, 204–5,
238, 258, 312
early career of, 275–78
Pulitzer Prize of, 205, 266, 270,
272–73
as vice-president of Dow Jones &
Company, 279–91
Hunt, Al, 4, 265, 278, 302
Hussein, King, 270
Hymnowitz, Carol, 287

IBM, 200–202
Indecent Exposure (McClintick), 162
Information Services Group, 9,
180–81, 183, 187, 328–30, 333
*Inside Job: The Looting of America's
Savings and Loans* (Pizzo,
Fricker, and Muolo), 295–99,
303
Interstate Commerce Commission,
19
Investor's Daily, 6

Jacobs, Eli, 247, 250, 252, 303
Jaworski, Leon, 269
Jennings, Peter, 269, 293
Jessop, John, 9–10, 336–37
Jobs, Steven, 166
Jones, Edward, 13, 15

Kann, Francesca Mayer, 129–33, 141
Kann, Peter Robert, 11–12, 86,
    129–42, 180, 191–92, 206–9
  advertising policy *Wall Street
    Journal* and, 261–62
  as associate publisher, 194–96
  as chief executive officer of Dow
    Jones & Company, 331, 337,
    339–43
  as chief executive officer of *Wall
    Street Journal*, 347–49
  House and, 265–78
  Pulitzer Prize of, 142–43, 267–69
Karmen, Monroe "Bud," 107
Keating, Charles, Jr., 300–301
Kellog, John H., 27
Kelly, Dan, 5, 272–73
Kennedy, Edward, 209–11
Kennedy, John F., 103
Kerby, William, 11–12, 33, 45–49,
    57–60, 80–83, 98, 120, 180
  as president of Dow Jones &
    Company, 57, 62–64, 79–90,
    93–95, 101
  a president of *Wall Street Journal*,
    106
Kersner, Scott, 298
Kilgore, James, 79
Kilgore, Leslie Bernard (Barney), 11,
    55–60, 110, 180, 349
  advertising policy of *Wall Street
    Journal* and, 61–69
  as chief executive officer of Dow
    Jones & Company, 57–89
  early career of, 33–43
  editorial style of *Wall Street
    Journal* and, 70–77, 152–54
  as president of Dow Jones &
    Company, 44–53, 55
Kilgore, Mary Louise Throop,
    39–40, 84–85
King, Rodney, 217
Kissane, Cy, 60
Kohlmeier, Louis, 107
Kovach, Bill, 293
Kravis, Henry, 243, 251
Krieger, Bill, 203–4, 247
Kwitny, Jonathan, 294–95, 303

Laffer, Arthur Prof., 211
La Guardia, Fiorello, 38–39
Lancaster, Paul, 107–9

Landro, Laura, 238–39
Lawrence Butner and Associates,
    198
Levine, Dennis, 305, 308
Lincoln Savings, 301–2
Lippmann, Walter, 32–33
Lipsky, Seth, 145
Lombard, Laurence M., 55, 57
Los Angeles Times, 6

McCarthy, John, 125
McClintick, David, 158–62
McCormack, Buren, 52, 77, 82, 90,
    185–86
MacDonald, Donald A., 69, 111–12,
    118–21, 123, 126, 129–33, 168,
    182–84, 191–94, 348
  advertising policy of *Wall Street
    Journal* and, 113, 121
  Book Digest and, 172–79
Macdougall, Kent A., 140
McKinsey & Company, 189–91, 199
McLoughlin, Richard M., 175–77
McWethy, John, 93
Magowan, Peter, 315–17
Manguno, Joseph, 273, 280–85
Mann, Horace, 96–97
Mapes, Glynn, 5, 258
Martin, William McChesney, 90,
    95, 187
Marx, William Henry, 192
Melloan, George, 210
Meyer, Geofrey, 261
Metz, Tim, 252–53
Milken, Michael, 12, 242, 304–8
Miller, Norman C. "Mike," 273–75,
    277
  Pulitzer Prize of, 107, 278
Moffitt, Don, 107, 237, 239, 240
Money Machine, The (Bartlett),
    250–51
Morgan, J. P., 19
Muolo, Paul, 298–99

Napes, Glynn, 271–72
National Observer, 83–84, 89, 156,
    166
  founding of, 81–83
Neilsen rating, 116–17
Neuharth, Al, 6, 328
Newsweek, 57–89
New York Stock Exchange, 7

New York Times, business coverage
    of, 6, 253, 256–59
Nordstrom, 315

O'Donnell, Lawrence, 160–62,
    194–96, 204, 247
O'Hara, John, 175–77
Orr, John, 191–92
Ottaway, James, Jr., 165, 280–85,
    289–90
Ottaway Community Newspapers, 8,
    89, 165–66
Otten, Alan, 128, 205, 269, 274, 280
Over-the-Counter Market, 7

Pantry Pride, 307–8
Paramount, 340
Parhi, Paul, 323–24
Park Chung Hee, 281
Paul, Bill, 240
Peabody, Chubb, 119
Pearlstine, Norman, 146–55,
    195–96, 203–4, 227–28, 230–35
    journalistic failures of *Wall Street
        Journal* and, 254, 304, 307–13
    as managing editor, 237–51
Penn, Stanley, 107
Perleman, Ron, 304
Perrone, Joe, 168, 197–99
Perry, James, 84
Peterson, Peter G., 249–50
Phillips, Warren H., 11–12, 87,
    91–109, 180–81
    advertising policy *Wall Street
        Journal* and, 200–202
    as chief executive officer of Dow
        Jones & Company, 95, 155–56,
        163–66, 168–71, 184–85,
        189–91, 230, 252
    early career of, 84–85, 98–103
    expansion of Dow Jones &
        Company and, 325–26, 335–36
    journalistic failures of *Wall Street
        Journal* and, 127–29
Pizzo, Stephen, 295–99
Pollack, Ellen, 346
Predator's Ball, The (Bruck), 292,
    304, 306
Prestbo, John, 257
Princeton Packet, 57–89, 135–36
Psychology Today, 169

Pulitzer Prizes
    Bogdanich's, 294
    Cony's, 106–7
    Faludi's, 318
    Grimes's, 49
    House's, 5
    Royster's, 71
    Stewart's, 238, 260, 293
Putka, Gary, 222, 231

Reader's Digest, 175
Reagan, Ronald, 189, 211–13,
    254–55
Reaganomics, 254–55, 296–97
Revlon, 307–8
Richard D. Irwin Textbook
    Publishing Company, 165–66
Ricklefs, Roger, 108
Rigier, Jim, 175–77
Roberts, George, 316–17
Roberts, Paul Craig, 214
Robertson, Cliff, 159–62
Robinson, James D., III, 240,
    242–44
Robinson, Linda Gosden, 239–44,
    306
Roh Tae Woo, 281–85
Roll, Ed, 126
Roman Catholic Church, 103–4
Roosevelt, Franklin Delano, 32–33
Rosenthal, Abe, 215
Royster, Vermont Connecticut, 33,
    70–72, 74–77, 206–7, 211, 217
    editorial on Kilgore by, 87–88
    Pulitzer Prize of, 71
Rustin, Dick, 221–23, 231, 247

Safeway Stores, 315–23
Safra, Edmond, 243
Salibury, Harrison, 129–32
Schamp, Eddie, 85
Schorr, Burt, 104–6
Schwarzman, Stephen, 250
Sebastian, Pamela, 347
Securities and Exchange
    Commission, 227, 229–30
Seib, Gerald, 258
"Seven Points to Better Reporting
    and Writing" (Barron), 24
Shaw, Ray, 192, 196–200, 327,
    329–30

Shearson-Lehman, 241–43
Silverado Savings and Loans, 302
Skinner, Peter G., 339–43
Smart Money (magazine), 311
Smith, Randy, 249–51
Soderlind, Sterling E. "Jim," 103–4, 156
Sokolov, Raymond, 177, 214–15
Solomon, Mack, 160
Sorenson, Bill, 129–33
Sorenson, Martha Mayer, 129–30
Sorokin, H. Lee, 345–46
South China Morning Post, 145, 175
South Korea, 281–85
Spiegel, Thomas, 306–9
Stabler, Charles, 288
Stanton, Frank, 167, 177–78
Stars and Stripes, 98
Steiger, Paul, 247–50, 253, 257, 309–11, 344, 346–47
Stesser, Stan, 107
Stewart, James, 235, 244, 260, 292–93, 313
    investigation of Milken and, 304–9
    Pulitzer Prize of, 238, 260, 293
Swartz, Steve, 249

Talese, Gay, 216
Taylor, Fred, 35, 107, 138–40, 147, 152–54, 195, 203–4, 238, 246–47, 345
    as managing editor, 156, 158
Telerate, 9, 264, 325–30, 334–39
Terranova, Joe, 9
Ticker tape machine, 12, 14, 19–20, 29, 40–42
Totenberg, Nina, 83
Trentonian, 219, 233
Trump, Donald, 309–11
Trump Organization, 309–10

USA Today, 6, 263–64

Valenti, Carl, 183–84, 188, 333, 336–37
Vanderbilt, Cornelius, 18
Vendetta (Burrough & Helyar), 243–44
Veronis, John, 167–71, 178
Vickers, Ray, 102–3

Videotext, 187
Vietnam war, 107–8, 127–29, 138–41
Volcker, Paul, 255

Wall Street Journal, 203–4
    advertising policy of, 61–69, 111, 117–18, 121, 170–71, 198–99, 200–202, 262
    Asian edition of, 143, 145–47, 183, 280–85, 289
    Atlanta bureau of, 104–6
    Barron and, 21–31
    Chicago bureau of, 27, 93–94, 101
    Dallas bureau of, 147–49
    Detroit bureau of, 27, 150
    early history of, 14, 21–27, 29
    editorial style of, 4–5, 24, 37, 42, 47–49, 52, 72–74, 211–17, 234–35, 344–55
    European edition of, 182–85, 256–57
    expansion of, 45, 49, 54–55, 61, 64–65, 68, 78, 92, 106, 110, 155, 193, 197–98
    financial reverses of, 40–41, 261–64
    future of, 347–49
    journalistic failures of, 7, 11–12, 127–29, 231, 247–54, 256–60, 292–313, 346–47
    Los Angeles bureau of, 152–54
    management style of, 143–45, 180–81, 195–96, 203–4
    readers of, 3–4
    Saigon bureau of, 138–41
    San Francisco bureau of, 37
    technology and, 6–7, 14, 30, 46–47, 185–87
    third section, 246
    Tokyo bureau of, 154–55
    two-section issue, 202–3
    Washington bureau of, 27, 34, 39, 75, 264–65
Wall Street Journal Circulation Center, 121
Walsh, Mary Williams, 285–87
Wanniski, Jude, 83, 210
Washington Post, The, 128
Wasserstein, Bruce, 251–52
Watergate affair, 127–29
Webb, Victor, 183–84

Wedtech affair, 345
Weinstock, Davis, 250
Wendt, Lloyd, 27
Westar, 186–87
Westinghouse Broadcasting, 340–43
Windsor Conger Clark, David, 225
Wojniak, Robert, 166

Woodlock, Thomas, 52, 73–74
Woodruff, Judy, 265
Woodward, Robert, 128
World War II, 44

Zimmerman, Fred, 277